Honoré de Balzac

The Thirteen: Histoire Des Treize

And Other Stories

Honoré de Balzac

The Thirteen: Histoire Des Treize
And Other Stories

ISBN/EAN: 9783337005573

Printed in Europe, USA, Canada, Australia, Japan

Cover: Foto ©Thomas Meinert / pixelio.de

More available books at **www.hansebooks.com**

H. DE BALZAC

The Thirteen

(Histoire des Treize)

AND OTHER STORIES

TRANSLATED BY

ELLEN MARRIAGE

WITH A PREFACE BY

GEORGE SAINTSBURY

PHILADELPHIA
THE GEBBIE PUBLISHING CO., Ltd.
1899

CONTENTS

	PAGE
PREFACE	ix
THE THIRTEEN—	
AUTHOR'S PREFACE	1
I. FERRAGUS	8
II. THE DUCHESSE DE LANGEAIS . . .	139
MAÎTRE CORNÉLIUS	298
GAMBARA	367

LIST OF ILLUSTRATIONS

MME. DE LANGEAIS RANG THE BELL (p. 235)	*Frontispiece*
	PAGE
"YOU ARE MISTAKEN, MADEMOISELLE, MY WIFE COULD NOT POSSIBLY —"	78
A GIRL'S BODY STRANDED THAT MORNING ON THE BANK	132
"SOUND YOURSELF; IF YOU HAVE NOT COURAGE ENOUGH, HERE IS MY DAGGER"	188
HE STOOD UNDER THE WALL TO HEAR THE MUSIC OF THE ORGAN	203

Drawn by W. Boucher

PREFACE.

IN its original form the "Histoire des Treize" consists—or, rather, it was originally built up—of three stories: "Ferragus" or the "Rue Soly," "La Duchesse de Langeais" or "Ne touchez-pas à la hache," and "La Fille aux Yeux d'Or." The last, in some respects one of Balzac's most brilliant effects, does not appear here, as it contains things that are inconvenient. It may be noted that he had at one time the audacity to think of calling it "La Femme aux Yeux Rouges."

To tell the truth, there is more power than taste throughout the "Histoire des Treize," and perhaps not very much less unreality than power. Balzac is very much better than Eugène Sue, though Eugène Sue also is better than it is the fashion to think him just now. But he is here, to a certain extent, competing with Sue on the latter's own ground. The notion of the "Dévorants"—of a secret society of men devoted to each other's interests. entirely free from any moral or legal scruple, possessed of considerable means in wealth, ability, and position, all working together, by fair means or foul, for good ends or bad—is, no doubt, rather seducing to the imagination at all times; and it so happened that it was particularly seducing to the imagination of that time. And its example has been powerful since; it gave us Mr. Stevenson's "New Arabian Nights" only, as it were, the other day.

But there is something a little schoolboyish in it; and I do not know that Balzac has succeeded entirely in eliminating this something. The pathos of the death, under persecution, of the innocent Clémence does not entirely make up for the unreasonableness of the whole situation. Nobody can say that the abominable misconduct of Maulincour—who is a hopeless "cad"—is too much punished, though an Englishman may think that Dr. Johnson's receipt of three or four footmen with cudgels, applied repeatedly and unsparingly, would have been better than elaborately prepared accidents and duels, which were too honorable for a Peeping Tom of this kind; and poisonings, which reduced the avengers to the level of their victim. But the imbroglio is of itself stupid; these fathers who cannot be made known to husbands are mere stage properties, and should never be fetched out of the theatrical lumber-room by literature.

"La Duchesse de Langeais" is, I think, a better story, with more romantic attraction, free from the objections just made to "Ferragus," and furnished with a powerful, if slightly theatrical catastrophe. It is as good as anything that its author has done of the kind, subject to those general considerations of probability and otherwise which have been already hinted at. For those who are not troubled by any such critical reflections, both, no doubt, will be highly satisfactory. And, indeed, I must confess that I should not think much of any boy who, beginning Balzac with the "Histoire des Treize," failed to go rather mad over it. I know there was a time when I used to like it best of all, and thought not merely "Eugénie Grandet," but "Le Père Goriot" (though not the "Peau de Chagrin"), dull in comparison. Some attention, however, must be paid to two remarkable characters, on whom it is quite clear that Balzac expended a great deal of pains, and one of whom he seems to have "caressed," as the French say, with a curious admixture of dislike and admiration.

The first, Bourignard or Ferragus, is, of course, another, though a somewhat minor example—Collin or Vautrin being the chief—of that strange tendency to take intense interest in criminals, which seems to be a pretty constant eccentricity of many human minds, and which laid an extraordinary grasp on the great French writers of Balzac's time. I must confess, though it may sink me very low in some eyes, that I have never been able fully to appreciate the attractions of crime and criminals, fictitious or real. Certain pleasant and profitable things, no doubt, retain their pleasure and their profit, to some extent, when they are done in the manner which is technically called criminal; but they seem to me to acquire no additional interest by being so. As the criminal of fact is, in the vast majority of cases, an exceedingly commonplace and dull person, the criminal of fiction seems to me only, or usually, to escape these curses by being absolutely improbable and unreal. But I know this is a terrible heresy.

Henri de Marsay is a much more ambitious and a much more interesting figure. In him are combined the attractions of criminality, beauty, brains, success, and, last of all, dandyism. It is a well-known and delightful fact that the most Anglophobe Frenchman—and Balzac might fairly be classed amongst them—have always regarded the English dandy with half-jealous, half-awful admiration. Indeed, our novelist, it will be seen, found it necessary to give Marsay English blood. But there is a tradition that this young Don Juan—not such a good fellow as Byron's, nor such a *grand seigneur* as Molière's—was partly intended to represent Charles de Rémusat, who is best known to this generation by very sober and serious philosophical works, and by his part in his mother's correspondence. I do not know that there ever were any imputations on M. de Rémusat's morals; but in memoirs of the time he is, I think, accused of a certain selfishness and *hauteur*, and he certainly made his way, partly by journalism, partly by society, to power very much as Marsay did. But Marsay would certainly not have written "Abelard" and the rest, or have returned to Ministerial rank in our time. Marsay, in fact, more fortunate than Rubempré, and of a higher stamp and flight than Rastignac, makes with them Balzac's trinity of sketches of the kind of personage whose part, in his day and since, every young Frenchman has aspired to play, and some have played. It cannot be said that "a moral man is Marsay;" it cannot be said that he has the element of good-nature which redeems Rastignac. But he bears a blame and a burden for which we Britons are responsible in part—the Byronic ideal of the guilty hero coming to cross and blacken the old French model of unscrupulous good humor. It is not a very pretty mixture or a very worthy ideal; but I am not so sure that it is not still a pretty common one.

The association of the three stories forming the "Histoire des Treize" is, in book form, original, inasmuch as they filled three out of the four volumes of "Études des Mœurs" published in 1834-35, and themselves forming part of the first collection of Scènes de la Vie Parisienne. But "Ferragus" had appeared in parts (with titles to each) in the "Revue de Paris" for March and April 1833, and part of "La Duchesse de Langeais" in the "Echo de la Jeune France" almost contemporaneously. There were divisions in this also. "Ferragus" and "La Duchesse" also appeared without "La Fille aux Yeux d'Or" in 1839, published in one volume by Charpentier, before their absorption at the usual time in the Comédie. G. S.

THE THIRTEEN.

AUTHOR'S PREFACE.

IN the Paris of the Empire there were banded together Thirteen men equally impressed with the same thought, equally endowed with energy enough to keep them true to it, while among themselves they were loyal to keep faith even when their interests chanced to clash. They were sufficiently strong to set themselves above all laws; bold enough to shrink from no enterprise; and so fortunate as to succeed in nearly everything that they undertook. So profoundly politic were they that they could dissemble the tie which bound them together. They ran the greatest risks and kept their failures to themselves. Fear never entered into their calculations; not one of them had trembled before princes, before the executioner's axe, before innocence. They had taken each other as they were, regardless of social prejudices. Criminals they doubtless were, yet none the less were they all remarkable for some one of the virtues which go to the making of great men, and their numbers were filled up only from among picked recruits. Finally, that nothing should be lacking to complete the dark, mysterious romance of their history, nobody to this day knows whom they were. The Thirteen once realized all the wildest ideas conjured up by tales of the occult powers of a Manfred, a Faust, or a Melmoth; and to-day the band is broken up or, at any rate, dispersed. Its members have quietly returned beneath the yoke of the civil law; much as Morgan, the Achilles of piracy, gave up buccaneering to be a peaceable planter; and, untroubled by qualms of conscience, sat himself down by the fireside to dispose of blood-stained booty acquired by the red light of blazing towns and slaughter.

After Napoleon's death, the band was dissolved by a chance event which the author is bound for the present to pass over in silence, and its mysterious existence, as curious, it may be, as the darkest novel by Mrs. Radcliffe, came to an end.

It was only lately that the present writer, detecting, as he fancied, a faint desire for celebrity in one of the anonymous heroes to whom the whole band once owed an occult allegiance, received the somewhat singular permission to make public certain of the adventures which befell that band, provided that, while telling the story in his own fashion, he observed certain limits.

The aforesaid leader was still an apparently young man with fair hair and blue eyes, and a soft, thin voice which might seem to indicate a feminine temperament. His face was pale, his ways mysterious. He chatted pleasantly, and told me that he was only just turned of forty. He might have belonged to the very upper class. The name which he gave was probably assumed, and no one answering to his description was known in society. Who is he, do you ask? No one knows.

Perhaps when he made his extraordinary disclosures to the present writer, he wished to see them in some sort reproduced; to enjoy the effect of the sensation on the multitude; to feel as Macpherson might have felt when the name of Ossian, his creation, passed into all languages. And, in truth, that Scottish advocate knew one of the keenest, or, at any rate, one of the rarest sensations in human experience. What was this but the incognito of genius? To write an "Itinerary from Paris to Jerusalem" is to take one's share in the glory of a century, but to give a Homer to one's country—this surely is a usurpation of the rights of God.

The writer is too well acquainted with the laws of narration to be unaware of the nature of the pledge given by this brief preface; but, at the same time, he knows enough of the history of the Thirteen to feel confident that he will not disap point any expectations raised by the programme. Tragedies dripping with gore, comedies piled up with horrors, tales of heads taken off in secret have been confided to him. If any reader has not had enough of the ghastly tales served up to the public for some time past, he has only to express his wish; the author is in a position to reveal cold-blooded atrocities and family secrets of a gloomy and astonishing nature. But in preference he has chosen those pleasanter stories in which stormy passions are succeeded by purer scenes, where the beauty and goodness of woman shine out the brighter for the darkness. And, to the honor of the Thirteen, such episodes as these are not wanting. Some day, perhaps, it may be thought worth while to give their whole history to the world; in which case it might form a pendant to the history of the buccaneers—that race apart so curiously energetic, so attractive in spite of their crimes.

When a writer has a true story to tell, he should scorn to turn it into a sort of puzzle-toy, after the manner of those novelists who take their reader for a walk through one cavern after another to show him a dried-up corpse at the end of the fourth volume, and inform him, by way of conclusion, that he has been frightened all along by a door hidden somewhere or other behind some tapestry; or a dead body, left by inadvertence, under the floor. So the present chronicler, in spite of his objection to prefaces, felt bound to introduce his fragment by a few remarks.

FERRAGUS, the first episode, is connected by invisible links with the history of the Thirteen, for the power which they acquired in a natural manner provides the apparently supernatural machinery.

Again, although a certain literary coquetry may be permissible to retailers of the marvelous, the sober chronicler is bound to forego such advantage as he may reap from an odd-sounding name, on which many ephemeral successes are founded in these days. Wherefore the present writer gives the following succinct statement of the reasons which induced him to adopt the unlikely sounding title and sub-title.

In accordance with old-established custom. FERRAGUS is a name taken by the head of a guild of Dévorants, or journeymen. Every chief on the day of his election chooses a pseudonym and continues a dynasty of Dévorants precisely as a pope changes his name on his accession to the triple tiara; and as the church has its Clement XIV., Gregory XII., Julius II., or Alexander VI., so the workmen have their "Trempe-la-Soupe IX., Ferragus XXII., Tutanus XIII., or Masche-Fer IV." Who are the Dévorants, do you ask?

The Dévorants are one among many tribes of companions whose origin can be traced to a great mystical association formed among the workmen of Christendom for the rebuilding of the Temple at Jerusalem. Companionism, to coin a word, is still a popular institution in France. Its traditions still exert a power over little-enlightened minds, over men so uneducated that they have not learned to break their oaths; and the various organizations might be turned to formidable account even yet if any rough-hewn man of genius arose to make use of them, for his instruments would be, for the most part, almost blind.

Wherever journeymen travel, they find a hostel for companions which has been in existence in the town from time immemorial. The *obade*, as they call it, is a kind of lodge with a "mother" in charge, an old, half-gypsy wife who has nothing to lose. She hears all that goes on in the countryside; and, either from fear or from long habit, is devoted to the interests of the tribe boarded and lodged by her. And as a result, this shifting population, subject as it is to an unalterable law of custom, has eyes in every place, and will carry out an order anywhere without asking questions; for the oldest journeyman is still at an age when a man has some beliefs left. What is more, the whole fraternity professes doctrines which, if unfolded never so little are both true enough and mysterious enough to electrify all the adepts with patriotism; and the brothers of the league are so attached to their rules that there have been bloody battles between different fraternities on a question of principle. Fortunately, however, for peace and public order, if a Dévorant is ambitious, he takes to building houses, makes a fortune, and leaves the guild.

A great many curious things might be told of their rivals, the *Compagnons du Devoir* (of the duty), of all the different sects of workmen, their manners and customs and brotherhoods, and of the resemblances between them and the Freemasons; but here, these particulars would be out of place. The author will merely add, that before the Revolution a Trempe-la-Soupe had been known in the King's service, which is to say, that he had the tenure of a place in his majesty's galleys for one hundred and one years; but even thence he ruled his guild, and was religiously consulted on all matters, and if he escaped from the hulks he met with help, succor, and respect wherever he went. To have a chief in the hulks is one of those misfortunes for which Providence is responsible; but a faithful lodge of Dévorants is bound, as before, to obey a power created by and set above themselves. Their lawful sovereign is in exile for the time being, but none the less is he their king. And now any romantic mystery hanging about the names Ferragus and the Dévorants is completely dispelled.

As for the Thirteen, the author feels that, on the strength of the details of this almost fantastic story, he can afford to give away yet another prerogative, though it is one of the greatest on record, and would possibly fetch a high price if brought into a literary auction mart; for the owner might inflict as many volumes on the public as La Contemporaine.*

The Thirteen were all of them men tempered like Byron's friend Trelawney, the original (so it is said) of "The Corsair." All of them were fatalists, men of spirit and poetic temperament; all of them were tired of the commonplace life

* A long series of so-called Memoirs, which appeared about 1830.

which they led; all felt attracted toward Asiatic pleasures by all the vehement strength of newly awakened and long dormant forces. One of these, chancing to take up " Venice Preserved " for the second time, admired the sublime friendship between Pier and Jaffier, and fell to musing on the virtues of outlaws, the loyalty of the hulks, the honor of thieves, and the immense power that a few men can wield if they bring their whole minds to bear upon the carrying out of a single will. It struck him that the individual man rose higher than men. Then he began to think that if a few picked men should band themselves together; and if, to natural wit, and education, and money, they could join a fanaticism hot enough to fuse, as it were, all these separate forces into a single one, then the whole world would be at their feet. From that time forth, with a tremendous power of concentration, they could wield an occult power against which the organization of society would be helpless; a power which would push obstacles aside and defeat the will of others; and the diabolical power of all would be at the service of each. A hostile world apart within the world, admitting none of the ideas, recognizing none of the laws of the world; submitting only to the sense of necessity, obedient only from devotion; acting all as one man in the interests of the comrade who should claim the aid of the rest; a band of buccaneers with carriages and yellow kid gloves; a close confederacy of men of extraordinary power, of amused and cool spectators of an artificial and pretty world which they cursed with smiling lips; conscious as they were that they could make all things bend to their caprice, weave ingenious schemes of revenge, and live with one life in thirteen hearts, to say nothing of the unfailing pleasure of facing the world of men with a hidden misanthropy, a sense that they were armed against their kind, and could retire into themselves with one idea which the most remarkable men had not—all this constituted a religion of pleasure and egoism which made fanatics of the Thirteen.

The history of the Society of Jesus was repeated for the devil's benefit. It was hideous and sublime.

The pact was made; and it lasted, precisely because it seemed impossible. And so it came to pass that in Paris there was a fraternity of thirteen men, each one bound, body and soul, to the rest, and all of them strangers to each other in the sight of the world. But evening found them gathered together like conspirators, and then they had no thoughts apart; riches, like the wealth of the Old Man of the Mountain, they possessed in common; they had their feet in every salon, their hands in every strong box, their elbows in the streets, their heads upon all pillows, they did not scruple to help themselves at their pleasure. No chief commanded them, nobody was strong enough. The liveliest passion, the most urgent need took precedence—that was all. They were thirteen unknown kings; unknown, but with all the power and more than the power of kings; for they were both judges and executioners, they had taken wings that they might traverse the heights and depths of society, scorning to take any place in it, since all was theirs. If the author learns the reason of their abdication of this power he will communicate it.

And now the author is free to give those episodes in the History of the Thirteen which, by reason of the Parisian flavor of the details or the strangeness of the contrasts, possessed a peculiar attraction for him.

PARIS, 1831.

THE THIRTEEN.

I.

FERRAGUS,

CHIEF OF THE DÉVORANTS.

To Hector Berlioz.

THERE are streets in Paris which have lost their character as hopelessly as a man guilty of some shameful action; there are likewise noble streets, streets that are simply honest and nothing more, young streets as to whose morality the public has as yet formed no opinion, and streets older than the oldest dowager. Then there are deadly streets, respectable streets, streets that are always clean, and streets that are invariably filthy; artisan, industrial, and commercial streets. The streets of Paris, in short, possess human qualities, so that you cannot help forming certain ideas of them on a first impression. There are low streets where you would not care to linger, and streets in which you would like to live. Some, like the Rue Montmartre, for instance, turn a fair face on you at the first and end in a fish's tail. The Rue de la Paix is a wide and imposing street, but it arouses none of the nobly gracious thoughts which take a susceptible nature at unawares in the Rue Royale, while it certainly lacks the majesty which pervades the Place Vendôme.

If you walk through the Ile Saint-Louis the loneliness of the spot, the dreary look of the houses and great empty mansions is enough to account for the melancholy which settles on your nerves. The Ile Saint-Louis, a corpse no longer tenanted by farmers-general, is the Venice of Paris. The Place de la Bourse is garrulous, bustling, common; it is only beautiful by moonlight; an epitomized Paris in broad day, by night a dreamlike vision of ancient Greece.

Is not the Rue Traversière Saint-Honoré plainly a shameless street, with its villainous little houses for mistresses, a couple of windows in width, and vice, and crime, and misery on every floor? And there are thoroughfares with a North aspect, visited by the sun only three or four times in the year; deadly streets are they, where life is taken with impunity, and the law looks on and never interferes. In olden days the Parliament would probably have summoned the lieutenant of police to hear a little plain speaking, or at least they would have passed a vote of censure on the street, just as on another occasion they recorded their dissatisfaction with the wigs worn by the Chapter of Beauvais. Yet, M. Benoiston de Châteauneuf has shown conclusively that the mortality in certain streets is twice as high as the normal death-rate! And to sum up the matter in a single example: what is the Rue Fromenteau but a haunt of vice and murder?

These observations may be dark sayings for those who live beyond the bounds of Paris; but they will be apprehended at once by those students, thinkers, poets, and men of pleasure, who know the art of walking the streets of Paris, and reap a harvest of delights borne in on the tides of life that ebb and flow within her walls with every hour. For these, Paris is the most fascinating of monsters; here she is a pretty woman, there a decrepit pauper; some quarters are spick and span as the coins of a new reign, and a nook here and there is elegant as a woman of fashion.

A monster, indeed, is the great city, in every sense of the word! In the garrets you find, as it were, its brain full of knowledge and genius; the second floor is a digestive apparatus, and the stores below are unmistakable feet, whence all the busy foot-traffic issues.

Oh! what a life of incessant activity the monster leads! The final vibration of the last carriage returning from the ball has scarcely died away before Its arms begin to stir a little at the barriers, and the City gives itself a gradual shake. All the gates begin to yawn, turning on their hinges like the membranes of some gigantic lobster invisibly controlled by some thirty thousand men and women. Each one of these thirty thousand must live in the alloted six square feet of space which serves as kitchen, workshop, nursery, bedroom, and garden; each one is bound to see everything, while there is scarce light enough to see anything. Imperceptibly the monster's joints creak, the stir of life spreads, the street finds a tongue, and by noon it is alive everywhere, the chimneys smoke, the monster feeds, and with a roar It stretches out its myraid paws. 'Tis a wonderful sight! And yet, oh Paris! who has not marveled at thy dark passages, thy fitful gleams of light, thy deep, soundless blind alleys? They who have not heard thy murmurs between midnight and two o'clock in the morning know nothing as yet of thy real poetry, of thy fantastic, broad contrast.

There are a very few amateurs, amateurs are they that can keep a steady head and take their Paris with gusto; and these know the physiognomy of the city so well that they know "even her spots, her blemishes, and her warts." Others may think of Paris as the monstrous marvel, as an astounding assemblage of brains and machinery in motion, as the City of a Hundred Thousand Romances, the head of the world. But for these who know her, Paris wears a dull or a gay face, she is ugly or fair, alive or dead; for them she is a living creature. Every room in a house is a lobe of the cellular tissue of the great courtesan, whose heart, and brain, and fantastic life they know to the uttermost. Therefore they are her lovers. They look up at a street corner, knowing that they shall see a clock face; they tell a friend with an empty snuff-box to "take such and such a turning, and you will find a tobacconist's store to the left, next-door to a confectioner that has a pretty wife."

For poets of this order, a walk through Paris is an expensive luxury. How refuse to spend a few minutes in watching the dramas, the accidents, the faces, the picturesque chance effects which importune you in the streets of the restless Queen of Cities that goes clad in placards, yet can boast not one clean corner, so complacent is she to the vices of the French nation. Who has not left home in the morning for the uttermost ends of Paris, and recognized by dinner-time the futility of his efforts to get away from the centre? Such as these will pardon these vagrant beginnings, which, after all, may be summed up by one eminently profitable and novel observation (so far as any observation can be novel in Paris where there is nothing new, not even the statue set up yesterday, on which the street urchin has left his mark already.

Well, then—there are certain streets, unknown for the most part by fashionable people, there are certain districts and certain houses to which a woman of fashion cannot go, unless she wishes that the most cruelly injurious constructions shall be put upon her errand. If she is a wealthy woman with a carriage of her own, and if she chooses to go on foot or disguised through one of these slums, her reputation as an honest woman is compromised. If, furthermore, it should so happen that she is seen about nine o'clock in the evening, the conjectures which an observer may permit himself are like to have appalling consequences. And, finally, if the woman is young and pretty; if she is seen to enter a house in one of these neighborhoods; if the house has a long, dark, damp, and reeking passage entry; if, at the end of the passage, a feeble, flickering lamp lights up the features of a hideous crone with bony fingers—then, to tell the truth in the interests of young and pretty women, that woman is lost. She is at the mercy of the first man of her acquaintance who chances to meet her in these foul ways.

And there is a street in Paris where such an encounter may end in a most dreadful and ghastly tragedy, a tragedy of blood, a tragedy in the modern vein. Unluckily, the convincingness of the situation and the dramatic element in it will be lost, like the modern drama, upon all save the very few; and a sad pity it is that the tale must be told to a public that cannot fully appreciate the truth of the local color. Still, who can flatter himself that he will ever be understood? We all die unappreciated. It is the lot of women and of men of letters.

At half-past eight one February evening, thirteen years ago, a young man chanced to turn the corner of the Rue Pagevin into the Rue des Vieux-Augustins precisely at the point where the Rue Soly enters it. Now, at that time there was not a wall in the Rue Pagevin but echoed a foul word; the Rue Soly was one of the narrowest and least practicable thoroughfares in Paris, not excepting the least frequented nooks in the most deserted streets of the city; and the young man came there by one of those chances that do not come twice in a lifetime. Arrived at this point, he was walking carelessly along when he saw a woman a few paces ahead of him, and fancied that he saw in her a vague resemblance to one of the prettiest women in Paris, a beautiful and modest woman whom he secretly and passionately loved; loved, too, without hope. She was married. In a moment his heart gave a bound. An intolerable heat, kindled in his diaphragm, spread through every vein. He felt a cold chill along his spine, a tingling sensation on the surface of his face.

He was young, he was in love, he knew Paris. His perspicacity would not allow him to shut his eyes to all the vile possibilities of the situation—a young, fair, and wealthy woman of fashion stealing along the street with a guilty, furtive step! That She should be in that filthy neighborhood at that hour of night!

His love seems romantic, no doubt, and the more so because he was an officer in the Guards. Of a man in an infantry regiment the thing is not inconceivable; but as a cavalry officer high in the service, he belonged to a division of the army that most desires rapid conquests. The cavalry are vain of their uniform, but they are vainer still of their success with women. Nevertheless, the officer's love was a genuine passion that will seem great to many a young heart. He loved the woman because she was virtuous. Her virtues, her reserved grace, the saintliness that awed him—these were the most precious treasures of his hidden passion. And she, in truth, was worthy of a Platonic love such as you sometimes find like a rare flower on the chronicler's page among the ruin and bloodshed of the Middle Ages. She was worthy to be the secret spring of all a young man's actions; the source of a love as high and pure as the blue heavens, a love without hope, to which a man clings because it never disappoints him, a love prodigal of uncontrolled delight, especially at an age when hearts are hot and imaginations poignant, and a man's eyes see very clearly.

There are strange, grotesque, inconceivable night effects to be seen in Paris; you cannot think, unless you have amused yourself with watching these, how fantastic a woman's shape can grow in the dusk. Sometimes the creature whom you follow by accident or design seems graceful and slender; sometimes a glimpse of a stocking, if it is very white, leads you to think that the outlines beneath are dainty and fine; a figure, muffled up, it may be, in a shawl or a pelisse, develops young luxuriant curves in the shadows; and as a last touch, the uncertain light from a store-window or a street lamp lends the stranger a fleeting halo, an illusion which stirs and kindles imagination to go beyond the truth. And then, the senses are stirred, color and life are put into everything, the woman is transfigured; her outward form grows fairer; there are moments when she is a woman no longer, she is an evil spirit, a will-of-the-wisp, drawing you farther and farther by a glowing magnetism until you reach—some decent dwelling, and the poor housewife, terrified by your menacing approach, and quaking at the sound of a man's boots, promptly shuts the door in your face without giving you so much as a glance.

Suddenly the flickering light from a shoemaker's window fell across the woman in front; it struck just across the hollow of the back. Ah! surely those curves belonged to Her only among women! Who else knew that secret of chaste movement which all innocently brings the beauty of the most attractive shape into relief.

It was the same shawl and velvet bonnet that she wore in the morning. Not a speck on her gray stockings; not a trace of mud on her shoes. The shawl clung tightly about the outlines of her bust, vaguely moulding its exquisite contours; but the young man had seen those white shoulders in the ballroom, and he knew what a wealth of beauty was hidden beneath the shawl.

An intelligent observer can guess by the way in which a Parisienne wraps her shawl about her shoulders, by her manner of lifting her foot, on what mysterious errand she is bent. There is an indescribable tremor and lightness about her and her movements; she seems to weigh less, she walks on and on, or rather she threads her way like a spinning star, flitting, borne along by a thought, which the folds of her dress, the flutter of her skirts, betray.

The young man quickened his pace, passed, and turned his head to look at her—— Presto! She had disappeared down an entry, a wicket with a bell attached slammed and tinkled after her. He turned back and caught sight of her as she climbed the staircase at the end of the passage, not without obsequious greetings on the part of an old portress below. It was a crooked staircase, the lamplight fell full on the lower steps, up which the lady sprang lightly and briskly, as an impatient woman might do.

"Why impatient?" he asked himself, as he went back to plant himself against the opposite wall. He gazed up, look-less wight, watching every story as narrowly as if he were a detective on the track of a conspirator.

It was a house like thousands of others in Paris, mean, commonplace, narrow, dingy, with three windows on each of the four floors. The store and the entresol belonged to the shoemaker. The second floor blinds were closed. Whither had the lady gone? He fancied that he heard the jingling of a door bell on the third floor. And, in fact, a light began to move in a room above, with two brightly illuminated windows, and presently appeared in a third window, hitherto in darkness, which seemed to belong to the parlor or dining room. In a moment the vague shadow of a woman's bonnet appeared on the ceiling, the door was closed, the first room relegated to darkness, and the two farther windows shone red as before. Just then a voice cried: "Look out!" and something struck against the young man's shoulder.

"You don't seem to mind in the least what you are about," said the gruff voice. It was a workman, carrying a long plank on his shoulder. He went by. The man might have been sent as a warning by Providence to ask the prying inquirer: "What are you meddling for? Mind your own business, and leave Parisiennes to their own little affairs."

The officer folded his arms; and being out of sight of every one, he allowed two tears of rage to roll down his cheeks. The sight of these shadows moving across the windows was painful to him; he looked away up the Rue des Vieux-Augustins, and saw a hackney-coach drawn up under a blind wall, at a distance from any house-door or store-window.

Is it she? Or is it not? Life or death for a lover. And the lover waited in suspense for an age of twenty minutes. Then she came downstairs, and he knew past mistake that this was the woman whom he loved in his secret soul. Yet even now he tried to doubt. The fair stranger went to the cab and stepped into it.

"The house is always there," thought he; "I can search

it at any time;" so he ran after the cab to make quite certain of the lady. Any remaining doubt was soon removed.

The vehicle stopped before an artificial flower store in the Rue de Richelieu, close to the Rue de Ménars. The lady alighted, entered the store, sent out the fare to the cabman, and chose some marabouts. Feather plumes for that black hair of hers, with her dark beauty! She brought the feathers close to her face to judge of the effect. The officer fancied he could hear the store woman speaking.

"Nothing more becoming, madame, to a dark complexion; there is something rather too hard about the contours of a brunette; the marabouts impart just the fluffy touch which is wanting. Her grace the Duchesse de Langeais says that the feathers lend something vague and Ossianic, and a great distinction to the face."

"Well, send them to me at once."

With that the lady tripped away round the corner into the Rue de Ménars and entered her own house. The door closed upon her, and the young lover, his hopes lost, and double misfortune, his cherished beliefs lost too, went through Paris like a drunken man, till before long he found himself at his own door, with no very clear knowledge how he came there. He flung himself into an easy-chair, rested his feet on the firedogs, and sat, with his head in his hands, while his soaked boots first dried and then scorched on the bars. It was a dreadful hour for him; he had come to one of those crises in a man's life when character is modified; and the course of action of the best of men depends upon the first lucky or unlucky step that he chances to take; upon Providence or Fate, whichever you choose.

He came of a good family, not that their nobility was of very ancient date; but there are so few old houses left in these days that any young man comes of an old family. One of his ancestors had purchased the post of councilor to the Parliament of Paris, and in course of time became president. His sons, with a fine fortune apiece, had entered the King's service, made good marriages, and arrived at Court. Then came the Revolution and swept them all away. One of them, however, an old and stubborn dowager, who had no mind to emigrate, remained in Paris, was put in prison, and lay there in danger of her life till the 9th Thermidor saved her, and finally she recovered her property. Afterward, at an auspicious moment in 1804, she sent for her grandson, Auguste de Maulincour, sole surviving scion of the Carbonnons de Maulincour, and in the characters of mother, noble, and self-willed dowager, brought him up with treble care.

At a later day, after the Restoration, Auguste de Maulincour, aged eighteen, entered the Maison Rouge, followed the Princes to Ghent, received a commission in the Guards, and at three-and-twenty was a major in a cavalry regiment—a superb position which he owed to his grandmother. And indeed, in spite of her age, the old lady knew her way at Court remarkably well.

This twofold biography, with some variations, is substantially the history of every family of emigrants, when blessed with debts and possessions, dowagers and tact.

Mme. la Baronne de Maulincour had a friend, the elderly Vidame de Pamiers, a sometime commander of the Knights of Malta. It was an eternal friendship of the kind that grows out of other ties formed sixty years ago, a friendship which nothing can destroy, because down in the depths of it lie secrets of the hearts of man and woman. These, if one had the time, would be well worth guessing; but such secrets, condensed into a score of lines, lose their savor; they should furnish forth instead some four volumes that might prove as interesting as "Le Doyen de Killerine"—a work which young men are wont to discuss and criticise and leave unread.

Auguste de Maulincour was connected, therefore, with the Faubourg Saint-Germain through his grandmother and the vidame; and with a name that dated two centuries back, he could assume the airs and opinions of others who traced their descent from Clovis. Tall, pale, slender, and delicate-looking, a man of honor, whose courage, moreover, was undoubted (for he had fought duels without hesitation for the least thing in life)—he had never yet been on a field of battle, yet wore the cross of the Legion of Honor at his button-hole. He represented, as you see, one of the mistakes of the Restoration, perhaps one of its more pardonable mistakes.

The young manhood of the Restoration period was unlike the youth of any other epoch, in that it was placed between memories of the Empire on the one hand, and of exile on the other; between the old traditions of the Court and the conscientious bourgeois system of training for appointments; between bigotry and fancy dress-balls; between a Louis XVIII., who saw nothing but the present moment, and a Charles X., who looked too far ahead. The young generation was always halting between two political creeds; blind and yet clairvoyant, bound to accept the will of the King, knowing the while that the Crown was entering on a mistaken policy. The older men counted the younger as naught, and jealously kept the reins of government in their enfeebled hands at a time when the Monarchy might have been saved by their withdrawal and the accession of that young France at whom the old-fashioned doctrinaires and *émigrés* of the Restoration are still pleased to laugh.

Auguste de Maulincour was one victim of the ideas that weighed upon the youth of those days. It was in this wise: The Vidame de Pamiers, even at the age of sixty-seven, was still a very lively personage, who had both seen and lived a great deal. He told a story well, he was a man of honor and gallantry, but so far as women were concerned he held the most detestable opinions. He fell in love, but he did not respect women. *Women's* honor, *women's* sentiments? Fiddle-de-dee! folly and make-believe. In the company of women he believed in them, did this *ci-devant* "monster;" he brought out their merits, he never contradicted a lady. But among friends, when women were the topic, the vidame laid it down as an axiom that the whole duty of a young man was to deceive women and to carry on several intrigues at once; and that when a young man attempted to meddle with affairs of State, he made a gross mistake.

It is sad to be obliged to sketch such a hackneyed character. Where has he not appeared? Is he not literally almost as worn out as the Imperial Grenadier? But over M. de Maulincour the vidame exercised an influence which must be recorded; he was a moralist after his own fashion, and he used to try to convert the young man to the doctrines of the great age of gallantry.

As for the dowager, she was a tender, pious woman, placed between her vidame and God; a pattern of grace and sweetness, but none the less endowed with a persistence which never went beyond the bounds of good taste, and always triumphed in the end. She had tried to preserve her grandson in all the fair illusions of life; she had brought him up on the best principles; she had given him all her own delicacy of feeling, and had made a diffident man of him, and to all appearance an absolute fool. His boyish sensibility, untouched by contact with the world, had met with no rubs without; so modest, so keenly sensitive was it, that actions and maxims to which the world attaches no importance grieved him sorely. He felt ashamed of his sensitiveness, hid it beneath a show of assurance, and suffered in silence, laughing in company at things which he reverenced in his secret heart. And therefore he was mistaken in his choice: for by a common freak of Fate he, the man of mild melancholy, who saw love in its spiritual aspects, must needs fall in love with a woman who detested German sentimentalism. He began to distrust himself. He grew moody, hugged himself on his troubles, and made moan because he was not understood. And then—since we always desire a thing more vehemently because it is hard to win—he continued to worship women with the ingenuous tenderness and feline delicacy of which they possess the secret; perhaps, too, they prefer to keep the monopoly of it. And, indeed, though women complain that men love amiss, they have very little taste for the semi-feminine nature in man. Their whole superiority consists in making the man believe that he is their inferior in love; for which reason they are quite ready to discard a lover when he is experienced enough to rob them of the fears in which they choose to deck themselves, to relieve them of the delicious torments of feigned jealousy, the troubles of disappointed hopes and vain suspense, and the whole train of dear feminine miseries, in short. Women hold Grandisons in abhorrence. What is more contrary to their nature than a tranquil, perfect love? They must have emotions. Bliss without storms for them is not bliss at all. A soul great enough to bring the Infinite into love is as uncommon among women as genius among men. A great passion is as rare as a masterpiece. Outside this love there lies nothing but arrangements and passing excitations, contemptible, like all petty things.

In the midst of the secret disasters of his heart, while he was seeking some one who should understand him (that quest, by the way, is the lover's folly of our time), Auguste found a perfect woman—a woman with that indescribable touch of sacredness and holiness which inspires such reverence that love needs all the support of a long intimacy to declare itself. He found her in a circle as far as possible from his own, in the second sphere of that financial world in which great capitalists take the first place.

Then Auguste gave himself up wholly to the bliss of the most moving and profound of passions; a purely contemplative love—a love made up of uncounted repressed longings, of shades of passion so vague, so deep, so fugitive, so vivid, that it is hard to find a comparison for them; they are like sweet scents, or sunlight, or cloud shadows, like all things that shine forth for a moment in the outer world to vanish, revive, and die, and leave a long wake of emotion in the heart. When a man is young enough to conceive melancholy and far-off hopes, to see in woman something more than a woman, can any greater happiness befall him than this—of loving so well that the mere contact of a white gloved hand, the light touch of a woman's hair, the sound of a voice, the chance of one look, fills him with a joy outpassing a fortunate lover's ecstasy of possession? And for this reason, none but slighted, shy, unattractive, unhappy men and women, unknown lovers, know all that there is in the sound of the voice of the one whom they love. It is because those fire-laden vibrations of the air have their source and origin in the soul itself that they bring hearts into communion with such violence, such lucid thought transferrence. So little misleading are they that a single modulation is often a revelation in itself. What enchantment is poured forth upon a poet's heart by the musical resonance of a low voice! What freshness it spreads through his soul, what visions it summons up! Love is in the voice before the eyes make confession.

Auguste, a poet after the manner of lovers—for there are poets who feel and poets who express, and the former are the happier—Auguste had known the sweetness of all those early joys, so far-reaching, so abundant. SHE was the possessor of such an entrancing voice as the most guileful of women might covet, that she might deceive others at her pleasure; hers were those silver notes, low only to the ear, that peal aloud through the heart, soothing the tumult and unrest that they stir.

And this was the woman who had gone at night to the Rue Soly in the neighborhood of the Rue Pagevin! He had seen her stealing into a house of ill-fame; and that most magnificent of passions had been brought low. The vidame's reasoning triumphed.

"If she is false to her husband, we will both avenge ourselves," said Auguste. And there was still love left in that "if." The suspended judgment of Cartesian philosophy is a homage always due to virtue. The clocks struck ten; and Auguste de Maulincour bethought himself that the woman he loved must surely be going to a dance at a house that he knew. He dressed, went thither, and made a furtive survey of the rooms. Mme. de Nucingen, seeing him thus intent, came to speak to him.

"You are looking for Madame Jules; she has not yet come."

"Good-evening, dear," said a voice.

Mme. de Nucingen and Auguste both turned. There stood Mme. Jules dressed in white, simple and noble, wearing those very feathers which the baron had watched her choose in the store. That voice of Love went to his heart. If he had only known how to assert the slightest claim to be jealous of the woman before him, he would have turned her to stone then and there with the exclamation: "Rue Soly!" But he, a stranger, might have repeated those words a hundred times in Mme. Jules' ear, and she in astonishment would merely ask him what he meant. He stared at her with dazed eyes.

Ill-natured men who scoff at everything may, perhaps, find it highly amusing to discover a woman's secret, to know that her chastity is a lie, that there are strange thoughts in the depths beneath the quiet surface, and an ugly tragedy behind the pure forehead. But there are others, no doubt, who are saddened at heart by it; and many of the scoffers, when at home and alone with themselves, curse the world, and despise such a woman. This was how Auguste de Maulincour felt as he confronted Mme. Jules. It was a strange position. He and this woman exchanged a few words seven or eight times in a season—that was all; yet he was charging her with stolen pleasure of which she knew nothing, and pronouncing judgment without telling her of the accusation.

Many a young man has done the same and gone home broken-hearted because all is over between him and some woman whom he once worshiped in his heart, and now scorns in his inmost soul. Then follow soliloquies heard of none, spoken to the walls of some lonely refuge; storms raised and quieted in the heart's depths, wonderful scenes of man's inner life which still await their painter.

M. Jules Desmarets made the round of the rooms, while his wife took a seat. But she seemed embarrassed in some way; and, as she chatted with her neighbor, she stole a glance now and again at her husband. M. Jules Desmarets was the Baron de Nucingen's stockbroker. And now for the history of the husband and wife.

M. Desmarets, five years before his marriage, was a clerk in a stockbroker's office; he had nothing in the world but his slender salary. But he was one of those men whom misfortune teaches to know life in a very few lessons, men who strike out their line and keep to it persistently as an insect; like other obstinate creatures he could sham death if anything stopped him, and weary out the patience of opponents by the perseverance of the woodlouse. Young as he was, he possessed all the republican virtues of the poor; he was sober, he never wasted his time, he set his face against pleasure. He was waiting. Nature, beside, had given him the immense advantage of a prepossessing exterior. His calm, pure forehead, the outlines of his placid yet expressive features, the simplicity of his manners, and everything about him, told of a hard-working, uncomplaining existence, of the high personal dignity which inspires awe in others, and of that quiet nobleness of spirit which is equal to all situations. His modesty impressed those who knew him with a certain respect. It was a solitary life, however, that he led in the midst of Paris. Society he saw only by glimpses during the few minutes spent on holidays in his employer's drawing-room.

In him, as in most men who lead such a life, there were astonishing depths of passion, inward forces too great to be brought into play by small occasions. His narrow means compelled him to live like an ascetic, and he subdued his fancies with hard work. After growing pale over figures, he sought relaxation in a dogged effort to acquire the wider knowledge so necessary to any man that would make his mark in these days, whether in business, at the bar, in politics or letters. The one reef in the careers of these finer natures is their very honesty. They come across some penniless girl, fall in love, and marry her, and afterward wear out their lives in the struggle for existence, with want on the one hand, love on the other. Housekeeping bills will extinguish the loftiest ambition. Jules Desmarets went straight ahead upon that reef.

One evening, at his employer's house, he met a young lady of the rarest beauty. Love rapidly made such havoc as a passion can make in a lonely and slighted heart, when an unhappy creature's affections have been starved, and the fair hours of youth consumed by continual work. So certain are they to love in earnest, so swiftly does their whole being centre itself upon the woman to whom they are attracted, that when she is present they are conscious of exquisite sensations, in none of which she shares. This is the most flattering form of egoism for the woman who can see, beneath the apparent immobility of passion, the feeling stirred in depths so remote that it is long before it reappears at the human surface. Such unfortunates as these are anchorites in the heart of Paris; they know all the joys of anchorites; sometimes, too, they may yield to their temptations; but it still more frequently happens that they are thwarted, betrayed, and misinterpreted; and only very seldom are they permitted to gather the sweet fruits of the love that seems to them like a power dropped down from heaven.

A smile from his wife, a mere modulation of her voice, was enough to gives Jules Desmarets a conception of the infinite of love. Happily the concentrated fire of passion within revealed itself artlessly to the woman for whom it burned.

And these two human creatures loved each other devoutly. To sum up all in a few words, they took each other by the hand without a blush, and went through the world together as two children, brother and sister, might pass through a crowd that makes way admiringly for them.

The young lady was in the odious position in which selfishness places some children at their birth. She had no recognized status; her name, Clémence, and her age were attested, not by a certificate of birth, but by a declaration made before a notary. As to her fortune, it was trifling. Jules Desmarets, hearing these bad tidings, was the happiest of men. If Clémence had belonged to some wealthy family, he would have despaired; but she was a poor love-child, the offspring of a dark, illicit passion. They were married. This was the beginning of a series of pieces of good fortune for Jules. Everybody envied him his luck; jealous tongues alleged that he succeeded by sheer good fortune, and left his merits and ability out of account.

Clémence's mother, nominally her godmother, bade Jules purchase a stockbroker's connection a few days after the wedding, promising to secure all the necessary capital. Such connections were still to be bought at moderate prices. On the great lady's recommendation, a wealthy capitalist made proposals on the most favorable terms to Jules Desmarets that evening in the stockbroker's own drawing-room, lent him money enough to exploit his business, and by the next day the fortunate clerk had bought his employer's connection.

In four years Jules Desmarets was one of the wealthiest members of his fraternity. Important clients had been added to the number of those left him by his predecessor. He inspired unbounded confidence; and from the manner in which business came to him, it was impossible but that he should recognize some occult influence due to his wife's mother, or, as he believed, to the mysterious protection of Providence.

Three years after the marriage Clémence lost her godmother.

By that time M. Jules, so called to distinguish him from his elder brother, whom he had established in Paris as a notary, was in receipt of an income of two hundred thousand livres. There was not such another happy couple in Paris. A five years' course of such unwonted love had been troubled but once by a slander, for which M. Jules took a single vengeance. One of his old associates said that M. Jules owed his success to his wife, and that influence in high places had been dearly bought. The inventor of the slander was killed in the duel that ensued. A passionate love so deeply rooted that it stood the test of marriage was much admired in society, though some women were displeased by it. It was pretty to see them together; they were respected, and made much of on all sides. M. and Mme. Jules were really popular, perhaps because there is no pleasanter sight than happy love; but they never stayed long in crowded rooms, and escaped to their nest as soon as they could, like two strayed doves.

The nest, however, was a fine large house in the Rue de Ménars, in which artistic feeling tempered the luxury which the city man is always supposed to display. Here, also, M. and Mme. Jules entertained splendidly. Social duties were somewhat irksome to them; but, nevertheless, Jules Desmarets submitted to such exactions, knowing that sooner or later a family will need acquaintances. He and his wife lived like plants in a hothouse in a stormy world. With very natural delicacy, Jules carefully kept the slander from his wife's knowledge as well as the death of the man that had almost troubled their felicity.

Mme. Jules, with her artistic temper and refinement, had inclinations toward luxury. In spite of the terrible lesson of the duel, there were incautious women to hint in whispers that Mme. Jules must often be pinched for money. Her husband allowed her twenty thousand francs for her dress and pocket-money, but this could not possibly be enough, they said, for her expenses. And, indeed, she was often more daintly dressed

in her own home than in other people's houses. She only
cared to adorn herself for her husband's eyes, trying in this way
to prove to him that for her he was all the world. This was love
indeed, pure love, and more than this, it was happy as clandes-
tine love sanctioned by the world can be. M. Jules was
still his wife's lover, and more in love every day. Everything in his wife, even her caprices, made him happy. When
she had no new fancy to gratify, he felt as much disturbed as
if this had been a symptom of bad health.

It was against this passion that Auguste de Maulincour, for
his misfortune, had dashed himself. He loved Madame Clem-
ence Jules to distraction. And yet even with a supreme
passion in his heart he was not ridiculous, and he lived the
regular garrison life, yet even with a glass of champagne in
his hand he wore an abstracted air. His was the quiet scorn
of existence, the clouded countenance worn alike on various
pretexts by jaded spirits, by men but little satisfied with the
hollowness of their lives, and by the victims of pulmonary
disease or heart troubles. A hopeless love or a distaste for
existence constitutes a sort of social position nowadays.

To take a queen's heart by storm were perhaps a more hope-
ful enterprise than a madly conceived passion for a woman
happily married. Auguste de Maulincour had sufficient excuse for his gravity and dejection. A queen has always the
vanity of her power; her height above her lover places her
at a disadvantage; but a well-principled bourgeoise, like a
hedgehog or an oyster, is encompassed about with awkward
defenses.

At this particular moment Auguste stood near his unde-
clared lady. She, certainly, was incapable of carrying on a
double intrigue. There sat Mme. Jules in childlike composure, the least guileful of women, gentle, full of queenly
serenity. What depths can there be in human nature? The
baron, before addressing her, kept his eyes on husband and
wife in turn. What reflections did he not make! In a minute's

space he recomposed a second version of Young's "Night Thoughts." And yet—the rooms were filled with dance music, and the light of hundreds of wax-tapers streamed down upon them. It was a banker's ball, one of those insolent fêtes by which the world of dull gold attempted to rival that other world of gilded rank and ormolu, the world where the high-born Faubourg Saint-Germain was laughing yet, all unconscious that a day was approaching when capitalists would invade the Luxembourg and seat a king on the throne. Conspiracy used to dance in those days, giving as little thought to future bankruptcies of Power as to failures ahead in the financial world. M. le Baron de Nucingen's gilded salons wore that look of animation which a fête in Paris is wont to wear; there is gayety, at any rate, on the surface. The wit of the cleverer men infects the fools, while the beaming expression characteristic of the latter spreads over the countenances of their superiors in intellect; and the whole room is brightened by the exchange. But gayety in Paris is always a little like a display of fireworks; pleasure, coquetry, and wit all coruscate, and then die out like spent rockets. To-morrow morning, wit, coquetry, and pleasure are put off and forgotten.

"Heigho!" thought Auguste, as he came to a conclusion, "are women really after all as the vidame sees them? Certain it is that of all the women dancing here to-night, not one seems so irreproachable as Madame Jules. And Madame Jules goes to the Rue Soly!"

The Rue Soly was like a disease, the mere word made his heart contract.

"Do you never dance, madame?" he began.

"This is the third time that you have asked me that question this winter," she answered, smiling.

"But perhaps you have never given me an answer."

"That is true."

"I knew quite well that you were false, like all women——"

Mme. Jules laughed again.

"Listen to me, monsieur. If I told you my real reason for not dancing, it would seem ridiculous to you. There is no insincerity, I think, in declining to give private reasons at which people usually laugh."

"Any confidence, madame, implies a degree of friendship of which I, no doubt, am unworthy. But it is impossible that you should have any but noble secrets, and can you think me capable of irreverent jesting?"

"Yes," she said. "You, like the rest of men, laugh at our purest feelings and misconstrue them. Beside, I have no secrets. I have a right to love my husband before all the world; I am proud of it, I tell you; and if you laugh at me when I say that I never dance with any one else, I shall have the worst opinion of your heart."

"Have you never danced with any one but your husband since your marriage?"

"No, monsieur. I have leaned on no other arm, no one else has come very close to me."

"Has not your doctor so much as felt your pulse?"

"Ah, well, now you are laughing."

"No, madame, I admire you because I can understand. But you suffer others to hear your voice, to see you, to—— In short, you permit our eyes to rest admiringly on you——"

"Ah, these things trouble me," she broke in. "If it were possible for husband and wife to live like lover and mistress, I would have it so; for in that case——"

"In that case, how came you to be out, on foot and disguised, a few hours ago, in the Rue Soly?"

"Where is the Rue Soly?" asked she, not a trace of emotion in her clear voice, not the faintest quiver in her features. She did not redden, she was quite composed.

"What! You did not go up the stairs to the third floor in a house at the corner of the Rue des Vieux-Augustins and the Rue Soly? You had not a cab waiting for you ten paces away? and you did not return to a store in the Rue de Richelieu, where you chose the feathers in your hair at this moment?"

"I did not leave my house this evening." She told the lie with an imperturbable laughing face; she fanned herself as she spoke; but any one who could have laid a hand on her girdle at the back, might perhaps have felt that it was damp. Auguste bethought himself of the vidame's teaching.

"Then it was some one extraordinarily like you," he rejoined with an air of belief.

"Sir," said she, "if you are capable of following a woman about to detect her secrets, you will permit me to tell you that such a thing is wrong, very wrong, and I do you the honor of declining to believe it of you."

The baron turned away, took up his position before the hearth, and seemed thoughtful. He bent his head, but his eyes were fixed stealthily upon Mme. Jules. She had forgotten the mirrors on the walls, and glanced toward him two or three times with an evident dread in her eyes. Then she beckoned to her husband, laid a hand upon his arm, and rose to go through the rooms. As she passed M. de Maulincour, who was talking with a friend, he said aloud, as if in answer to a question—

"A woman that certainly will not sleep quietly to-night——"

Mme. Jules stopped, flung him a crushing, disdainful glance, and walked away, all unaware that one more such glance, if her husband chanced to see it, would imperil the happiness and the lives of two men.

Auguste, consumed with rage smouldering in the depths of his soul, soon afterward left the room, vowing to get to the bottom of this intrigue. He looked around for Mme. Jules before he went, but she had disappeared.

Here were the elements of a tragedy suddenly put into a young head, an eminently romantic head, as is generally the case with those who have not realized their dreamed-of love to the full. He adored Mme. Jules in a new aspect; he loved her with the fury of jealousy, with the agonized frenzy of despair. The woman was false to her husband; she had come down to the ordinary level. Auguste might give himself up to all the felicity of success, imagination opened out for him the vast field of the transports of possession. In short, if he had lost an angel, he had found the most tantalizing of devils. He lay down to build castles in the air, and to justify Mme. Jules. Some errand of charity had brought her there, he told himself, but he did not believe it. He made up his mind to devote himself entirely to the investigation of the causes and motives involved in this mysteriously hidden knot. It was a romance to read; or better, it was a drama to act, and he was cast for a part in it.

It is a very fine thing to play the detective for one's own ends and for passion's sake. Is it not an honest man's chance of enjoying the amusements of the thief? Still, you must be prepared to boil with helpless rage, to growl with impatience, to stand in mud till your feet are frozen, to shiver and burn and choke down false hopes. You must follow up any indication to an end unknown; and miss your chance, storm, improvise lamentations and dithyrambs for your own benefit, and utter insensate exclamations before some harmless passer-by, who stares back at you in amazement. You take to your heels and overturn good souls with their apple-baskets, you wait and hang about under a window, you make guesses by the running hundred. Still it is sport, and Parisian sport; sport with all its accessories save dogs, and guns, and tally-ho. Nothing, except some moments in the gambler's life, can compare with it. A man's heart must needs be swelling with love and revenge before he will lie in ambush ready to spring like a tiger on his prey; before he can find enjoyment in watching all that goes on in the quarter; for interest of many kinds abounds in Paris without the added pleasure of stalking game. How should one soul suffice a man for all this? What is it but a life made up of a thousand passions, a thousand feelings, and thoughts?

Auguste de Maulincour flung himself heart and soul into this feverish life, because he felt all its troubles and joys. He went about Paris in disguise; he watched every corner of the Rue Pagevin and the Rue des Vieux-Augustins. He ran like a lamplighter from the Rue de Ménars to the Rue Soly, and back again from the Rue Soly to the Rue de Ménars, all unconscious of the punishment or the reward in store for so many pains, such measures, such shifts! And even so, he had not yet reached the degree of impatience which gnaws the vitals and brings the sweat to a man's brow; he hung about in hope. It occurred to him that Mme. Jules would scarcely risk another visit for some few days after detection. So he devoted those first few days to an initiation into the mysteries of the street. Being but a novice in the craft, he did not dare to go to the house itself and question the janitor and the shoemaker; but he had hopes of securing a post of observation in rooms exactly opposite those inscrutable apartments. He made a careful survey of the ground; he was trying to reconcile caution with impatience, his great love, and the inscrutable secret.

By the beginning of March he was in the midst of his preparations for making a great decisive move, when official duties summoned him from his chessboard one afternoon about four o'clock, after an assiduous course of sentry-duty, for which he was not a whit the wiser. In the Rue Coquillière he was caught by one of the heavy showers which swell the stream in the gutters in a moment, while every drop falling into the roadside puddles raises a bell-shaped splash. A foot-passenger in such a predicament is driven to take refuge in a store or café if he can afford to pay for shelter; or, at urgent need, to hurry into some entry, the asylum of the poor and shabbily dressed. How is it that as yet no French painter has tried to give us that characteristic group, a crowd of Parisians weather-bound under an archway? Where will you find better material for a picture?

To begin with, is there not the pensive or philosophical pedestrian who finds a pleasure in watching the slantwise streaks of rain in the air against the gray background of sky—a fine chased work something like the whimsical shapes taken by spun glass? Or he looks up at the whirlpools of white water, blown by the wind like a luminous dust over the house-roofs, or at the fitful discharges of the wet, foaming gutter-pipes. There are, in fact, a thousand nothings to wonder at, and the idlers are studying them with keen relish, although the owner of the premises treats them to occasional thumps from the broom-handle while pretending to be sweeping out the gateway.

There is the chatty person who grumbles and talks with the porter's wife, while she rests on her broom as a grenadier leans on his gun; there is the poverty-stricken individual glued fantastically to the wall—he has nothing to dread from such contact; for his rags, they are already so well acquainted with the street; there is the man of education who studies, spells out, or even reads the advertisements, and never gets to the end of them; there is the humorous person who laughs at the mud-bedraggled women, and makes eyes at the people in the windows opposite; there is the mute refugee that scans every casement on every floor, and the working man or woman with a mallet or a bundle, as the case may be, translating the shower into probable losses or gains. Then there is the amiable man, who bounces in like a bombshell with an "Oh! what weather, gentlemen!" and raises his hat to the company; and, finally, there is your true Parisian bourgeois, a weatherwise citizen who never comes out without his umbrella; he knew beforehand that it was going to rain, but he came out in spite of his wife's advice, and now he is sitting in the porter's chair.

Each member of this chance assembled group watches the

sky in his own characteristic fashion, and then skips away for fear of splashing his boots, or goes because he is in a hurry and sees other citizens walking past in spite of wind and weather, or because the courtyard is damp and like to give you your death of cold—the selvedge, as the saying goes, being worse than the cloth. Every one has his own reasons for going, until no one is left but the prudent pedestrian, who waits to see a few blue chinks among the clouds before he goes on his way.

M. de Maulincour, therefore, took refuge with a tribe of foot-passengers under the porch of an old-fashioned house with a courtyard not unlike a gigantic chimney-shaft. There were so many stories rising to a height on all sides, and the four plastered walls, covered with greenish stains and saltpetre ooze, were traversed by such a multitude of gutters and spouts, that they would have put you in mind of the cascades of St. Cloud. From every direction came the sound of falling water; it foamed, splashed, and gurgled; it gushed forth in streams, or black, or white, or blue, or green; it hissed and gathered volume under the broom wielded by the janitor's wife, a toothless crone of great experience in storms, who seemed to bless the waters as she swept down a host of odds and ends into the street. A curious inventory of the rubbish would have told you a good deal about the lives and habits of the lodgers on every floor. There were tea-leaves, cuttings of chintz, discolored and spoilt petals of artificial flowers, vegetable refuse, paper, and scraps of metal. Every stroke of the old woman's broom laid bare the heart of the gutter, that black channel paved with chessboard squares, on which every janitor wages desperate war. The luckless lover gazed intently at this picture, one of the many thousands which bustling Paris composes every day; but he saw it all with unseeing eyes, until he looked up and found himself face to face with a man that had just come in.

This man was, at any rate to all appearance, a beggar.

Not a Parisian beggar, that human creature for which human speech has found no name as yet; but a novel type, a beggar cast in some different mould, and apart from all the associations called up by that word. The stranger was not by any means remarkable for that peculiarly Parisian character, which frequently startles us in those unfortunates whom Charlet drew, and often enough with a rare felicity; the Paris beggar with the coarse face plastered with mud, the red bulbous nose, the toothless but menacing mouth, the eyes lighted up by a profound intelligence which seems out of place—a servile terrific figure. Some of the impudent vagabonds have mottled, chapped, and veined countenances, rugged foreheads, and thin, dirty locks that put you in mind of a worn-out wig lying in the gutter. Jolly in their degradation and degraded amid their jollity, debauchery has set its unmistakable mark on them, they hurl their silence at you like a reproach, their attitude expresses appalling thoughts. They are ruthless, are these dwellers between beggary and crime; they circle at a safe distance round the gallows, steering clear of the law in the midst of vice, and vicious within the bounds of law. While they often provoke a smile, they set you thinking.

One, for instance, represents stunted civilization; he comprehends it all, thieves' honor, patriotism, and manhood, with the perverse ingenuity of the common criminal and the subtlety of kid-gloved rascality. Another is resigned to his lot; he is pastmaster in mimicry, but a dull creature. None of them are exempt from passing fancies for work and thrift; but the social machinery thrusts them down into their filth, without caring to discover whether there may not be poets, or great men, or brave men, or a whole wonderful organization among the beggars in the streets, those gypsies of Paris. Like all masses of men who have suffered, the beggar tribes are supremely good and superlatively wicked; they are accustomed to endure nameless ills, and a fatal power keeps them on a level with the mud of the streets. And every one of them has a dream, a hope, a happiness of his own, which takes the shape of gambling, or the lottery, or drink.

There was nothing of this strange life about the man who was propping himself, very much at his ease, against the wall opposite M. de Maulincour; he looked like a fancy portrait sketched by an ingenious artist on the back of some canvas returned to the studio.

He was lank and lean; his leaden-hued visage revealed glacial depths of thought; his ironical bearing, and a dark look, which plainly conveyed his claim to treat every man as his equal, dried up any feeling of compassion in the hearts of the curious. His complexion was a dingy white; his wrinkled, hairless head bore a vague resemblance to a block of granite. A few grizzled, lank locks on either side of his face straggled over the collar of a filthy overcoat buttoned up to the chin. There was something of a Voltaire about him, something, too, of a Don Quixote; melancholy, scornful, sarcastic, full of philosophical ideas, but half insane. Apparently he wore no shirt. His beard was long. His shabby black cravat was so slit and worn that it left his neck on exhibition, and a protuberant, deeply furrowed throat, on which the thick veins stood out like cords. There were wide, dark bruised circles about his eyes. He must have been at least sixty years old. His hands were white and clean. His shoes were full of holes, and trodden down at the heels. A pair of much-mended blue trousers, covered with a kind of pale fluff, added to the squalor of his appearance.

Perhaps the man's wet clothes exhaled a nauseous stench; perhaps at any time he had about him that odor of poverty peculiar to Paris slums—for slums, like offices, vestries, and hospitals, have a special smell, and a stale, rancid, fetid, unimaginable reek it is. At any rate, the man's neighbors edged away and left him alone. He glanced round at them, and then at the officer; it was an unmoved, expressionless look; the look for which M. de Talleyrand was so famous, a survey made by lack-lustre eyes with no warmth in them. Such a look is an inscrutable veil beneath which a strong mind can hide deep feeling, and the most accurate calculations as to men, affairs, and events. Not a wrinkle deepened in his countenance. Mouth and forehead were alike impassive, but his eyes fell, and there was something noble, almost tragic, in their slow movement. A whole drama lay in that droop of the withered eyelids.

The sight of this stoical face started M. de Maulincour upon those musings that begin with some commonplace question and wander off into a whole world of ideas before they end. The storm was over and gone. M. de Maulincour saw no more of the man than the skirts of his overcoat trailing on the curb-stone; but as he turned to go he saw that a letter had just dropped at his feet, and guessed that it belonged to the stranger, for he had noticed that he put a bandana handkerchief back into his pocket. M. de Maulincour picked up the letter to return it to its owner, and unthinkingly read the address—

MOSIEUR FERRAGUSSE,

Rue des Grands-Augustins, at the corner of the
Rue Soly.

PARIS.

To MOSIEUR.

There was no postmark on the letter, and at sight of the address M. de Maulincour hesitated to return it; for there are few passions which will not turn base in the long length. Some presentiment of the opportuneness of the treasure-trove crossed the baron's mind. He would keep the letter, and so acquire a right to enter the mysterious house, never doubting but that the man lived therein. Even now a suspicion, vague as the beginning of daylight, connected the stranger with Mme. Jules. Jealous lovers will suppose anything; and it is by this very process of supposing everything and selecting the more probable conjectures that examining magistrates, spies, lovers, and observers get at the truth which they have an interest in discovering.

"Does the letter belong to him? Is it from Mme. Jules?"

His restless imagination flung a host of questions to him at once, but at the first words of the letter he smiled. Here it follows word for word in the glory of its artless phrases; it was impossible to add anything to it, and short of omitting the letter itself, nothing could be taken away. It has been necessary, however, to revise the orthography and the punctuation; for in the original there are neither commas nor stops, nor so much as a note of exclamation, a fact that strikes at the root of the system by which modern authors endeavor to render the effect of the great disasters of every kind of passion:

"HENRY" (so it ran), "of all the sacrifices that I have had to make for your sake, this is the hardest, that I mayn't give you news of myself. There is a voice that I must obey, which tells me I ought to let you know all the wrong you've done me. I know beforehand that you are that hardened by vice that you will not stoop to pity me. Your heart must be deaf to all feeling; is it not deaf to the cry of nature? Not that it matters much. I am bound to let you know the degree to which you are to blame, and the horror of the position in which you have put me. You knew how I suffered for my first fall, Henry, yet you could bring me to the same pass again, and leave me in my pain and despair. Yes, I own I used to think you loved and respected me, and that helped me to bear up. And now what is left to me? I have lost all that I cared most about, all that I lived for, parents, friends, and relations, and character, and all through you. I have given up everything for you, and now I have nothing before me but shame and disgrace and, I don't blush to say it, want. It only needed your scorn and hatred to make my

misery complete; and now I have that as well, I shall have
courage to carry out my plans. I have made up my mind—
it's for the credit of my family—I shall put an end to my
troubles. You must not think hardly of the thing that I am
going to do, Henry. It is wicked, I know, but I can't help
myself. No help, no money, no sweetheart to comfort me—
can I live? No, I can't. What must be, must. So in two
days, Henry, two days from now, your Ida will not be worthy
of your respect; but take back the solemn promise I made
you, so as I may have an easy conscience, for I shall not be
unworthy of your regard. Oh, Henry, my friend, for I
shall never change to you, promise to forgive me for the life
I'm going to lead. It is love that gives me courage, and it
is love that will keep me right. My heart will be so full of
your image that I shall still be true to you. I pray heaven
on my bended knees not to punish you for all the wrong you
have done, for I feel that there is only one thing wanting
among my troubles, and that is the pain of knowing that you
are unhappy. In spite of my plight, I will not take any help
from you. If you had cared about me, I might have taken
anything as coming from friendship; but my soul rises up
against a kindness as comes from pity, and I should demean
myself more by taking it than him that offered it. I have
one favor to ask. I don't know how long I shall have to
stop with Mme. Meynardie, but be generous enough to keep
out of my sight there. Your last two visits hurt me so that it
was a long time before I got over it; but I don't mean to go
into any particulars of your behavior in that respect. You
hate me—you said so; the words are written on my heart,
and freeze it with cold. Alas! just when I want all my courage, my wits desert me. Henry dear, before I put this bar
between us, let me know for the last time that you respect me
still; write me, send me an answer, say that you respect me
if you don't love me any more. I shall always be able to
look you in the face, but I don't ask for a sight of you; I am

so weak, and I love you so, that I don't know what I might do. But, for pity's sake, write me a line at once; it will give me courage to bear my misery. Farewell, you have brought all my troubles upon me, but you are the one friend that my heart has chosen, and will never forget.   IDA."

This young girl's life, her disappointed love, her ill-starred joys, her grief, her dreadful resignation to her lot, the humble poem summed up in so few words, produced a moment's effect upon M. de Maulincour. He asked himself, as he read the obscure but essentially Parisian tragedy written upon the soiled sheet, whether this Ida might not be connected in some way with Mme. Jules; whether the assignation that he chanced to witness that evening was not some charitable effort on her part. Could that aged, poverty-stricken man be Ida's betrayer? The thing bordered on the marvelous. Amusing himself in a maze of involved and incompatible ideas, the baron reached the neighborhood of the Rue Pagevin just in time to see a hack stop at the end of the Rue des Vieux-Augustins nearest the Rue Montmartre. Every driver on the stand had something to say to the new arrival.

"Can *she* be in it?" he thought.

His heart beat with hot, feverish throbs. He pushed open the wicket with the tinkling bell, but he lowered his head as he entered; he felt ashamed of himself, a voice in his inmost soul cried:

"Why meddle in this mystery?"

At the top of a short flight of steps he confronted the old woman.

"Monsieur Ferragus?"

"Don't know the name——"

"What! Doesn't Monsieur Ferragus live here?"

"No name of the sort in the house."

"But my good woman——"

"I'm not a 'good woman,' sir; I am the portress."

"But, madame, I have a letter here for Monsieur Ferragus."

"Oh! if you have a letter, sir," said she, with a change of tone, "that is quite another thing. Will you just let me see it—that letter?"

Auguste produced the folded sheet. The old woman shook her head dubiously over it, hesitated, and seemed on the point of leaving her lodge to acquaint the mysterious Ferragus with this unexpected incident. At last she said: "Very well, go upstairs, sir. You ought to know your way up——"

Without staying to answer a remark which the cunning crone possibly meant as a trap, the young officer bounded up the stairs and rang loudly at the third-floor door. His lover's instinct told him: "*She* is here."

The stranger of the archway, the "orther" of Ida's troubles, answered the door himself, and showed a clean countenance, a flowered gown, a pair of white flannel trousers, and a neat pair of carpet-slippers. Mme. Jules' face appeared behind him in the doorway of the inner room; she grew white, and dropped into a chair.

"What is the matter, madame?" exclaimed Auguste, as he sprang toward her.

But Ferragus stretched out an arm and stopped the young man short with such a well-delivered blow that Auguste reeled as if an iron bar had struck him on the chest.

"Stand back, sir! What do you want with us? You have been prowling about the quarter these five or six days. Perhaps you are a spy?"

"Are you Monsieur Ferragus?" retorted the baron.

"No, sir."

"At any rate, it is my duty to return this paper which you dropped under an archway where we both took shelter from the rain."

As he spoke and held out the letter, he glanced round the room in spite of himself. Ferragus' room was well but plainly furnished. There was a fire in the grate. A table was set, more sumptuously than the man's apparent position and the low rent of the house seemed to warrant. And lastly, he caught a glimpse of a heap of gold coins on a *console* just inside the next room, and heard a sound from thence which could only be a woman's sobbing.

"The letter is mine, thank you," said the stranger, turning round in a way intended to convey the hint that the baron had better go, and that at once.

Too inquisitive to notice that he himself was being submitted to a thorough scrutiny, Auguste did not see the semi-magnetic glances, the devouring gaze which the stranger turned upon him. If he had met those basilisk eyes, he would have seen his danger, but he was too violently in love to think of himself. He raised his hat, went downstairs, and back to his own home. What could a meeting of three such persons as Ida, Ferragus, and Mme. Jules mean? He might as well have taken up a Chinese puzzle, and tried to fit the odd-shaped bits of wood together without a clue.

But Mme. Jules had seen him; Mme. Jules went to the house; Mme. Jules had lied to him. Next day he would call upon her; she would not dare to refuse to see him; he was now her accomplice; he was hand and foot in this shady intrigue. Already he began to play the sultan, and thought how he would summon Mme. Jules to deliver up all her secrets.

Paris was afflicted in those days with a rage for building. If Paris is a monster, it is assuredly of all monsters the most subject to sudden rage. The city takes up with a thousand whimsies. Sometimes Paris begins to build like some great lord with a passion for bricks and mortar; then the trowel is dropped in an attack of military fever, every one turns out in a National Guard's uniform, and goes through the drill and smokes cigars, but the fit does not last; martial exercises are suddenly abandoned, and the cigar is thrown away. Then Paris begins to feel low, becomes insolvent, sells its effects in

the Place du Châtelet, and files its petition; but in a few
days all is straight again, and the city puts on festival array
and dances. One day the city fills hands and mouth with
barley-sugar, yesterday it bought "Papier Weynen;" to-day
the monster has the toothache, and plasters every wall with
advertisements of Alexipharmaques, and to-morrow it will lay
in a store of cough lozenges. Paris has the craze of the
season or of the month as well as the rage of the day; and at
this particular time everybody was building or pulling down
something. What they built or pulled down no one knows to
this day, but there was scarce a street in which you did not see
erections of scaffolding, poles, planks, and cross-bars lashed
together at every story. The fragile structures, covered with
white plaster dust, quivered under the tread of the Limousin
bricklayers and shook with the vibrations of every passing
carriage in spite of the protection of wooden hoardings, which
people are bound to erect around the monumental buildings
that never rise above their foundations. There is a nautical
suggestion about the mast-like poles and ladders and rigging
and the shouts of the bricklayers.

One of these temporary erections stood not a dozen paces
away from the Hôtel Maulincour, in front of a house that was
being built of blocks of free-stone. Next day, just as the
Baron de Maulincour's cab passed by the scaffolding on the
way to Mme. Jules, a block two feet square slipped from its
rope-cradle at the top of the pole, turned a somersault, fell,
and killed the manservant at the back of the vehicle. A cry
of terror shook the scaffolding and the bricklayers. One of
the two, in peril of his neck, could scarcely cling to the pole;
it seemed that the block struck him in passing. A crowd
quickly gathered. The men came down in a body, with
shouts and oaths, declaring that M. de Maulincour's cab had
shaken their crane. Two inches more, and the stone would
have fallen on the baron's head. It was an event in the
quarter. It got into the newspapers.

M. de Maulincour, sure that he had touched nothing, brought an action for damages. The law stepped in. It turned out upon inquiry that a boy with a wooden lath had mounted guard to warn passengers to give the building a wide berth, and with that the affair came to an end. M. de Maulincour must even put up with the loss of his manservant and the fright that he had had. He kept his bed for several days, for he had been bruised by the breakage of the cab, and he was feverish after the shock to his nerves. So there was no visit paid to Mme. Jules.

Ten days later, when he went out of doors for the first time, he drove to the Bois de Boulogne in the now repaired cab. He turned down the Rue de Bourgogne, and had reached the sewer just opposite the Chamber of Deputies, when the axle snapped in the middle. The baron was driving so fast that the two wheels swerved and met with a shock that must have fractured his skull if it had not been for the hood of the vehicle, and, as it was, he sustained serious injury to the ribs. So for the second time in ten days he was brought home more dead than alive to the weeping dowager.

This second accident aroused his suspicions. He thought, vaguely however, of Mme. Jules and Ferragus; and by way of clearing up his suspicions, he had the broken axle brought into his bedroom, and sent for his coach-builder. The man inspected the fracture, and proved two things to M. Maulincour's mind. First, that the axle never came from his establishment, for he made a practice of cutting his initials roughly on every one that he supplied. How this axle had been exchanged for the previous one he was at a loss to explain. And secondly, he found that there was a very ingeniously contrived flaw in the iron bar, a kind of cavity made by a blowpipe while the metal was hot.

"Eh! Monsieur le Baron, a man had need to be pretty clever to turn out an axle-tree on that pattern; you could swear it was natural——"

M. de Maulincour asked the man to keep his own counsel, and considered that he had had a sufficient warning. The two attempts on his life had been plotted with a skill which showed that his were no common enemies.

"It is a war of extermination," said he, turning restlessly on his bed, "a warfare of savages, ambushes, and treachery, a war declared in the name of Madame Jules. In whose hands is she? And what power can this Ferragus wield?"

M. de Maulincour, brave man and soldier though he was, could not help shivering when all was done and said. Among the thoughts that beset him, there was one which found him defenseless and afraid. How if these mysterious enemies of his should resort next to poison? Terror, exaggerated by fever and low diet, got the better of him in his weak condition. He sent for an old attached servant of his grandmother's, a woman who loved him with that almost motherly affection through which an ordinary nature reaches the sublime. Without telling her all that was in his mind, he bade her buy all necessary articles of food for him, secretly, and every day at a fresh place; and at the same time, he warned her to keep everything under lock and key, and to allow no one whatsoever to be present while she prepared his meals. In short, he took the most minute precautions against this kind of death. He was lying ill in bed; he had therefore full leisure to consider his best way of defending himself, and love of life is the only craving sufficiently clairvoyant to allow human egoism to forget nothing. But the luckless patient had himself poisoned his own life with dread. Every hour was overshadowed by a gloomy suspicion that he could not throw off. Still, the two lessons in murder had taught him one qualification indispensable to a politic man; he understood how greatly dissimulation is needed in the complex action of the great interests of life. To keep a secret is nothing; but to be silent beforehand, to forget, if necessary, for thirty years, like Ali Pasha, the better to ensure a revenge pondered during those thirty years—this is a fine study in a country where few men can dissemble for thirty days together.

By this time Mme. Jules was Auguste de Maulincour's whole life. His mind was always intently examining the means by which he might win a triumph in his mysterious duel with unknown antagonists. His desire for this woman grew the greater by every obstacle. Amid all his thoughts Mme. Jules was always present in his heart of hearts; there she stood more irresistible now in her imputed sin than she used to be with all the undoubted virtues for which he had once worshiped her.

The sick man, wishing to reconnoitre the enemy's position, thought there could be no danger in letting the old commander into the secret. The commander loved Auguste as a father loves his wife's children; he was shrewd and adroit, he was of a diplomatic turn of mind. So the commander came, heard the baron's story, and shook his head, and the two held counsel. Auguste maintained that in the days in which they lived the detective force and the powers that be were equal to finding out any mysteries, and that if there was absolutely no other way the police would prove powerful auxiliaries. The commander, the vidame, did not share his young friend's confidence or his convictions.

"The police are the biggest bunglers on earth, dear boy, and the powers that be are the feeblest of all things where individuals are concerned. Neither the authorities nor the police can get to the bottom of people's minds. If they discover the causes of a fact that is all that can reasonably be expected of them. Now the authorities and the police are eminently unsuited to a business of this kind; the personal interest which is not satisfied till everything is found out is essentially lacking in them. No human power can prevent a murderer or a poisoner from reaching a prince's heart or an honest man's stomach. It is passion that makes the complete detective."

With that the vidame strongly advised his young friend the baron to travel. Let him go to Italy, and from Italy to Greece, and from Greece to Syria and Asia, and come back only when his mysterious enemies should be convinced of his repentance. In his way he would conclude a tacit peace with them. Or, if he stayed, he had better keep to his house, and even to his room, since there he could secure himself against the attacks of this Ferragus, and never leave it except to crush the enemy once for all.

"A man should never touch his enemy except to smite off his head," the vidame said gravely.

Nevertheless, the old man promised his favorite that he would bring all the astuteness with which heaven had gifted him to bear on the case, and that, without committing any one, he would send a reconnoitring party into the enemy's camp, know all that went on there, and prepare a victory.

The vidame had in his service a retired Figaro, as mischievous a monkey as ever took human shape. In former times the man had been diabolically clever, and a convict's physical frame could not have responded better to all demands made upon it; he was agile as a thief and subtle as a woman, but he had fallen into the decadence of genius for want of practice. New social conditions in Paris have reformed the old valets of comedy. The emeritus Scapin was attached to his master as to a being of superior order; but the crafty vidame used to increase the annual wage of his sometime provost of gallantry by a tolerably substantial sum, in such sort that the natural ties of good-will were strengthened by the bond of interest, and the old vidame received in return such watchful attention as the tenderest of mistresses could scarcely devise in a lover's illness. In this relic of the eighteenth century, this peril of old-world stage-servants, this minister incorruptible (since all his desires were gratified)— the vidame and M. de Maulincour both put their trust.

"Monsieur le Baron would spoil it all," said the great man

in livery, summoned by the vidame to the council. "Let monsieur eat and drink and sleep in peace. I will take it all upon myself."

And indeed, a week afterward, when M. de Maulincour, now perfectly recovered, was breakfasting with his grandmother and the vidame, Justin appeared to make his report. The dowager went back to her rooms, and he began with that false modesty which men of genius affect—

"Ferragus is not the real name of the enemy in pursuit of Monsieur le Baron. The man, the devil rather, is called Gratien, Henri, Victor, Jean-Joseph Bourignard. The said Gratien Bourignard used to be a builder and contractor; he was a very rich man at one time; and most of all, he was one of the prettiest fellows in Paris, a Lovelace that might have led Grandison himself astray. My information goes no further. He once was a common workman; the journeymen of the order of Dévorants elected him as their head, with the name of Ferragus XXIII. The police should know that, if they are there to know anything. The man has moved, and at present is lodging in the Rue Joquelet. Madame Jules Desmarets often goes to see him. Her husband pretty often sets her down in the Rue Vivienne on his way to the Bourse; or she leaves her husband at the Bourse, and comes back that way. Monsieur le Vidame knows so much in these matters that he will not expect me to tell him whether the husband rules the wife or the wife rules her husband, but Madame Jules is so pretty that I should bet on her. All this is absolutely certain. My Bourignard often goes to gamble at number 129. He is a gay dog, with a liking for women, saving your presence, and has his amours like a man of condition. As for the rest, he is frequently in luck, he makes up like an actor and can take on any face he likes; he just leads the queerest life you ever heard of. He has several addresses, I have no doubt, for he nearly always escapes what Monsieur le Vidame calls 'parliamentary investigation.' If monsieur wishes, however, the man can be got rid of decently, leading such a life as he does. It is always easy to get rid of a man with a weakness for women. Still, the capitalist is talking of moving again. Now, have Monsieur le Vidame and Monsieur le Baron any orders to give?"

"I am pleased with you, Justin. Go no further in the affair without instructions, but keep an eye on everything here, so that Monsieur le Baron shall have nothing to fear." He turned to Maulincour. "Live as before, dear boy," he said, "and forget Madame Jules."

"No, no," said Auguste, "I will not give her up to Gratien Bourignard; I mean to have him bound hand and foot and Madame Jules as well."

That evening Auguste de Maulincour, recently promoted to a higher rank in the Guards, went to a ball in Mme. la Duchesse de Berri's apartments at the Élysée-Bourbon. There, surely, was no fear of the slightest danger; and yet the Baron de Maulincour came away with an affair of honor on his hands, and no hope of arranging it. His antagonist, the Marquis de Ronquerolles, had the strongest reasons for complaining of him; the quarrel arose out of an old flirtation with M. de Ronquerolle's sister, the Comtesse de Sérizy. This lady, who could not endure high-flown German sentiment, was all the more particular with regard to every detail of the prude's costume in which she appeared in public. Some fatal inexplicable prompting moved Auguste to make a harmless joke, Mme. de Sérizy took it in very bad part, and her brother took offense. Explanations took place in whispers in a corner of the room. Both behaved like men of the world, there was no fuss of any kind; and not till next day did the Faubourg Saint-Honoré, the Faubourg Saint-Germain, and the château hear what had happened. Mme. de Sérizy was warmly defended; all the blame was thrown on Maulincour. August persons intervened. Seconds of the highest rank were imposed on M. de Maulincour and M. de Ronquerolles; every precaution was taken on the ground to prevent a fatal termination.

Auguste's antagonist was a man of pleasure, not wanting, as every one admitted, in a sense of honor; it was impossible to think of the marquis as a tool in the hands of Ferragus, Chief of Dévorants; and yet, as Auguste de Maulincour stood up before his man, in his own mind he felt a wish to obey an unaccountable instinct, and to put a question to him.

"Gentlemen," he said, addressing his seconds, "I emphatically do not refuse to stand Monsieur de Ronquerolles' fire; but, first, I own that I was in fault, I will make the apology which he is sure to require, and even in public if he wishes it; for, when a lady is in the case, there is nothing, I think, dishonoring to a gentleman in such an apology. So I appeal to his commonsense and generosity, isn't there something rather senseless in fighting a duel when the better cause may happen to get the worst of it?"

But M. de Ronquerolles would not hear of such a way out of the affair. The baron's suspicions were confirmed. He went across to his opponent.

"Well, Monsieur le Marquis," he said, "will you pledge me your word as a noble, before these gentlemen, that you bear me no grudge save the one for which ostensibly we are to fight?"

"Monsieur, that is a question which ought not to be put to me."

M. de Ronquerolles returned to his place. It was agreed beforehand that only one shot should be fired on either side. The antagonists were so far apart that a fatal end for M. de Maulincour seemed problematical, not to say impossible; but Auguste dropped. The bullet had passed through his ribs, missing the heart by two finger-breadths. Luckily, the extent of the injury was not great.

"This was no question of revenge for a dead passion; you aimed too well, monsieur, for that," said the baron.

M. de Ronquerolles, thinking that he had killed his man, could not keep back a sardonic smile.

"Julius Cæsar's sister, monsieur, must be above suspicion."

"Madame Jules again!" exclaimed Auguste, and he fainted away before he could finish the caustic sarcasm that died on his lips. He had lost a good deal of blood, but his wound was not dangerous. For a fortnight his grandmother and the vidame nursed him with the lavish care which none but the old, wise with the experience of a lifetime, can give. Then one morning he received a rude shock. It came from his grandmother. She told him that her old age, the last days of her life, were filled with deadly anxiety. A letter addressed to her and signed " F." gave her the history of the espionage to which her grandson had stooped; it was given in full from point to point. M. de Maulincour was accused of conduct unworthy a man of honor. He had posted an old woman (so it was stated) near the hack-stand in the Rue de Ménars. Nominally his wrinkled spy supplied water to the cabmen, but really she was stationed there to watch Mme. Jules Desmarets. He had deliberately set himself to play the detective on one of the most harmless men in the world, and tried to find out all about him when secrets which concerned the lives of three persons were involved. Of his own accord he had entered upon a pitiless struggle, in which he had been wounded three times already, and must inevitably succumb at last; for his death had been sworn; every human power would be exerted to compass it. It was too late for M. de Maulincour to escape his doom by a promise to respect the mysterious life of these three persons; for it was impossible to believe the word of a gentleman who could sink so low as the level of a police spy. And for what reason? To disturb, without cause, the existence of an innocent woman and a respectable old man.

The letter was as nothing to Auguste compared with the Baronne de Maulincour's loving reproaches. How could he fail to trust and respect a woman? How could he play the spy on her when he had no right to do so? Had any man a right to spy on the woman whom he loved? There followed a torrent of excellent reasoning which never proves anything. It put the young man for the first time of his life into one of those towering passions from which the most decisive actions of life are apt to spring.

"If this is to be a duel to the death" (so he concluded), "I am justified in using every means in my power to kill my enemy."

Forthwith the vidame, on behalf of M. de Maulincour, waited on the superintendent of the detective force in Paris, and gave him a full account of the adventure, without bringing Mme. Jules' name into the story, although she was the secret knot of all the threads. He told him, in confidence, of the fears of the Maulincour family, thus threatened by some unknown person, an enemy daring enough to vow such vengeance on an officer in the Guards, in the teeth of the law and the police. He of the police was so much surprised that he raised his green spectacles, blew his nose two or three times, and offered his mull to the vidame, who said, to save his dignity, that he never took snuff, though his countenance was bedabbled with rappee. The head of the department took his notes, and promised that, with the help of Vidocq and his sleuth hounds, the enemy of the Maulincour family should be accounted for in a very short time; there were no mysteries, so he was pleased to say, for the Paris police.

A few days afterward, the superintendent came to the Hôtel Maulincour to see M. le Vidame, and found the baron perfectly recovered from his last injuries. He thanked the family in formal style for the particulars which they had been so good as to communicate, and informed them that the man Bourignard was a convict sentenced to twenty years' penal servitude, and that in some miraculous way he made his escape from the gang on the way from Bicêtre to Toulon. The police had made fruitless efforts to catch him for the past fifteen years;

they learned that he had very recklessly come back to live in Paris; and there, though he was constantly implicated in all sorts of shady affairs, hitherto he had eluded the most active search. To cut it short, the man, whose life presented a great many most curious details, was certain to be seized at one of his numerous addresses and given up to justice. This redtape personage concluded his official report with the remark that, if M. de Maulincour attached sufficient importance to the affair to care to be present at Bourignard's capture, he might repair to such and such a number in the Rue SainteFoi at eight o'clock next morning. M. de Maulincour, however, felt that he could dispense with this method of making certain; he shared the feeling of awe which the police inspires in Paris; he felt every confidence in the diligence of the local authorities.

Three days afterward, as he saw nothing in the newspapers about an arrest which surely would have supplied material for an interesting article, M. de Maulincour was beginning to feel uncomfortable, when the following letter relieved his mind:

"MONSIEUR LE BARON:—I have the honor to announce that you need no longer entertain any fears whatsoever with regard to the matter in hand. The man Gratien Bourignard, alias Ferragus, died yesterday at his address, number 7 Rue Joquelet. The suspicions which we were bound to raise as to his identity were completely set at rest by facts. The doctor of the prefecture was specially sent by us to act in concert with the doctor of the mayor's office, and the superintendent of the preventive police made all the necessary verifications, so that the identity of the body might be established beyond question. The personal character, moreover, of the witnesses who signed the certificate of death, and the confirmatory evidence of those who were present at the time of the said Bourignard's death—including that of the curé of the Bonne-

Nouvelle, to whom he made a last confession (for he made a Christian end)—all these things taken together do not permit us to retain the slightest doubt.

"Permit me, M. le Baron, to remain, etc."

M. de Maulincour, the dowager, and the commander drew a breath of unspeakable relief. She, good woman, kissed her grandson while a tear stole down her cheeks, and then crept away to give thanks to God. The dear dowager had made a nine days' prayer for Auguste's safety, and believed that she had been heard.

"Well," said the vidame, "now you can go to that ball that you were speaking about; I have no more objections to make."

M. de Maulincour was the more eager to go to this ball since Mme. Jules was sure to be there. It was an entertainment given by the prefect of the Seine in whose house the two worlds of Paris society met as on a neutral ground. Auguste de Maulincour went quickly through the rooms, but the woman who exerted so great an influence on his life was not to be seen. He went into a still empty card-room, where the tables awaited players, sat himself down on a sofa, and gave himself up to the most contradictory thoughts of Mme. Jules, when some one grasped him by the arm; and, to his utter amazement, he beheld the beggar of the Rue Coquillière, Ida's Ferragus, the man who lived in the Rue Soly, Justin's Bourignard, the convict that had died the day before.

"Not a sound, not a word, sir!" said Bourignard. Auguste knew that voice, though to any other it would surely have seemed unrecognizable.

The man was very well dressed; he wore the insignia of the Golden Fleece and the star of the Legion of Honor.

"Sir," he hissed out like a hyena, "you warrant all my attempts on your life by allying yourself with the police. You shall die, sir. There is no help for it. Are you in love with

Madame Jules? Did she once love you? What right have you to trouble her peace and smirch her reputation?"

Somebody else came up. Ferragus rose to go.

"Do you know this man?" asked M. de Maulincour, seizing Ferragus by the collar.

But Ferragus slipped briskly out of his grasp, caught M. de Maulincour by the hair, and shook him playfully several times.

"Is there absolutely nothing but a dose of lead that will bring you to your senses?" he replied.

"I am not personally acquainted with him," said de Marsay, who had witnessed this scene, "but I know that this gentleman is Monsieur de Funcal, a very rich Portuguese."

M. de Funcal had vanished. The baron went off in pursuit, he could not overtake him, but he reached the peristyle in time to see a splendid equipage and the sneer on Ferragus' face, before he was whirled away out of sight.

"For pity's sake, tell me where Monsieur de Funcal lives," said Auguste, betaking himself to de Marsay, who happened to be an acquaintance.

"I do not know, but somebody here no doubt can tell you."

In answer to a question put to the prefect, Auguste learned that the Comte de Funcal's address was at the Portuguese embassy. At that moment, while he fancied that he could still feel those ice-cold fingers in his hair, he saw Mme. Jules, in all the splendor of that beauty, fresh, graceful, unaffected, radiant with the sanctity of womanhood, which drew him to her at the first. For him this creature was infernal; Auguste felt nothing for her now but hate—hate that overflowed in murderous, terrible glances. He watched for an opportunity of speaking to her alone.

"Madame," he said, "three times already your bravos have missed me——"

"What do you mean, sir?" she answered, reddening. "I heard with much concern that several bad accidents had befallen you; but how can I have had anything to do with them?"

"You knew that the man in the Rue Soly has hired ruffians on my track?"

"Sir!"

"Madame, henceforth I must call you to account not only for my happiness, but also for my life-blood——"

Jules Desmarets came up at that moment.

"What are you saying to my wife, sir?"

"Come to my house to inquire if you are curious to know." And Maulincour went. Mme. Jules looked white and ready to faint.

There are very few women who have not been called upon, once in their lives, to face a definite, pointed, trenchant question with regard to some undeniable fact, one of those questions which a husband puts in a pitiless way. The bare thought of it sends a cold shiver through a woman; the first word pierces her heart like a steel blade. Hence the axiom, "All women are liars." They tell lies to spare the feelings of others, white lies, heroic lies, hideous lies; but falsehood is incumbent upon them. Once admit this, does it not follow of necessity that the lies ought to be well told? Women tell lies to admiration in France. Our manners are an excellent school for dissimulation. And, after all, women are so artlessly insolent, so charming, so graceful, so true amid falsehood, so perfectly well aware of the value of insincerity as a means of avoiding the rude shocks which put happiness in peril, that falsehood is as indispensable to them as cotton-batting for their jewelry. Insincerity furnishes forth the staple of their talk, and truth is only brought out occasionally. They speak truth, as they are virtuous, from caprice or speculation. The methods vary with the individual character. Some women laugh and lie, others weep, or grow grave, or put themselves in a passion.

They begin life with a feigned indifference to the homage

which gratifies them most; they often end by insincerity with
themselves. Who has not admired their seeming loftiness
when they are trembling the while for the mysterious treasure
of love? Who has not studied the ease, the ready wit, the
mental disengagement with which they confront the greatest
embarrassments of life? Everything is quite natural; deceit
flows out as snowflakes fall from the sky.

And yet what skill women have to discover the truth in
another! How subtly they can use the hardest logic, in
answer to the passionately uttered question that never fails to
yield up some heart secret belonging to their interlocutor, if
a man is so guileless as to begin with questioning a woman.
If a man begins to question a woman, he delivers himself into
her hand. Will she not find out anything that he means to
hide, while she talks and says nothing? And yet there are
men that have the audacity to enter upon a contest of wits
with a Parisienne—a woman who can put herself out of reach
of a thrust with "You are very inquisitive!" "What does
it matter to you?" "Oh! you are jealous!" "And how
if I do not choose to answer you?" A Parisienne, in short,
has a hundred and thirty-seven thousand ways of saying No,
while her variations on the word YES surpass computation.
Surely one of the finest diplomatic, philosophic, logographic,
and moral performances which remain to be made would be
a treatise on No and YES. But who save an androgynous
being could accomplish the diabolical feat? For which reason it will never be attempted. Yet of all unpublished works,
is there one better known or more constantly in use among
women?

Have you ever studied the conduct, the pose, the *disinvoltura* of a lie? Look at it now. Mme. Jules was sitting in
the right-hand corner of her carriage, and her husband to her
left. She had contrived to repress her emotion as she left the
ballroom, and by this time her face was quite composed.
Her husband had said nothing to her then; he said nothing

now. Jules was staring out of the window at the dark walls of the silent houses as they drove past; but suddenly, just as they turned the corner of a street, he seemed to come to some determination, he looked intently at his wife. She seemed to feel cold in spite of the fur-lined pelisse in which she was wrapped; she looked pensive, he thought, and perhaps she really was pensive. Of all subtly communicable moods, gravity and reflection are the most contagious.

"What can Monsieur de Maulincour have said to move you so deeply?" began Jules. "And what is this that he wishes me to hear at his house?"

"Why, he can tell you nothing at his house that I cannot tell you now," she replied.

And with that woman's subtlety, which is always slightly dishonoring to virtue, Mme. Jules waited for another question. But her husband turned his head away and resumed his study of arched gateways. Would it not mean suspicion and distrust if he asked any more? It is a crime in love to suspect a woman; and Jules had already killed a man, without a doubt of his wife. Clémence did not know how much deep passion and reflection lay beneath her husband's silence; and little did Jules imagine the extraordinary drama which locked his wife's heart from him. And the carriage went on and on through silent Paris, and the husband and wife, two lovers who idolized each other, nestled softly and closely together among the silken cushions, a deep gulf yawning between them all the while.

How many strange scenes take place in the elegant coupés which pass through the streets between midnight and one o'clock in the morning after a ball! The carriages alluded to, be it understood, are fitted with transparent panes of glass, and lamps that not merely light up the brougham itself, but the whole street as well on either side; they belong to law-sanctioned love, and the law gives a man a right to sulk and fall out with his wife, and kiss and make it up again, in a coupé or anywhere else. So married couples are at liberty to quarrel without fear of being seen by passers-by. And how many secrets are revealed to foot-passengers in the dark streets, to the young bachelors who drove to the ball and, for some reason or other, are walking home afterward! For the first time in their lives, Jules and Clémence leaned back in their respective corners; usually Desmarets pressed close to his wife's side.

"It is very cold," said Mme. Jules. But her husband heard nothing; he was intent on reading all the dark signs above the stores.

"Clémence," he began at last, "forgive me for this question that I am about to ask?"

He came nearer, put his arm about her waist, and drew her toward him.

"Oh, dear! here it comes!" thought poor Clémence.

"Well," she said aloud, anticipating the question, "you wish to know what Monsieur de Maulincour was saying to me? I will tell you, Jules; but, I am afraid. Ah, God! can we have secrets from each other? A moment ago I knew that you were struggling between the consciousness that we love each other and a vague dread; but that consciousness that we love each other is unclouded, is it not? and do not your doubts seem very shadowy to you? Why not stay in the light that you love? When I have told you everything, you will wish to know more; and, after all, I myself do not know what is lurking under that man's strange words. And then, perhaps, there would be a duel, ending in a death. I would far rather that we both put that unpleasant moment out of our minds. But, in any case, give me your word to wait till this most extraordinary adventure is entirely cleared up in some natural way.

"Monsieur de Maulincour declared that those three accidents of which you heard—the block of stone that killed his servant, the carriage accident, and the duel about Madame de

Sérizy—were all brought upon him by a plot which I had woven against him. And he threatened to explain my reasons for wishing to murder him to you.

"Can you make anything out of all this? It was his face that disturbed me; there was madness in it; his eyes were haggard; he was so excited that he could not bring out his words. I felt sure that he was mad. That was all. Now, I should not be a woman if I did not know that, for a year past, Monsieur de Maulincour has been, as they say, quite wild about me. He has never met me except at dances; we have never exchanged any words but ballroom small-talk. Perhaps he wants to separate us, so that I may be left defenseless and alone some day. You see how it is! You are frowning already. Oh, I detest the world with all my heart! We are so happy without it, why should we go in search of society? Jules, I beg of you, promise me that you will forget all this! I expect we shall hear to-morrow that Monsieur de Maulincour has gone out of his mind."

"What an extraordinary thing!" said Jules to himself, as he stepped out into the peristyle of his own abode.

And here, if this story is to be developed by giving it in all its truth of detail, by following its course through all its intricacies, there must be a revelation of some of the secrets of love—secrets learned by slipping under the canopy of a bed-chamber, not brazenly, but after the manner of Puck, without startling either Jeanie or Dougal, or anybody else. For this venture, one had need be chaste as our noble French language consents to be, and daring as Gérard's brush in his picture of Daphnis and Chloe.

Mme. Jules' bedroom was a sacred place. No one but her husband and her maid was allowed to enter it. Wealth has great privileges, and the most enviable of them all is the power of carrying out thoughts and feelings to the uttermost; of quickening sensibility by fulfilling its myriad caprices; of encompassing that inner life with a splendor that exalts it, elegance that refines, and the subtle shades of expression that enhance the charm of love.

If you particularly detest picnic dinners and meals badly served; if you feel a certain pleasure at the sight of dazzling white damask, plate, exquisite porcelain, and richly carved and gilded tables lit up by translucent tapers; if you have a taste for miracles of the most refined culinary art beneath silver coverings with armorial bearings; then, if you have a mind to be consistent, you must come down from the heights of your garret, and you must leave the grisettes in the street. Garrets and grisettes, like umbrellas and hinged clogs, must be left to people who bring tickets to the doors of restaurants to pay for their dinners; and you must think of love as something rudimentary, only to be developed in all its charm by a gilded fireside, in a room made deaf to all sound from without by drawn blinds and closed shutters and thick curtain folds, while the opal light of a Parian lamp falls over soft carpets from the Savonnerie and the silken hangings on the walls. You must have mirrors to reflect each other, to give you an infinite series of pictures of the woman in whom you would fain find many women, of her to whom Love gives so many forms. There should be long, low sofas, and a bed like a secret which you guess before it is revealed; and soft furs spread for bare feet on the floor of the dainty chamber, and wax tapers under glass shades, and white gauze draperies, so that you can see to read at any hour of the night; and flowers without too heavy-sweet a scent, and linen fine enough to satisfy Anne of Austria.*

This delicious scheme had been carried out by Mme. Jules. But that is nothing; any woman of taste might do as much; though, nevertheless, there is a certain touch of personality in the arrangement of these things, a something which stamps this ornament or that detail with a character of its own. The fanatical cult of individuality is more prevalent than ever in

---

* Her chemise could be passed through a finger ring.

these days. Rich people in France are beginning to grow more and more exclusive in their tastes and belongings than they have been for the past thirty years. Mme. Jules knew that her programme must be carried out consistently; that everything about her must be part of a harmonious whole of luxury which make a fit setting for love.

"Fifteen hundred francs and my Sophie," or "Love in a Cottage," is the sort of talk to expect from famished creatures, and brown bread does very well at first; but if the pair are really in love, their palates grow nicer, and in the end they sigh for the riches of the kitchen. Love holds toil and want in abhorrence, and would rather die at once than live a miserable life of hand to mouth.

Most women after a ball are impatient for sleep. Their rooms are strewn with limp flowers, scentless bouquets, and ball-gowns. Their little thick shoes are left under an armchair, they totter across the floor in their high-heeled slippers, take the combs out of their hair, and shake down their tresses without a thought of their appearance. Little do they care if they disclose to their husbands' eyes the clasps and pins and cunning contrivances which maintained the dainty fabric in erection. All mystery is laid aside, all pretense dropped for the husband—there is no make-up for him. The corset of the reparative kind, fearfully and wonderfully made, is left lying about if the sleepy waiting-woman forgets to put it away. Whalebone stiffening, sleeves encased in buckram, delusive finery, hair supplied by the coiffeur, the whole factitious woman, in fact, lies scattered about. *Disjecta membra poetæ*, the artificial poetry so much admired by those for whose benefit the whole was conceived and elaborated, the remains of the pretty woman of an hour ago, encumber every corner, while the genuine woman in slatternly disorder, and the crumpled nightcap of yesterday, to-day, and to-morrow, presents herself yawning to the arms of a husband who yawns likewise.

"For, really, monsieur, if you want a pretty nightcap to rumple every night, you must increase my allowance."

Such is life as it is. A woman is always old and unattractive to her husband; always smart, dainty, and dressed in her best for that Other, every husband's rival, the world that slanders women or picks them to pieces.

Mme. Jules did quite otherwise. Love, like all other beings, has its own instinct of self-preservation. Inspired by love, constantly rewarded by happiness, she never failed in the scrupulous performance of little duties in which no one can grow slack, for by such means love is kept unimpaired by time. Are not these pains, these tasks imposed by a self-respect which becomes her passing well? What are they but sweet flatteries, a way of reverencing the beloved in one's own person?

So Mme. Jules had closed the door of her dressing-room on her husband; there she changed her ball-gown and came out dressed for the night, mysteriously adorned for the mysterious festival of her heart. The chamber was always exquisite and dainty; Jules, when he entered it, found a woman coquettishly wrapped in a graceful, loose gown, with her thick hair twisted simply about her head. She had nothing to fear from dishevelment; she robbed Love's sight and touch of nothing. This woman was always simpler and more beautiful for him than for the world—a woman revived by her toilet, a woman whose whole art consisted in being whiter than the cambrics that she wore, fresher than the freshest scent, more irresistible than the wiliest courtesan. In a word, she was always loving, and therefore always beloved. In this admirable skill in *le métier de femme*—in the art and mystery of being a woman—lay the great secret of Josephine's charm for Napoleon, of Cesonia's influence over Caligula in older times, of the ascendency of Diane de Poitiers over Henri II. And if this secret is so potent in the hands of women who have counted seven or eight lustres, what a weapon is it for a young wife! The prescribed happiness of fidelity becomes rapture.

Mme. Jules had been particularly careful of her toilet for the night. After that conversation which froze the blood in her veins with terror, and still caused her the liveliest anxiety, she meant to be exquisitely charming, and she succeeded. She fastened her cambric dressing-gown, leaving it loose at the throat, and let her dark hair fall loosely over her shoulders. An intoxicating fragrance clung about her after her scented bath, her bare feet were thrust into velvet slippers. Jules, in his dressing-gown, was standing meditatively by the fire, with his elbow on the mantelpiece, and one foot on the fender. Feeling strong on her vantage-ground, she tripped across to him and laid a hand over his eyes. Then she whispered, close to his ear, so closely that he could feel her warm breath on him and the tips of her teeth: "What are you thinking about, monsieur?"

With quick tact, she held him closely to her and put her arms about him to snatch him away from his gloomy thoughts. A woman who loves knows well how to use her power; and the better the woman, the more irresistible is her coquetry.

"Of you," said he.

"Only of me?"

"Yes!"

"Oh! that was a very doubtful 'Yes!'"

They went to bed. As Mme. Jules fell asleep she thought: "Decidedly, de Maulincour will bring about some misfortune. Jules is preoccupied and absent-minded; he has thoughts which he does not tell me."

Toward three o'clock in the morning Mme. Jules was awakened by a foreboding that knocked at her heart while she slept. She felt, physically and mentally, that her husband was not beside her. She missed Jules' arm, on which her head had lain nightly for five years, while she slept happily and peacefully, an arm that never wearied of the weight. A voice cried: "Jules is in pain! Jules is weeping!" She lifted her head, sat upright, felt that her husband's place was cold, and saw him sitting by the fire, his feet on the fender, his head leaning back in the great armchair. There were tears on his cheeks. Poor Clémence was out of bed in a moment, and sprang to her husband's knee.

"Jules, what is it? Are you not feeling well? Speak, tell me; oh, speak to me, if you love me."

She poured out a hundred words of the deepest tenderness. Jules, at his wife's feet, kissed her knees, her hands. The tears flowed afresh as he answered—

"Clémence, dear, I am very wretched. It is not love if you cannot trust your mistress, and you are my mistress. I worship you, Clémence, even while I doubt you. The things that man said last night went to my heart; and, in spite of me, they stay there to trouble me. There is some mystery underneath this. Indeed, I blush to say it, but your explanation did not satisfy me. Commonsense sheds a light on it which love bids me reject. It is a dreadful struggle. How could I lie there with your head on my shoulder and think that there were thoughts in your mind that I did not know? Oh, I believe you, I believe in you," he exclaimed, as she smiled sadly and seemed about to speak "Say not a word, reproach me with nothing. The least little word from you would break my heart. And, beside, could you say a single thing that I have not said to myself for the last three hours? Yes, for three hours I lay, watching you as you slept, so beautiful you were, your forehead looked so quiet and pure. Ah! yes, you have always told me all your thoughts, have you not? I am alone in your inmost heart. When I look into the depths of your eyes, I read all that lies there. Your life is always as pure as those clear eyes. Ah! no, there is no secret beneath their transparent gaze."

He rose and kissed her eyelids.

"Let me confess it to you, beloved; all through these five

years one thing has made me happier day by day, I have been glad that you should have none of the natural affections which always encroach a little upon love. You had neither sister nor father nor mother nor friend; I was neither above nor below any other in thy heart; I was there alone. Clémence, say over again for me all the intimate sweet words that you have spoken so often; do not scold me; comfort me, I am very wretched. I have a hateful suspicion to reproach myself with, while you have nothing burning in your heart. Tell me, my darling, may I stay by your side? How should two that are so truly one rest their heads on the same pillow, when one is at peace and the other in pain? What can you be thinking of?" he cried abruptly, as Clémence looked meditative and confused, and could not keep back the tears.

"I am thinking of my mother," she said gravely. "You could not know, Jules, how it hurt your Clémence to recall her mother's last farewells, while your voice, the sweetest of all music, was sounding in her ears; to remember the solemn pressure of the chill hand of a dying woman, while I felt your caresses, and the overpowering sense of the sweetness of your love."

She made him rise, and held him tightly, with far more than man's strength, in her arms; she kissed his hair, her tears fell over him.

"Oh! I could be hacked into pieces for you! Tell me, beyond doubt, that I make you happy, that for you I am the fairest of women, that I am a thousand women for you. But you are loved as no other man can ever be loved. I do not know what the words 'duty,' 'virtue' mean. Jules, I love you for your own sake; it makes me happy to love you; I shall always love you; better and better, till my last sigh. I take a kind of pride in my love. I am sure that I am fated to know but the one great love in my life. Perhaps this that I am going to say is wicked, but I am glad to have no children, I wish for none. I feel that I am more a wife than a mother. Have you any fears? Listen to me, my love; promise me to forget, not this hour of mingled love and doubt, but that madman's words. I ask it, Jules. Promise me not to see him again, to keep away from his house. I have a feeling that if you go a single step further in that labyrinth, we shall both sink into depths where I shall die, with your name still on my lips, your heart in my heart. Why do you put me so high in your inmost life, and so low in the outer? You can take so many men's fortunes on trust, and you cannot give me the alms of one doubt? And when, for the first time in your life, you can prove that your faith in me is unbounded, would you dethrone me in your heart? Between a lunatic and your wife, you believe the lunatic's word? Oh! Jules——"

She broke off, flung back the hair that fell over her forehead and throat, and in heart-rending tones she added, "I have said too much. A word should be enough. If there is still a shadow across your mind and your forehead, however faint it may be, mind, it will kill me."

She shivered in spite of herself, and her face grew white.

"Oh! I will kill that man," said Jules to himself, as he caught up his wife and carried her to the bed. "Let us sleep in peace, dear angel," he said aloud; "I have put it all out of mind, I give you my word."

The loving words were repeated more lovingly, and Clémence slept. Jules, watching his sleeping wife, told himself, "She is right. When love is so pure, a suspicion is like a blight. Yes, and a blight on so innocent a soul, so delicate a flower, is certain death."

If between two human creatures, each full of love for the other, with a common life at every moment, there should arise a cloud, the cloud will vanish away, but not without leaving some trace of its passage behind. Perhaps their love grows deeper, as earth is fairer after the rain; or perhaps the shock reverberates like distant thunder in a blue sky; but, at any rate, they cannot take up life where it was before, love must increase or diminish. At breakfast, M. and Mme. Jules showed each other an exaggerated attention. In their glances there was an almost forced gayety which might have been expected of people eager to be deceived. Jules had involuntary suspicions; his wife, a definite dread. And yet, feeling sure of each other, they had slept. Was the embarrassment due to want of trust? to the recollection of the scene in the night? They themselves could not tell. But they loved each other, and were loved so sincerely, that the bitter-sweet impression could not fail to leave its traces; and each, beside, was so anxious to be the first to efface them, to be the first to return, that they could not but remember the original cause of a first discord. For those who love, vexation is out of the question, and pain is still afar off, but the feeling is still a kind of mourning, difficult to describe. If there is a parallel between colors and the moods of the mind; if, as Locke's blind man said, scarlet produces the same effect on the eyes as the blast of a trumpet on the ears, then this melancholy reaction may be compared with sober gray tints. Yet saddened love, love conscious of its real happiness beneath the momentary trouble, knows a wholly new luxurious blending of pain and pleasure. Jules dwelt on the tones of his wife's voice, and watched for her glances with the young passion that stirred him in the early days of their love; and memories of five perfectly happy years, Clémence's beauty, her artless love, soon effaced (for the time) the last pangs of an intolerable ache.

It was Sunday. There was no Bourse and no business. Husband and wife could spend the whole day together, and each made more progress in the other's heart than ever before, as two children in a moment's terror cling closely and tightly together, instinctively united against danger. Where two have but one life, they know such hours of perfect happiness sent by chance, flowers of a day, which have nothing to do with yesterday or to-morrow.

To Jules and Clémence it was a day of exquisite enjoyment. They might almost have felt a dim foreboding that this was to be the last day of their life as lovers. What name can be given to the mysterious impulse which hastens the traveler's steps before the storm has given warning?—it fills the dying with a glow of life and beauty a few days before the end, and sets them making the most joyous plans; it counsels the learned man to raise the flame of the midnight lamp when it burns most brightly; it wakens a mother's fears when some keen-sighted observer looks too intently at her child. We all feel this influence in great crises in our lives, yet we have neither studied it nor found a name for it. It is something more than a presentiment, something less than vision.

All went well till the next day. It was Monday, Jules Desmarets was obliged to be at the Bourse at the usual time; and, according to his custom, he asked his wife before he went if she would take the opportunity of driving with him.

"No," she said; "the weather is too bad."

And, indeed, it was pouring with rain. It was about half-past two o'clock. M. Desmarets went on the market, and thence to the Treasury. At four o'clock, when he came out, he confronted M. de Maulincour, who was waiting for him with the pertinacity bred of hate and revenge.

"I have some important information to give you, sir," he said, taking Desmarets by the arm. "Listen to me. I am an honorable man; I do not wish to send anonymous letters which would trouble your peace of mind; I prefer to speak directly. In short, you may believe that if my life were not at stake, I should never interfere between husband and wife, even if I believed that I had a right so to do."

"If you are going to say anything that concerns Madame Desmarets," answered Jules, "I beg you to be silent, sir."

"If I keep silence, sir, you may see Madame Jules in the dock beside a convict before very long. Now, am I to be silent?"

Jules' handsome face grew white, but seemingly he was calm again in a moment. He drew Maulincour under one of the porches of the temporary building then frequented by stockbrokers, and spoke, his voice unsteady with deep emotion—

"I am listening, sir, but there will be a duel to the death between us if——"

"Oh! I am quite willing," exclaimed M. de Maulincour. "I have the greatest respect for you. Do you speak of death, sir? You are not aware, I expect, that your wife probably employed somebody to poison me on Saturday evening? Yes, sir, since the day before yesterday, some extraordinary change has taken place in me. All the hairs of my head distill a fever and mortal languor that pierces through the bone; and I know perfectly well what man it was that touched my head at the dance."

M. de Maulincour told the whole story of his Platonic love for Mme. Jules and the details of the adventure with which this Scene opens. Anybody would have listened to him as attentively as Desmarets, but Mme. Jules' husband might be expected to be more astonished than anybody else in the world. And here his character showed itself—he was more surprised than overwhelmed. Thus constituted the judge, and the judge of an adored wife, in his inmost mind he assumed a judicial directness and inflexibility of mind. He was a lover still; he thought less of his own broken life than of the woman; he heard, not his own grief, but a far-off voice crying to him: "Clémence could not lie! Why should she be false to you?"

"I felt certain that in Monsieur de Funcal I recognized this Ferragus, whom the police believe to be dead," concluded M. de Maulincour, "so I put an intelligent man on his track at once. As I went home, I fortunately chanced to call to mind a Madame Meynardie, mentioned in this Ida's letter, Ida being apparently my persecutor's mistress. With this one bit of information, my emissary speedily cleared up this ghastly adventure, for he is more skilled at finding out the truth than the police themselves."

"I am unable to thank you, sir, for your confidence," said Desmarets. "You speak of proof and witnesses; I am waiting for them. I shall not flinch from tracking down the truth in this extraordinary business; but you will permit me to suspend my judgment until the case is proved by circumstantial evidence. In any case, you shall have satisfaction, for you must understand that we both require it."

Jules went home.

"What is it?" asked his wife. "You look so pale you frighten me!"

"It is a cold day," he said, as he walked slowly away to the bedroom, where everything spoke of happiness and love, the so quiet chamber where a deadly storm was brewing.

"Have you been out to-day?" he asked, with seeming carelessness. The question, no doubt, was prompted by the last of a thousand thoughts, which had gathered unconsciously in his mind, till they took the shape of a single lucid reflection, which his jealousy brought out on the spur of the moment.

"No," she answered, and her voice sounded frank.

Even as she spoke, Jules, glancing through the dressing-room door, noticed drops of rain on the bonnet which his wife used to wear in the morning. Jules was a violent-tempered man, but he was likewise extremely sensitive; he shrank from confronting his wife with a lie. And yet those drops of water shed, as it were, a gleam of light which tortured his brain. He went downstairs to the porter's room.

"Fouquereau," he said, when he had made sure that they were alone, "three hundred francs per annum to you if you tell me the truth; if you deceive me, out you go; and if you mention my question and your answer to any one else, you will get nothing at all."

He stopped, looked steadily at the man, and then drawing him to the light of the window, he asked—

"Did your mistress go out this morning?"

"Madame went out at a quarter to three, and I think I saw her come in again half-an-hour ago."

"Is that true, upon your honor?"

"Yes, sir."

"You shall have the annual sum I promised you. But if you mention it, remember what I said; for if you do, you lose it all."

Jules went back to his wife.

"Clémence," he said, "I want to put my house accounts a bit straight, so do not be vexed if I ask you something. I have let you have forty thousand francs this year, have I not?"

"More than that," she answered. "Forty-seven."

"Could you tell me exactly how it was spent?"

"Why, yes. First of all, there were several outstanding bills from last year——"

"I shall find out nothing in this way," thought Jules. "I have gone the wrong way to work."

Just at that moment the man brought in a note. Jules opened it for the sake of appearances, but seeing the signature at the foot, he read it eagerly:

"Monsieur:—To set your mind and our minds at rest, I take the step of writing you, although I have not the privilege of being known to you; but my position, my age, and the fear that some misfortune may befall, compels me to beseech your forbearance in the distressing situation in which our afflicted family is placed. For some days past, M. Auguste de Maulincour has shown unmistakable symptoms of mental derangement; and we are afraid that he may disturb your happiness with the wild fancies of which he spoke to M. le Commandeur de Pamiers and to me, in the first fit of fever. We desire to give you warning of a malady which is still curable, no doubt; and as it might have very serious consequences for the honor of the family and my grandson's future, I count upon your discretion. If M. le Commandeur or I, monsieur, had been able to make the journey to your house, we should have dispensed with a written communication; but you will comply, I do not doubt, with the request of a mother who beseeches you to burn this letter.

"Permit me to add that I am with the highest regard,

"BARONNE DE MAULINCOUR *née* DE RIEUX."

"What tortures!" exclaimed Jules.

"What can be passing in your thoughts?" asked his wife, with intense anxiety in her face.

"I have come to this!" cried Jules; "I ask myself whether you have had this note sent to me to dispel my suspicions. So judge what I am suffering," he added, tossing the letter to her.

"The unhappy man," said Mme. Jules, letting the sheet fall; "I am sorry for him, though he has given me a great deal of pain."

"You know that he spoke to me?"

"Oh! Did you go to see him when you had given your word?" was her terror-stricken answer.

"Clémence, our love is in danger; we are outside all the ordinary laws of life, so let us leave minor considerations in great perils. Now, tell me, why did you go out this morning? Women think they are privileged to tell us fibs now and again. You often amuse yourselves with preparing pleasant surprises for us, do you not? Just now you said one thing and meant another no doubt; you said a 'No' for a 'Yes.'"

He brought her bonnet out of the dressing-room.

"Look here! Without meaning to play the Bartholo here, your bonnet has betrayed you. Are these not rain-drops? Then you must have gone out and caught the drops of rain as you looked about for a cab, or in coming in or out of the house to which you drove. Still, a woman can go out even if she has told her husband that she means to stay indoors; there is no harm in that. There are so many reasons for changing one's mind. A whim, a woman has a right to be whimsical, is that not so? You are not bound to be consistent with yourselves. Perhaps you forgot something; something to be done for somebody else, or a call, or a charitable errand? But there can be nothing to prevent a wife from telling her husband what she has done. How should one ever blush on a friend's breast? And it is not a jealous husband who speaks, my Clémence; it is the friend, the lover, the comrade."

He flung himself passionately at her feet.

"Speak, not to justify yourself, but to soothe an intolerable pain. I know for certain that you left the house. Well, what did you do? Where did you go?"

"Yes, Jules, I left the house," she said, and though her voice shook, her face was composed. "But do not ask me anything more. Wait and trust me, or you may lay up lifelong regrets for yourself. Jules, my Jules, trust is love's great virtue. I confess it, I am too much troubled to answer you at this moment; I am a woman inept at lying, and I love you, you know I love you."

"With all that shakes a man's belief and rouses his jealousy —for I am not the first in your heart, Clémence, it seems; I am not your very self!—well, with it all, I would still rather trust you, Clémence, trust your voice and those eyes of yours. If you are deceiving me, you would deserve——"

"Oh! a thousand deaths," she broke in.

"And I have not one thought hidden from you, while——"

"Hush," she cried, "our happiness depends upon silence between us."

"Ah! I will know all!" he shouted, with a burst of violent anger.

As he spoke a sound reached them, a shrill-tongued woman's voice raised to a scream in the antechamber.

"I will come in, I tell you! Yes, I will come in, I want to see her, I will see her!" somebody cried.

Jules and Clémence hurried into the drawing-room, and in another moment the door was flung open. A young woman suddenly appeared with two servants behind her.

"This woman would come in, sir, in spite of us. We told her once before that madame was not at home. She said she knew quite well that madame had gone out, but she had just seen her come in. She threatens to stop at the house-door until she has spoken to madame."

"You can go," said M. Desmarets, addressing the servants.

"What do you want, mademoiselle?" he added, turning to the visitor.

The "young lady" was a feminine type known only in Paris; a type as much a product of the city as the mud or the curb-stones in the streets, or the Seine water which is filtered through half a score of great reservoirs before it sparkles clear and pure in cut-glass decanters, all its muddy sediment left behind. She is, moreover, a truly characteristic product. Pencil and pen and charcoal, painter and caricaturist and draughtsman, have caught her likeness repeatedly; yet she eludes analysis, because you can no more grasp her in all her moods than you can grasp Nature, or the fantastic city herself. Her circle has but one point of contact with vice, from which the rest of its circumference is far removed. Yet the one flaw in her character is the only trait that reveals her; all her fine qualities lie out of sight while she flaunts her ingenuous shamelessness. The plays and books that bring her before the public, with all the illusion that clings about her, give but a very inadequate idea of her; she never is, and never will be, herself except in her garret; elsewhere she is either worse or better than she really is. Give her wealth, she degenerates;

in poverty she is misconstrued. How should it be otherwise? She has so many faults and so many virtues; she lives too close to a tragic end in the river on the one hand, and a branding laugh upon the other; she is too fair and too foul; too much like a personification of that Paris which she provides with toothless old portresses, washerwomen, street-sweepers, and beggars; sometimes too with insolent countesses and admired and applauded actresses and opera singers. Twice in former times she even gave two queens, in all but name, to the Monarchy. Who could seize such a Protean woman-shape?

She is a very woman, less than a woman, and more than a woman. The painter of contemporary life can only give a few details, the general effect of so vast a subject, and some idea of its boundlessness.

This was a Paris grisette—a grisette, however, in her glory. She was the grisette that drives about in a cab; a happy, handsome, and fresh young person, but still a grisette, a grisette with claws and scissors; bold as a Spaniard, quarrelsome as an English prude instituting a suit for restitution of conjugal rights, coquettish as a great lady, and more outspoken; equal to all occasions, a typical "lioness," issuing from her little apartment.

Many and many a time she had dreamed of that establishment with its red cotton curtains and its furniture covered with Utrecht velvet, of the tea-table and the hand-painted china tea-service and the settee; the small square of velvet-pile carpet, the alabaster timepiece and vases under glass shades, the yellow bedroom, the soft eiderdown quilt—of all the joys of a grisette's life, in short. Now she had a servant, a superannuated member of her own profession, a veteran grisette with mustaches and good-conduct stripes. Now she went to the theatres and had as many sweetmeats as she liked; she had silk dresses and finery to soil and draggle, and all the joys of life from the point of view of the milliner's assistant, except a carriage of her own, a carriage being to the milliner's assistant's dreams what the marshal's baton is for the private soldier. Yes, all these things this particular grisette possessed in return for a real affection, or perhaps in spite of a real affection on her part; for others of her class will often exact as much for one hour in the day, a sort of toll carelessly paid for by a brief space in some old man's clutches, whom she utilizes as her banker.

The young person now confronting M. and Mme. Jules wore shoes, which displayed so much white stocking that they looked like an almost invisible black boundary line against the carpet. The kind of foot-gear, very neatly rendered by French comic drawings, is one of the Parisian grisette's peculiar charms of dress; but a still more unmistakable sign for observant eyes is the precision with which her gown is moulded to her figure, which is very clearly outlined. Moreover, the visitor was "turned out" in a green dress, to use the picturesque expression coined by the French soldier, a dress with a chemisette, which revealed a fine figure, fully displayed, for her Ternaux shawl would have slipped down to the floor if she had not held the two loosely knotted ends in her grasp. She had a delicate face, a white skin and color in her cheeks, sparkling gray eyes, a very prominent rounded forehead, and carefully waved hair, which escaped from under a little bonnet, and fell in large curls about her neck.

"My name is Ida, sir. And if that is Madame Jules whom I have the privilege of addressing, I have come to tell her all that I have against her on my mind. It is a shame, when she has made her bargain, and has such furniture as you have here, to try to take away the man to whom a poor girl is as good as married, and him talking of making it all right by marrying me at the registry office. There's quite plenty nice young men in the world—isn't there, sir?—for her to fancy without her coming and taking a man well on in years away from me when I am happy with him. Yah! I haven't a fine house, I haven't, I have only my love! I *distest* your fine-looking men and money; I am all heart and——"

Mme. Jules turned to her husband—

"You will permit me, sir, to hear no more of this," said she, and went back to her room.

"If the lady is living with you, I have made a hash of it, so far as I can see; but so much the worser," continued Ida. "What business has she to come and see Monsieur Ferragus every day?"

"You are mistaken, mademoiselle," said Jules, in dull amazement; "my wife could not possibly——"

"Oh! so you are married, are you, the two of you?" said the grisette, evidently rather surprised. "Then it's far worse, sir, is it not, when a woman has a lawful husband of her own to have anything to do with a man like Henri——"

"But what Henri?" said Jules, taking Ida aside into another room lest his wife should overhear anything further.

"Well, then, Monsieur Ferragus."

"But he is dead," protested Jules.

"What stuff! I went to Franconi's yesterday evening, and he brought me home again, as he ought to do. Your lady too can give you news of him. Didn't she go to see him at three o'clock? That she did, I know, for I was waiting for her in the street; being as a very nice man, Monsieur Justin—perhaps you know him? a little old fogey that wears stays and has seals on his watchchain—it was he that told me that I had a Madame Jules for my rival. That name, sir, is well known among fancy names; asking your pardon, since it's your own, but Madame Jules might be a duchess at Court, Henri is so rich he can afford all his whims. It is my business to look after my own, as I have a right to do; for I love Henri, I do. He was my first fancy, and my love and the rest of my life is at stake. I am afraid of nothing, sir; I am honest, and I never told a lie yet, nor took a thing belonging to anybody whatever. If I had an empress for my rival I

should go right straight to her, and if she took my husband that is to be from me, I feel that I could kill her, was she never so much an empress, for one fine woman is as good as another, sir——"

"That will do, that will do!" interrupted Jules. "Where do you live?"

"Number 14 Rue de la Corderie du Temple, sir. Ida Gruget, corset-maker, at your service, sir; for we make a good many corsets for gentlemen."

"And this man Ferragus, as you call him, where does he live?"

"Why, sir" (tightening her lips), "in the first place, he is not just 'a man'—he is a gentleman, and better off than you are, maybe. But what makes you ask me for his address, when your wife knows where he lives? He told me I was not to give it to nobody. Am I bound to give you an answer? I am not in the police court nor the confessional, the Lord be thanked, and I am not beholden to any one."

"And how if I offer you twenty, thirty, forty thousand francs to tell me his address?"

"Oh, not quite, my little dear; it's no go," said she, with a gesture learned in the streets, as accompaniment to her singular answer. "No amount of money would get that out of me. I have the honor to wish you good-evening. Which way do you get out of this?"

Jules allowed her to go. He was stricken to earth. The whole world seemed to be crumbling away under him, the sky above had fallen with a crash.

"Dinner is ready, sir," said the footman.

For fifteen minutes the footman and Desmarets' manservant waited in the dining-room, but no one appeared. The maid came in to say that "the mistress would not take dinner."

"Why, what is the matter, Joséphine?" asked the footman.

"I don't know. The mistress is crying, and she is going to bed. The master has a fancy somewhere else, I expect, and it has been found out at an awkward time; do you understand? I would not answer for the mistress' life. Men are all so clumsy, always making scenes without thinking in the least."

"Not a bit of it," said the man, lowering his voice; "on the contrary, it is the mistress who—in short, you understand. What time could the master have for gadding about, when he hasn't spent a night out these five years, and goes down to his office at ten o'clock, and only comes up to lunch at twelve? In fact, his life is open and regular, while the mistress goes off pretty nearly every day at three o'clock, no one knows where."

"So does the master," said the maid, taking her mistress' part.

"But he goes to the Bourse, the master does. This is the third time I have told him that dinner is ready," he added, after a pause; "you might as well talk to a *statute*."

Jules came in.

"Where is your mistress?" asked he.

"Madame has gone to bed, she has a sick headache," said the maid, assuming an important air.

"You can take the dinner away," said Jules, with much cool self-possession. "I shall keep madame company." And he went to his wife. She was crying, and stifling her sobs with her handkerchief.

"Why do you cry?" said Jules, using the formal *vous*. "You have no violence, no reproaches, to expect from me. Why should I avenge myself? If you have not been faithful to my love, it is because you were not worthy of it——"

"Not worthy!"

The words repeated amid her sobs, and the tone in which they were spoken, would have softened any man but Jules.

"To kill you, a man must love more, perhaps, than I," he resumed; "but I have not the heart to do it, I would sooner make away with myself and leave you to your—your happiness —and to—whom——?"

He broke off.

"Make away with yourself!" cried Clémence. She flung herself at Jules' feet and clung about them; but he tried to shake her off, and dragged her to the bed.

"Leave me alone," said he.

"No, no, Jules! If you love me no longer, I shall die. Do you wish to know all?"

"Yes." He took her, held her forcibly in his grasp, sat down on the bedside, and held her between his knees; then he gazed dry-eyed at the fair face, now red as fire and seamed with tear-stains. "Now, tell me," he said for the second time.

Clémence began to sob afresh.

"I cannot. It is a secret of life and death. If I told you, I—— No, I *cannot*. Have pity, Jules!"

"You are deceiving me still," he said, but he replaced the formal *vous* by *tu* (you by thou).

"Ah!" she cried, at this sign of relenting. "Yes, Jules, you may believe that I am deceiving you, now you shall know everything very soon."

"But this Ferragus, this convict that you go to see, this man enriched by crime. if he is not your lover, if you are not his——"

"Oh, Jules!"

"Well, is he your unknown benefactor, the man to whom we owe our success, as people have said before this?"

"Who said so!"

"A man whom I killed in a duel."

"Oh, God! one man dead already."

"If he is not your protector, if he does not give you money, and you take money to him, is he your brother?"

"Well," she said, "and if he were?"

M. Desmarets folded his arms.

"Why should this have been kept from my knowledge?" returned he. "Did you both deceive me—you and your mother? And do people go to see their brothers every day, or nearly every day, eh?"

But his wife fell swooning at his feet.

He pulled the bell-rope, summoned Joséphine, and laid Clémence on the bed.

"She is dead," he thought, "and how if I am wrong?"

"This will kill me," murmured Mme. Jules, as she came to herself.

"Joséphine," exclaimed M. Desmarets, "go for Monsieur Desplein; and then go to my brother's house and ask him to come as soon as possible."

"Why your brother?" asked Clémence.

But Jules had already left the room.

For the first time in five years Mme. Jules slept alone in her bed, and was obliged to allow a doctor to enter the sanctuary, two troubles that she felt keenly.

Desplein found Mme. Jules very ill; never had violent emotion been worse timed. He postponed his decision on the case till the morrow, and left diverse prescriptions which were not carried out, all physical suffering was forgotten in heart distress. Daylight was at hand, and still Clémence lay awake. Her thoughts were busy with the murmur of conversation, which lasted for several hours, between the others, but no single word reached her through the thickness of the walls to give a clue to the meaning of the prolonged conference. M. Desmarets, the notary, went at length; and then, in the stillness of the night, with a strange stimulation of the senses that comes with passion, Clémence could hear the squeaking of a pen and the unconscious movements made by some one busily writing. Those who are accustomed to sit up through the night, and have noticed the effect of deep silence on the laws of acoustics, know that a faint sound at intervals is easily heard, when a continuous and even murmur is scarcely distinguishable.

Clémence rose, anxious and trembling. She forgot her condition, forgot that she was damp with perspiration, and, barefooted and without a dressing-gown, went across and opened the door. Luckily it turned noiselessly on its hinges. She saw her husband, pen in hand, sitting fast asleep in his easy-chair. The candles were burning low in the sockets. She crept forward, and on an envelope that lay sealed already she saw the words: "My Will."

She knelt down, as if at a graveside, and kissed her husband's hand. He woke at once.

"Jules, dear, even criminals condemned to death are given a few days' respite," she said, looking at him with eyes shining with love and fever. "Your innocent wife asks for two days—only two days. Leave me, then, free for two days, and—wait. After that I shall die happy; at any rate, you will be sorry."

"You shall have the delay, Clémence."

And while she kissed her husband's hands in a pathetic outpouring of her heart, Jules, fascinated by that cry of innocence, took her in his arms and kissed her on the forehead, utterly ashamed that he should still submit to the power of that noble beauty.

Next morning, after a few hours of sleep, Jules went to his wife's room, mechanically obedient to his custom of never leaving home without first seeing her. Clémence was asleep. A ray of light from a chink in the highest window fell on the face of a woman worn out with grief. Sorrow had left traces on her brow already, and faded the fresh red of her lips. A lover's eyes could not mistake the significance of the dark marbled streaks and the pallor of illness, which took the place of the even color in her cheeks and the white velvet of her skin, the transparent surface over which all the feelings that stirred that fair soul so unconsciously flitted.

"She is not well," thought Jules. "Poor Clémence, may God protect us!"

He kissed her very gently on the forehead; she awoke, looked into her husband's face, and understood. She could not speak, but she took his hand, and her eyes grew soft with tears.

"I am innocent," she said, finishing her dream.

"You will not go out to-day, will you?" said Jules.

"No; I feel too weak to get up."

"If you change your mind, wait till I come home," said Jules, and he went down to the porter's lodge.

"Fouquereau, you must keep a strict watch to-day," he said. "I wish to know every one who comes in or out."

With that, Jules sprang into a cab, bade the man drive to the Hôtel de Maulincour, and asked for the baron.

"Monsieur is ill," was the reply.

Jules insisted, and sent in his name. If he could not see M. de Maulincour, he would see the vidame or the dowager. He waited for some time in the old baroness' drawing-room; she came at last, however, to say that her grandson was far too ill to see him.

"I know the nature of his illness, madame," said Jules, "from the letter which you did me the honor to send, and I entreat you to believe——"

"A letter, monsieur? A letter that I sent to you?" broke in the baroness. "I have not written a word. And what am I supposed to say, monsieur, in this letter?"

"Madame, as I meant to call on Monsieur de Maulincour this very day, and to return the note to you, I thought I need not destroy it in spite of the request at the end. Here it is."

The dowager rang for her double-strength spectacles, and glanced down the sheet with every sign of the greatest astonishment.

"The handwriting is so exactly like mine, monsieur, that if we were not speaking of a quite recent event, I should be deceived by it myself. My grandson certainly is ill, monsieur, but his mind has not been affected the least bit in the world. We are puppets in the hands of wicked people; still, I cannot guess the object of this piece of impertinence. You shall see my grandson, monsieur, and you will admit that he is perfectly sane."

She rang the bell again to ask if it were possible for the baron to receive a visit from M. Desmarets. The footman brought an answer in the affirmative. Jules went up to Auguste de Maulincour's room, and found that young officer seated in an armchair by the fireside. He was too weak to rise, and greeted his visitor with a melancholy inclination of the head. The Vidame de Pamiers was keeping him company.

"Monsieur le Baron," began Jules, "I have something to say of so private a nature that I should wish to speak with you alone."

"Monsieur," said Auguste, "Monsieur le Commandeur knows all about this affair; you need not fear to speak before him."

"Monsieur le Baron, you have disturbed and almost destroyed my happiness; and you had no right to do so. Until we know which of us must ask or give satisfaction to the other, you are bound to give me your assistance in the dark ways to which you have suddenly brought me. So I have come to inquire the present address of this mysterious being who exercises such an unlucky influence on our lives, and seems to have some supernatural power at his orders. I received this letter yesterday, just as I came in after hearing your account of yourself."

Jules handed the forged letter.

"This Ferragus or Bourignard or Monsieur de Funcal is a fiend incarnate!" shouted Maulincour. "In what hideous labyrinth have I set foot? Whither am I going? I was wrong, monsieur," he added, looking full at Jules, "but death surely is the greatest expiation of all, and I am dying. So you can ask me anything you wish; I am at your service."

"You should know where this strange man lives; I absolutely must get to the bottom of this mystery, if it costs me all that I have; and with such a cruelly ingenious enemy every moment is precious."

"Justin will tell us all about it directly," replied the baron. The vidame fidgeted upon his chair. Auguste rang the bell.

"Justin is not in the house," exclaimed the vidame in a hasty fashion, which said a good deal more than the words.

"Well," Auguste said quickly, "and if he is not, our servants here know where he is. A man on horseback shall go at once to find him. Your servant is in Paris, is he not? They will find him somewhere."

The old Vidame de Pamiers was visibly troubled.

"Justin will not come, dear fellow," he said. "I wanted to keep the accident from your knowledge, but——"

"Is he dead?" exclaimed M. de Maulincour. "And when? and how?"

"It happened yesterday night. He went out to supper with some old friends, and got drunk, no doubt; his friends, being also the worse for wine, must have left him to lie in the street; a heavy carriage drove right over him——"

"The convict did not fail that time; he killed his man at the first attempt," said Auguste. "He was not so lucky with me; he had to try four times."

Jules grew moody and thoughtful.

"So I shall find out nothing, it seems," he exclaimed, after a long pause. "Perhaps your man was rightly served; he went beyond your orders when he slandered Madame Desmarets to one 'Ida,' to stir up the girl's jealousy and let her loose upon us."

"Ah, monsieur, in my fury I gave over Madame Jules to him."

"Sir!" exclaimed Mme. Jules' husband, stung to the quick; but Maulincour silenced him with a wave of the hand.

"Oh! now I am prepared for all that may happen. What is done is done, and you will do no better; nor can you say anything that my own conscience has not told me already. I am expecting the most famous specialist in toxicology to learn my fate. If the pain is likely to be intolerable, I have made up my mind; I shall blow my brains out."

"You are talking like a boy," cried the old vidame, aghast at the baron's coolness. "Your grandmother would die of grief!"

"And so, monsieur, there is no way of finding out in what part of Paris this extraordinary man lives?" asked Monsieur Jules.

"I think, monsieur, that I heard this poor Justin say that Monsieur de Funcal was to be found at the Portuguese or else the Brazilian embassy," said the vidame. "Monsieur de Funcal is of a good family; he belongs to both countries. As for the convict, he is dead and buried. Your persecutor, whoever he may be, is so powerful, it seems to me, that you had better accept him in his new metamorphosis until you are in a position to overwhelm him with confusion and crush him; but set about it prudently, my dear sir. If Monsieur de Maulincour had taken my advice, nothing of all this would have happened."

Jules withdrew, coolly but politely. He was at his wits' end to find Ferragus. As he came in, the porter came out to inform him that madame had gone out to put a letter into the box opposite the Rue de Ménars. Jules felt humiliated by the profound intelligence with which the man aided and abetted his scheme, and by the very skill with which he found means to serve him. The zeal and peculiar ingenuity which inferiors will show to compromise their betters, when their betters compromise themselves, were well known to Jules, and he appreciated the danger of having such accomplices in any affair whatsoever; but he had forgotten his personal dignity till he suddenly saw how far he had fallen. What a triumph for a serf, unable to rise to his master, to bring that master down to his own level!

Jules was stern and abrupt with the man. Another blunder. But he was so wretched! His life, till then so straight and clean, had grown crooked; and now there was nothing for it but to use craft and lies. And Clémence, too, was using lies and craft with him. It was a sickening moment. Lost in depths of bitter thought, he stood forgetful of himself and motionless on the door-step. Sometimes he gave way to despair which counseled flight; he would leave France and carry with him his love and all the illusions of unproved guilt; and then again, never doubting but that Clémence's letter was addressed to Ferragus, he cast about for ways of intercepting the reply sent by that mysterious being. Again, examining into his singular success since his marriage, he asked himself whether that slander which he had avenged was not after all a truth. At length, returning to Ferragus' answer, he reasoned with himself on this wise:

"But will this Ferragus, so profoundly astute as he is, so consequent in the least things that he does; this man who sees, and foresees, and calculates, and even guesses our thoughts, will he send an answer? Is he not sure to employ some means in keeping with his power? Can he not send a reply by some ingenious scoundrel, or, more likely still, in a jewel case brought by some unsuspecting, honest creature, or in a parcel with a pair of shoes which some working-girl, in all innocence, brings home for my wife? Suppose that there should be an understanding between him and Clémence?"

He could trust nothing and nobody. He made a hurried survey of the boundless field, the shoreless sea of conjecture; and after drifting hither and thither, and in every possible direction, it occurred to him that he was stronger in his own house than anywhere else; so he resolved to stay at home and watch like an ant-lion at the bottom of its funnel in the sand.

"Fouquereau," he said, "if any one asks for me, I am not at home. But if any one wishes to speak with madame, or brings anything for her, ring twice. And you must let me see every letter left here, no matter to whom it is addressed. And so," he thought within himself, as he went into his office on the entresol, "and so I shall outwit Master Ferragus. And if his messenger is cunning enough to ask for me, so as to find out whether madame is alone, at any rate I shall not be gulled like a fool."

His office windows looked into the street. As he stood with his face pressed against the panes, jealousy inspired him with a final stratagem. He determined to send his head-clerk to the Bourse in his carriage; the clerk should take a letter to a friend of his, another stockbroker, to whom he would explain his business transactions—he would beg his friend to take his place. His most difficult business he put off till the morrow, regardless of the rise and fall of stocks, and all the funds of Europe. Fair prerogative of love! Love eclipses all things else. The rest of the world fades away before it; and altar, throne, and government securities are as though they were not. At half-past three o'clock, just when the Bourse is all agog with rates and premiums, rises and falls, current accounts, and the rest of it, Jules looked up and saw Fouquereau with a beaming countenance.

"An old woman has just been here, sir; she is as sharp as they make them. Oh! she is an artful one. I can tell you. She asked for you, and seemed put out to find you were not at home; then she gave me this letter here for madame."

Jules broke the seal with fevered anguish, but he dropped exhausted into his chair. The letter was a string of meaningless words, and quite unintelligible without a key. It was written in cipher.

"You can go. Fouquereau."

The man went.

"This mystery is deeper than the unplumbed sea. Oh,

this is love beyond a doubt. Love, and love only, could be as sagacious, as ingenious as the writer of this letter. Oh, God! I will kill Clémence."

Even at that moment a bright idea burst upon his brain, and struck him so forcibly, that it seemed almost like the breaking out of light. In the old days of poverty and hard work before his marriage, Jules had made a real friend. The excessive delicacy with which Jules spared the susceptibilities of a poor and shy comrade, the respect that he paid his friend, the tactful ingenuity with which he made that friend accept a share of his good fortune without a blush—all these things had increased their friendship since those days. In spite of Desmarets' prosperity, Jacquet was faithful to him.

Jacquet, an honest man, and a toiler of austere life, had slowly made his way in that department which of all others employs most rascality and most honesty. He was in the Foreign Office; the most delicate part of its archives was in his charge. He was a kind of departmental glow-worm, shedding light during his working hours on secret correspondence, deciphering and classifying dispatches. Rather above the rank and file of the middle-classes, he held the highest (subaltern) post at the Foreign Office, and lived unrecognized; rejoicing in an obscurity which put him beyond reverses of fortune, and content to pay his debt to his fatherland in small coin. A born assistant-registrar, he enjoyed the respect that was due to him, in newspaper language. And, as an unknown patriot in a Government Department, he resigned himself to groan, by his fireside, over the aberrations of the Government that he served. His position, thanks to Jules, had been improved by a suitable marriage. In his own home, Jacquet was a debonair king, a " man with an umbrella," as they say, who hired a carriage for his wife which he never entered himself; and as a final touch to this portrait of an unconscious philosopher, it should be added that he had never yet suspected, and never would suspect, how much he might make out of his position, with a stockbroker for his intimate friend, and a knowledge of State secrets. A hero after the manner of that unknown private soldier who died to save Napoleon with a cry of "Who goes there?" he was faithful to his Department.

In another ten minutes Jules stood in Jacquet's private office. His friend brought forward a chair, laid his green silk eye-shade down methodically upon the table, rubbed his hands, took out his snuff-box, rose to his feet, threw out his chest with a crack of the shoulder-blades, and said—

"What chance brings you here, Mo'sieur Desmarets? What do you want with me?"

"I want you to find out a secret for me, Jacquet; it is a matter of life and death."

"It is not about politics?"

"You are not the man I should come to if I wanted to know anything of that kind," said Jules. "No, it is a private affair, and I must ask you to keep it as secret as possible."

"Claude-Joseph Jacquet, professional mute. Why, don't you know me?" laughed he. "My line of business is discretion."

Jules put the letter before him.

"This is addressed to my wife; I must have it read to me," he said.

"The devil! the devil! a bad business," said Jacquet, scrutinizing the document as a money-lender examines a negotiable bill. "Aha! a stencil cipher. Wait!"

He left Jules alone in the office, but came back pretty soon.

"Tomfoolery, my friend. It is written with an old stencil cipher which the Portuguese ambassador used in Monsieur de Choiseul's time after the expulsion of the jesuits. Stay, look here."

Jacquet took up a sheet of paper with holes cut in it at regular intervals; it looked rather like the lace paper which confectioners put over their sugar-plums. When this was set over the sheet below, Jules could easily make sense of the words left uncovered:

"MY DEAR CLÉMENCE:—Do not trouble yourself any more; no one shall trouble our happiness again, and your husband will put his suspicions aside. I cannot go to see you. However ill you may be, you must gather up your courage to come to me; summon up your strength, love will give it to you. I have been through a most cruel operation for your sake, and I cannot stir out of bed. Moxas were applied yesterday evening to the nape of the neck and across the shoulders; it was necessary to cauterize pretty deeply. Do you understand? But I thought of you, and found the pain not intolerable. I have left the sheltering roof of the Embassy to baffle Maulincour, who shall not persecute us much longer; and here I am safe from all search at Number 12 Rue des Enfants-Rouges, with an old woman, one Mme. Étienne Gruget, mother of that Ida, who shall shortly pay dear for her silly prank. Come to-morrow at nine o'clock. My room can only be reached by an inner staircase. Ask for M. Camuset. Adieu till to-morrow. I kiss thy forehead, my darling."

Jacquet gazed at Jules with a kind of shocked expression with a very real sympathy in it, and brought out his favorite invocation: "The devil! the devil!" in two distinct intonations.

"It seems clear to you, doesn't it?" said Jules. "Well, and yet, in the bottom of my heart a voice pleads for my wife, and that voice rises above all the pangs of jealousy. I shall endure the most horrid torture until to-morrow; but at last, to-morrow between nine and ten, I shall know all. I shall either be wretched or happy for life. Think of me, Jacquet."

"I will be at your house at eight o'clock. We will go yonder together. I will wait outside in the street for you, if you like. There may be risks to run; you ought to have some one you can trust within call, a sure hand that can take a hint. Count upon me."

"Even to help me to kill a man?"

"The devil! the devil!" Jacquet said quickly, repeating, so to speak, the same musical note. "I have two children and a wife——"

Jules squeezed Claude Jacquet's hand and went out. But he came back in haste.

"I am forgetting the letter," said he. "And that is not all; it must be sealed again."

"The devil! the devil! you opened it without taking an impression; but, luckily, the edge of the fracture is pretty clean. There, let me have it, I will give it you back again *secundum scripturam* (according to the Scriptures)."

"When?"

"By half-past five——"

"If I am not in, simply give it to the porter, and tell him to send it up to madame."

"Do you want me to-morrow?"

"No. Farewell."

Jules soon reached the Place de la Rotonde du Temple, dismissed his cabriolet, and walked down to the Rue des Enfants-Rouges, to take a look at Mme. Étienne Gruget's abode. The mystery on which so many lives hung was to be cleared up there. Ferragus was there, and Ferragus held all the ends of the threads in this obscure business. Was not the connection between Mme. Jules, her husband, and this man the Gordian knot of a tragedy stained even now with blood? Nor should the blade be wanting to cut asunder the tightest of all bonds.

The house belonged to the class commonly known as *cabajoutis*—an expressive name given by working people in Paris to patchwork buildings, as they may be called. Several houses, originally separate, have some time been run into one, according to the fancy of the various proprietors who successively enlarged them; or they were begun and left unfinished for a time, and afterward resumed and completed. Unlucky dwellings are they that have passed, like sundry nations, under the rule of several dynasties of capricious rulers. The various stories and the windows do not belong to each other, to borrow one of the most picturesque of painter's words; every detail, even the decorations outside, clashes with the rest of the building. The *cabajoutis* is to Parisian street architecture what the *capharnaüm*, or lumber-room, is to the house—a regular rubbish-heap, where the most unlikely things are shot down together pell-mell.

"Mme. Étienne?" Jules asked of the portress.

That functionary was installed in the great centre doorway in a sort of hencoop, a little wooden house on wheels, not unlike the cabins which the police authorities put up at every cabstand.

"Eh?" said the portress, laying down the stocking which she was knitting. The living accessories which contribute to the general effect of any portion of the great monster, Paris, fit in, as a rule, remarkably well with the character of their surroundings. The porter, janitor, concierge, Swiss, or whatever you may choose to call this indispensable muscle in the monster's economy, is always in keeping with the quarter of which he is an integral part; very often he is the Quarter incarnate. The concierge of the Faubourg Saint-Germain, an idle being embroidered at every seam, speculates in stocks and shares; in the Chaussée d'Antin, the porter is a comfortable personage; in the neighborhood of the Bourse, he reads the newspaper; in the Faubourg Montmartre, he carries on some industry or other. In low neighborhoods the portress is a worn-out prostitute; in the Marais she keeps herself respectable, she is apt to be peevish and cross-grained, she has her "ways."

At sight of Jules, the portress of the Rue des Enfants-Rouges stirred up the dying embers of block fuel in her foot-warmer, taking a knife for the purpose. Then she said:

"You want Madame Étienne; do you mean Madame Étienne Gruget?"

"Yes," said Jules Desmarets, with a touch of vexation.

"She that works at trimmings?"

"Yes."

"Very well, sir," and, emerging from her cage, she laid a hand on Jules' arm and drew him to the farther end of a long narrow passage, vaulted like a cellar; "you go up the second staircase opposite, just across the yard. Do you see the windows with the wallflowers? That's where Madame Étienne lives."

"Thank you, madame. Is she alone, do you think?"

"Why shouldn't she be alone when she is a lone woman?"

Jules sprang noiselessly up a very dark staircase, every step incrusted with dried lumps of mud deposited by the lodgers' boots. He found three doors on the second floor, but no sign of wallflowers. Luckily for him, some words were written in chalk on the grimiest and greasiest of the three—*Ida will be back at nine o'clock to-night.*

"Here it is," said Jules to himself.

He tugged at an old blackened bell-pull, with a fawn's foot attached, and heard the smothered tinkle of a little cracked bell, and the yapping of an asthmatic little dog. He could tell by the sound that the bell made inside that the room was so lumbered up with things that there was no room for an echo—a characteristic trait of workmen's lodgings and little households generally, where there is neither space nor air. Jules looked about involuntarily for the wallflowers, and found them at last on the window-sill, between two pestiferous sinks. Here were flowers, a garden two feet long and six inches wide, and a sprouting grain of wheat—all life condensed into that narrow space, and not one of life's miseries lacking! A ray of sunlight shone down, as if in pity on the sickly blossoms and the superb green column of wheat-stalk, bringing out the indescribable color peculiar to Paris slums; dust, grease, and inconceivable filth incrusted and corroded the rubbed, discolored damp walls, the worm-eaten balusters, the gaping window-sashes, the doors that once had been painted red. In another moment he heard an old woman's cough and the sound of heavy feet dragging painfully along in list slippers. This must be Ida Gruget's mother. She opened the door, came out upon the landing, raised her face to his, and said—

"Ah! it's M'sieur Bocquilion! Why, no it isn't. My word! how like you are to M'sieur Bocquillon! You are a brother of his perhaps? What can I do for you, sir? Just step inside."

Jules followed her into the first room, and caught a general impression of bird-cages, pots and pans, stoves, furniture, little earthenware dishes full of broken meat, or milk for the dog and the cats; a wooden clock-case, blankets, Eisen's engravings, and a heap of old ironware piled up with the most curiously grotesque effect. It was a genuine Parisian *capharnaüm;* nothing was lacking, not even a few odd numbers of the "Constitutionnel."

"Just come in here and warm yourself," said the Widow Gruget, but prudence prevailed. Jules was afraid that Ferragus might overhear, and wondered whether the bargain which he proposed to make had not better be concluded in the outer room; just then, however, a hen came cackling down a staircase and cut short his inward conference. He made up his mind and followed Ida's mother into the next room, where a fire was burning. A wheezy little pug-dog, a dumb spectator, followed them, and scrambled up on an old stool. Mme. Gruget's request to come in and get warm was prompted by the very coxcombry of poverty on the brink of destitution. Her stock-pot completely hid a couple of smouldering sticks which ostentatiously shunned each other. A skimmer lay on the floor, with the handle among the ashes. On the wooden ledge above the fireplace, amid a litter of wools, cotton-reels, and odds and ends, needed for the manufacture of trimmings, stood a little waxen crucifix under a shade made of pieces of glass joined together with strips of bluish paper. Jules looked round at the furniture with a curiosity in which self-interest was blended, and in spite of himself he showed his secret satisfaction.

"Well, sir, do you think you can buy any of my furniture?" inquired the widow, sitting down in a yellow caneseated armchair, her headquarters apparently; for it contained her pocket-handkerchief, her snuff-box, some half-peeled vegetables, her spectacles, an almanack, a length of galoon on which she was at work, a pack of greasy playing-cards, and a couple of novels. All this sounded hollow. The piece of furniture on which the widow was "descending the river of life" was something like the comprehensive bag which women take on a journey, a sort of house in miniature, containing everything from the husband's portrait to the drop of balm tea in case she feels faint, from the sugar-plums for the little ones to English court-plaster for cut fingers.

Jules made a careful survey of it all. He looked very closely at Mme. Gruget herself, with her gray eyes, denuded of lashes and eyebrows, at her toothless mouth, at the dark shades in her wrinkles, at her rusty net cap, with its yet more rusty frill, at her tattered cotton petticoats, her worn slippers, and charred foot-warmer, and then at the table covered with crockery, silks, and patterns of work in worsted and cotton, with the neck of a wine-bottle rising out of the middle of the litter, and said within himself: "This woman has some passion, some failing that she keeps quiet: she is in my power." Aloud he said with a significant gesture: "I have come to order some galoon of you, madame;" then lowered his voice to add: "I know that you have a lodger here, a man that goes by the name of Camuset."

The old woman looked up at once, but there was not a sign of surprise in her countenance.

"Look here, can he overhear us? There is a fortune involved for you, mind you."

"You can speak, sir, there is nothing to be afraid of; there is nobody here. There is somebody upstairs, but it is quite impossible that he should hear you."

"Ah! cunning old thing! She can give you a Norman's answer," thought Jules. "We may come to terms. You need not trouble yourself to tell a lie, madame. To begin with, bear in mind that I mean no harm whatever to you, nor your invalid lodger with his blisters, nor to your daughter Ida the stay-maker, Ferragus' sweetheart. You see, I know all about it. Never mind, I have nothing to do with the police, and I want nothing that is likely to hurt your conscience.

"A young lady will come here to-morrow between nine and ten to have some talk with your daughter's sweetheart. I want to be somewhere near, so that I can hear and see everything without being heard or seen. You must arrange this for me, and I will give you two thousand francs down, and an annuity of six hundred francs. My notary shall draw up the agreement this evening in your presence, and I will give the money into his hands to pay over to you to-morrow after this meeting at which I wish to be present, when I shall have proof of your good faith."

"It will not do any harm to my daughter, will it, my dear gentleman?" she returned, on the watch like a suspicious cat.

"None whatever, madame. But, at the same time, your daughter is behaving very badly to you, it seems to me. When a man as rich and powerful as Ferragus is fond of her, it ought to be easy to make you more comfortable than you appear to be."

"Ah, my dear gentleman, not so much as a miserable ticket for the Ambigu or the Gaieté, where she can go whenever she likes. It is shameful. And I that sold my silver spoons, and am eating now off German silver in my old age, all to apprentice that girl, and give her a business where she could coin gold if she chose. For as to that, she takes after her mother; she is as neat-fingered as a fairy, it must be said in justice to her. At any rate, she might as well hand over her old silk dresses to me, so fond as I am of wearing silk; but no, sir. She goes to the Cadran Bleu, to dine at fifty francs a head, and rolls in her carriage like a princess, and doesn't care a rap for her mother. God Almighty! we bring these scatter-brained girls into the world, and it is not the best that could be said for us. A mother, sir, and a good mother, too, for I have hidden her giddiness, and cosseted her to that degree that I took the bread out of my mouth to stuff her with all that I had! Well, and that is not enough, but she must come and coax you, and then wish you 'Good-day, mother!' That is the way they do their duty to them that brought them into the world! Just let them go their ways. But she will have children some day or other, and then she will know what it is for herself; bad bargains they are, but one loves them, all the same."

"What, does she do nothing for you?"

"Nothing? Oh, no, sir, I don't say that. If she did nothing at all for me, it would be rather too bad. She pays the rent, and she gives me firewood and thirty-six francs a month. But is it right, sir, that I should have to go on working at my age; I am fifty-two, and my eyes are weak of an evening? And what is more, why won't she have me with her? If she is ashamed of me, she may as well say so at once. You had need to bury yourself, and that is the truth, for these beastly children that forget all about you before they have so much as shut the door.'

She drew her handkerchief from her pocket, and a lottery ticket fell out, but she picked it up in a moment.

"Hi? that is the tax-collector's receipt."

Jules suddenly guessed the reason of the prudent parsimony of which the mother complained, and felt the more sure that the Widow Gruget would agree to his proposal.

"Very well, madame," he said, "in that case you will accept my offer."

"Two thousand francs down, did you say, sir? and six hundred francs a year?"

"I have changed my mind, madame. I will promise you only three hundred francs of annuity. The arrangement suits me better. But I will pay you five thousand francs down. You would rather have it so, would you not?"

"Lord, yes, sir."

"You will be more comfortable, you can go to the Ambigu Comique, or Franconi's, or anywhere else, and go comfortably in a hackney-coach."

"Oh, I do not care about Franconi's at all, being as you don't hear talk there. And if I agree to take the money, sir, it is because it will be a fine thing for my child. And I shall not be living on her. Poor little thing, after all, I don't grudge her such pleasure as she gets. Young things must have amusement, sir. And so, if you will assure me that I shall be doing nobody any harm——"

"Nobody," repeated Jules. "But see now, how are you going to set about it?"

"Oh, well, sir, if Monsieur Ferragus has just a little drink of poppy water to-night, he will sleep sound, the dear man! And much he stands in need of sleep, in such pain as he is, for he suffers so that it makes you sorry to see it. And by-the-by, just tell me what sort of a notion it is for a healthy man to have his back burnt to cure the neuralgia that does not trouble him once in two years? But to go back to our business, sir. My neighbor that lives just above has left her key with me; her room is next door to Monsieur Ferragus' bedroom. She has gone to the country for ten days. So if you have a hole made to-night in the partition wall, you can look in and hear at your ease. There is a locksmith, a great friend of mine, a very nice man, that talks like an angel; he will do that for me, and nobody any the wiser."

"Here are a hundred francs for him. You must come this evening to Monsieur Desmarets'; he is a notary; here is his address. The paper will be ready at nine o'clock, but—mum!"

"Right; mum as you say. Good-day, sir."

Jules went home again, almost soothed by the certainty of knowing everything to-morrow. He found the letter, sealed flawlessly again, in the porter's room.

"How are you?" he asked his wife, in spite of the coolness between them, so difficult is it to break from the old habits of affection.

"Rather better, Jules," she answered in winning tones; "will you dine here with me?"

"Yes. Stay, here is something that Fouquereau gave me for you," and he handed her the letter. At the sight of it Clémence's white face flushed a deep red; the sudden crimson sent an intolerable pang through her husband.

"Is that joy?" laughed he, "or relief from suspense?"

"Oh! many things," she said, as she looked at the seal.

"I will leave you, madame."

He went down to his office and wrote to his brother about the annuity for the Widow Gruget. When he came back again dinner was ready on a little table by Clémence's bedside, and Joséphine waited upon them.

"If I were not lying in bed, what a pleasure it would be to me to serve you!" she said, when Joséphine had gone. "Oh, and even on my knees," she went on, passing her white fingers through Jules' hair. "Dear noble heart! you were very merciful and good to me just now. You have done me more good by your trust in me than all the doctors in the world could do with their prescriptions. Your woman's delicacy—for you can love as a woman can—shed balm in my soul; I feel almost well again. There is a truce. Jules, come closer, let me kiss you."

Jules could not forego the joy of Clémence's kiss, and yet it was not without something like remorse in his heart. He felt small before this woman, in whose innocence he was always tempted to believe. There was a sort of sorrowful gladness about Clémence. A chastened hope shone through the troubled expression of her face. They seemed both alike unhappy that the deceit must be kept up; another kiss, and they must tell each other all; they could endure their pain no longer.

"To-morrow evening, Clémence?"

"No, monsieur, to-morrow at noon you shall know everything, and you will kneel before your wife. Ah! no, you shall not humble yourself. No, all is forgiven you. No, you have done no wrong. Listen. Yesterday you shattered me very ruthlessly, but life perhaps might not have been complete if I had not known that anguish; it is a dark shadow to bring out the brightness of days like heaven."

"You are bewitching me," Jules exclaimed, "and you would give me remorse."

"Poor love, fate overrules us, and I cannot help my destiny. I am going out to-morrow."

"When?"

"At half-past nine."

"Clémence, you must be very careful. You must consult Dr. Desplein and old Haudry."

"I shall consult my own heart and courage only."

"I will leave you free. I shall not come to see you till noon."

"Will you not stay with me a little while to-night? I am not ill now——"

Jules finished his work and came back to sit with her. He could not keep away. Love was stronger in him than all his griefs.

Next morning, at nine o'clock, Jules slipped out of the house, hurried to the Rue des Enfants-Rouges, climbed the stairs, and rang the bell at the Widow Gruget's door.

"Ah! You are a man of your word, punctual as sunrise," was old Mme. Gruget's greeting. "Come in, sir. I have a cup of coffee and cream ready for you in case——" she added, when the door was closed. "Oh! and genuine cream, a little jar that I saw them fill with my own eyes at the cowkeeper's near by in the Enfants-Rouges market."

"Thank you, no, madame, nothing. Show me upstairs——"

"Very good, my dear gentleman. Step this way."

She showed Jules into a room just above her own, and pointed triumphantly to a hole about as large as a two-franc piece, cut during the night so as to correspond with a rose in the pattern of the paper in Ferragus' room. The opening had been made above a cupboard on either side the wall; the locksmith had left no trace of his handiwork; and from below it was very difficult to see this improvised loophole in a dark corner. If Jules meant to see or hear anything, he was obliged to stay there in a tolerably cramped position, perched on the top of a step which the Widow Gruget had thoughtfully placed for him.

"There's a gentleman with him," she said, as she went. And, in fact, Jules saw that some one was busy dressing a line of blisters raised on Ferragus' shoulders. He recognized Ferragus from M. de Maulincour's description of the man.

"When shall I be all right, do you think?" asked the patient.

"I do not know," said the other; "but, from what the doctors say, seven or eight more dressings will be needed at least."

"Very well, see you again this evening," returned Ferragus, holding out a hand to the man as he adjusted the last bandage.

"This evening," returned the other, shaking Ferragus cordially by the hand. "I should be glad to see you out of your pain."

"At last Monsieur de Funcal's papers are to be handed over to-morrow, and Henry Bourignard is really dead," continued

Ferragus. "Those two unlucky letters that cost us so dear have been destroyed, so I shall be somebody, socially speaking; a man among men again, and I am quite as good as the sailor whom the fishes have eaten. God knows whether it is for my own sake that I have taken a count's title."

"Poor Gratien! you are the best head among us, our beloved brother, the Benjamin of the band. You know that."

"Farewell; take good care of my Maulincour."

"You can set your mind at rest on that score."

"Ho! stay, marquis!" cried the convict.

"What is it?"

"Ida is capable of anything after the scene yesterday evening. If she flings herself into the river, I certainly shall not fish her out; she will the better keep the secret of my name, the only secret she knows; but look after her, for, after all, she is a kind creature."

"Very well."

The stranger went. Ten minutes afterward Jules heard the unmistakable rustle of silk, and almost knew the sound of his wife's footsteps, not without a fevered shiver.

"Well, father, poor father, how are you? How brave you are!" It was Clémence who spoke.

"Come here, child," said Ferragus, holding out his hand. And Clémence bent her forehead for his kiss.

"Let us see you, what is it, poor little girl? What new troubles——?"

"Troubles, father? It is killing me, killing the daughter who loves you so. As I wrote telling you yesterday, you absolutely must use that fertile brain of yours to find some way of seeing poor Jules this very day. If you only knew how good he has been to me in spite of suspicions that seemed so well founded! Love is my life, father. Do you wish to see me die? Oh! I have been through so much as it is, and my life is in danger, I feel it."

"To lose you, my child! to lose you for a miserable Parisian's curiosity! I would set Paris on fire. Ah! you know what a lover is, but what a father is you do not, you cannot, know."

"You frighten me, father, when you look like that. Do not put two such different sentiments in the balance. I had my husband before I knew that my father was living——"

"If your husband was the first to set a kiss upon your forehead, I was the first to let tears fall there," said Ferragus. "Reassure yourself, Clémence; open your heart to me. I love you well enough to be happy in the knowledge that you are happy; although your father is almost nothing in your heart, while you fill his."

"Ah, God! such words make me too happy. You make me love you more than ever, and it seems to me that I am robbing something from my Jules. But just think that he is in despair, my good father. What shall I tell him in two hours' time?"

"Child, do you think that I waited for your letter to save you from this threatened unhappiness? What came to those who took it into their heads to meddle with your happy life, or to come between us? Why, have you never recognized a second Providence watching over you? And you do not know twelve men, full of vigor in mind and body, are like an escort about your love and your life, always ready to do any deed to save you? And the father who used to risk his life to see you as you took your walks; or came at night to see you in your little cot in your mother's room; that father who, from the memory of your childish kisses, and from these alone, drew strength to live when a man of honor must take his own life to escape a shameful fate: how should not he— how should not I, in short, that draw breath only through your lips—see only with your eyes, feel through your heart, how should I not defend you with a lion's claws and a father's soul, when you are all that I have, my only blessing, my life, my daughter? Why, since that angel died, that was your mother, I have dreamed only one dream—of the joy of calling you my daughter openly, of clasping you in my arms before heaven and earth, of killing the convict——" (he paused for a moment)—"of giving you a father," he continued; "I saw a time when I could grasp your husband's hand without a blush, and live fearlessly in both your hearts, and say to the world: 'This is my child!'—in short, I had visions of being a father at my ease."

"Oh! father, father!"

"After many efforts, after searching the world over, my friends have found me a man's shape to fill," continued Ferragus. "In a few days' time I shall be Monsieur de Funcal, a Portuguese count. There, dear child, there are few men of my age that would have patience to learn Portuguese and English, with which that confounded naval officer was perfectly acquainted."

"My dear father!"

"Every contingency is provided for. In a few days his majesty, John VI., King of Portugal, will be my accomplice. So you only need a little patience when your father has had so much. But for me it was quite natural. What would I not do to reward your devotion during these three years? To come so dutifully to see your old father, risking your happiness as you did."

"Father!" Clémence took Ferragus' hands and kissed them.

"Come! a little more courage, Clémence; let us keep the fatal secret to the end. Jules is not an ordinary man; and yet, do we know whether with his lofty character and great love he will not feel something like disrespect for the daughter of——"

"Ah! you have read your child's soul," cried Clémence; "I have no fear but that," she added, in a heart-rending tone. "The thought freezes my blood. But remember, father, I have promised him the truth in two hours."

"Well, my child, tell him to go to the Portuguese embassy to see the Comte de Funcal, your father; I will be there."

"And how about Monsieur de Maulincour who talked about Ferragus? Ah, dear! to tell lie upon lie, what torture, father!"

"To whom are you speaking? Yet a few days, and no man alive can give me the lie. And beside, Monsieur de Maulincour is in no condition to remember anything by this time—— There, there, silly child, dry your tears, and bear in mind that——"

A dreadful cry rang from the next room, where Jules Desmarets was hiding.

"My girl, my poor girl!" The wail came through the loophole above the cupboard; Ferragus and Mme. Jules were terror-stricken by it.

"Go and see what it is, Clémence."

Clémence fled down the narrow staircase, found the door of Mme. Gruget's room standing wide open, and heard her voice ring out overhead. The sound of sobbing attracted her to the fatal room, and these words reached her ears as she entered—

"It is you, sir, with your notions, that have been the death of her!"

"Hush, wretched woman!" exclaimed Jules, trying to stop her cries with his pocket-handkerchief.

"Murder! Help!" cried the Widow Gruget. At that moment Clémence came in, saw her husband, shrieked aloud, and fled.

There was a long pause. "Who will save my daughter?" asked Mme. Gruget. "You have murdered her."

"And how?" asked Jules mechanically, stupefied by the thought that his wife had recognized him.

"Read that, sir," said she, bursting into tears. "Will any money comfort me for this?" and she held out a letter:

"Farewell, mother. I leave you all I have. I ask your pardon for my faults, and for this last grief I am bringing on you by making away with myself. Henry, that I love better than myself, said that I had done him harm, and he would have no more to do with me afterward; I have lost all hopes of establishing myself, and I shall go and throw myself into the river. I am going down below Neuilly, so as they shall never put me in the Morgue. If Henry doesn't hate me after I've punished myself with death, ask him to bury a poor girl whose heart only beat for him, and to forgive me, for I did wrong to meddle with what was no concern of mine. Dress his blisters carefully.' He has suffered a deal, the poor dear. But I shall have as much courage to drown myself as he had to have himself burnt. There are some corsets ready; see that they are sent home. And pray God for your daughter.

"IDA."

"Take the letter to Monsieur de Funcal, in the next room. He is the only man that can save your daughter, if it is not too late." And Jules vanished, flying like a criminal when the deed is done. His legs shook under him. His swelling heart was sending a hotter and fuller tide through his veins, with a mightier pulse than he had ever known before. The most conflicting thoughts filled his mind, and yet one idea prevailed above them all. He had been disloyal to the one whom he loved best in the world; he could not compound with his conscience, its voice grew in proportion to the extent of the wrong that he had done, till the clamor filled him, as passion had filled his inmost being during the bitterest hours of the suspense which had shaken him but a short while ago. He dared not go home, and spent most of the day in wandering about Paris. Upright as he was, he shrank from confronting the blameless brow of the wife he had not rightly valued. The sin is in proportion to the purity of the conscience; and an act which for some is scarcely a mistake will weigh like a crime upon a few white souls. Is there not, indeed, a divine significance in that word white? and does not the slightest spot on a virgin's garments degrade them at once to the level of the beggar's rags? Between the two there is but the difference between misfortune and error. Repentance is not proportioned to the sin; God makes no distinctions; it is as hard to wipe out one stain as to wash away the sins of a lifetime.

These thoughts lay heavily on Jules' soul. Justice is not more inexorable than passion, nor more ruthless in its reasoning; for passion has a conscience of its own, infallible as instinct. He went home again in despair, overwhelmed with a sense of the wrong he had done; but, in spite of himself, joy in his wife's innocence was visible in his pale face. He went to her room with a fast-throbbing heart, and found her lying in bed. She was in a high fever. He sat down by the bedside, took her hand, and kissed it and covered it with tears.

"Dear angel, they are the tears of repentance," he said, when they were alone.

"And for what?" she asked.

She bent her head down on the pillow as she spoke, and shut her eyes, and lay quite still, fearing, with a mother's, an angel's delicacy, to betray her pain and alarm her husband. The whole woman was summed up in those words. There was a long silence. Jules, fancying that Clémence was asleep, stole out to ask Joséphine about her mistress.

"Madame came in half-dead, sir. We sent for Monsieur Haudry."

"Has he been? What did he say?"

"Nothing, sir. He did not seem satisfied; he said that no one was to be allowed in the room except the nurse, and he would come again in the course of the evening."

Jules stole softly back to his wife, and sat down in an armchair by the bedside. He did not move; his eyes never left hers. Whenever Clémence looked up she met their gaze, and from under her lashes there escaped a tender, sorrowful, impassioned glance—a glance that fell like a fiery dart in the inmost soul of the man thus generously absolved, and loved through everything by her whom he had done to death. Forebodings of death lay between them; death was a presence felt alike by both. Their looks were blended in the same agony, as their two hearts had been made one through love equally felt and shared. There were no questions now, but a dreadful certainty. In the wife, a perfect generosity; in the husband, a hideous remorse; and in both their souls one vision of the end, and the same consciousness of the inevitable.

There was a moment when Jules, thinking that his wife was asleep, kissed her softly on the forehead, gazed long at her, and said to himself: "Ah, God! leave this angel with me yet a while longer, that I may expiate my sins by long adoration. Heroic as a daughter; what word could describe her as a wife?"

Clémence opened her eyes; they were full of tears.

"You hurt me," she said in a weak voice.

It was growing late. Dr. Haudry came and asked Jules to leave the room while he saw his patient; and when he came out afterward there was no need to ask any questions—a gesture told all.

"Send for any of my colleagues in whom you have most confidence," said the doctor; "I may be mistaken."

"But, doctor, tell me the truth. I am not a child, I can hear it; and beside, I have the strongest reasons for wishing to know it, there are accounts to settle——"

"Madame Jules is death-stricken," said the doctor. "There is something on her mind which complicates the physical illness; the situation was dangerous as it was, and repeated imprudence has made it worse. Getting out of bed in the night with barefeet; going out on foot yesterday, and in the carriage to-day, when I forbade it, she must have meant to kill herself. Still my verdict is not final; there is youth, and astonishing nervous strength—it might be worth while to risk all to save all by some violent reagent; but I could not take it upon myself to prescribe the treatment, I should not even advise it. I should oppose it in consultation."

Jules went back to the room again. For eleven days he stayed night and day by his wife's bedside, sleeping only in the daytime, with his head on the bedfoot. Never did any man carry the ambition of devotion so far as Jules Desmarets. In a jealous anxiety to do everything himself, he would not allow any one else to perform the least service for his wife; he sat with her hand in his, as if in this way he could give of his own vitality to her. There were times of doubt and fallacious joy, good days, and an improvement, and crises, and the dreadful reverberations of the coming death, that hesitates while life hangs in the balance, but strikes at last. Mme. Jules was never too weak to smile; she was sorry for her husband, knowing that very soon he would be left alone. It was the twofold agony of life and love; but as life ebbed, love grew stronger.

Then came a dreadful night, when Clémence suffered from the delirium that always comes before death in young creatures. She talked aloud of her happy love, of her father, of her mother's death-bed revelations, and the charge she had laid upon her daughter. Clémence was struggling, not for life, but for the passionate love that she could not let go.

"God in heaven!" she cried out, "do not let him know how I want to have him die with me."

Jules, unable to bear the sight, happened to be in the next room, and so did not hear the wish that he would have fulfilled.

When the crisis was over, Mme. Jules found strength. Next day she looked lovely and peaceful once more; she talked, she began to hope, and made a pretty invalid's toilet. She wanted to be alone all day, and entreated her husband to leave her so earnestly, that he was fain to grant her wish, as a child's pleading is always granted. Jules, moreover, had need of the day. He went to M. de Maulincour to claim the duel to which both had agreed. He obtained an interview with the cause of his troubles, not without great difficulty; but the vidame, informed that it was an affair of honor, gave way in obedience to the chivalrous prejudices which had always ruled his life, and brought Monsieur Jules up to the Baron de Maulincour.

Monsieur Desmarets looked about him in a vain search for his antagonist.

"Oh, it really is he," said the commander, indicating the figure in the armchair by the fireside.

"He? who? Jules?" asked the dying man, in a broken voice.

Auguste had lost the one central faculty by which we live—memory. At sight of him M. Desmarets shrank back in horror. He could not recognize the youthful, fine gentleman in this Thing, for which there was no name in any language, to quote Bossuet's saying. It was, in truth, a white-haired corpse, a skeleton scarcely covered by the wrinkled, shriveled, withered skin. The eyes were pale and fixed, the mouth gaped hideously, like the mouth of an imbecile, or of some debauchee dying of excess. Not the faintest spark of intelligence was left to the forehead, nor indeed to any other feature; nor was there any appearance of color or of circulating blood in the flabby flesh. These were the shrunken, dissolving remains of what had been a human being, a man reduced to the condition of the monstrosities preserved in spirits at the Museum. Jules fancied he could see Ferragus' terrible head rising above that visage, and his hate shrank appalled at the completeness of the vengeance. Clémence's husband could find it in his heart to pity the unrecognizable wreck of what had been so lately a young man.

"The duel has taken place," said the vidame.

"Monsieur de Maulincour has taken many lives," Jules exclaimed in distress.

"And the lives of his nearest and dearest," added the old noble. "His grandmother is dying of grief, and I, perhaps, shall follow her to the tomb."

Mme. Jules grew worse from hour to hour on the day after the visit. She took advantage of a momentary strength to draw a letter from her pillow, and gave it quickly to Jules with a sign which no one could mistake; she wished to spend her last breath of life in a kiss. He took it, and she died.

Jules dropped down half-dead, and was taken away to his brother's house. There, as in the midst of tears and ravings he bewailed his absence of the day before, his brother told him how anxious Clémence had been that he should not be present during the church's administration of the last sacrament to the dying, that rite so terribly impressive for a sensitive imagination.

"You could not have borne it," said his brother. "I myself could scarcely endure to see it, and every one broke out into weeping. Clémence looked like a saint. She summoned up her strength to bid us farewell: it was heart-rending to hear that voice for the last time. And when she asked pardon for any involuntary unkindness to those who had served her, a wail went up among the sobs, a wail——"

"Enough, that will do."

He wanted to be alone to read his wife's last thoughts, now that she, the woman whom the world had admired, had faded away like a flower:

"This is my will, my dearest. Why should not people dispose of their heart's treasures, as of everything else that is theirs? The love in my heart—was it not all that I had? And here I want to think of nothing but love: it was all that your Clémence brought you, it is all that she can leave you when she dies. Jules, I am loved again, I can die a happy woman. The doctors will have their theories of my death; but no one knows the real cause but myself. I will tell you about it, in spite of the pain it may give you. I am dying because I kept a secret that could not be told, but I will not carry away a secret unsaid in the heart that is wholly yours.

"I was nurtured and brought up in complete solitude, far away from the vices and deceits of the world, by the amiable woman whom you knew, Jules. Society did justice to the conventional qualities by which a woman gains social popularity; but I, in secret, enjoyed communion with an angel's soul; I could love the mother who gave me a childhood of joy without bitterness, knowing well why I loved her. Which means, does it not, that she was twice loved? Yes. I loved and feared and respected her, yet neither the fear nor the respect oppressed my heart. I was all in all to her; she was all in all to me. Through nineteen years of happiness known to the full, nineteen years without a care, my soul, lonely amid the world which murmured about me, mirrored nothing but the one most pure vision of my mother, and my heart beat for her alone. I was conscientiously devout. I was glad to lead a pure life in the sight of God. My mother cultivated all noble and lofty feelings and thoughts in me. Ah! it gladdens me to own it, Jules. I know now that my girlhood was complete, that I came to you with a maiden heart.

"When I came out of the profound solitude; when for the first time I smoothed my hair beneath a wreath of almond blossom, and added a few knots of satin ribbon to my white gown, thinking how pretty they looked, and wondering about this world that I was to see, and felt curious about; well, Jules, even then, that simple girlish coquetry was for you; at my first entrance into that new world I saw *you*—— I saw your face; it stood out from all the others; you were handsome, I thought; your voice and your manner prepossessed me in your favor; and when you came up and spoke to me, and your forehead flushed and your voice was tremulous—the memory of that moment sets my heart throbbing even now as I write you to-day, when I think of it for the last time. Our love has been from the first the keenest of sympathies, and it was not long before we divined each other, and began to share, as we have shared ever since, the uncounted joys of love.

"From that day my mother had but the second place in my heart. I told her so, and she smiled, my adorable mother! And since then I have been yours—yours wholly. That is my life, my whole life, my dear husband.

"And this is what remains to be said:

"One evening, a few days before my mother died, she told me the secret of her life, not without hot tears. I loved her more, far more, when I heard in the presence of the priest who absolved her that there was such a thing as passion condemned by the world and the church. Yet, surely, God must be merciful when love is the sin of souls as loving as hers, even though that angel could not bring herself to repent of it. She loved with all her heart, Jules, for all her heart was love. And so I prayed for her every day, without judging her. From that time I knew why her mother's love had been so deep and tender; from that time I knew, too, that in Paris there was some one living for whom I was everything—life and love. I knew, beside, that your success was due to him, and that he liked you, and that he was an outlaw with a blighted name, and that these things troubled him less for his own sake than for mine—for both our sakes. My mother had been his one comfort; I promised to take her place now that she was dead. With all the enthusiasm of an unsophisticated nature, I thought of nothing but the joy of sweetening the bitterness of her last moments, so I pledged myself to continue her work of secret charity—the charity of the heart.

"I saw my father for the first time by the bed on which my mother had just drawn her last breath. When he raised his tear-filled eyes, it was to find all his dead hopes once more in me. I vowed, not to lie, but to keep silence; and what woman could have broken that silence? Therein lay my mistake—a mistake expiated by death—I could not trust you, Jules. But fear is so natural to a woman, especially to a wife who knows all that she has to lose. I was afraid for my love. It seemed to me that my father's secret might cost me my happiness; and the more I loved, the more I dreaded the loss of love. I dared not confess this to my father; it would have hurt him, and in his position any wound smarts keenly. But while he said not a word to me, he felt my fears. The true father's heart trembled for my happiness, and I trembled for myself, and shrank from speaking of it with the same delicacy which kept me mute.

"Yes, Jules, I thought that some day you might not love Gratien's daughter as you loved your Clémence. But for that dread in the depths of my heart, could I have hidden anything from you—from you that filled even this inmost recess?

"When that odious, miserable officer spoke to you, I was forced to tell a lie. That day I knew sorrow for the second time in my life, and that sorrow has grown day by day till this last moment of converse with you. What does my father's position matter now? You know everything. With love to aid me, I might have wrestled with disease and borne any pain; but I cannot smother the voice of doubt. Is it not possible that the knowledge of my origin may take something from your love, Jules, and weaken it, and spoil its purity? And this fear nothing can extinguish in me. *This* is the cause of my death.

"I could not live in continual dread of a word or a look, one word which might never be uttered, one glance that would never be given; but, I cannot help it—*I am afraid!* I have your love till I die, that comforts me. I have known for four years past that my father and his friends have all but turned the world upside down to act a lie to the world. They have bought a dead man, a reputation, and a fortune, and all to give a new life to a living man, and a social position to me—

all this for your sake, for our sakes! We were to know nothing about it. Well, my death will probably save my father from the necessity of further falsehood, for he will die when I am dead.

"So, farewell, Jules. I have put my whole heart here in this letter. When I show you my love in the innocence of its dread, do I not leave you my very soul? I should not have had strength to tell you this, but I could write it for you.

"I have just made confession of the sins of my lifetime to God; I have promised, it is true, to think of nothing now but the Father in heaven; but I could not resist the pleasure of confession to you, that are all to me upon earth. Alas! who would not forgive me this last sigh between the life that is no more and the life to come? So, farewell, Jules, my beloved; I am going to God, with whom there is love unclouded for evermore, to whom you also will one day come. There, at the foot of the Throne of God, together for evermore, we shall love through all the ages. That hope alone can comfort me. If I am worthy to go first, I shall follow you through your life, my spirit will be with you and around you, for you must live on here below awhile. Lead a holy life, to rejoin me the more surely. You can do so much good here on this earth! Is it not an angel's mission for a stricken soul to spread happiness around, to give that which he has not?

"I leave the unhappy to your care; how should I be jealous of their smiles, their tears? We shall find a great charm in these sweet charities. Cannot we be together still, if you will associate my name, your Clémence's name, with every kindly deed? When two have loved as we have loved, Jules, there is nothing left but God; God does not lie, God does not fail. Give all your love to Him, I ask it of you. Cultivate good in those who suffer, comfort the afflicted among the church on earth.

"Adieu, dear heart that I have filled. I know you, I know

that you will not love twice; and I can die happy in a thought that would make any wife glad. Yes, I shall lie buried in your heart. Now that I have told you the story of my childhood, is not my whole life poured into your heart? I shall never be driven from it after I am dead. You have only known me in the flower of my youth; I shall leave nothing but regrets behind, and no disenchantment. Jules, that is a very happy death.

"May I ask one thing of you that have understood me so well, one thing needless to ask, no doubt—the fulfillment of a woman's fancy, of a wish prompted by a jealousy to which all women are subject. I beg of you to burn all that belonged to us, to destroy our room, and everything that may recall our love.

"Once again, farewell, a last farewell full of love, as my last thought will be, and my latest breath."

Jules finished the letter, and a frantic grief came upon his heart in terrible paroxysms which cannot be described. Every agony takes its own course, and obeys no fixed rule; some men stop their ears to hear no sound, women sometimes close their eyes to shut out all sights; and here and there a great and powerful soul plunges into sorrow as into an abyss. Despair makes an end of all insincerities. Jules escaped from his brother's house, and returned to the Rue de Ménars, meaning to spend the night at his wife's side, and to keep that divine creature in sight till the last. As he went, with the recklessness of a man brought to the lowest depths of misery, he began to understand why Asiatic laws forbid widows to survive their husbands. He wanted to die. He was in the fever of sorrow; the collapse had not yet set in.

He reached the sacred chamber without hindrance, saw Clémence lying on her death-bed, fair as a saint, her hair smoothed over her brows, her hands folded. She had been laid already in her shroud. The light of the tall candles fell upon a priest at his prayers, on Joséphine, who was crying in a corner, and on two men by the bed. One of these was Ferragus. He stood erect and motionless, gazing dry-eyed at his daughter, you might have taken his face for a bronze statue; he did not see Jules. The other was Jacquet— Jacquet, to whom Mme. Jules had always been kind. He had felt for her the respectful friendship that brings warmth to the heart without troubling it, a softened passion, love without its longings and its tumult, and now he had come religiously to pay his debt of tears, to bid a long adieu to his friend's wife, and set a first and last kiss on the forehead of the woman of whom he had tacitly made his sister.

All was silent there. This was not the terrible death of the church, nor the pageantry of death that passes through the streets; it was death that glides in under the roof, death in his pathetic aspects; this was a lying in state for the heart amid tears shed in secret.

Jules sat down beside Jacquet, squeezed his friend's hand, and thus without a word they stayed till the morning. When the candles burnt faintly in the dawn, Jacquet thought of the painful scenes to come, and led Jules away into the next room. For a moment Clémence's husband looked full at her father, and Ferragus looked at Jules. Anguish questioned and sounded the depths of anguish, and both understood at a glance. A flash of rage glittered for an instant in Ferragus' eyes.

"It is your doing!" he thought.

"Why not have trusted me?" the other one seemed to retort.

So might two tigers have seen the uselessness of a conflict, after eyeing each other during a moment of hesitation, without so much as a growl.

"Jacquet, did you see to everything?" asked Jules.

"Yes, to everything; and everywhere some one else had been before me and given orders and paid."

"He is snatching his daughter from me!" shouted Jules, in a paroxysm of despair.

He dashed into the bedroom. The father had gone. Clémence had been laid in her leaden coffin. One or two workmen were preparing to solder down the lid, and Jules retreated aghast. At the sound of the hammer he broke out into dull weeping.

"Jacquet," he said at length, "one idea stays with me after this dreadful night, just one thought, but I must realize it, cost what it may. Clémence shall not lie in a Paris cemetery. She shall be cremated, and I will keep her ashes beside me. Do not say a word about it to me, but just arrange to have it done. I shall shut myself up in *her* room and stay there till I am ready to go. No one shall come in but you to tell me what you have done. There, spare for nothing."

That morning Mme. Jules' coffin lay under the archway with lighted candles round it, and was afterward removed to St. Roch. The whole church was hung with black. The kind of display made for the funeral service had attracted a great many people. Everything, even the most heartfelt anguish, is a theatrical spectacle in Paris. There are people who will stand at the windows to watch curiously while a son weeps in his mother's funeral procession, just as there are others who want good seats to see an execution. No people in the world have such voracious eyes. But the curious in St. Roch were particularly astonished to find the six side-chapels in the church likewise draped with black, and two men in mourning attending a mass for the dead in each. In the choir there were but two persons present at the funeral—M. Desmarets the notary and Jacquet—the servants were beyond the screen. The hangers-on of the church were puzzled by the splendor of the funeral and the insignificant number of mourners. Jules would have no indifferent persons.

High mass was celebrated with all the sombre grandeur of the funeral service. Thirteen priests from various parishes were there beside the officiating clergy of St. Roch. The sound of blended voices rose as the eight chanters, the priests, and the boy-choristers sang antiphonally; and never, perhaps, was the *Dies iræ* more deeply impressive than at that moment, never did it strike an icier chill to the nerves of Christians by accident of birth, assembled there by chance, curiosity, and greed of sensation. From the side-chapels twelve other childish voices, shrill with grief, rose wailing in the chorus. A dull note of dismay reverberated through the church; cries of anguish answered wails of terror on every side. That awful music spoke of agony unknown on earth, of secret friendship weeping for the dead. Never has any known religion given so powerful a rendering of the terrors of the soul, stripped violently of the body, and tossed as by tempest into the presence of the intolerable Majesty of God. Before that clamor of clamors, artists and their most impassioned work must shrink abashed. No, nothing can stand beside that music which gathers up all human passions, galvanizing them into a life beyond the grave, bringing them, yet palpitating, into the presence of the living God, the Avenger. Man's life, with all its developments, is embraced by that Canticle of Death; for the cries of children, mingled with the notes of deeper voices, recall the pains of cradled infancy, swelled by the sum of all the pain of life's later stages, by the full-toned bass, and the quavering notes of old men and of priests. Does not the volume of strident melody, full of thunder and lightnings, speak to the most undaunted imagination, to the ice-bound heart, nay, to philosophers themselves? As you hear it, it seems that God thunders. The vaults of every chapel are cold no longer; they quiver, and find a voice, and pour forth fear with all the might of their echoes. You seem to see visions of the uncounted dead rising and holding up their hands. It is not a father, a wife or child, that lies beneath the black drapery; it is Humanity emerging from the dust. It is impossible to be just to the Apostolic and Roman Catholic

Church until you have passed through a supreme sorrow, and wept for the beloved dead lying beneath the cenotaph; until you have heard all the emotion which fills your heart, interpreted by that Hymn of Despair, by those cries that overwhelm the soul, by the religious awe that rises from strophe to strophe, eddying up to heaven, appalling, diminishing, exalting the soul, till as the last verse comes to an end you are left with the sense of Eternity. You have been wrestling with the vast idea of the Infinite; and now all is hushed in the church. Not a word is uttered there. Unbelievers themselves "know not what ails them." Spanish genius alone could invest unspeakable sorrow with such transcendent majesty.

When the solemn ceremony was over, twelve men in mourning emerged from the chapels, and stood grouped around the coffin to hear the chant of hope which the church raises for the Christian's soul before the human form is committed to earth. Then each of them entered a mourning coach, Jacquet and M. Desmarets took the thirteenth, and the servants followed on foot.

An hour afterward the twelve strangers were gathered about a grave, dug at the highest point of the cemetery familiarly known as Père-Lachaise; the coffin had just been lowered; a curious crowd had gathered from all parts of that public garden. The priest recited a short prayer, and flung a handful of earth over the mortal remains; and the sexton and his men, having claimed their fee, hastily began to fill up the grave before going to another.

And here this story would seem to finish. Yet perhaps it would be incomplete if the practical effects of death should be forgotten at the close of a slight sketch of Parisian life, and its capricious undulations. Death in Paris is unlike death in any other great city; few people know what it is to bring a heartfelt sorrow into conflict with civilization in the shape of the municipal authorities of Paris. Perhaps, too, the reader may feel sufficient interest in Ferragus XXIII. and Jules Desmarets to care to know what became of them. And in any case, there are plenty of people who like to know all about everything; and, as the most ingenious of French critics once said, would find out the chemistry of the combustion of the oil of Aladdin's lamp if they could.

Jacquet, being a civil servant, naturally applied to the authorities for permission to exhume and cremate Mme. Jules' body. The dead sleep under the protection of the prefect of police; to the prefect of police, therefore, Jacquet betook himself. That functionary required a formal application. A sheet of stamped paper must be purchased, sorrow must appear in the regulation form; and when a man is so overwhelmed with grief that words fail him, he must express himself in the peculiar idiom of red-tape, and translate his wishes into business-like phrases with a marginal note:

"The petitioner prays permission to cremate
the body of his wife."

The head of the department, whose duty it was to draw up a report for the prefect of police, a member of the Council of State, glanced over the marginal note, in which the object of the request was clearly stated by his own instruction, and said—

"But this is a serious question. It is impossible to draw up a report in less than a week."

Jacquet was obliged to explain the delay, and Jules thought of the words he had heard Ferragus utter: "Set Paris on fire!" Nothing seemed more natural than a thorough destruction of that receptacle of monstrous things.

"Why, there is nothing for it but to apply to the Secretary of the Interior and set your Minister on to him." he told Jacquet.

Jacquet accordingly applied to the Home Office, and asked for an audience, which he obtained—for that day two weeks.

Jacquet was naturally persistent. He went, therefore, from department to department, and succeeded in reaching the private secretary of the Minister of Foreign Affairs. With such influence he received a promise of a private interview with the pasha of the Home Office, and a few lines written by the autocrat of Foreign Affairs by way of passport. Jacquet now had hopes of carrying his point by storm. He was ready for every emergency with arguments and categorical answers. All ended in failure.

"This is no affair of mine," said the Minister. "The thing concerns the prefect of police. And what is more: no law gives a husband the custody of his wife's body, nor has a father a right to a child's corpse. It is a serious matter. It ought to be looked into, beside, in the interests of the public. The city of Paris might suffer. In short, if the matter were referred directly to me, I could not give a decision *hic et nunc;* a report would be required."

In the administrative system a "report" answers much the same end as limbo or paradise does in theology. Jacquet had met with the "report" craze before; nor had he neglected previous opportunities of groaning over the absurdities of red tape. He knew that since the administrative Revolution of 1804, when the report had carried all before it in Government departments, the minister had not yet been found that would take it upon himself to have an opinion, or give a decision on any matter, however small, until the thing had been winnowed, sifted, and thoroughly scrutinized by the scribblers and scratchers and sublime official intelligences of his department.

Jacquet—the man deserved to have a Plutarch for his biographer—Jacquet saw that he had set off on the wrong tack, and defeated his own ends by trying to proceed by the proper forms. He should simply have removed Mme. Jules' coffin after the service to one of the Desmarets' houses in the country. There the mayor of the village would have made no difficulty about gratifying the sorrowing widower's request. Constitutional and administrative legalism is sterile; it is a barren monster for nations and kings and the interests of private individuals; but the nations as yet have only learned to spell those principles that are written in blood; and as the evils of ruling by the letter of the law are never accompanied by strife and bloodshed, legalism reduces a nation to a dead level, and there is an end of it.

Jacquet, being a stickler for liberty, returned home, meditating by the way on the blessings of arbitrary government; for a man only criticises the law of the land by the light of his own passions. But when he came to talk to Jules, there was nothing for it but to deceive his friend; the unhappy man was in a high fever, and for a couple of days he stayed in bed.

That evening at dinner the minister chanced to mention that the fancy had taken some one in Paris to have his wife's body cremated in the Roman fashion. And for a moment classical funeral rites were the talk of the clubs. As things ancient were coming into fashion, several people were of the opinion that it would be a fine thing to revive the funeral pyre for distinguished personages. Some were for, and others against, the idea. Some held that there were so many great men that the practice would raise the price of fuel; they opined that with a nation so fond of the mental exercise of changing its opinions, it would be a ridiculous thing to see a whole Longchamp of ancestors trotted out in their urns at the expiration of a lease; while, if the urns happened to be valuable, creditors (a race that never respects anything) would seize upon them, and they, with their contents of honorable dust, would be put up to public auction. Others retorted that it was scarcely possible for a man to insure a permanent residence for his grandparents in Père-Lachaise; for that in time the city of Paris would be compelled to order a St. Bartholomew of its dead. The cemeteries were invading the open country, and threatened to encroach upon the grain land of le Brie. In short, the question raised one of the futile and ingenious discussions which, in Paris, too often aggravates deep-seated evils. Happily for Jules, he knew nothing of the conversation, jokes, and epigrams with which his sorrow supplied the town.

The prefect of police took offense because M. Jacquet had gone straight to the minister to avoid the delays and matured wisdom of the Board of Works. The exhumation of Mme. Jules' body was a question within the jurisdiction of the municipal police. Wherefore the police department was elaborating a sharp answer to the petition. A single demand is enough, the administration has a tight hold, and a thing once in its grasp is like to go a long way. Any matter, moreover, may be referred to the Council of State, another piece of machinery very hard to set in motion. Another day went by, and Jacquet made his friend understand that the idea must be given up; that in a city where the number of " tears " embroidered on the black trappings are prescribed, where the law recognizes seven classes of funerals, where land in which to bury the dead is sold by its weight in silver, where grief is exploited on a system of double entry, and the prayers of the church are sold dear, or the vestry puts in a claim for a few extra voices in the *Dies iræ*—any deviation from the beaten rut traced out for grief by the authorities was impossible.

" It would have been one joy in my misery," said Jules ; " I meant to go somewhere, a long way off, to die, and I wished when I lay in the grave to have Clémence in my arms. I did not know that officialdom could put out its claws to reach us even in our coffins."

He would go to see whether there was a little room for him beside his wife. So the friends went together to Père-Lachaise. At the gateway they found a crowd of ciceroni waiting to guide sight-seers through the labyrinth, as if Père-Lachaise were a museum or the Cour des Diligences or some other sight. It was impossible that Jules or Jacquet should find Clémence's tomb. Terrible agony! They went to consult the gatekeeper.

The dead have a gatekeeper, and there are hours at which the dead cannot receive visitors. Only by shaking all the rules and regulations from top to bottom can any one obtain the right to go thither in the darkness to weep in silence and solitude over the grave which holds his beloved dead. There are summer regulations and winter regulations. Of all the concierges of Paris, the gatekeeper of Père-Lachaise is the best off. There is no cord to pull, to begin with. Instead of a single room, he has a house, an establishment that cannot exactly be described as a government department, although there is a considerable staff attached, and the jurisdiction is wide, and the governor of the dead draws a salary and wields an immense power over a population who cannot possibly complain of him; he plays the despot at his ease. Neither is his abode exactly a place of business, albeit there are offices and books to be kept, and clerks to keep them, and receipts and expenditure and profits. And the gatekeeper himself is neither a Swiss nor a concierge nor a porter, for the door is always yawning wide for the dead; and though there certainly are monuments to be kept in order, he is not there to look after them. He is, in short, an anomaly which cannot be defined; his office is akin in one way or another to every power in existence, and yet he is a nobody, for his authority, like Death, by which it lives, lies completely beyond the pale. Nevertheless, exception as he is, he holds his tenure from the City of Paris, a creature as chimerical as the emblematical vessel on her coat of arms; an imaginary being swayed by hundreds of paws and claws which seldom move in concert; and, as a result, her public servants are, to all intents and purposes, fixtures. The cemetery-keeper, therefore, is the concierge promoted to the rank of a public servant, a permanent element amid dissolution.

His place, for that matter, is no sinecure. No one can be

buried till the gatekeeper has seen the permit ; and he is bound to give account of his dead. He can lay his finger on a spot in that huge burying ground to point out the six feet of earth in which some day you will lay all that you love, or hate, as the case may be—the mistress you love or your unloved cousin. For, mind you, to this lodge all loves and hates must come at the last, and are duly docketed and passed through the office. The man keeps a register of sleeping-places for the dead ; they go down on his list when they go down into the grave.

The gatekeeper has custodians under him, and gardeners and grave-diggers and assistants. He is a personage. Mourners are not brought into direct contact with him as a rule ; he only comes forward if something serious occurs, if one dead man is mistaken for another, or if a body is exhumed for a murder case, or a corpse comes to life again. The bust of the reigning sovereign presides in his room. Possibly he keeps other busts of departed monarchs, with various royal, imperial, or semi-royal persons, in a cupboard somewhere, a sort of miniature Père-Lachaise for changes in the Government. In other respects, he is a public servant ; an excellent man, a good husband and father, epitaphs apart ; but—so much varied emotion has passed under his eyes in the shape of hearses ! he has seen so many tears shed, both sham and real, and been acquainted with grief in so many shapes and in so many faces—with six millions of eternal sorrows, in short ! For him, grief means a stone slab an inch thick, four feet high by twenty-two inches wide. As for regrets, they are one of the things to be put up with in his profession, and he never dines but he has witnessed torrents of tears shed by inconsolable affliction. Every other emotion finds him kindly and sympathetic ; he, too, can shed tears over the tragic end of a stage hero like M. Germeuil in L'Auberge des Adrets, he is moved when the man in the butter-colored breeches is murdered by Robert Macaire ; but when it comes to a real genuine death, his heart is ossified. Deaths mean rows of figures for him; it is his business to tabulate statistics of the dead. And, as a last word, twice, or perhaps thrice in a century, it may happen that he has a sublime part to play, and then he is a hero at every hour—in time of pestilence.

When Jacquet went in search of this absolute monarch, his majesty's temper had suffered somewhat.

"I told you," he cried, "to water all the flowers from the Rue Massèna to the Place Regnault de Saint-Jean d'Angely! You fellows simply took not the least notice of what I told you. My patience! if the relatives take it into their heads to come, as it is a fine day, they will be throwing all the blame on me. They will call out as if they had been burnt, and say frightful things about us up here, and our characters will be taken away——"

"Sir," put in Jacquet, "we should like to know where Madame Jules was buried."

"Madame Jules *who?* We have had three Jules this week. Ah!" (interrupting himself as he glanced at the gate), "here comes Colonel de Maulincour's funeral, go out for the permit. My word! it is a fine funeral," he added. "He has not been long about following his grandmother. Some families seem to drop off for a wager. They have such bad blood, have those Parisians!"

Jacquet tapped him on the arm.

"Sir, the person of whom I am speaking was Madame Jules Desmarets, the stockbroker's wife."

"Oh, I know!" returned he, looking at Jacquet. "Thirteen mourning coaches at the funeral, weren't there? and only one relation apiece in the first dozen. It was so queer that we noticed it——"

"Take care, sir; Monsieur Jules is with me, he might overhear you; and you ought not to talk like that."

"I beg your pardon, sir, you are right. Excuse me, I took you for the next-of-kin. Madame Jules is in the Rue du

Maréchal Lefebvre, side-walk Number 4," he continued, after consulting a plan of the ground; "she lies between Mademoiselle Raucourt of the Comédie Française and Monsieur Moreau-Malvin, a butcher in a big way of business. There is a white marble monument on order for him; it will be one of the finest things to be seen in the cemetery here, and that's a fact."

"We are no nearer, sir," Jacquet broke in.

"And that is true," said the other, looking round.

"Jean!" he called, as a man came in sight. "Show these gentlemen the way to Madame Jules' grave, the stockbroker's wife. You know! Next to Mademoiselle Raucourt's where there is a bust."

And the friends set out with their conductor; but before they reached the steep path which leads to the higher part of the cemetery they must run the gantlet of a score or more of stone-cutters, carvers, and makers of wrought-iron work, who came up to insinuate in honeyed accents that, "if monsieur would like to have something put up, we could do it for him very reasonably——"

Jacquet was glad enough to be there to stand between his friend and words intolerable for bleeding hearts. They reached the spot where she lay. At the sight of the rough sods and the row of pegs driven in by the laborers to mark out the space for the iron railings, Jules leaned upon Jacquet's shoulder, raising his head at intervals to give a long look at the little patch of clay where he must leave all that remained of her for whom and through whom he still lived.

"How hard for her to lie there!"

"But she is not there!" protested Jacquet; "she lives in your memory. Come away; let us leave this horrid place, where the dead are tricked out like women at a ball," he continued.

"How if we took her out of it?"

"Is it possible?"

"All things are possible!" cried Jules. Then, after a pause: "So I shall come here some day; there is room for me."

Jacquet succeeded in getting him out of the inclosure. The tombs inclosed in those sprucely kept chessboard compartments marked out by iron railings are covered with inscriptions and sculptured palms, and tears as cold as the marble on which survivors record their regrets and their coats-of-arms. You may read jests there, carved in black letters, epigrams at the expense of the curious, pompous biographies, and ingeniously worded farewells. Here some one bides tryst, and, as usual in such cases, bides alone. Here you behold a floriated thyrsus, there a lance-head railing; farther on there are Egyptian vases and now and again cannon; while spangles, tinsel, and trash meet your eyes wherever you turn them. You see trade-signs in every direction. Every style—Moorish, Grecian, and Gothic—is represented, together with every variety of decoration—friezes, egg-mouldings, paintings, urns, genii, and temples, among any quantity of dead rose-bushes and faded immortelles. It is a scandalous comedy! Here is Paris over again—streets, trade-signs, industries, houses and all complete; but it is a Paris seen through the wrong end of the perspective glass, a microscopic city, a Paris diminished to a shadow of itself, and shrunk to the measure of these chrysalides of the dead, this human species that has dwindled so much in everything save vanity.

Jules caught a glimpse of the view. At his feet, in the long valley of the Seine, between the low ridges of Vaugirard and Meudon, Belleville and Montmartre, lay the real Paris, in a blue haze of its own smoke, now sunlit and transparent. He glanced from under his eyelids over the forty thousand houses of the city, and waved his hand toward the space between the column of the Place Vendôme and the cupola of the Invalides.

"There she was taken from me," he cried, "by the fatal

curiosity of a world which seeks bustle and excitement for the sake of excitement and bustle."

Eight or nine miles farther away down the Seine valley, in a little village on one of the lower slopes of those ridges of hill, between which the great, restless city lies, like a child in its cradle, another sad death scene was taking place; but here there was none of the funeral pomp of Paris—there were no torches, no tall candle, no mourning-coaches hung with black, no prayers of the church; this was death reduced to the bare fact. And this was the fact. A girl's body stranded that morning on the bank, among the reeds that grow in the Seine mud. Some sand-dredgers on their way to work caught sight of it as they went up the river in their crazy boat.

"Halloo! fifty francs for us!" cried one.

"Right you are!" said the other.

They came close up to the dead body.

"She is a very fine girl."

"Let us go and give notice."

And the two dredgers, first covering the corpse with their jackets, went off to the mayor; and that worthy was not a little puzzled to know how to draw up an official report of the discovery.

The rumor spread with the telegraphic speed peculiar to neighborhoods where communications are uninterrupted; the gossip on which the world battens, and scandal, tittle-tattle, and slander, rush in to fill the vacuum between any given points. In a very short time people came to the mayor's office to relieve that gentleman of any difficulty, and among them they converted the official report into an ordinary certificate of death. Through their assiduity the girl's body was identified; it was proven to be that of Mlle. Ida Gruget, staymaker, of No. 14 Rue de la Corderie du Temple. At this stage of the proceedings the police intervened, and the Widow Gruget, the girl's mother, appeared with her daughter's fare-

A GIRL'S BODY STRANDED THAT MORNING ON THE BANK

well letter. While the mother sighed and groaned, a medical man ascertained that death had ensued from asphyxia and an access of venous blood to the pulmonary organs. That was all.

The inquest being over, and particulars filled in, the authorities gave permission for the burial of the body. The curé of the place declined to allow the procession to enter the church or to pray for the repose of the dead.* So an old peasant-woman sewed Ida Gruget in her shroud, she was laid in a rough coffin made of pine-boards, and carried to the churchyard on four men's shoulders. Some few country-women had the curiosity to follow, telling the story of the death with comments of pitying surprise. An old lady charitably kept the widow, and would not allow her to join the sad little procession. A man, who fulfilled the threefold office of sexton, beadle, and bell-ringer, dug a grave in the churchyard, a half acre of ground at the back of the well-known church, a classical building with a square tower buttressed at the corners, and a slate-covered spire. The churchyard, bounded by crumbling walls, lies behind the round apse; there are no marble headstones there, and no visitors; but not one, surely, of all the mounds that furrow the space, lacked the tears and heartfelt regrets which no one gave to Ida Gruget. They put her down out of sight in a corner among the nettles and tall grasses; the bier was lowered into its place in that field so idyllic in its simplicity, and in another moment the grave-digger was left alone to fill in the grave in the gathering dusk. He stopped now and again to look over into the road below the wall: once, with his hand on his pickaxe, he gazed intently at the Seine which had brought this body for him to bury.

"Poor girl!" exclaimed a voice; and suddenly a man came up.

"How you startled me, sir!" said the sexton.

* Interment in consecrated ground is denied the body of a suicide.

"Was there any service for this woman that you are burying?"

"No, sir. Monsieur the Curé would not allow it. She is the first person buried here that is not of this parish. Everybody knows everybody else hereabout. Does monsieur——? Halloo! he is gone!"

Several days slipped by. A man in black came to the house in the Rue de Ménars; the stranger did not wish to speak to Jules; he went to Mme. Jules' room and left a large porphyry vase there, bearing the inscription—

INVITA LEGE,
CONJUGI MŒRENTI
FILIOLÆ CINERES
RESTITUIT
AMICIS XII JUVANTIBUS
MORIBUNDUS PATER.

"What a man!" exclaimed Jules, bursting into tears.

In one week Jules had carried out all his wife's wishes, and set his own affairs in order. He sold his professional connection to a brother of Martin Falleix, and left Paris behind him, while the municipality was still debating whether or not a citizen had any legal claim to his wife's dead body.

Who has not met on the Paris boulevards, at a street corner, under the arcades of the Palais Royal—anywhere, in short, as chance may determine—some stranger, man or woman, whose face sets a host of confused thoughts springing up in his brain? It grows suddenly interesting at sight, perhaps because some personal singularity suggests a stormy life; perhaps gestures, gait, air, and costume all combine to present a curious whole; perhaps because a searching glance or an indescribable something makes a sudden, strong impression before you can explain the cause very clearly to yourself. On the morrow, other thoughts, other pictures of Paris life sweep away the passing dream. But if you happen to meet the same person again; if he is always passing along the street at the same hour (like a clerk at the registrar's office, for instance, whose presence is required at marriages eight hours daily); if he is one of those wandering mortals who seem to be a part of the furniture of the streets of Paris, and you see him again and again in public places, on first nights, or in those restaurants of which he is the fairest ornament—— then that figure becomes a tenant in your memory, and stays there like an odd volume of a novel without a conclusion.

You are tempted to go up to the stranger and ask: "Who are you? Why are you sauntering about the streets? What right have you to wear a crumpled collar, a cane with an ivory knob, and a seedy vest? Why those blue spectacles with double glasses?" or "What makes you cling to that old-style cravat?"

Some among these errant creatures belong to the progeny of Terminus, god of boundaries; they say nothing to your soul. There they are; that is all. Why are they there? Nobody knows. They are conventional signs, like the hackneyed figures used by sculptors to represent the Four Seasons, or Commerce, or Plenty. Others, again, retired attorneys, or storekeepers, or antique generals, walk about, and always appear to be much the same. They never seem to be a part of the torrent of Paris, with its throng of young bustling men; rather, they remind you of half-uprooted trees by a river-side. It is impossible to say whether other people forgot to bury them, or whether they escaped out of their coffins. They have reached a semi-fossil condition.

One of these Paris Melmoths had come for several days past to make one of a sedate, self-contained little crowd which never fails to fill the space between the Southern gate of the Luxembourg Gardens and the North gate of the Observatory, whenever the weather is bright. It is a place by itself, a neutral space in Paris. It lies out of the city, as it were, and yet the city is all about it. It partakes of the nature of a square, a thoroughfare, a boulevard, a fortification, a garden, an avenue, and a highway; it is provincial and Parisian; it is every one of these things, and not one of them; it is a desert. All about that nameless spot rise the walls of the Foundling Hospital, the Hôpital Cochin, the Capuchins, La Bourbe, the Hospice de la Rochefoucauld, the Deaf and Dumb Asylum, and the hospital of the Val-de-Grâce. All the sin and suffering of Paris, in fact, finds a refuge in its neighborhood; and that nothing may be wanting in so philanthropic a quarter, students of science repair thither to study the ebb and flow of the tides and latitude and longitude. M. de Chateaubriand too established the Marie-Thérèse Infirmary not very far away, and the Carmelites founded a convent near by. In that desert the sound of bells never ceases, every stroke represents one of the solemn moments in man's life; the mother in travail, the newborn babe, the dying laborer, the nun at prayer, perishing vice, shivering age, disappointed genius. Only a few paces away lies the Mont-Parnasse Cemetery, whither shabby funerals go all day long from the crowded Faubourg Saint-Marceau.

Players at bowls have monopolized this esplanade with its view of Paris—gray-headed, homely, good-natured worthies are they, who continue the line of our ancestors, and can only be compared as to externals with their public, the moving gallery which follows them about. The man before alluded to as new to this deserted quarter was an assiduous spectator of the game, and certainly might be said to be the most striking figure in these groups; for if it is permissible to classify Parisians zoologically, the other bystanders unmistakably belonged to the mollusc species. The new-comer would walk sympathetically with the jack, the small ball—the *cochonnet*, at which the other balls are aimed, the centre of interest in the game; and when it came to a stand, he would lean against a tree, and watch as a dog watches his master, while the bowls flew or rolled past. You might have taken him for the fantastic tutelar spirit of the jack. He never uttered a word. The players themselves, as zealous fanatics as could be found in any religious sect, had never taken him to task for his persistent silence, though some free-thinkers among them held that the man was deaf and dumb. Whenever there was occasion to measure the distance between the bowls and the jack, the stranger's cane was taken as the standard of measurement. The players used to take it from his ice-cold fingers without a word, or even a friendly nod. The loan of the cane was a kind of "easement" which he tacitly permitted. If a shower came on he stayed beside the jack—the slave of the bowls, the guardian of the unfinished game. He took rain and fine weather equally as a matter of course; like the players, he was a sort of intermediate species between the stupidest Parisian and the most intelligent of brutes. In other respects he was pale and withered-looking, absent-minded, and careless of his dress. He often came without his hat. His square-shaped head and bald, sallow cranium showed through his white hair, like a beggar's knee thrust through a hole in his breeches. He shambled uncertainly about with his mouth open; his vacant eyes were never turned to the sky, he never raised them indeed, and always seemed to be looking for something on the ground. At four o'clock an old woman would come for him and take him away somewhere or other, towing him after her as a girl tugs a capricious goat which insists on browsing when it is time to go back to the shed. It was something dreadful to see the old man.

It was afternoon. Jules, sitting alone in his traveling carriage, was driven rapidly along the Rue de l'Est, and came out upon the Carrefour de l'Observatoire, just as the old man, leaning against a tree, allowed himself to be despoiled of his cane amid the vociferous clamor of the players, in pacific dispute over their game. Jules, fancying that he knew the face, called to the postillion to stop, and the carriage came to a stand there and then. As a matter of fact, the postillion, wedged in among heavy carts, was in nowise anxious to ask the insurgent players at bowls to allow him to pass; he had too much respect for uproars, had that postillion.

"It is he!" Jules exclaimed, finally recognizing Ferragus XXIII., Chef des Dévorants, in that human wreck. "How he loved her!" he added after a pause. "Go on, postillion!" he shouted.

PARIS, *February*, 1833.

II.

THE DUCHESSE DE LANGEAIS.

To Franz Liszt.

In a Spanish city on an island in the Mediterranean there stands a convent of the order of Barefooted Carmelites, where the rule instituted by St. Theresa is still preserved with all the first rigor of the reformation brought about by that illustrious woman. Extraordinary as this may seem, it is none the less true. Almost every religious house in the peninsula, or in Europe for that matter, was either destroyed or disorganized by the outbreak of the French Revolution and the Napoleonic wars; but as this island was protected through those times by the English fleet, its wealthy convent and peaceable inhabitants were secure from the general trouble and spoliation. The storms of many kinds which shook the first fifteen years of the nineteenth century spent their force before they reached those cliffs at so short a distance from the coast of Andalusia.

If the Emperor's name so much as reached the shore of the island, it is doubtful whether the holy women kneeling in the cloisters grasped the reality of his dream-like progress of glory, or the majesty that blazed in flame across kingdom after kingdom during his meteor life.

In the minds of the Roman Catholic world, the convent stood out preëminent for a stern discipline which nothing had changed; the purity of its rule had attracted unhappy women from the farthest parts of Europe, women deprived of all human ties, sighing after the long suicide accomplished in the breast of God. No convent, indeed, was so well fitted for that complete detachment of the soul from all earthly things, which is demanded by the religious life, albeit on the continent of Europe there are many convents magnificently adapted to the purpose of their existence. Buried away in the loneliest valleys, hanging in mid-air on the steepest mountain-sides, set down on the brink of precipices, in every place man has sought for the poetry of the Infinite, the solemn awe of Silence; in every place man has striven to draw closer to God, seeking Him on mountain-peaks, in the depths below the crags, at the cliff's edge; and everywhere man has found God. But nowhere, save on this half-European, half-African ledge of rock could you find so many different harmonies, combining so to raise the soul, that the sharpest pain comes to be like other memories; the strongest impressions are dulled, till the sorrows of life are laid to rest in the depths.

The convent stands on the highest point of the crags at the uttermost end of the island. On the side toward the sea the rock was once rent sheer away in some globe-cataclysm; it rises up a straight wall from the base where the waves gnaw at the stone below high-water mark. Any assault is made impossible by the dangerous reefs that stretch far out to sea, with the sparkling waves of the Mediterranean playing over them. So, only from the sea can you discern the square mass of the convent built conformably to the minute rules laid down as to the shape, height, doors, and windows of monastic buildings. From the side of the town, the church completely hides the solid structure of the cloisters and their roofs, covered with broad slabs of stone impervious to sun or storm or gales of wind.

The church itself, built by the munificence of a Spanish family, is the crowning edifice of the town. Its fine, bold front gives an imposing and picturesque look to the little city in the sea. The sight of such a city, with its close-huddled roofs, arranged for the most part amphitheatre-wise above a picturesque harbor, and crowned by a glorious cathedral front with triple-arched Gothic doorways, belfry towers, and filigree spires, is a spectacle surely in every way the sublimest on earth. Religion towering above daily life, to put men continually in mind of the end and the way, is in truth a thoroughly Spanish conception. But now surround this picture by the Mediterranean, and a burning sky, imagine a few palms here and there, a few stunted evergreen trees mingling their waving leaves with the motionless flowers and foliage of carved stone; look out over the reef with its white fringes of foam in contrast to the sapphire sea; and then turn to the city, with its galleries and terraces whither the inhabitants come to take the flower-scented air as it rises of an evening above the houses and the tops of the trees in their little gardens; add a few sails down in the harbor; and lastly, in the stillness of falling night, listen to the organ music, the chanting of the services, the wonderful sound of bells pealing out over the open sea. There is sound and silence everywhere; oftener still there is silence over all.

Within the church is divided into a sombre, mysterious nave and narrow aisles. For some reason, probably because the winds are so high, the architect was unable to build the flying buttresses and intervening chapels which adorn almost all cathedrals, nor are there openings of any kind in the walls which support the weight of the roof. Outside there is simply the heavy wall structure, a solid mass of gray stone further strengthened by huge piers placed at intervals. Inside, the nave and its little side-galleries are lighted entirely by the great stained-glass rose-window suspended by a miracle of art above the centre doorway; for upon that side the exposure permits of the display of lacework in stone and of other beauties peculiar to the style improperly called Gothic.

The larger part of the three naves was left for the townsfolk, who came and went and heard mass there. The choir was shut off from the rest of the church by a grating and thick folds of brown curtain, left slightly apart in the middle in such a way that nothing of the choir could be seen from the church except the high altar and the officiating priest. The grating itself was divided up by the pillars which supported the organ loft; and this part of the structure, with its carved wooden columns, completed the line of the arcading in the gallery carried by the shafts in the nave. If any inquisitive person, therefore, had been bold enough to climb upon the narrow balustrade in the gallery to look down into the choir, he could have seen nothing but the tall eight-sided windows of stained glass beyond the high altar.

At the time of the French expedition into Spain to establish Ferdinand VII. once more on the throne, a French general came to the island after the taking of Cadiz, ostensibly to require the recognition of the King's government, really to see the convent and to find some means of entering it. The undertaking was certainly a delicate one; but a man of passionate temper, whose life had been, as it were, but one series of poems in action, a man who all his life long had lived romances instead of writing them, a man preëminently a Doer, was sure to be tempted by a deed which seemed to be impossible.

To open the doors of a convent of nuns by lawful means! The metropolitan or the Pope would scarcely have permitted it! And as for force or stratagem—might not any indiscretion cost him his position, his whole career as a soldier, and the end in view to boot? The Duc d'Angoulême was still in Spain; and of all the crimes which a man in favor with the commander-in-chief might commit, this one alone was certain to find him inexorable. The general had asked for the mission to gratify private motives of curiosity, though never was curiosity more hopeless. This final attempt was a matter of conscience. The Carmelite convent on the island was the only nunnery in Spain which had baffled his search.

As he crossed from the mainland, scarcely an hour's distance, he felt a presentiment that his hopes were to be fulfilled; and afterward, when as yet he had seen nothing of the convent but its walls, and of the nuns not so much as their robes; while he had merely heard the chanting of the service, there were dim auguries under the walls and in the sound of the voices to justify his frail hope. And, indeed, however faint those so unaccountable presentiments might be, never was human passion more vehemently excited than the general's curiosity at that moment. There are no small events for the heart; the heart exaggerates everything; the heart weighs the fall of a fourteen-year-old Empire and the dropping of a woman's glove in the same scales, and the glove is nearly always the heavier of the two. So here are the facts in all their prosaic simplicity. The facts first, the emotions will follow.

An hour after the general landed on the island, the royal authority was reëstablished there. Some few Constitutional Spaniards who had found their way thither after the fall of Cadiz were allowed to charter a vessel and sail for London. So there was neither resistance nor reaction. But the change of government could not be effected in the little town without a mass, at which the two divisions under the general's command were obliged to be present. Now, it was upon this mass that the general had built his hopes of gaining some information as to the sisters in the convent; he was quite unaware how absolutely the Carmelites were cut off from the world; but he knew that there might be among them one whom he held dearer than life, dearer than honor.

His hopes were cruelly dashed at once. Mass, it is true, was celebrated with great pomp. In honor of such a solemnity, the curtains which always hid the choir were drawn back to display its riches, its valuable paintings and shrines so bright with gems that they eclipsed the glories of the votive offerings of gold and silver hung up by sailors of the port on the columns in the naves. But all the nuns had sought seclusion in the organ-loft. And yet, in spite of this first check, during this very mass of thanksgiving, the most intimately thrilling drama that ever set a man's heart beating opened out widely before him.

The sister who played the organ aroused such intense enthusiasm, that not a single man regretted that he had come to the service. Even the men in the ranks were delighted, and the officers were in ecstasy. As for the general, he was seemingly calm and indifferent. The sensations stirred in him as the sister played one piece after another belong to the small number of things which it is not lawful to utter; words are powerless to express them; like Death, God, Eternity, they can only be realized through their one point of contact with humanity. Strangely enough, the organ music seemed to belong to the school of Rossini, the musician who brings most human passion into his art. Some day his works, by their number and extent, will receive the reverence due to the Homer of music. From among all the scores that we owe to his great genius, the nun seemed to have chosen "Moses in Egypt" for special study, doubtless because the spirit of sacred music finds therein its supreme expression. Perhaps the soul of the great musician, so gloriously known to Europe, and the soul of this unknown executant had met in the intuitive apprehension of the same poetry. So at least thought two dilettanti officers who must have missed the Theatre Favart in their Spanish exile.

At last in the Te Deum no one could fail to discern a French soul in the sudden change that came over the music. Joy for the victory of the Most Christian King evidently stirred this nun's heart to the depths. She was a Frenchwoman beyond mistake. Soon the love of country shone out, breaking forth like shafts of light from the fugue, as the sister introduced variations with all a Parisienne's fastidious taste, and blended vague suggestions of our grandest national airs with her music. A Spaniard's fingers would not have brought this warmth into a graceful tribute paid to the victorious arms of France. The musician's nationality was revealed.

"We find France everywhere, it seems," said one of the men.

The general had left the church during the Te Deum; he could not listen any longer. The nun's music had been a revelation of a woman loved to frenzy; a woman so carefully hidden from the world's eyes, so deeply buried in the bosom of the church, that hitherto the most ingenious and persistent efforts made by men who brought great influence and unusual powers to bear upon the search had failed to find her. The suspicion aroused in the general's heart became all but a certainty with the vague reminiscence of a sad, delicious melody, the air of "Fleuve du Tage."* The woman he loved had played the prelude to the ballet in a boudoir in Paris, how often! and now this nun had chosen the song to express an exile's longing, amid the joy of those that triumphed. Terrible sensation! To hope for the resurrection of a lost love, to find her only to know that she was lost, to catch a mysterious glimpse of her after five years—five years, in which the pent-up passion, chafing in an empty life, had grown the mightier for every fruitless effort to satisfy it!

Who has not known, at least once in his life, what it is to lose some precious thing; and after hunting through his papers, ransacking his memory, and turning his house upside down; after one or two days spent in vain search, and hope, and despair; after a prodigious expenditure of the liveliest irritation of soul, who has not known the ineffable pleasure of finding that all-important nothing which had come to be a kind of monomania? Very good. Now, spread that fury of search over five years; put a woman, put a heart, put Love in the place of the trifle; transpose the monomania into the key of high passion; and, furthermore, let the seeker be a man of ardent temper, with a lion's heart and a leonine head and mane, a man to inspire awe and fear in those who come in contact with him—realize this, and you may, perhaps, understand why the general walked abruptly out of the church when the first notes of a ballad, which he used to hear with a rap-

* The Tagus River.

ture of delight in a gilt-paneled boudoir, began to vibrate along the aisles of the church in the sea.

The general walked away down the steep street which led to the port, and only stopped when he could not hear the deep notes of the organ. Unable to think of anything but the love which broke out in volcanic eruption, filling his heart with fire, he only knew that the Te Deum was over when the Spanish congregation came pouring out of the church. Feeling that his behavior and attitude might seem ridiculous, he went back to head the procession, telling the alcalde and the governor that, feeling suddenly faint, he had gone out into the air. Casting about for a plea for prolonging his stay, it at once occurred to him to make the most of this excuse, framed on the spur of the moment. He declined, on a plea of increasing indisposition, to preside at the banquet given by the town to the French officers, betook himself to his bed, and sent a message to the major-general, to the effect that temporary illness obliged him to leave the colonel in command of the troops for the time being. This commonplace but very plausible stratagem relieved him of all responsibility for the time necessary to carry out his plans. The general, nothing if not "Catholic and monarchical," took occasion to inform himself of the hours of the services, and manifested the greatest zeal for the performance of his religious duties, piety which caused no remark in Spain.

The very next day, while the division was marching out of the town, the general went to the convent to be present at vespers. He found an empty church. The townsfolk, devout though they were, had all gone down to the quay to watch the embarkation of the troops. He felt glad to be the only man there. He tramped noisily up the nave, clanking his spurs till the vaulted roof rang with the sound; he coughed, he talked aloud to himself to let the nuns know, and more particularly to let the organist know that if the troops were gone, one Frenchman was left behind. Was this singular warning heard and understood? He thought so. It seemed to him that in the *Magnificat* the organ made response which was borne to him on the vibrating air. The nun's spirit found wings in music and fled toward him, throbbing with the rhythmical pulse of the sounds. Then, in all its might, the music burst forth and filled the church with warmth. The Song of Joy set apart in the sublime liturgy of Latin Christianity to express the exaltation of the soul in the presence of the glory of the Ever-living God became the utterance of a heart almost terrified by its gladness in the presence of the glory of a mortal love; a love that yet lived, a love that had risen to trouble her even beyond the grave in which the nun is laid, that she may rise again the bride of Christ.

The organ is in truth the grandest, the most daring, the most magnificent of all instruments invented by human genius. It is a whole orchestra in itself. It can express anything in response to a skilled touch. Surely it is in some sort a pedestal on which the soul poises for a flight forth into space, essaying on her course to draw picture after picture in an endless series, to paint human life, to cross the Infinite that separates heaven from earth? And the longer a dreamer listens to those giant harmonies, the better he realizes that nothing save this hundred-voiced choir on earth can fill all the space between kneeling men and a God hidden by the blinding light of the sanctuary. The music is the one interpreter strong enough to bear up the prayers of humanity to heaven, prayer in its omnipotent moods, prayer tinged by the melancholy of many different natures, colored by meditative ecstasy, upspringing with the impulse of repentance—blended with the myriad fancies of every creed. Yes. In those long vaulted aisles the melodies inspired by the sense of things divine are blent with a grandeur unknown before, are decked with new glory and might. Out of the dim daylight, and the deep silence broken by the chanting of the choir in response to the thunder of the organ, a veil is woven for God, and the brightness of His attributes shines through it.

And this wealth of holy things seemed to be flung down like a grain of incense upon the fragile altar raised to Love beneath the eternal throne of a jealous and avenging God. Indeed, in the joy of the nun there was little of that awe and gravity which should harmonize with the solemnities of the *Magnificat*. She had enriched the music with graceful variations, earthly gladness throbbing through the rhythm of each. In such brilliant quivering cadences some great singer might strive to find a voice for her love, her melodies fluttered as a bird carols buoyantly about its mate. There were moments when she seemed to leap back into the past, to dally there, now with laughter, now with tears. Her changing moods, as it were, ran riot. She was like a woman excited and happy over her lover's return.

But at length, after the swaying fugues of delirium, after the marvelous rendering of a vision of the past, a revulsion swept over the soul that thus found utterance for itself. With a swift transition from the major to the minor, the organist told her hearer of her present lot. She gave the story of long melancholy broodings, of the slow course of her moral malady. How day by day she deadened the senses, how every night cut off one more thought, how her heart was slowly reduced to ashes. The sadness deepened shade after shade through languid modulations, and in a little while the echoes were pouring out a torrent of grief. Then, on a sudden, high notes rang out like the voices of angels singing together, as if to tell the lost but not forgotten lover that their spirits now could only meet in heaven. Pathetic hope! Then followed the Amen. No more joy, no more tears in the air, no sadness, no regrets. The Amen was the return to God. The final chord was deep, solemn, even terrible; for the last rumblings of the bass sent a shiver through the audience that raised the hair on their heads; the nun shook out her veiling of crepe, and seemed to sink again into the tomb from which she had risen for a moment. Slowly the reverberations died away; it seemed as if the church, but now so full of musical light, had returned to thick darkness.

The general had been caught up and borne swiftly away by this strong-winged spirit; he had followed the course of its flight from beginning to end. He understood to the fullest extent the imagery of that burning symphony; for him the chords reached deep and far. For him, as for the sister, the poem meant future, present, and past. Is not music, and even opera music, a sort of text, which a susceptible or poetic temper, or a sore and stricken heart, may expand as memories shall determine? If a musician must needs have the heart of a poet, must not the listener, too, be in a manner a poet and a lover to hear all that lies in great music? Religion, love, and music—what are they but a threefold expression of the same fact, of that craving for expansion which stirs in every noble soul. And these three forms of poetry ascend to God, in whom all passion on earth finds its end. Wherefore the holy human trinity finds a place amid the infinite glories of God; of God, whom we always represent surrounded with the fires of love and cymbals of gold—music and light and harmony. Is not He the Cause and the End of all our strivings?

The French general guessed rightly that here in the desert, on this bare rock in the sea, the nun had seized upon music as an outpouring of the passion that still consumed her. Was this her manner of offering up her love as a sacrifice to God? Or was it Love exultant in triumph over God? The questions were hard to answer. But one thing at least the general could not mistake—in this heart, dead to the world, the fire of passion burned as fiercely as in his own.

Vespers over, he went back to the alcalde's house upon whom he was quartered. In the all-absorbing joy which comes in such full measure when a satisfaction sought long and painfully is attained at last, he could see nothing beyond this—

he was still loved! In her heart love had grown in loneliness, even as his love had grown stronger as he surmounted one barrier after another which this woman had set between them! The glow of soul came to its natural end. There followed a longing to see her again, to contend with God for her, to snatch her away—a rash scheme, which appealed to a daring nature. He went to bed, when the meal was over, to avoid questions; to be alone and think at his ease; and he lay absorbed by deep thought till day broke.

He rose early to go to mass. He went to the church and knelt close to the screen, with his forehead touching the curtain; he would have torn a hole in it if he had been alone, but his host had come with him out of politeness, and the least imprudence might compromise the whole future of his love and ruin the new-found hopes.

The organ sounded, but it was another player, and not the nun of the last two days whose hands touched the keys. It was all colorless and cold for the general. Was the woman he loved prostrated by emotion which well-nigh overcame a strong man's heart? Had she so fully realized and shared an unchanged, longed-for love, that now she lay dying on her bed in her cell? While innumerable thoughts of this kind perplexed his mind, the voice of the woman he worshiped rang out close beside him; he knew its clear resonant soprano. It was her voice, with that faint tremor in it which gave it all the charm that shyness and diffidence give to a young girl; her voice, distinct from the mass of singing as a prima donna's in the chorus of a finale. It was like a golden or silver thread in dark frieze.

It was she! There could be no mistake. Parisienne now as ever, she had not laid coquetry aside when she threw off worldly adornments for the veil and the Carmelite's coarse serge. She who had affirmed her love last evening in the praise sent up to God seemed now to say to her lover: "Yes, it is I. I am here. My love is unchanged, but I am beyond the reach of love. You will hear my voice, my soul shall enfold you, and I shall abide here under the brown shroud in the choir from which no power on earth can tear me. Thou canst never see me more!"

"It is she indeed!" the general said to himself, raising his head. He had leant his face on his hands, unable at first to bear the intolerable emotion that surged like a whirlpool in his heart, when that well-known voice vibrated under the arcading, with the sound of the sea for accompaniment.

Storm was without, and calm within the sanctuary. Still that rich voice poured out all its caressing notes; it fell like balm on the lover's burning heart; it blossomed upon the air—the air that a man would fain breathe more deeply to receive the affluence of a soul breathed forth with love in the words of the prayer. The alcalde coming to join his guest found him in tears during the elevation, while the nun was singing, and brought him back to his house. Surprised to find so much piety in a French military officer, the worthy magistrate invited the confessor of the convent to meet his guest. Never had news given the general more pleasure; he paid the ecclesiastic a good deal of attention at supper, and confirmed his Spanish hosts in the high opinion they had formed of his piety by a not wholly disinterested respect. He inquired with gravity how many sisters there were in the convent, and asked for particulars of its endowment and revenues, as if from courtesy he wished to hear the good priest discourse on the subject most interesting to him. He informed himself as to the manner of life led by the holy women. Were they allowed to go out of the convent, or to see visitors?

"Señor," replied the venerable churchman, "the rule is strict. A woman cannot enter a monastery of the order of St. Bruno without a special permission from his holiness, and the rule here is equally stringent. No man may enter a convent of Barefooted Carmelites unless he is a priest specially attached to the services of the house by the archbishop. None of the nuns may leave the convent; though the great saint, Mother Theresa, often left her cell. The visitor or the mothers superior can alone give permission, subject to an authorization from the archbishop, for a nun to see a visitor, and then especially in a case of illness. Now we are one of the principal houses, and consequently we have a mother superior here. Among other foreign sisters there is one Frenchwoman, Sister Theresa; she it is who directs the music in the chapel."

"Oh!" said the general, with feigned surprise. "She must have rejoiced over the victory of the House of Bourbon."

"I told them the reason of the mass; they are always a little bit inquisitive."

"But Sister Theresa may have interests in France. Perhaps she would like to send some message or to hear news."

"I do not think so. She would have spoken to me."

"As a fellow-countryman, I should be quite curious to see her," said the general. "If it is possible, if the lady superior consents, if——"

"Even at the grating, and in the reverend mother's presence, an interview would be quite impossible for anybody whatsoever; but strict as the mother is, for a deliverer of our holy religion and the throne of his Catholic majesty, the rule might be relaxed for a moment," said the confessor, blinking. "I will speak about it."

"How old is Sister Theresa?" inquired the lover. He dared not ask any questions of the priest as to the nun's beauty.

"She does not reckon years now," the good man answered, with a simplicity that made the general shudder.

Next day before siesta, the confessor came to inform the French general that Sister Theresa and the mother consented to receive him at the grating in the parlor before vespers. The general spent the siesta in pacing to and fro along the quay in the noonday heat. Thither the priest came to find him, and brought him to the convent by way of the gallery round the cemetery. Fountains, green trees, and rows of arcading maintained a cool freshness in keeping with the place.

At the farther end of the long gallery the priest led the way into a large room divided in two by a grating covered with a brown curtain. In the first, and in some sort public half of the apartment, where the confessor left the new-comer, a wooden bench ran round the wall, and two or three chairs, also of wood, were placed near the grating. The ceiling consisted of bare unornamented joists and cross-beams of ilex wood. As the two windows were both on the inner side of the grating, and the dark surface of the wood was a bad reflector, the light in the place was so dim that you could scarcely see the great black crucifix, the portrait of Sainte-Theresa, and a picture of the Madonna which adorned the gray parlor walls. Tumultuous as the general's feelings were, they took something of the melancholy of the place. He grew calm in that homely quiet. A sense of something vast as the tomb took possession of him beneath the chill unceiled roof. Here, as in the grave, was there not eternal silence, deep peace—the sense of the Infinite? And beside this there was the quiet and the fixed thought of the cloister—a thought which you felt like a subtle presence in the air, and in the dim dusk of the room; an all-pervasive thought nowhere definitely expressed, and looming the larger in the imagination; for in the cloister the great saying: "Peace in the Lord," enters the least religious soul as a living force.

The monk's life is scarcely comprehensible. A man seems confessed a weakling in a monastery; he was born to act, to live out a life of work; he is evading a man's destiny in his cell. But what man's strength, blended with pathetic weakness, is implied by a woman's choice of the convent life! A man may have any number of motives for burying himself in a monastery; for him it is the leap over the precipice. A woman has but one motive—she does not unsex herself; she betroths herself to a heavenly bridegroom. Of the monk you may ask: "Why did you not fight your battle?" But if a woman immures herself in the cloister, is there not always a sublime battle fought first?

At length it seemed to the general that that still room and the lonely convent in the sea were full of thoughts of him. Love seldom attains to solemnity; yet surely a love still faithful in the breast of God was something solemn, something more than a man had a right to look for as things are in this nineteenth century? The infinite grandeur of the situation might well produce an effect upon the general's mind; he had precisely enough elevation of soul to forget politics, honors, Spain, and society in Paris, and to rise to the height of this lofty climax. And what in truth could be more tragic? How much must pass in the souls of these two lovers, brought together in a place of strangers, on a ledge of granite in the sea; yet held apart by an intangible, unsurmountable barrier! Try to imagine the man saying within himself: "Shall I triumph over God in her heart?" when a faint rustling sound made him quiver, and the curtain was drawn aside.

Between him and the light stood a woman. Her face was hidden by the veil that drooped from the folds upon her head; she was dressed according to the rule of the order in a gown of the color become proverbial. Her bare feet were hidden; if the general could have seen them, he would have known how appallingly thin she had grown; and yet in spite of the thick folds of her coarse gown, a mere covering and no ornament, he could guess how tears, and prayer, and passion, and loneliness had wasted the woman before him.

An ice-cold hand, belonging, no doubt, to the mother superior, held back the curtain. The general gave the enforced witness of their interview a searching glance, and met the dark, inscrutable gaze of an aged recluse. The mother might have been a century old, but the bright, youthful eyes belied the wrinkles that furrowed her pale face.

"Madame la Duchesse," he began, his voice shaken with emotion, "does your companion understand French?" The veiled figure bowed her head at the sound of his voice.

"There is no duchess here," she replied. "It is Sister Theresa whom you see before you. She whom you lightly call my companion is my mother in God, my superior here on earth."

The words were so meekly spoken by the voice that sounded in other years amid harmonious surroundings of refined luxury, the voice of a queen of fashion in Paris. Such words from the lips that once spoke so lightly and flippantly struck the general dumb with amazement.

"The holy mother only speaks Latin and Spanish," she added.

"I understand neither. Dear Antoinette, make my excuses to her."

The light fell full upon the nun's figure; a thrill of deep emotion betrayed itself in a faint quiver of her veil as she heard her name softly spoken by the man who had been so hard in the past.

"My brother," she said, drawing her sleeve under her veil, perhaps to brush tears away, "I am Sister Theresa."

Then, turning to the superior, she spoke in Spanish; the general knew enough of the language to understand what she said perfectly well; possibly he could have spoken it had he chosen to do so.

"Dear mother, the gentleman presents his respects to you, and begs you to pardon him if he cannot pay them himself, but he knows neither of the languages which you speak——"

The aged nun bent her head slowly, with an expression of angelic sweetness, enhanced at the same time by the consciousness of her power and dignity.

"You know this gentleman?" she asked, with a keen glance.

"Yes, mother."

"Go back to your cell, my daughter!" said the mother imperiously.

The general slipped aside behind the curtain lest the dreadful tumult within him should appear in his face; even in the shadow it seemed to him that he could still see the superior's piercing eyes. He was afraid of her; she held his little, frail, hard-won happiness in her hands; and he, who had never quailed under a triple row of guns, now trembled before this nun. The duchess went toward the door, but she turned back.

"Mother," she said, with dreadful calmness, "the Frenchman is one of my brothers."

"Then stay, my daughter," said the superior, after a pause.

The piece of admirable jesuitry told of such love and regret, that a man less strongly constituted might have broken down under the keen delight in the midst of a great and, for him, an entirely novel peril. Oh! how precious words, looks, and gestures became when love must baffle lynx eyes and tiger's claws! Sister Theresa came back.

"You see, my brother, what I have dared to do only to speak to you for a moment of your salvation and of the prayers that my soul puts up for your soul daily. I am committing mortal sin. I have told a lie. How many days of penance must expiate that lie! But I shall endure it for your sake. My brother, you do not know what happiness it is to love in heaven; to feel that you can confess love purified by religion, love transported into the highest heights of all, so that we are permitted to lose sight of all but the soul. If the doctrine and the spirit of the saint to whom we owe this refuge had not raised me above earth's anguish, and caught me up and set me, far indeed beneath the Sphere wherein she dwells, yet truly above this world, I should not have seen you again.

But now I can see you, and hear your voice, and remain calm——"

The general broke in: "But, Antoinette, let me see you, you whom I love passionately, desperately, as you could have wished me to love you."

"Do not call me Antoinette, I implore you. Memories of the past hurt me. You must see no one here but Sister Theresa, a creature who trusts in the Divine mercy." She paused for a little, and then added: "You must control yourself, my brother. Our mother would separate us without pity if there is any worldly passion in your face, or if you allow the tears to fall from your eyes."

The general bowed his head to regain self-control; when he looked up again he saw her face beyond the grating—the thin, white, but still impassioned face of the nun. All the magic charm of youth that once bloomed there, all the fair contrast of velvet whiteness and the color of the Bengal rose, had given place to a burning glow as of a porcelain jar with a faint light shining through it. The wonderful hair in which she took such pride had been shaven; there was a bandage round her forehead and about her face. An ascetic life had left dark traces about the eyes, which still sometimes shot out fevered glances; their ordinary calm expression was but a veil. In a few words, she was but the ghost of her former self.

"Ah! you that have come to be my life, you must come out of this tomb! You were mine; you had no right to give yourself, even to God. Did you not promise me to give up all at the least command from me? You may, perhaps, think me worthy of that promise now when you hear what I have done for you. I have sought you all through the world. You have been in my thoughts at every moment for five years; my life has been given to you. My friends, very powerful friends, as you know, have helped with all their might to search every convent in France, Italy, Spain, Sicily, and America. Love burned more brightly for every vain search. Again and again

I made long journeys with a false hope; I have wasted my life and the heaviest throbbings of my heart in vain under many a dark convent wall. I am not speaking of a faithfulness that knows no bounds, for what is it?—nothing compared with the infinite longings of my love. If your remorse long ago was sincere, you certainly ought not to hesitate to follow me to-day."

"You forget that I am not free."

"The duke is dead," he answered quickly.

Sister Theresa flushed red.

"May heaven be open to him!" she cried with a quick rush of feeling. "He was generous to me. But I did not mean such ties; it was one of my sins that I was ready to break them all without scruple—for you."

"Are you speaking of your vows?" the general asked, frowning. "I did not think that anything weighed heavier with your heart than love. But do not fear, Antoinette; the Holy Father himself shall absolve you of your oath. I will surely go to Rome, I will entreat all the powers on earth; if God could come down from heaven, I would——"

"Do not blaspheme."

"So do not fear the anger of God. Ah! I would far rather hear that you would leave your prison for me; that this very night you would let yourself down into a boat at the foot of the cliffs. And we would go away to be happy somewhere at the world's end, I know not where. And, with me at your side, you should come back to life and health under the wings of love."

"You must not talk like this," said Sister Theresa: "you do not know what you are to me now. I love you far better than I ever loved you before. Every day I pray for you; I see you with other eyes. Armand, if you but knew the happiness of giving yourself up, without shame, to a pure friendship which God watches over! You do not know what joy it is to me to pray for heaven's blessing on you. I never pray for myself: **God** will do with me according to His will; but, at the price of my soul, I wish I could be sure that you are happy here on earth, and that you will be happy hereafter throughout all ages. My eternal life is all that trouble has left me to offer up to you. I am old now with weeping; I am neither young nor fair; and in any case, you could not respect the nun who became a wife; no love, not even motherhood, could give me absolution. What can you say to outweigh the uncounted thoughts that have gathered in my heart during the past five years, thoughts that have changed, and worn, and blighted it? I ought to have given a heart less sorrowful to God."

"What can I say? Dear Antoinette, I will say this, that I love you; that affection, love, a great love, the joy of living in another heart that is ours, utterly and wholly ours, is so rare a thing and so hard to find, that I doubted you, and put you to sharp proof; but now, to-day, I love you, Antoinette, with all my soul's strength. If you will follow me into solitude, I will hear no voice but yours. I will see no other face."

"Hush, Armand! You are shortening the little time that we may be together here on earth."

"Antoinette, will you come with me?"

"I am never away from you. My life is in your heart, not through the selfish ties of earthly happiness, or vanity, or enjoyment; pale and withered as I am, I live here for you, in the breast of God. As God is just, you shall be happy——"

"Words, words all of it! Pale and withered? How if I want you? How if I cannot be happy without you? Do you still think of nothing but duty with your lover before you? Is he never to come first and above all things else in your heart? In time past you put social success, yourself, heaven knows what, before him; now it is God, it is the welfare of my soul! In Sister Theresa I find the duchess over again, ignorant of the happiness of love, insensible as ever, beneath the semblance of sensibility. You do not love me; you have never loved me——"

"Oh, my brother——!"

"You do not wish to leave this tomb. You love my soul, do you say? Very well, through you it will be lost for ever. I shall make away with myself——"

"Mother!" Sister Theresa called aloud in Spanish, "I have lied to you; this man is my lover!"

The curtain fell at once. The general, in his stupor, scarcely heard the doors within as they clanged together with violence.

"Ah! she loves me still!" he cried, understanding all the sublimity of that cry of hers. "She loves me still. She must be carried off."

The general left the island, returned to headquarters on the peninsular, pleaded ill-health, asked for leave of absence, and forthwith took his departure for France.

And now for the incidents which brought the two personages in this Scene into their present relation to each other.

The thing known in France as the Faubourg Saint-Germain is neither a quarter, nor a sect, nor an institution, nor anything else that admits of a precise definition. There are great houses in the Place Royale, the Faubourg Saint-Honoré, and the Chaussée d'Antin, in any one of which you may breathe the atmosphere of the Faubourg Saint-Germain. So, to begin with, the whole faubourg is not within the faubourg. There are men and women born far enough away from its influences who respond to them and take their place in the circle; and again there are others, born within its limits, who may yet be driven forth for ever. For the last forty years the manners, and customs, and speech, in a word, the tradition of the Faubourg Saint-Germain, have been to Paris what the Court used to be to it in other times; it is what the Hôtel Saint-Paul was to the fourteenth century; the Louvre to the fifteenth; the Palais, the Hôtel Rambouillet, and the Place Royale to the sixteenth; and lastly, as Versailles was to the seventeenth and the eighteenth.

Just as the ordinary work-a-day Paris will always centre about some point; so, through all periods of history, the Paris of the nobles and the upper classes converges toward some particular spot. It is a periodically recurrent phenomenon which presents ample matter for reflection to those who are fain to observe or describe the various social zones; and possibly an inquiry into the causes that bring about this centralization may do more than merely justify the probability of this episode; it may be of service to serious interests which some day will be more deeply rooted in the commonwealth, unless, indeed, experience is as meaningless for political parties as it is for youth.

In every age the great nobles, and the rich who always ape the great nobles, build their houses as far as possible from crowded streets. When the Duc d'Uzès built his splendid hôtel in the Rue Montmartre in the reign of Louis XIV., and set the fountain at his gates—for which beneficent action, to say nothing of his other virtues, he was held in such veneration that the whole quarter turned out in a body to follow his funeral—when the duke, I say, chose this site for his house, he did so because that part of Paris was almost deserted in those days. But when the fortifications were pulled down, and the market gardens beyond the line of the boulevards began to fill with houses, then the d'Uzès family left their fine mansion, and in our time it was occupied by a banker. Later still, the noblesse began to find themselves out of their element among storekeepers, left the Place Royale and the centre of Paris for good, and crossed the river to breathe freely in the Faubourg Saint-Germain, where palaces were reared already about the great hôtel built by Louis XIV.* for

* Louis the Great.

the Duc de Maine—the Benjamin of his legitimatized sons. And indeed, for people accustomed to a stately life, can there be more unseemly surroundings than the bustle, the mud, the street cries, the bad smells, and narrow thoroughfares of a populous quarter? The very habits of life in a mercantile or manufacturing district are completely at variance with the lives of nobles. The storekeeper and artisan are just going to bed when the great world is thinking of dinner; and the noisy stir of life begins among the former when the latter have gone to rest. Their day's calculations never coincide; the one class represents the expenditure, the other the receipts. Consequently their manners and customs are diametrically opposed.

Nothing contemptuous is intended by this statement. An aristocracy is in a manner the intellect of the social system, as the middle classes and the proletariat may be said to be its organizing and working power. It naturally follows that these forces are differently situated; and of their antagonism there is bred a seeming antipathy produced by the performance of different functions, all of them, however, existing for one common end.

Such social dissonances are so inevitably the outcome of any charter of the Constitution, that however much a Liberal may be disposed to complain of them, as of treason against those sublime ideas with which the ambitious plebeian is apt to cover his designs, he would none the less think it a preposterous notion that M. le Prince de Montmorency, for instance, should continue to live in the Rue Saint-Martin at the corner of the street which bears that nobleman's name; or that M. le Duc de Fitz-James, descendant of the royal house of Scotland, should have his hôtel at the angle of the Rue Marie Stuart and the Rue Montorgueil. *Sint ut sunt, aut non sint*, the grand words of the jesuit, might be taken as a motto by the great in all countries. These social differences are patent in all ages; the fact is always accepted by the people; its "reasons of state" are self-evident; it is at once cause and effect, a principle and a law. The commonsense of the masses never deserts them until demagogues stir them up to gain ends of their own; that commonsense is based on the verities of social order; and the social order is the same everywhere, in Moscow as in London, in Geneva as in Calcutta. Given a certain number of families of unequal fortune in any given space, you will see an aristocracy forming under your eyes; there will be the patricians, the upper classes, and yet other ranks below them. Equality may be a *right*, but no power on earth can convert it into *fact*. It would be a good thing for France if this idea could be popularized. The benefits of political harmony are obvious to the least intelligent classes. Harmony is, as it were, the poetry of order, and order is a matter of vital importance to the working population. And what is order, reduced to its simplest expression, but the agreement of things among themselves—unity, in short? Architecture, music, and poetry, everything in France, and in France more than in any other country, is based upon this principle; it is written upon the very foundations of her clear, accurate language, and a language must always be the most infallible index of national character. In the same way you may note that the French popular airs are those most calculated to strike the imagination, the best modulated melodies are taken over by the people; clearness of thought, the intellectual simplicity of an idea attracts them; they like the incisive sayings that hold the greatest number of ideas. France is the one country in the world where a little phrase may bring about a great revolution. Whenever the masses have risen, it has been to bring men, affairs, and principles into agreement. No nation has a clearer conception of that idea of unity which should permeate the life of an aristocracy; possibly no other nation has so intelligent a comprehension of a political necessity; history will never find her behind the time. France has been led astray many a time, but she is deluded, woman-like, by generous ideas, by a glow of enthusiasm which at first outstrips sober reason.

So, to begin with, the most striking characteristic of the faubourg is the splendor of its great mansions, its great gardens, and a surrounding quiet in keeping with princely revenues drawn from great estates. And what is this distance set between a class and a whole metropolis but the visible and outward expression of the widely different attitude of mind which must inevitably keep them apart? The position of the head is well defined in every organism. If by any chance a nation allows its head to fall at its feet, it is pretty sure sooner or later to discover that this is a suicidal measure; and since nations have no desire to perish, they set to work at once to grow a new head. If they lack the strength for this, they perish as Rome perished, and Venice, and so many other states.

This distinction between the upper and lower spheres of social activity, emphasized by differences in their manner of living, necessarily implies that in the highest aristocracy there is real worth and some distinguishing merit. In any State, no matter what form of "government" is affected, so soon as the patrician class fails to maintain that complete superiority which is the condition of its existence, it ceases to be a force, and is pulled down at once by the populace. The people always wish to see money, power, and initiative in their leaders, hands, hearts, and heads; they must be the spokesmen, they must represent the intelligence and the glory of the nation. Nations, like women, love strength in those who rule them; they cannot give love without respect; they refuse utterly to obey those of whom they do not stand in awe. An aristocracy fallen into contempt is a *roi fainéant*,* a husband in petticoats; first it ceases to be itself, and then it ceases to be.

And in this way the isolation of the great, the sharply marked distinction in their manner of life, or in a word, the

* Lit.: a lazy king.

general custom of the patrician caste is at once the sign of a real power, and their destruction so soon as that power is lost. The Faubourg Saint-Germain failed to recognize the conditions of its being, while it would still have been easy to perpetuate its existence, and therefore was brought low for a time. The faubourg should have looked the facts fairly in the face, as the English aristocracy did before them; they should have seen that every institution has its climacteric periods, when words lose their old meanings, and ideas reappear in a new guise, and the whole condition of politics wears a changed aspect, while the underlying realities undergo no essential alteration.

These ideas demand further developments which form an essential part of this episode; they are given here both as a succinct statement of the causes and an explanation of the things which happen in the course of the story.

The stateliness of the castles and palaces where nobles dwell; the luxury of the details; the constantly maintained sumptuousness of the furniture; the "atmosphere" in which the fortunate owner of landed estates (a rich man before he was born) lives and moves easily and without friction; the habit of mind which never descends to calculate the petty work-a-day gains of existence; the leisure; the higher education attainable at a much earlier age; and lastly, the aristocratic tradition that makes of him a social force, for which his opponents, by dint of study and a strong will and tenacity of vocation, are scarcely a match—all these things should contribute to form a lofty spirit in a man, possessed of such privileges from his youth up; they should stamp his character with that high self-respect, of which the least consequence is a nobleness of heart in harmony with the noble name that he bears. And in some few families all this is realized. There are noble characters here and there in the faubourg, but they are marked exceptions to a general rule of egoism which has been the ruin of this world within a world. The privileges above enumerated are the birthright of the French noblesse, as of every patrician efflorescence ever formed on the surface of a nation ; and will continue to be theirs so long as their existence is based upon real estate, or money ; *domaine-sol* (domain of the soil) and *domaine-argent* (domain of money) alike, the only solid bases of an organized society; but such privileges are held upon the understanding that the patricians must continue to justify their existence. There is a sort of moral fief held on a tenure of service rendered to the sovereign, and here in France the people are undoubtedly the sovereigns nowadays. The times are changed, and so are the weapons. The knight-banneret of old wore a coat of chain-armor and a hauberk ; he could handle a lance well and display his pennon, and no more was required of him ; to-day he is bound to give proof of his intelligence. A stout heart was enough in the days of old ; in our days he is required to have a capacious brain-pan. Skill and knowledge and capital—these three points mark out a social triangle on which the escutcheon of power is blazoned ; our modern aristocracy must take its stand on these.

A fine theorem is as good as a great name. The Rothschilds, the Fuggers of the nineteenth century, are princes *de facto*. A great artist is in reality an oligarch ; he represents a whole century, and almost always he is a law to others. And the art of words, the high-pressure machinery of the writer, the poet's genius, the merchant's steady endurance, the strong will of the statesman who concentrates a thousand dazzling qualities in himself, the general's sword—all these victories, in short, which a single individual will win, that he may tower above the rest of the world, the patrician class is now bound to win and keep exclusively. They must head the new forces as they once headed the material forces ; how should they keep the position unless they are worthy of it ? How, unless they are the soul and brain of a nation, shall they set its hand moving ? How lead a people without the power of command? And what is the marshal's baton without the innate power of the captain in the man who wields it? The Faubourg Saint-Germain took to playing with batons, and fancied that all the power was in its hands. It inverted the terms of the proposition which called it into existence. And instead of flinging away the insignia which offended the people, and quietly grasping the power, it allowed the bourgeoisie to seize the authority, clung with fatal obstinacy to its shadow, and over and over again forgot the laws which a minority must observe if it would live. When an aristocracy is scarce a thousandth part of the body social, it is bound to-day, as of old, to multiply its points of action, so as to counterbalance the weight of the masses in a great crisis. And in our days those means of action must be living forces, and not historical memories.

In France, unluckily, the noblesse were still so puffed up with the notion of their ancient and vanished power, that it was difficult to contend against a kind of innate presumption in themselves. Perhaps this is a national defect. The Frenchman is less given than any one else to undervalue himself; it comes natural to him to go from his degree to the one above it: and while it is a rare thing for him to pity the unfortunates over whose heads he rises, he always groans in spirit to see so many fortunate people above him. He is very far from heartless, but too often he prefers to listen to his intellect. The national instinct which brings the Frenchman to the front, the vanity that wastes his substance, is as much a dominant passion as thrift in the Dutch. For three centuries it swayed the noblesse, who, in this respect, were certainly preëminently French. The scion of the Faubourg Saint-Germain, beholding his material superiority, was fully persuaded of his intellectual superiority. And everything contributed to confirm him in his belief; for ever since the Faubourg Saint-Germain existed at all—which is to say, ever since Versailles ceased to be the royal residence—the faubourg, with some few gaps in continuity, was always backed up by the central power, which in France seldom fails to support that side. Thence its downfall in 1830.

At that time the party of the Faubourg Saint-Germain was rather like an army without a base of operations. It had utterly failed to take advantage of the peace to plant itself in the heart of the nation. It sinned for want of learning its lesson, and through an utter incapability of regarding its interests as a whole. A future certainty was sacrificed to a doubtful present gain. This blunder in policy may perhaps be attributed to the following cause:

The class-isolation so strenuously kept up by the noblesse brought about fatal results during the last forty years; even caste-patriotism was extinguished by it, and rivalry fostered among themselves. When the French noblesse of other times were rich and powerful, the nobles (*gentilhommes*) could choose their chiefs and obey them in the hour of danger. As their power diminished, they grew less amenable to discipline; and as in the last days of the Byzantine Empire, every one wished to be emperor. They mistook their uniform weakness for uniform strength.

Each family ruined by the Revolution and the abolition of the law of primogeniture thought only of itself, and not at all of the great family of its caste. It seemed to them that as each individual grew rich, the party as a whole would gain in strength. And herein lay their mistake. Money, likewise, is only the outward and visible sign of power. All these families were made up of persons who preserved a high tradition of courtesy, of true graciousness of life, of refined speech, with a family pride, and a squeamish sense of *noblesse oblige** which suited well with the kind of life they led; a life wholly filled with occupations which become contemptible so soon as they cease to be accessories and take the chief place in existence. There was a certain intrinsic merit in all these

---

* The obligations of a noble's life.

people, but the merit was on the surface, and none of them were worth their face-value.

Not a single one among those families had courage to ask itself the question, "Are we strong enough for the responsibility of power?" They were cast on the top, like the lawyers of 1830; and instead of taking the patron's place, like a great man, the Faubourg Saint-Germain showed itself greedy as an upstart. The most intelligent nation in the world perceived clearly that the restored nobles were organizing everything for their own particular benefit. From that day the noblesse was doomed. The Faubourg Saint-Germain tried to be an aristocracy when it could only be an oligarchy—two very different systems, as any man may see for himself if he gives an intelligent perusal to the list of the patronymics of the House of Peers.

The King's Government certainly meant well; but the maxim that the people must be made to *will* everything, even their own welfare, was pretty constantly forgotten, nor did they bear in mind that La France is a woman and capricious, and must be happy or chastised at her own good pleasure. If there had been many dukes like the Duc de Laval, whose modesty made him worthy of the name he bore, the elder branch would have been as securely seated on the throne as the House of Hanover at this day.

In 1814 the noblesse of France were called upon to assert their superiority over the most aristocratic bourgeoisie in the most feminine of all countries, to take the lead in the most highly educated epoch the world had yet seen. And this was even more notably the case in 1820. The Faubourg Saint-Germain might very easily have led and amused the middle classes in days when people's heads were turned with distinctions, and art and science were all the rage. But the narrow-minded leaders of a time of great intellectual progress all of them detested art and science. They had not even the wit to present religion in attractive colors, though they needed its support. While Lamartine, Lamennais, Montalembert, and other writers were putting new life and elevation into men's ideas of religion, and gilding it with poetry, these bunglers in the Government chose to make the harshness of their creed felt all over the country. Never was nation in a more tractable humor; La France, like a tired woman, was ready to agree to anything; never was mismanagement so clumsy; and La France, like a woman, would have forgiven wrongs more easily than bungling.

If the noblesse meant to reinstate themselves, the better to found a strong oligarchy, they should have honestly and diligently searched their houses for men of the stamp that Napoleon used; they should have turned themselves inside out to see if peradventure there was a Constitutionalist Richelieu lurking in the entrails of the faubourg; and if that genius was not forthcoming from among them, they should have set out to find him, even in the fireless garret where he might happen to be perishing of cold; they should have assimilated him, as the English House of Lords continually assimilates aristocrats made by chance; and finally ordered him to be ruthless, to lop away the old wood, and cut the tree down to the living shoots. But, in the first place, the great system of English Toryism was far too large for narrow minds; the importation required time, and in France a tardy success is no better than a fiasco. So far, moreover, from adopting a policy of redemption, and looking for new forces where God puts them, these petty great folk took a dislike to any capacity that did not issue from their midst; and, lastly, instead of growing young again, the Faubourg Saint-Germain grew positively older.

Etiquette, not an institution of primary necessity, might have been maintained if it had appeared only on state occasions, but as it was, there was a daily wrangle over precedence; it ceased to be a matter of art or Court ceremonial, it became a question of power. And if from the outset the Crown lacked an adviser equal to so great a crisis, the aristocracy was still more lacking in a sense of its wider interests, an instinct which might have supplied the deficiency. They stood nice about M. de Talleyrand's marriage, when M. de Talleyrand was the one man among them with the steel-encompassed brains that can forge a new political system and begin a new career of glory for a nation. The faubourg scoffed at a minister if he was not gentle born, and produced no one of gentle birth that was fit to be a minister. There were plenty of nobles fitted to serve their country by raising the dignity of justices of the peace, by improving the land, by opening out roads and canals, and taking an active and leading part as country gentlemen; but these had sold their estates to gamble on the Stock Exchange. Again, the faubourg might have absorbed the energetic men among the bourgeoise, and opened their ranks to the ambition which was undermining authority; they preferred instead to fight, and to fight unarmed, for of all that they once possessed there was nothing left but tradition. For their misfortune there was just precisely enough of their former wealth left them as a class to keep up their bitter pride. They were content with their past. Not one of them seriously thought of bidding the son of the house take up arms from the pile of weapons which the nineteenth century flings down in the market-place. Young men, shut out from office, were dancing at MADAME's balls, while they should have been doing the work done under the Republic and the Empire by young, conscientious, harmlessly employed energies. It was their place to carry out at Paris the programme which their seniors should have been following in the country. The heads of houses might have won back recognition of their titles by unremitting attention to local interests, by falling in with the spirit of the age, by recasting their order to suit the taste of the times.

But, pent up together in the Faubourg Saint-Germain, where the spirit of the ancient Court and traditions of bygone feuds between the nobles and the Crown still lingered on, the aristocracy was not whole-hearted in its allegiance to the Tuileries, and so much the more easily defeated because it was concentrated in the Chamber of Peers, and badly organized even there. If the noblesse had woven themselves into a network over the country, they could have held their own; but cooped up in their faubourg, with their backs against the château, or spread at full length over the budget, a single blow cut the thread of a fast-expiring life, and a petty, smug-faced lawyer came forward with the axe. In spite of M. Royer-Collard's admirable discourse, the hereditary peerage and law of entail fell before the lampoons of a man who made it a boast that he had adroitly argued some few heads out of the executioner's clutches, and now forsooth must clumsily proceed to the slaying of old institutions.

There are examples and lessons for the future in all this. For if there were not still a future before the French aristocracy, there would be no need to do more than find a suitable sarcophagus; it were something pitilessly cruel to burn the dead body of it with fire of Tophet. But though the surgeon's scalpel is ruthless, it sometimes gives back life to a dying man; and the Faubourg Saint-Germain may wax more powerful under persecution than in its day of triumph, if it but chooses to organize itself under a leader.

And now it is easy to give a summary of this semi-political survey. The wish to reëstablish a large fortune was uppermost in every one's mind; a lack of broad views, and a mass of small defects, a real need of religion as a political factor, combined with a thirst for pleasure which damaged the cause of religion and necessitated a good deal of hypocrisy; a certain attitude of protest on the part of loftier and clearer-sighted men who set their faces against Court jealousies; and the disaffection of the provincial families, who often came of purer descent than the nobles of the Court which alienated them from itself—all these things combined to bring about a most discordant state of things in the Faubourg Saint-Germain. It was neither compact in its organization, nor consequent in its action; neither completely moral, nor frankly dissolute; it did not corrupt, nor was it corrupted; it would neither wholly abandon the disputed points which damaged its cause, nor yet adopt the policy that might have saved it. In short, however effete individuals might be, the party as a whole was none the less armed with all the great principles which lie at the roots of national existence. What was there in the faubourg that it should perish in its strength?

It was very hard to please in the choice of candidates; the faubourg had good taste, it was scornfully fastidious, yet there was nothing very glorious nor chivalrous truly about its fall.

In the Emigration of 1789 there were some traces of a loftier feeling; but in the Emigration of 1830 from Paris into the country there was nothing discernible but self-interest. A few famous men of letters, a few oratorical triumphs in the Chambers, M. de Talleyrand's attitude in the Congress, the taking of Algiers, and not a few names that found their way from the battlefield into the pages of history—all these things were so many examples set before the French noblesse to show that it was still open to them to take their part in the national existence, and to win recognition of their claims, if, indeed, they could condescend thus far. In every living organism the work of bringing the whole into harmony within itself is always going on. If a man is indolent, the indolence shows itself in everything that he does; and, in the same manner, the general spirit of a class is pretty plainly manifested in the face it turns on the world, and the soul informs the body.

The women of the Restoration displayed neither the proud disregard of public opinion shown by the Court ladies of olden time in their wantonness nor yet the simple grandeur of the tardy virtues by which they expiated their sins and shed so bright a glory about their names. There was nothing either very frivolous or very serious about the woman of the Restoration. She was hypocritical as a rule in her passion, and compounded, so to speak, with its pleasures. Some few families led the domestic life of the Duchesse d'Orléans, whose connubial couch was exhibited so absurdly to visitors at the Palais Royal. Two or three kept up the traditions of the Regency, filling cleverer women with something like disgust. The great lady of the new school exercised no influence at all over the manners of the time; and yet she might have done much. She might, at worst, have presented as dignified a spectacle as Englishwomen of the same rank. But she hesitated feebly among old precedents, became a bigot by force of circumstances, and allowed nothing of herself to appear, not even her better qualities.

Not one among the Frenchwomen of that day had the ability to create a salon whither leaders of fashion might come to take lessons in taste and elegance. Their voices, which once laid down the law to literature, that living expression of a time, now counted absolutely for naught. Now when a literature lacks a general system, it fails to shape a body for itself, and dies out with its period.

When in a nation at any time there is a people apart thus constituted, the historian is pretty certain to find some representative figure, some central personage, who embodies the qualities and the defects of the whole party to which he belongs; there is Coligny, for instance, among the Huguenots, the Coadjuteur in the time of the Fronde, the Maréchal de Richelieu under Louis XV., Danton during the Terror. It is in the nature of things that the man should be identified with the company in which history finds him. How is it possible to lead a party without conforming to its ideas? or to shine in any epoch unless a man represents the ideas of his time? The wise and prudent head of a party is continually obliged to bow to the prejudices and follies of its rear; and this is the cause of actions for which he is afterward criticised by this or that historian sitting at a safer distance from terrific popular explosions, coolly judging the passion and ferment without which the great struggles of the world could not be carried on at all. And if this is true of the Historical Comedy of the centuries, it is equally true in a more restricted sphere in the detached scenes of the national drama known as the "Manners of the Age."

At the beginning of that ephemeral life led by the Faubourg Saint-Germain under the Restoration, to which, if there is any truth in the above reflections, they failed to give stability, the most perfect type of the aristocratic caste in its weakness and strength, its greatness and littleness, might have been found for a brief space in a young married woman who belonged to it. This was a woman artificially educated, but in reality ignorant; a woman whose instincts and feelings were lofty, while the thought which should have controlled them was wanting. She squandered the wealth of her nature in obedience to social conventions; she was ready to brave society, yet she hesitated till her scruples degenerated into artifice. With more willfulness than real force of character, impressionable rather than enthusiastic, gifted with more brain than heart; she was supremely a woman, supremely a coquette, and above all things a Parisienne, loving a brilliant life and gayety, reflecting never, or too late; imprudent to the verge of poetry, and humble in the depths of her heart, in spite of her charming insolence. Like some straight-growing reed, she made a show of independence; yet, like the reed, she was ready to bend to a strong hand. She talked much of religion, and had it not at heart, though she was prepared to find in it a solution of her life. How explain a creature so complex? Capable of heroism, yet sinking unconsciously from heroic heights to utter a spiteful word; young and sweet-natured, not so much old at heart as aged by the maxims of those about her; versed in a selfish philosophy in which she was all unpracticed, she had all the vices of a courtier, all the nobleness of developing womanhood. She trusted nothing and no one, yet there were times when she quitted her skeptical attitude for a submissive credulity.

How should any portrait be anything but incomplete of her, in whom the play of swiftly changing color made discord only to produce a poetic confusion? for in her there shone a divine brightness, a radiance of youth that blended all her bewildering characteristics in a certain completeness and unity informed by her charm. Nothing was feigned. The passion or semi-passion, the ineffectual high aspirations, the actual pettiness, the coolness of sentiment and warmth of impulse, were all spontaneous and unaffected, and as much the outcome of her own position as of the position of the aristocracy to which she belonged. She was wholly self-contained; she held herself proudly above the world and beneath the shelter of her name. There was something of the egoism of Medea in her life, as in the life of the aristocracy that lay a-dying, and would not so much as raise itself or stretch out a hand to any political physician; so well aware of its feebleness, or so conscious that it was already dust, that it refused to touch or be touched.

The Duchesse de Langeais (for that was her name) had been married for about four years when the Restoration was finally consummated, which is to say, in 1816. By that time the revolution of the Hundred Days had let in the light on the mind of Louis XVIII. In spite of his surroundings, he comprehended the situation and the age in which he was living; and it was only later, when this Louis XI., without the axe, lay stricken down by disease, that those about him got the upper hand. The Duchesse de Langeais, a Navarreins by birth, came of a ducal house which had made a point of never marrying below its rank since the reign of Louis XIV. Every daughter of the house had the right and must sooner or later take a *tabouret* (seat) at Court. So, Antoinette de Navarreins, at the age of eighteen, came out of the profound solitude in which her girlhood had been spent to marry the Duc de Langeais' eldest son. The two families at that time were living quite out of the world; but after the invasion of France, the return of the Bourbons seemed to every Royalist mind the only possible way of putting an end to the miseries of the war.

The Ducs de Navarreins and de Langeais had been faithful throughout to the exiled princes, nobly resisting all the temptations of glory under the Empire. Under the circumstances they naturally followed out the old family policy; and Mlle. Antoinette, a beautiful and portionless girl, was married to M. le Marquis de Langeais only a few months before the death of the duke his father.

After the return of the Bourbons, the families resumed their rank, offices, and dignity at Court; once more they entered public life, from which hitherto they had held aloof, and took their place high on the sun-lit summits of the new political world. In that time of general baseness and sham political conversions, the public conscience was glad to recognize the unstained loyalty of the two houses, and a consistency in political and private life for which all parties involuntarily respected them. But, unfortunately, as so often happens in a time of transition, the most disinterested persons, the men whose loftiness of view and wise principles would have gained the confidence of the French nation and led them to believe in the generosity of a novel and spirited policy; these men, to repeat, were taken out of affairs, and public business was allowed to fall into the hands of others, who found it to their interest to push principles to their extreme consequences by way of proving their devotion.

The families of Langeais and Navarreins remained about the Court, condemned to perform the duties required by Court ceremonial amid the reproaches and sneers of the Liberal party. They were accused of gorging themselves with riches and honors, and all the while their family estates were no larger than before, and liberal allowances from the civil list were wholly expended in keeping up the state necessary for any European government, even if it be a republic.

In 1818, M. le Duc de Langeais commanded a division of the army, and the duchess held a post about one of the princesses, in virtue of which she was free to live in Paris and apart from her husband without scandal. The duke, moreover, beside his military duties, had a place at Court, to which he came during his term of waiting, leaving his major-general in command. The duke and duchess were leading lives entirely apart, separated both in fact and feeling, the world none the wiser. Their marriage of convention shared the fate of nearly all family arrangements of the kind. Two more antipathetic dispositions could not well have been found; they were brought together; they jarred upon each other; there was soreness on either side; thus they were divided once for all. Then they went their separate ways, with a due regard for appearances. The Duc de Langeais, by nature as methodical as the Chevalier de Folard, gave himself up methodically to his own tastes and amusements, and left his wife at liberty to do as she pleased so soon as he felt sure of her character. He recognized in her a spirit preëminently proud, a cold heart, a profound submissiveness to the usages of the world, and a youthful loyalty. Under the eyes of great relations, with the light of a prudish and bigoted Court turned full upon the duchess, his honor was safe.

So the duke calmly did as the great lords of the eighteenth century did before him, and left a young wife of two-and-twenty to her own devices. He had deeply offended that wife, and in her nature there was one appalling characteristic —she would never forgive an offense when woman's vanity and self-love, with all that was best in her nature, perhaps, had been slighted, wounded in secret. Insult and injury in the face of the world a woman loves to forget; there is a way open to her of showing herself great; she is a woman in her forgiveness; but a secret offense women never pardon; for secret baseness, as for hidden virtues and hidden love, they have no kindness.

This was Mme. la Duchesse de Langeais' real position, unknown to the world. She herself did not reflect upon it. It was the time of the rejoicings over the Duc de Berri's marriage. The Court and the faubourg roused itself from its listlessness and reserve. This was the real beginning of that unheard-of splendor which the Government of the Restoration carried too far. At that time the duchess, whether for reasons of her own, or from vanity, never appeared in public without a following of women equally distinguished by name and fortune. As queen of fashion she had her *dames d'ateurs*, her ladies, who modeled their manner and their wit on hers. They had been cleverly chosen. None of her satellites belonged to the inmost Court circle, not to the highest level of the Faubourg Saint-Germain; but they had set their minds upon admission to those inner sanctuaries. Being as yet simple dominations, they wished to rise to the neighborhood of the throne, and mingle with the seraphic powers in the high sphere known as "le petit château." Thus surrounded, the duchess' position was stronger and more commanding and secure. Her "ladies" defended her character and helped her to play her detestable part of a woman of fashion. She could laugh at men at her ease, play with fire, receive the homage on which the feminine nature is nourished, and remain mistress of herself.

At Paris, in the highest society of all, a woman is a woman still; she lives on incense, adulation, and honors. No beauty, however undoubted, no face, however fair, is anything without admiration. Flattery and a lover are proofs of power. And what is power without recognition? Nothing. If the prettiest of women were left alone in a corner of a drawing-room, she would droop. Put her in the very centre and summit of socia. grandeur, she will at once aspire to reign over all hearts—often because it is out of her power to be the happy queen of one. Dress and manner and coquetry are all meant to please one of the poorest creatures extant—the brainless coxcomb, whose handsome face is his sole merit; it was for such as these that women threw themselves away. The gilded wooden idols of the Restoration, for they were neither more nor less, had neither the antecedents of the *petits maîtres* (little masters) of the time of the Fronde, nor the rough sterling worth of Napoleon's heroes, not the wit and fine manners of their grandsires; but something of all three they meant to be without any trouble to themselves. Brave they were, like all young Frenchmen; ability they possessed, no doubt, if they had had a chance of proving it, but their places were filled up by the old worn-out men, who kept them in leading strings. It was a day of small things, a cold prosaic era. Perhaps it takes a long time for a Restoration to become a Monarchy.

For the past eighteen months the Duchesse de Langeais had been leading this empty life, filled with balls and subsequent visits, objectless triumphs, and the transient loves that spring up and die in an evening's space. All eyes were turned on her when she entered a room; she reaped her harvest of flatteries and some few words of warmer admiration, which she encouraged by a gesture or a glance, but never suffered to penetrate deeper than the skin. Her tone and bearing and everything else about her imposed her will upon others. Her life was a sort of fever of vanity and perpetual enjoyment, which turned her head. She was daring enough in conversation; she would listen to anything, corrupting the surface, as it were, of her heart. Yet, when she returned home, she often blushed at the story that had made her laugh; at the scandalous tale that supplied the details, on the strength of which she analyzed the love that she had never known, and marked the subtle distinctions of modern passion, not without comment on the part of complacent hypocrites. For women know how to say everything among themselves, and more of them are ruined by each other than corrupted by men.

There came a moment when she discerned that not until a women is loved will the world fully recognize her beauty and her wit. What does a husband prove? Simply that a girl or woman was endowed with wealth, or well brought up; that her mother managed cleverly; that in some way she satisfied a man's ambitions. A lover constantly bears witness to her personal perfections. Then followed the discovery, still in Mme. de Langeais' early womanhood, that it was possible to be loved without committing herself, without permission, without vouchsafing any satisfaction beyond the most meagre dues. There was more than one demure feminine hypocrite to instruct her in the art of playing such dangerous comedies.

So the duchess had her court, and the number of her adorers and courtiers guaranteed her virtue. She was amiable and fascinating; she flirted till the ball or the evening's gayety was at an end. Then the curtain dropped. She was cold, indifferent, self-contained again, till the next day brought its renewed sensations, superficial as before. Two or three men were completely deceived, and fell in love in earnest. She laughed at them, she was utterly insensible. "I am loved!" she told herself. "He loves me!" The certainty sufficed her. It is enough for the miser to know that his every whim might be fulfilled if he chose; so it was with the duchess, and perhaps she did not even go so far as to form a wish.

One evening she chanced to be at the house of an intimate friend, Mme. la Vicomtesse de Fontaine, one of the humble rivals who cordially detested her, and went with her everywhere. In a "friendship" of this sort both sides are on their guard, and never lay their armor aside; confidences are ingeniously indiscreet, and not infrequently treacherous. Mme. de Langeais had distributed her little patronizing, friendly, or freezing bows, with the air natural to a woman who knows the worth of her smiles, when her eyes fell upon a total stranger. Something in the man's large gravity of aspect startled her, and, with a feeling almost like dread, she turned to Mme. de Maufrigneuse with: "Who is the new-comer, dear?"

"Some one that you have heard of, no doubt. The Marquis de Montriveau."

"Oh! is it he?"

She took up her eyeglass and submitted him to a very insolent scrutiny, as if he had been a picture meant to receive glances, not to return them.

"Do introduce him; he ought to be interesting."

"Nobody more tiresome and dull, dear. But he is the fashion."

M. Armand de Montriveau, at that moment all unwittingly the object of general curiosity, better deserved attention than any of the idols that Paris needs must set up to worship for a brief space, for the city is vexed by periodical fits of craving, a passion for infatuation and sham enthusiasm, which must be satisfied. The marquis was the only son of General de Montriveau, one of the *ci-devants* who served the Republic nobly, and fell by Joubert's side at Novi. Bonaparte had placed his son at the school at Châlons, with the orphans of other generals who fell on the battlefield, leaving their children under the protection of the Republic. Armand de Montriveau left school with his way to make, entered the artillery, and had only reached a major's rank at the time of the Fontainebleau disaster. In his section of the service the chances of advancement were not many. There are fewer officers, in the first place, among the gunners than in any other corps; and in the second place, the feeling in the artillery was decidedly Liberal, not to say Republican; and the Emperor, feeling little confidence in a body of highly educated men who were apt to think for themselves, gave promotion grudgingly in the service. In the artillery, accordingly, the general rule of the army did not apply; the commanding officers were not invariably the most remarkable men in their department, because there was less to be feared from mediocrities. The artillery was a separate corps in those days, and only came under Napoleon in action.

Beside these general causes, other reasons, inherent in Armand de Montriveau's character, were sufficient in themselves to account for his tardy promotion. He was alone in the world. He had been thrown at the age of twenty into the whirlwind of men directed by Napoleon; his interests were bounded by himself, any day he might lose his life; it became a habit of mind with him to live by his own self-respect and the consciousness that he had done his duty. Like all shy men, he was habitually silent; but his shyness sprang by no means from timidity; it was a kind of modesty in him; he found any demonstration of vanity intolerable. There was no sort of swagger about his fearlessness in action; nothing escaped his eyes; he could give sensible advice to his chums with unshaken coolness; he could go under fire, and dodge upon occasion to avoid bullets. He was kindly; but his expression was haughty and stern, and his face gained him this character. In everything he was rigorous as arithmetic; he never permitted the slightest deviation from duty on any plausible pretext, nor blinked the consequences of a fact. He would lend himself to nothing of which he was ashamed; he never asked anything for himself: in short, Armand de Montriveau was one of many great men unknown to fame, and philosophical enough to despise it; living without attaching themselves to life, because they have not found their opportunity of developing to the full their power to do and feel.

People were afraid of Montriveau: they respected him, but he was not very popular. Men may indeed allow you to rise above them, but to decline to descend as low as they is the one unpardonable sin. In their feeling toward loftier natures, there is a trace of hate and fear. Too much honor with them implies censure of themselves, a thing forgiven neither to the living nor to the dead.

After the Emperor's farewell at Fontainebleau, Montriveau, noble though he was, was put on half-pay. Perhaps the heads of the War Office took fright at uncompromising uprightness worthy of antiquity, or perhaps it was known that he felt bound by his oath to the imperial eagle. During the Hundred Days he was made a colonel of the Guard, and left on the field of Waterloo. His wounds kept him in Belgium; he was not present at the disbanding of the Army of the Loire, but the King's government declined to recognize promotion made during the Hundred Days, and Armand de Montriveau left France.

An adventurous spirit, a loftiness of thought hitherto satisfied by the hazards of war, drove him on an exploring expedition through Upper Egypt; his sanity of impulse directed his enthusiasm to a project of great importance, he turned his attention to that unexplored Central Africa which occupies the learned of to-day. The scientific expedition was long and unfortunate. He had made a valuable collection of notes bearing on various geographical and commercial problems, of which solutions are still eagerly sought; and succeeded, after surmounting many obstacles, in reaching the heart of the continent, when he was betrayed into the hands of a hostile native tribe. Then, stripped of all that he had, for two years he led a wandering life in the desert, the slave of savages, threatened with death at every moment, and more cruelly treated than a dumb animal in the power of pitiless children. Physical strength, and a mind braced to endurance, enabled him to survive the horrors of that captivity; but his miraculous escape well-nigh exhausted his energies. When he reached the French colony at Senegal, a half-dead fugitive covered with rags, his memories of his former life were dim and shapeless. The great sacrifices made in his travels were all forgotten like his studies of African dialects, his discoveries, and observations. One story will give an idea of all that he passed through. Once for several days the children of the sheikh of the tribe amused themselves by putting him up for a mark and flinging horses' knuckle-bones at his head.

Montriveau came back to Paris in 1818 a ruined man. He had no interest, and wished for none. He would have died twenty times over sooner than ask a favor of any one; he would not even press the recognition of his claims. Adversity and hardship had developed his energy even in trifles, while the habit of preserving his self-respect before that spiritual self which we call conscience led him to attach consequence to the most apparently trivial actions. His merits and adventures became known, however, through his acquaintances, among the principal men of science in Paris, and some few well-read military men. The incidents of his slavery and subsequent escape bore witness to a courage, intelligence, and coolness which won him celebrity without his knowledge, and that transient fame of which Paris salons are lavish, though the artist that fain would keep it must make untold efforts.

Montriveau's position suddenly changed toward the end of that year. He had been a poor man, he was now rich; or, externally at any rate, he had all the advantages of wealth. The King's government, trying to attach capable men to itself and to strengthen the army, made concessions about that time to Napoleon's old officers if their known loyalty and character offered guarantees of fidelity. M. de Montriveau's name once more appeared in the army list with the rank of colonel; he received his arrears of pay and passed into the Guards. All these favors, one after another, came to seek the Marquis de Montriveau; he had asked for nothing, however small. Friends had taken the steps for him which he would have refused to take for himself.

After this, his habits were modified all at once; contrary to his custom, he went into society. He was well received, everywhere he met with great deference and respect. He seemed to have found some end in life; but everything passed within the man, there were no external signs; in society he was silent and cold, and wore a grave, reserved face. His social success was great, precisely because he stood out in such strong contrast to the conventional facts which line the walls of Paris salons. He was, indeed, something quite new there. Terse of speech, like a hermit or a savage, his shyness was thought to be haughtiness, and people were greatly taken with it. He was something strange and great. Women generally were so much the more smitten with this original person because he was not to be caught by their flatteries, however adroit, nor by the wiles with which they circumvent the strongest men and corrode the steel temper. Their Parisian grimaces were lost upon M. de Montriveau; his nature only responded to the sonorous vibration of lofty thought and feeling. And he would very promptly have been dropped but for the romance that hung about his adventures and his life; but for the men who cried him up behind his back; but for a woman who looked for a triumph for her vanity, the woman who was to fill his thoughts.

For these reasons the Duchesse de Langeais' curiosity was no less lively than natural. Chance had so ordered it that her interest in the man before her had been aroused only the day before, when she heard the story of one of M. de Montriveau's adventures, a story calculated to make the strongest impression upon a woman's ever-changing fancy.

During M. de Montriveau's voyage of discovery to the sources of the Nile, he had had an argument with one of his guides, surely the most extraordinary debate in the annals of travel. The district that he wished to explore could only be reached on foot across a tract of desert. Only one of his guides knew the way; no traveler had penetrated before into that part of the country, where the undaunted officer hoped to find a solution of several scientific problems. In spite of the representations made to him by the guide and the older men of the place, he started upon the formidable journey. Summoning up courage, already highly strung by the prospect of dreadful difficulties, he set out in the morning.

The loose sand shifted under his feet at every step; and when, at the end of a long day's march, he lay down to sleep on the ground, he had never been so tired in his life. He knew, however, that he must be up and on his way before dawn next day, and his guide assured him that they should reach the end of their journey toward noon. That promise kept up his courage and gave him new strength. In spite of his sufferings, he continued his march, with some blasphemings against science; he was ashamed to complain to his guide, and kept his pain to himself. After marching for a third of the day, he felt his strength failing, his feet were bleeding, he asked if they should reach the place soon. "In an hour's time," said the guide. Armand braced himself for another hour's march, and they went on.

The hour slipped by; he could not so much as see against the sky the palm-trees and crests of hill that should tell of the end of the journey near at hand; the horizon-line of sand was vast as the circle of the open sea.

He came to a stand, refused to go farther, and threatened the guide—he had deceived him, murdered him; tears of rage and weariness flowed over his fevered cheeks; he was bowed down with fatigue upon fatigue, his throat seemed to be glued by the desert thirst. The guide meanwhile stood motionless, listening to these complaints with an ironical expression, studying the while, with the apparent indifference of an Oriental, the scarcely perceptible indications in the lay of the sands, which looked almost black in its reflections, like burnished gold.

"I have made a mistake," he remarked coolly. "I could not make out the track, it is so long since I came this way; we are most surely on it now, but we must push on for two hours longer."

"The man is right," thought M. de Montriveau.

So he went on again, struggling to follow the pitiless native. It seemed as if he were bound to his guide by some cord like the invisible bond between the condemned man and the headsman. But the two hours went by, Montriveau had spent his last drops of energy, and the sky-line was a blank, there were no palm-trees, no hills. He could neither cry out nor groan, he lay down on the sand to die, but his eyes would have frightened the boldest; something in his face seemed to say that he would not die alone. His guide, like a very fiend, gave him back a cool glance like a man that knows his power, left him to lie there, and kept at a safe distance out of reach of his desperate victim. At last M. Montriveau recovered strength enough for a last curse. The guide came nearer, silenced him with a steady look, and said: "Was it not your own will to go where I am taking you, in spite of us all? You say that I have lied to you. If I had not, you would not be even here. Do you want the truth? Here it is: *We have still another five hours' march before us, and we cannot go back.* Sound yourself; if you have not courage enough, here is my dagger."

Startled by this dreadful knowledge of pain and human strength, M. de Montriveau would not be behind a savage; he drew a fresh stock of courage from his pride as a European, rose to his feet, and followed his guide. The five hours were at an end, and still M. de Montriveau saw nothing, he turned his failing eyes upon his guide; but the Nubian hoisted him on his shoulders, and showed him a wide pool of water with greenness all about it, and a noble forest lighted up by the sunset. It lay only a hundred paces away; a vast ledge of granite hid the glorious landscape. It seemed to Armand that he had taken a new lease of life. His guide, that giant in courage and intelligence, finished his work of devotion by carrying him across the hot, slippery, scarcely discernible track on the granite. Behind him lay the hell of burning

"SOUND YOURSELF, IF YOU HAVE THE COURAGE ENOUGH,
HERE IS MY DAGGER."

sand, before him the earthly paradise of the most beautiful oasis in the desert.

The duchess, struck from the first by the appearance of this romantic figure, was even more impressed when she learned that this was that Marquis de Montriveau of whom she had dreamed during the night. She had been with him among the hot desert sands, he had been the companion of her nightmare wanderings; for such a woman was not this a delightful presage of a new interest in her life? And never was a man's exterior a better exponent of his character; never were curious glances so well justified. The principal characteristic of his great, square-hewn head was the thick, luxuriant black hair which framed his face, and gave him a strikingly close resemblance to General Kléber; and the likeness still held good in the vigorous forehead, in the outlines of his face, the quiet fearlessness of his eyes, and a kind of fiery vehemence expressed by strongly marked features. He was short, deep-chested, and muscular as a lion. There was something of the despot about him, and an indescribable suggestion of the security of strength in his gait, bearing, and slightest movement. He seemed to know that his will was irresistible, perhaps because he willed only that which was right. And yet, like all really strong men, he was mild of speech, simple in his manners, and kindly natured; although it seemed as if, in the stress of a great crisis, all these finer qualities must disappear, and the man would show himself implacable, unshaken in his resolve, terrific in action. There was a certain drawing in of the inner line of the lips which, to a close observer, indicated an ironical bent.

The Duchesse de Langeais, realizing that a fleeting glory was to be won by such a conquest, made up her mind to gain a lover in Armand de Montriveau during the brief interval before the Duchesse de Maufrigneuse brought him to be introduced. She would prefer him above the others; she would attach him to herself, display all her powers of coquetry for him. It was a fancy, such a mere duchess' whim as furnished a Lope or a Calderon with the plot of the "Dog in the Manger." She would not suffer another woman to engross him; but she had not the remotest intention of being his.

Nature had given the duchess every qualification for the part of coquette, and education had perfected her. Women envied her, and men fell in love with her, not without reason. Nothing that can inspire love, justify it, and give it lasting empire was wanting in her. Her style of beauty, her manner, her voice, her bearing, all combined to give her that instinctive coquetry which seems to be the consciousness of power. Her shape was graceful; perhaps there was a trace of self-consciousness in her changes of movement, the one affectation that could be laid to her charge; but everything about her was a part of her personality, from her least little gesture to the peculiar turn of her phrases, the demure glance of her eyes. Her great lady's grace, her most striking characteristic, had not destroyed the very French quick mobility of her person. There was an extraordinary fascination in her swift, incessant changes of attitude. She seemed as if she surely would be a most delicious mistress when her corset and the encumbering costume of her part was laid aside. All the rapture of love surely was latent in the freedom of her expressive glances, in her caressing tones, in the charm of her words. She gave glimpses of the high-born courtesan within her, vainly protesting against the creeds of the duchess.

You might sit near her through an evening, she would be gay and melancholy in turn, and her gayety, like her sadness, seemed spontaneous. She could be gracious, disdainful, insolent, or confiding at will. Her apparent good-nature was real; she had no temptation to descend to malignity. But at each moment her mood changed; she was full of confidence or craft; her moving tenderness would give place to a heart-breaking hardness and insensibility. Yet how paint her as she was, without bringing together all the extremes of feminine nature? In a word, the duchess was anything that she wished to be or to seem. Her face was slightly too long. There was a grace in it, and a certain thinness and fineness that recalled the portraits of the Middle Ages. Her skin was white, with a faint rose tint. Everything about her erred, as it were, by an excess of delicacy.

M. de Montriveau willingly consented to be introduced to the Duchesse de Langeais; and she, after the manner of persons whose sensitive taste leads them to avoid banalities, refrained from overwhelming him with questions and compliments. She received him with a gracious deference which could not fail to flatter a man of more than ordinary powers, for the fact that a man rises above the ordinary level implies that he possesses something of that tact which makes women quick to read feeling. If the duchess showed any curiosity, it was by her glances; her compliments were conveyed in her manner; there was a winning grace displayed in her words, a subtle suggestion of a desire to please which she of all women knew the art of manifesting. Yet her whole conversation was but, in a manner, the body of the letter; the postscript with the principal thought in it was still to come. After half an hour spent in ordinary chat, in which the words gained all their value from her tone and smiles, M. de Montriveau was about to retire discreetly, when the duchess stopped him with an expressive gesture.

"I do not know, monsieur, whether these few minutes during which I have had the pleasure of talking to you proved so sufficiently attractive that I may venture to ask you to call upon me; I am afraid that it may be very selfish of me to wish to have you all to myself. If I should be so fortunate as to find that my house is agreeable to you, you will always find me at home in the evening until ten o'clock."

The invitation was given with such irresistible grace that M. de Montriveau could not refuse to accept it. When he fell back again among the groups of men gathered at a distance from the women, his friends congratulated him, half laughingly, half in earnest, on the extraordinary reception vouchsafed him by the Duchesse de Langeais. The difficult and brilliant conquest had been made beyond a doubt, and the glory of it was reserved for the Artillery of the Guard. It is easy to imagine the jests, good and bad, when this topic had once been started; the world of Paris salons is so eager for amusement, and a joke lasts for such a short time, that every one is eager to pluck the flower while it blooms.

All unconsciously, the general felt flattered by this nonsense. From his place where he had taken his stand, his eyes were drawn again and again to the duchess by countless wavering reflections. He could not help admitting to himself that of all the women whose beauty had captivated his eyes, not one had seemed to be a more exquisite embodiment of faults and fair qualities blended in a completeness that might realize the dreams of earliest manhood. Is there a man in any rank of life that has not felt indefinable rapture in his secret soul over the woman singled out (if only in his dreams) to be his own; when she, in body, soul, and social aspects, satisfies his every requirement, a thrice perfect woman? And if this threefold perfection that flatters his pride is no argument for loving her, it is beyond cavil one of the great inducements to the sentiment. Love would soon be convalescent, as the eighteenth-century moralist remarked, were it not for vanity. And it is certainly true that for every one, man or woman, there is a wealth of pleasure in the superiority of the beloved. Is she set so high by birth that a contemptuous glance can never wound her? is she wealthy enough to surround herself with state which falls nothing short of royalty of kings of finance during their short reign of splendor? is she so ready-witted that a keen-edged jest never brings her into confusion? beautiful enough to rival any woman? Is it such a small thing to know that your self-love will never suffer through her? A man makes these reflections in the twinkling of an eye. And how if, in the future opened out by early ripened passion, he catches glimpses of the changeful delight of her charm, the frank innocence of a maiden soul, the perils of love's voyage, the thousand folds of the veil of coquetry? Is not this enough to move the coldest man's heart?

This, therefore, was M. de Montriveau's position with regard to woman; his past life in some measure explaining the extraordinary fact. He had been thrown, when little more than a boy, into the hurricane of Napoleon's wars; his life had been spent on fields of battle. Of women he knew just so much as a traveler knows of a country when he travels across it in haste from one inn to another. The verdict which Voltaire passed upon his eighty years of life might, perhaps, have been applied by Montriveau to his own thirty-seven years of existence; had he not thirty-seven follies with which to reproach himself? At his age he was as much a novice in love as the lad that has just been furtively reading "Faublas." Of women he had nothing to learn; of love he knew nothing; and thus, desires, quite unknown before, sprang from this virginity of feeling.

There are men here and there as much engrossed in the work demanded of them by poverty or ambition, art or science, as M. de Montriveau by war and a life of adventure—these know what it is to be in this unusual position if they very seldom confess to it. Every man in Paris is supposed to have been in love. No woman in Paris cares to take what other women have passed over. The dread of being taken for a fool is the source of the coxcomb's bragging so common in France; for in France to have the reputation of a fool is to be a foreigner in one's own country. Vehement desire seized on M. de Montriveau, desire that had gathered strength from the heat of the desert and the first stirrings of a heart unknown as yet in its suppressed turbulence. A strong man, and violent as he was strong, he could keep mastery over himself; but as he talked of indifferent things, he retired within himself, and swore to possess this woman, for through that thought lay the only way to love for him. Desire became a solemn compact made with himself, an oath after the manner of the Arabs among whom he had lived; for among them a vow is a kind of contract made with Destiny, a man's whole future is solemnly pledged to fulfill it, and everything, even his own death, is regarded simply as a means to the one end.

A younger man would have said to himself: "I should very much like to have the duchess for my mistress!" or, "If the Duchesse de Langeais cared for a man, he would be a very lucky rascal!" But the general said: "I will have Madame de Langeais for my mistress." And if a man takes such an idea into his head when his heart has never been touched before, and love begins to be a kind of religion with him, he little knows into what a hell he has set his foot.

Armand de Montriveau suddenly took flight and went home in the first hot fever-fit of the first love that he had known. When a man has kept all his boyish beliefs, illusions, frankness, and impetuosity into middle age, his first impulse is, as it were, to stretch out a hand to take the thing that he desires; a little later he realizes that there is a gulf set between them, and that it is all but impossible to cross it. A sort of childish impatience seizes him, he wants the thing the more, and trembles or cries. Wherefore, the next day, after the stormiest reflections that had yet perturbed his mind, Armand de Montriveau discovered that he was under the yoke of the senses, and his bondage made the heavier by his love.

The woman so cavalierly treated in his thoughts of yesterday had become a most sacred and dreadful power. She was to be his world, his life, from this time forth. The greatest joy, the keenest anguish, that he had yet known grew colorless before the bare recollection of the least sensation stirred in him by her. The swiftest revolutions in a man's outward life only touch his interests, while passion brings a complete revulsion of feeling. And so in those who live by feeling, rather than by self-interest, the doers rather than the reasoners, the sanguine rather than the lymphatic temperaments, love works a complete revolution. In a flash, with one single reflection, Armand de Montriveau wiped out his whole past life.

A score of times he asked himself, like a boy: "Shall I go, or shall I not?" and then at last he dressed, went to the Hôtel de Langeais toward eight o'clock that evening, and was admitted. He was to see the woman—ah! not the woman—the idol that he had seen yesterday, among lights, a fresh innocent girl in gauze and silken lace and veiling. He burst in upon her to declare his love, as if it were a question of firing the first shot on a field of battle.

Poor novice! He found his ethereal sylphide shrouded in a brown cashmere dressing-gown ingeniously befrilled, lying languidly stretched out upon a divan in a dimly lighted boudoir. Mme. de Langeais did not so much as rise, nothing was visible of her but her face; her hair was loose but confined by a scarf. A hand indicated a seat, a hand that seemed white as marble to Montriveau by the flickering light of a single candle at the farther side of the room, and a voice as soft as the light said—

"If it had been any one else, Monsieur le Marquis, a friend with whom I could dispense with ceremony, or a mere acquaintance in whom I felt but slight interest, I should have closed my door. I am exceedingly unwell."

"I will go," Armand said to himself.

"But I do not know how it is," she continued (and the simple warrior attributed the shining of her eyes to fever), "perhaps it was a presentiment of your kind visit (and no one can be more sensible of the prompt attention than I), but the vapors have left my head."

"Then may I stay?"

"Oh, I should be very sorry to have you go. I told myself this morning that it was impossible that I should have made the slightest impression on your mind, and that in all probability you took my request for one of the commonplaces of which Parisians are lavish on every occasion. And I forgave your ingratitude in advance. An explorer from the deserts is not supposed to know how exclusive we are in our friendships in the faubourg."

The gracious, half-murmured words dropped one by one, as if they had been weighted with the gladness that apparently brought them to her lips. The duchess meant to have the full benefit of her headache, and her speculation was fully successful. The general, poor man, was really distressed by the lady's simulated distress. Like Crillon listening to the story of the Crucifixion, he was ready to draw his sword against the vapors. How could a man dare to speak just then to this suffering woman of the love that she inspired? Armand had already felt that it would be absurd to fire off a declaration of love point-blank at one so far above other women. With a single thought came understanding of the delicacies of feeling, of the soul's requirements. To love: what was that but to know how to plead, to beg for alms, to wait? And as for the love that he felt, must he not prove it? His tongue was mute, it was frozen by the conventions of the noble faubourg, the majesty of a sick headache, the bashfulness of love. But no power on earth could veil his glances; the heat and the Infinite of the desert blazed in eyes, calm as a panther's, beneath the lids that fell so seldom. The duchess enjoyed the steady gaze that enveloped her in light and warmth.

"Madame la Duchesse," he answered, "I am afraid I express my gratitude for your goodness very badly. At this moment I have but one desire—I wish it were in my power to cure the pain."

"Permit me to throw this off. I feel too warm now."

she said, gracefully tossing aside a cushion that covered her feet.

"Madame, in Asia your feet would be worth some ten thousand sequins."

"A traveler's compliment!" smiled she.

It pleased the sprightly lady to involve a rough soldier in a labyrinth of nonsense, commonplaces, and meaningless talk, in which he manœuvred, in military language, as Prince Charles* might have done at close quarters with Napoleon. She took a mischievous amusement in reconnoitring the extent of his infatuation by the number of foolish speeches extracted from a novice whom she led step by step into a hopeless maze, meaning to leave him there in confusion. She began by laughing at him, but nevertheless it pleased her to make him forget how time went.

The length of a first visit is frequently a compliment, but Armand was innocent of any such intent. The famous explorer spent an hour in chat on all sorts of subjects, said nothing that he meant to say, and was feeling that he was only an instrument on whom this woman played, when she rose, sat upright, drew the scarf from her hair, and wrapped it about her throat, leaned her elbow on the cushions, did him the honor of a complete cure, and rang for lights. The most graceful movements succeeded to complete repose. She turned to M. de Montriveau, from whom she had just extracted a confidence which seemed to interest her deeply, and said—

"You wish to make game of me by trying to make me believe that you have never loved. It is a man's great pretension with us. And we always believe it! Out of pure politeness. Do we not know what to expect from it for ourselves? Where is the man that has found but a single opportunity of losing his heart? But you love to deceive us, and we submit to be deceived, poor foolish creatures that we are; for your hypoc-

* Commander in chief of the Austrian army on the Rhine.

risy is, after all, a homage paid to the superiority of our sentiments, which are all purity."

The last words were spoken with a disdainful pride that made the novice in love feel like a worthless bale flung into the deep, while the duchess was an angel soaring back to her particular heaven.

"Confound it!" thought Armand de Montriveau, "how am I to tell this wild thing that I love her?"

He had told her already a score of times; or, rather, the duchess had a score of times read his secret in his eyes; and the passion in this unmistakably great man promised her amusement and an interest in her empty life. So she prepared with no little dexterity to raise a certain number of redoubts for him to carry by storm before he should gain an entrance into her heart. Montriveau should overleap one difficulty after another; he should be a plaything for her caprice, just as an insect teased by children is made to jump from one finger to another, and in spite of all its pains is kept in the same place by its mischievous tormentor. And yet it gave the duchess inexpressible happiness to see that this strong man had told her the truth. Armand had never loved, as he had said. He was about to go, in a bad humor with himself, and still more out of humor with her; but it delighted her to see a sullenness that she could conjure away with a word, a glance, or a gesture.

"Will you come to-morrow evening?" she asked. "I am going to a ball, but I shall stay at home for you until ten o'clock."

Montriveau spent most of the next day in smoking an indeterminate quantity of cigars in his study window, and so he got through the hours till he could dress and go to the Hôtel de Langeais. To any one who had known the magnificent worth of the man, it would have been grievous to see him grown so small, so distrustful of himself; the mind that might have shed light over undiscovered worlds shrunk to the proportions of a she-coxcomb's boudoir. Even he himself felt that he had fallen so low already in his happiness that to save his life he could not have told his love to one of his closest friends. Is there not always a trace of shame in the lover's bashfulness, and perhaps in woman a certain exultation over diminished masculine stature? Indeed, but for a host of motives of this kind, how explain why women are nearly always the first to betray the secret?—a secret of which, perhaps, they soon weary.

"Madame la Duchesse cannot yet see visitors, monsieur," said the man; "she is dressing, she begs you to wait for her here."

Armand walked up and down the drawing-room, studying her taste in the least details. He admired Mme. de Langeais herself in the objects of her choosing; they revealed her life before he could grasp her personality and ideas. About an hour later the duchess came noiselessly out of her chamber. Montriveau turned, saw her flit like a shadow across the room, and trembled. She came up to him, not with a bourgeoise's inquiry: "How do I look?" She was sure of herself; her steady eyes said plainly, "I am adorned to please you."

No one surely, save the old fairy godmother of some princess in disguise, could have wound a cloud of gauze about the dainty throat, so that the dazzling satin skin beneath should gleam through the gleaming folds. The duchess was dazzling. The pale blue color of her gown, repeated in the flowers in her hair, appeared by the richness of its hue to lend substance to a fragile form grown too wholly ethereal, for as she glided toward Armand, the loose ends of her scarf floated about her, putting that valiant warrior in mind of the bright, blue damosel flies* that hover now over water, now over the flowers with which they seem to mingle and blend.

"I have kept you waiting," she said, with the tone that a

* The *agrion*, a small blue dragon-fly.

woman can always bring into her voice for the man whom she wishes to please.

"I would wait patiently through an eternity," said he, "if I were sure of finding a divinity so fair; but it is no compliment to speak of your beauty to you; nothing save worship could touch you. Suffer me only to kiss your scarf."

"Oh, fie!" she said, with a commanding gesture, "I esteem you enough to give you my hand."

She held it out for his kiss. A woman's hand, still moist from the scented bath, has a soft freshness, a velvet smoothness that sends a tingling thrill from the lips to the soul. And if a man is attracted to a woman, and his senses are as quick to feel pleasure as his heart is full of love, such a kiss, though chaste in appearance, may conjure up a terrific storm.

"Will you always give it me thus?" the general asked humbly, when he had pressed that dangerous hand respectfully to his lips.

"Yes, but there we must stop," she said, smiling. She sat down, and seemed very slow over putting on her gloves, trying to slip the unstretched kid over all her fingers at once, while she watched M. de Montriveau; and he was lost in admiration of the duchess and those repeated graceful movements of hers.

"Ah! you were punctual," she said; "that is right. I like punctuality. It is the courtesy of kings, his majesty says; but to my thinking, from you men it is the most respectful flattery of all. Now, is it not? Just tell me."

Again she gave him a side-glance to express her insidious friendship, for he was dumb with happiness—sheer happiness through such nothings as these! Oh, the duchess understood *son métier de femme*—the art and mystery of being a woman— most marvelously well; she knew, to admiration, how to raise a man in his own esteem as he humbled himself to her; how to reward every step of the descent to sentimental folly with hollow flatteries.

"You will never forget to come at nine o'clock."

"No; but are you going to a ball every night?"

"Do I know?" she answered, with a little childlike shrug of the shoulders; the gesture was meant to say that she was nothing if not capricious, and that a lover must take her as she was. "Beside," she added, "what is that to you? You shall be my escort."

"That would be difficult to-night," he objected; "I am not properly dressed."

"It seems to me," she returned loftily, "that if any one has a right to complain of your costume, it is I. Know, therefore, *monsieur le voyageur*,* that if I accept a man's arm, he is forthwith above the laws of fashion, nobody would venture to criticise him. You do not know the world, I see; I like you the better for it."

And even as she spoke she swept him into the pettiness of that world by the attempt to initiate him into the vanities of a woman of fashion.

"If she chooses to do a foolish thing for me, I should be a simpleton to prevent her," said Armand to himself. "She has a liking for me beyond a doubt; and, as for the world, she cannot despise it more than I do. So, now for the ball if she likes."

The duchess probably thought that if the general came with her and appeared in a ballroom in boots and a black tie, nobody would hesitate to believe that he was violently in love with her. And the general was well pleased that the queen of fashion should think of compromising herself for him; hope gave him wit. He had gained confidence, he brought out his thoughts and views; he felt nothing of the restraint that weighed on his spirits yesterday. His talk was interesting and animated, and full of those first confidences so sweet to make and to receive.

Was Mme. de Langeais really carried away by his talk, or

* Mister Traveler.

had she devised this charming piece of coquetry? At any rate, she looked up mischievously as the clock struck twelve.

"Ah! you have made me too late for the ball!" she exclaimed, surprised and vexed that she had forgotten how time was going.

The next moment she approved the exchange of pleasures with a smile that made Armand's heart give a sudden leap.

"I certainly promised Madame de Beauséant," she added. "They are all expecting me."

"Very well—go."

"No—go on. I will stay. Your Eastern adventures fascinate me. Tell me the whole story of your life. I love to share in a brave man's hardships, and I feel them all, indeed I do!"

She was playing with her scarf, twisting it and pulling it to pieces, with jerky, impatient movements that seemed to tell of inward dissatisfaction and deep reflection.

"Women are fit for nothing," she went on. "Ah! we are contemptible, selfish, frivolous creatures. We can bore ourselves with amusements, and that is all we can do. Not one of us that understands that she has a part to play in life. In old days in France, women were beneficent lights; they lived to comfort those that mourned, to encourage high virtues, to reward artists and stir new life with noble thoughts. If the world has grown so petty, ours is the fault. You make me loathe the ball and this world in which I live. No, I am not giving up much for you."

She had plucked her scarf to pieces, as a child plays with a flower, pulling away all the petals one by one; and now she crushed it into a ball, and flung it away. She could show her swan's neck.

She rang the bell. "I shall not go out to-night," she told the footman. Her long, blue eyes turned timidly to Armand; and by the look of misgiving in them, he knew that he was meant to take the order for a confession, for a first and great favor. There was a pause, filled with many thoughts, before she spoke with that tenderness which is often in women's voices, and not so often in their hearts. "You have had a hard life," she said.

"No," returned Armand. "Until to-day I did not know what happiness was."

"Then you know it now?" she asked, looking at him with a demure, keen glance.

"What is happiness for me henceforth but this—to see you, to hear you? Until now I have only known privation; now I know that I can be unhappy——"

"That will do, that will do," she said. "You must go; it is past midnight. Let us regard appearances. People must not talk about us. I do not know quite what I shall say; but the headache is a good-natured friend, and tells no tales."

"Is there to be a ball to-morrow night?"

"You would grow accustomed to the life, I think. Very well. Yes, we will go to another ball to-morrow night."

There was not a happier man in the world than Armand when he went out from her. Every evening he came to Mme. de Langeais' at the hour kept for him by a tacit understanding.

It would be tedious, and, for the many young men who carry a redundance of such sweet memories in their hearts, it were superfluous to follow the story step by step—the progress of a romance growing in those hours spent together, a romance controlled entirely by a woman's will. If sentiment went too fast, she would raise a quarrel over a word, or when words flagged behind her thoughts, she appealed to the feelings. Perhaps the only way of following such Penelope's progress is by marking its outward and visible signs.

As, for instance, within a few days of their first meeting, the assiduous general had won and kept the right to kiss his lady's insatiable hands. Wherever Mme. de Langeais went, M. de Montriveau was certain to be seen, till people jokingly called him "her grace's orderly." And already he had made enemies; others were jealous, and envied him his position. Mme. de Langeais had attained her end. The Marquis de Montriveau was among her numerous train of adorers, and a means of humiliating those who boasted of their progress in her good graces, for she publicly gave him preference over them all.

"Decidedly, Monsieur de Montriveau is the man for whom the duchess shows a preference," pronounced Madame de Sérizy.

And who in Paris does not know what it means when a woman "shows a preference?" All went on therefore according to prescribed rule. The anecdotes which people were pleased to circulate concerning the general put that warrior in so formidable a light, that the more adroit quietly dropped their pretensions to the duchess, and remained in her train merely to turn the position to account, and to use her name and personality to make better terms for themselves with certain stars of the second magnitude. And those lesser powers were delighted to take a lover away from Mme. de Langeais. The duchess was keen-sighted enough to see these desertions and treaties with the enemy; and her pride would not suffer her to be the dupe of them. As M. de Talleyrand, one of her great admirers, said, she knew how to take a second edition of revenge, laying the two-edged blade of a sarcasm between the pairs in these "morganatic"* unions. Her mocking disdain contributed not a little to increase her reputation as an extremely clever woman and a person to be feared. Her character for virtue was consolidated while she amused herself with other people's secrets, and kept her own to herself. Yet, after two months of assiduities, she saw with a vague dread in the depths of her soul that M. de Montriveau understood nothing of the subtleties of flirtation after the manner of the Faubourg Saint-Germain; he was taking a Parisienne's coquetry in earnest.

* Left-handed.

"You will not tame *him*, dear duchess," the old Vidame de Pamiers had said. "'Tis a first cousin to the eagle; he will carry you off to his eyrie if you do not take care."

Then Mme. de Langeais felt afraid. The shrewd old noble's words sounded like a prophecy. The next day she tried to turn love to hate. She was harsh, exacting, irritable, unbearable; Montriveau disarmed her with angelic sweetness. She so little knew the great generosity of a large nature, that the kindly jests with which her first complaints were met went to her heart. She sought a quarrel, and found proofs of affection. She persisted.

"When a man idolizes you, how can he have vexed you?" asked Armand.

"You do not vex me," she answered, suddenly growing gentle and submissive. "But why do you wish to compromise me? For me you ought to be nothing but a *friend*. Do you not know it? I wish I could see that you had the instincts, the delicacy of real friendship, so that I might lose neither your respect nor the pleasure that your presence gives me."

"Nothing but your *friend!*" he cried out. The terrible word sent an electric shock through his brain. "On the faith of these happy hours that you grant me, I sleep and wake in your heart. And now to-day, for no reason, you are pleased to destroy all the secret hopes by which I live. You have required promises of such constancy in me, you have said so much of your horror of women made up of nothing but caprice; and now do you wish me to understand that, like other women here in Paris, you have passions, and know nothing of love? If so, why did you ask my life of me? why did you accept it?"

"I was wrong, my friend. Oh, it is wrong of a woman to yield to such intoxication when she must not and cannot make any return."

"I understand. You have been merely coquetting with me, and———"

"Coquetting?" she repeated. "I detest coquetry. A coquette, Armand, makes promises to many, and gives herself to none; and a woman who keeps such promises is a libertine. This much I believed I had grasped of our code. But to be melancholy with humorists, gay with the frivolous, and politic with ambitious souls; to listen to a babbler with every appearance of admiration, to talk of war with a soldier, wax enthusiastic with philanthropists over the good of the nation, and to give to each one his little dole of flattery—it seems to me that this is as much a matter of necessity as dress, diamonds, and gloves, or flowers in one's hair. Such talk is the moral counterpart of the toilet. You take it up and lay it aside with the plumed head-dress. Do you call this coquetry? Why, I have never treated you as I treat every one else. With you, my friend, I am sincere. Have I not always shared your views, and when you convinced me after a discussion was I not always perfectly glad? In short, I love you, but only as a devout and pure woman may love. I have thought it over. I am a married woman, Armand. My way of life with Monsieur de Langeais gives me liberty to bestow my heart; but law and custom leave me no right to dispose of my person. If a woman loses her honor, she is an outcast in any rank of life? and I have yet to meet with a single example of a man that realizes all that our sacrifices demand of him in such a case. Quite otherwise. Any one can foresee the rupture between Madame de Beauséant and Monsieur d'Ajuda (for he is going to marry Mademoiselle de Rochefide, it seems); that affair made it clear to my mind that these very sacrifices on the woman's part are almost always the cause of the man's desertion. If you had loved me sincerely, you would have kept away for a time. Now, I will lay aside all vanity for you; is not that something? What will not people say of a woman to whom no man attaches himself? Oh, she is heartless, brainless, soulless ; and what is more, devoid of charm ! Coquettes will not spare me. They will rob me of the very qualities that mortify them. So long as my reputation is safe, what do I care if my rivals deny my merits? They certainly will not inherit them. Come, my friend ; give up something for her who sacrifices so much for you. Do not come quite so often ; I shall love you none the less."

"Ah!" said Armand, with the profound irony of a wounded heart in his words and tone. "Love, so the scribblers say, only feeds on illusions. Nothing could be truer, I see ; I am expected to imagine that I am loved. But, there! —there are some thoughts like wounds, from which there is no recovery. My belief in you was one of the last left to me, and now I see that there is nothing left to believe in this earth."

She began to smile.

"Yes," Montriveau went on in an unsteady voice, "this Catholic faith to which you wish to convert me is a lie that men make for themselves; hope is a lie at the expense of the future ; pride, a lie between us and our fellows ; and pity, and prudence, and terror are cunning lies. And now my happiness is to be one more, lying delusion : I am expected to delude myself, to be willing to give gold coin for silver to the end. If you can so easily dispense with my visits; if you can confess me neither as your friend nor your lover, you do not care for me ! And I, poor fool that I am, tell myself this, and know it, and love you ! "

"But dear me, poor Armand, you are flying into a passion ! "

"I flying into a passion ? "

"Yes. You think that the whole thing is ended because I ask you to be careful."

In her heart of hearts she was delighted with the anger that leaped out in her lover's eyes. Even as she tortured him, she was criticising him, watching every slightest change that passed over his face. If the general had been so unluckily inspired as to show himself generous without discussion (as happens occasionally with some artless souls), he would have been a banished man for ever, accused and convicted of not knowing how to love. Most women are not displeased to have their code of right and wrong broken through. Do they not flatter themselves that they never yield except to force? But Armand was not learned enough in this kind of lore to see the limed snare so ingeniously spread for him by the knowing duchess. So much of the child was there in the strong man in love.

"If all you want is to preserve appearances," he began in his simplicity, "I am willing to——"

"Simply to preserve appearances!" the lady broke in; "why, what idea can you have of me? Have I given you the slightest reason to suppose that I can ever be yours?"

"Why, what else are we talking about?" demanded Montriveau.

"Monsieur, you frighten me! No, pardon me. Thank you," she added, coldly; "thank you, Armand. You have given me timely warning of imprudence; committed quite unconsciously, believe it, my friend. You know how to endure, you say. I also know how to endure. We will not see each other for a time; and then, when both of us have contrived to recover calmness to some extent, we will think about arrangements for a happiness sanctioned by the world. I am young, Armand; a man with no delicacy might tempt a woman of four-and-twenty to do many foolish, wild things for his sake. But you! You will be my friend, promise me that you will?"

"The woman of four-and-twenty," returned he, "knows what she is about."

He sat down on the divan in the boudoir, and leaned his head on his hands.

"Do you love me, madame?" he asked at length, raising

his head, and turning a face full of resolution upon her. "Say it straight out: Yes or No!"

His direct question dismayed the duchess more than a threat of suicide could have done; indeed, the woman of the century is not to be frightened by that stale stratagem, the sword has ceased to be a part of the masculine costume. But in the effect of eyelids and lashes, in the contraction of the gaze, in the twitching of the lips, is there not some influence that communicates the terror which they express with such vivid magnetic power?

"Ah, if I were free, if——"

"Oh! is it only your husband that stands in the way?" the general exclaimed joyfully, as he strode to and fro in the boudoir. "Dear Antoinette, I wield a more absolute power than the autocrat of all the Russias. I have a compact with Fate; I can advance or retard destiny, so far as men are concerned, at my fancy, as you alter the hands of a watch. If you can direct the course of fate in our political machinery, it simply means (does it not?) that you understand the ins and outs of it. You shall be free before very long, and then you must remember your promise."

"Armand!" she cried. "What do you mean? Great heavens! Can you imagine that I am to be the prize of a crime? Do you want to kill me? Why! you cannot have any religion in you! For my own part, I fear God. Monsieur de Langeais may have given me reason to hate him, but I wish him no manner of harm."

M. de Montriveau beat a tattoo on the marble mantel, and only looked composedly at the lady.

"Dear," continued she, "respect him. He does not love me, he is not kind to me, but I have duties to perform with regard to him. What would I not do to avert the calamities with which you threaten him? Listen." she continued after a pause, "I will not say another word about separation; you shall come here as in the past, and I will still give you my forehead to kiss. If I refused once or twice, it was pure coquetry, indeed it was. But let us understand each other," she added as he came closer. "You will permit me to add to the number of my satellites, to receive even more visitors in the morning than heretofore; I mean to be twice as frivolous, I mean to use you to all appearance very badly; to feign a rupture; you must come not quite so often, and then, afterward——"

While she spoke she had allowed him to put an arm about her waist, Montriveau was holding her tightly to him, and she seemed to feel the exceeding pleasure that women usually feel in that close contact, an earnest of the bliss of a closer union. And then, doubtless, she meant to elicit some confidence, for she raised herself on tiptoe, and laid her forehead against Armand's burning lips.

"And then," Montriveau finished her sentence for her, "you shall not speak to me of your husband. You ought not to think of him again."

Mme. de Langeais was silent awhile.

"At least," she said, after a significant pause, "at least you will do all that I wish without grumbling, you will not be naughty; tell me so, my friend? You wanted to frighten me, did you not? Come now, confess it. You are too good ever to think of crimes. But is it possible that you can have secrets that I do not know? How can you control Fate?"

"Now, when you confirm the gift of the heart that you have already given me, I am far too happy to know exactly how to answer you. I can trust you, Antoinette; I shall have no suspicion, no unfounded jealousy of you. *But* if accident should set you free, we shall be one——"

"Accident, Armand?" (with that little dainty turn of the head that seems to say so many things, a gesture that such women as the duchess can use on light occasions, as a great singer can act with her voice). "Pure accident!" she repeated. "Mind that. If anything should happen to Monsieur de Langeais by your fault, I should never be yours," she added as a parting shot.

And so they parted, mutually content. The duchess had made a pact that left her free to prove to the world by words and deeds that M. de Montriveau was no lover of hers. And as for him, the wily duchess vowed to tire him out. He should have nothing of her beyond the little concessions snatched in the course of contests that she could incite or stop at her pleasure. She had so pretty an art of revoking the grant of yesterday, she was so much in earnest in her purpose to remain technically virtuous, that she felt that there was not the slightest danger for her in preliminaries fraught with peril for a woman less sure of her self-command. After all, the duchess was practically separated from her husband, a marriage long since annulled was no great sacrifice to make to her love.

Montriveau on his side was quite happy to win the vaguest promise, glad once for all to sweep aside, with all scruples of conjugal fidelity, her stock of excuses for refusing herself to his love. He had gained ground a little, and congratulated himself And so for a time he took unfair advantage of the rights so hardily won. More a boy than he had ever been in his life, he gave himself up to all the childishness that makes first love the flower of life. He was a child again as he poured out all his soul, all the thwarted forces that passion had given him, upon her hands, upon the dazzling forehead that looked so pure to his eyes; upon her fair hair; on the tufted curls where his lips were pressed. And the duchess, on whom his love was poured like a flood, was vanquished by the magnetic influence of her lover's warmth; she hesitated to begin the quarrel that must part them for ever. She was more a woman than she thought, this slight creature, in her effort to reconcile the demands of religion with the ever-new sensations of vanity, the semblance of pleasure which turns a Parisienne's head. Every Sunday she went to mass; she never missed a service; then, when evening came, she was

steeped in the intoxicating bliss of repressed desire. Armand
and Mme. de Langeais, like Hindoo fakirs, found the reward
of their continence in the temptations to which it gave rise.
Possibly, the duchess had ended by resolving love into frater-
nal caresses, harmless enough, as it might have seemed to the
rest of the world, while they borrowed extremes of degradation from the license of her thoughts. How else explain
the incomprehensible mystery of her continual fluctuations?
Every morning she proposed to herself to shut her door on
the Marquis de Montriveau; every evening, at the appointed
hour, she fell under the charm of his presence. There was a
languid defense; then she grew less unkind. Her words were
sweet and soothing. They were lovers—lovers only could
have been thus. For him the duchess would display her most
sparkling wit, her most captivating wiles; and when at last
she had wrought upon his senses and his soul, she might submit herself passively to his fierce caresses, but she had her
ne plus ultra of passion; and when once it was reached, she
grew angry if he lost the mastery of himself and made as
though he would pass beyond. No woman on earth can
brave the consequences of refusal without some motive; nothing is more natural than to yield to love; wherefore Mme. de
Langeais promptly raised a second line of fortification, a
stronghold less easy to carry than the first. She evoked the
terrors of religion. Never did father of the church, however
eloquent, plead the cause of God better than the duchess.
Never was the wrath of the Most High better proclaimed than
by her voice. She used no preacher's commonplaces, no
rhetorical amplifications. No. She had a "pulpit-tremor"
of her own. To Armand's most passionate entreaty, she replied with a tearful gaze, and a gesture in which a terrible
plenitude of emotion found expression. She stopped his
mouth with an appeal for mercy. She would not hear
another word; if she did, she must succumb; and better
death than criminal happiness.

"Is it nothing to disobey God?" she asked him, recovering a voice grown faint in the crises of inward struggles, through which the fair actress appeared to find it hard to preserve her self-control. "I would sacrifice society, I would give up the whole world for you, gladly; but it is very selfish of you to ask my whole after-life of me for a moment of pleasure. Come, now! are you not happy?" she added, holding out her hand; and certainly in her careless toilette the sight of her afforded consolations to her lover, who made the most of them.

Sometimes from policy, to keep her hold on a man whose ardent passion gave her emotions unknown before, sometimes in weakness, she suffered him to snatch a swift kiss; and immediately, in feigned terror, she flushed red and exiled Armand from the lounge so soon as it became dangerous ground.

"Your joys are sins for me to expiate, Armand; they are paid for by penitence and remorse," she cried.

And Montriveau, now at two chairs' distance from that aristocratic petticoat, betook himself to blasphemy and railed against Providence. The duchess grew angry at such times.

"My friend," she would say drily, "I do not understand why you decline to believe in God, for it is impossible to believe in man. Hush, do not talk like that. You have too great a nature to take up their Liberal nonsense with its pretension to abolish God."

Theological and political disputes acted like a cold douche on Montriveau; he calmed down; he could not return to love when the duchess stirred up his wrath by suddenly setting him down a thousand miles away from the boudoir, discussing theories of absolute monarchy, which she defended to admiration. Few women venture to be democrats; the attitude of democratic champion is scarcely compatible with tyrannous feminine sway. But often, on the other hand, the general shook out his mane, dropped politics with a leonine growling and lashing of the flanks, and sprang upon his prey; he was no longer capable of carrying a heart and brain at such variance for very far; he came back, terrible with love, to his mistress. And she, if she felt the prick of fancy stimulated to a dangerous point, knew that it was time to leave her boudoir; she came out of the atmosphere surcharged with desires that she drew in with her breath, sat down to the piano, and sang the most exquisite songs of modern music, and so baffled the physical attraction which at times showed her no mercy, though she was strong enough to fight it down.

At such times she was something sublime in Armand's eyes; she was not acting, she was genuine; the unhappy lover was convinced that she loved him. Her egoistic resistance deluded him into a belief that she was a pure and sainted woman; he resigned himself; he talked of Platonic love, did this artillery officer!

When Mme. de Langeais had played with religion sufficiently to suit her own purposes, she played with it again for Armand's benefit. She wanted to bring him back to a Christian frame of mind; she brought out her edition of "The Genius of Christianity," adapted for the use of military men. Montriveau chafed; his yoke was heavy. Oh! at that, possessed by the spirit of contradiction, she dinned religion into his ears, to see whether God might not rid her of this suitor, for the man's persistence was beginning to frighten her. And in any case she was glad to prolong any quarrel, if it bade fair to keep the dispute on moral grounds for an indefinite period; the material struggle which followed it was more dangerous.

But if the time of her opposition on the ground of the marriage law might be said to be the civil epoch of this sentimental warfare, the ensuing phase which might be taken to constitute the religious epoch had also its crisis and consequent decline of severity.

Armand, happening to come in very early one evening, found M. l'Abbé Gondrand, the duchess' spiritual director, established in an armchair by the fireside, looking as a spiritual director might be expected to look while digesting his dinner and the charming sins of his penitent. In the ecclesiastic's bearing there was a stateliness befitting a dignitary of the church; and the episcopal violet hue already appeared in his dress. At sight of his fresh, well-preserved complexion, smooth forehead, and ascetic's mouth, Montriveau's countenance grew uncommonly dark; he said not a word under the malicious scrutiny of the other's gaze, and greeted neither the lady nor the priest. The lover apart, Montriveau was not wanting in tact; so a few glances exchanged with the bishop-designate told him that here was the real forger of the duchess' armory of scruples.

That an ambitious abbé should control the happiness of a man of Montriveau's temper, and by underhand ways! The thought burst in a furious tide over his face, clenched his fists, and set him chafing and pacing to and fro; but when he came back to his place intending to make a scene, a single look from the duchess was enough. He was quiet.

Any other woman would have been put out by her lover's gloomy silence; it was quite otherwise with Mme. de Langeais. She continued her conversation with M. de Gondrand on the necessity of reëstablishing the church in its ancient splendor. And she talked brilliantly. The church, she maintained, ought to be a temporal as well as a spiritual power, stating her case better than the abbé had done, and regretting that the Chamber of Peers, unlike the English House of Lords, had no bench of bishops. Nevertheless, the abbé rose, yielded his place to the general, and took his leave, knowing that in Lent he could play a return game. As for the duchess, Montriveau's behavior had excited her curiosity to such a pitch that she scarcely rose to return her director's low bow.

"What is the matter with you, my friend?"

"Why, I cannot stomach that abbé of yours."

"Why did you not take a book?" she asked, careless whether the abbé, then closing the door, heard her or not.

The general paused, for the gesture which accompanied the duchess' speech further increased the exceeding insolence of her words.

"My dear Antoinette, thank you for giving love precedence of the church; but, for pity's sake, allow me to ask one question——"

"Oh! you are questioning me! I am quite willing. You are my friend, are you not? I certainly can open the bottom of my heart to you; you will see only one image there."

"Do you talk about our love to that man?"

"He is my confessor."

"Does he know that I love you?"

"Monsieur de Montriveau, you cannot claim, I think, to penetrate the secrets of the confessional?"

"Does that man know all about our quarrels and my love for you?——"

"That man, monsieur; say God!"

"God again! I ought to be alone in your heart. But leave God alone where He is, for the love of God and me. Madame, you *shall not* go to confession again, or——"

"Or?" she repeated sweetly.

"Or I will never come back here."

"Then go, Armand. Farewell, farewell for ever."

She arose and went to her boudoir without so much as a glance at Armand, as he stood with his hand on the back of a chair. How long he stood there motionless he himself never knew. The soul within has the mysterious power of expanding as of contracting space.

He opened the door of the boudoir. It was dark within. A faint voice was raised to say sharply—

"I did not ring. What made you come in without orders? Go away, Suzette."

"Then you suffer," exclaimed Montriveau.

"Stand up, monsieur, and go out of the room for a minute at any rate," she said, ringing the bell.

"Madame la Duchesse rang for lights," said he to the footman, coming in with the candles. When the lovers were alone together, Mme. de Langeais still lay on her couch; she was just as silent and motionless as if Montriveau had not been there.

"Dear, I was wrong," he began, a note of pain and a sublime kindness in his voice. "Indeed, I would not have you without religion——"

"It is fortunate that you can recognize the necessity of a conscience," she said in a hard voice, without looking at him. "I thank you in God's name."

The general was broken down by her harshness; this woman seemed as if she could be at will a sister or a stranger to him. He made one despairing stride toward the door. He would leave her forever without another word. He was wretched; and the duchess was laughing within herself over mental anguish far more cruel than the old judicial torture. But as for going away, it was not in his power to do it. In any sort of crisis, a woman is, as it were, bursting with a certain quantity of things to say; so long as she has not delivered herself of them, she experiences the sensation which we are apt to feel at the sight of something incomplete. Mme. de Langeais had not said all that was in her mind. She took up her parable and said—

"We have not the same convictions, general, I am pained to think. It would be dreadful if a woman could not believe in a religion which permits us to love beyond the grave. I set Christian sentiments aside; you cannot understand them. Let me simply speak to you of expediency. Would you forbid a woman at Court the table of the Lord, for which confession is necessary, when it is customary to take the sacrament at Easter? People must certainly do something for their party. The Liberals, whatever they may wish to do, will never destroy the religious instinct. Religion will always be a political necessity. Would you undertake to govern a nation of logic-choppers? Napoleon was afraid to try; he persecuted ideologists. If you want to keep people from reasoning, you must give them something to feel. So let us accept the Roman Catholic Church with all its consequences. And if we would have France go to mass, ought we not to begin by going ourselves? Religion, you see, Armand, is a bond uniting all the conservative principles which enable the rich to live in tranquillity. Religion and the rights of property are intimately connected. It is certainly a finer thing to lead a nation by ideas of morality than by fear of the scaffold, as in the time of the Terror—the one method by which your odious Revolution could enforce obedience. The priest and the King—that means you, and me, and the princess my neighbor; and, in a word, the interests of all honest people personified. There, my friend, just be so good as to belong to your party, you that might be its Sulla if you had the slightest ambition that way. I know nothing about politics myself; I argue from my own feelings; but still I know enough to guess that society would be overturned if people were always calling its foundations in question——"

"If that is how your Court and your Government think, I am sorry for you," broke in Montriveau. "The Restoration, madame, ought to say, like Catherine dei Medici, when she heard that the battle of Dreux was lost: 'Very well; now we will go to their meeting-houses.' Now 1815 was your battle of Dreux. Like the royal power of those days, you won in fact, while you lost in right. Political Protestantism has gained an ascendency over people's minds. If you have no mind to issue your Edict of Nantes; or if, when it is issued, you publish a Revocation; if you should one day be accused and convicted of repudiating the Charter, which is simply a pledge given to maintain the interests established under the

Republic, then the Revolution will rise again, terrible in her strength, and strike but a single blow. It will not be the Revolution that will go into exile; she is the very soil of France. Men die, but people's interests do not die—— Eh, great heavens! what are France and the crown and rightful sovereigns, and the whole world beside, to us? Idle words compared with my happiness. Let them reign or be hurled from the throne, little do I care. Where am I now?"

"In the Duchesse de Langeais' boudoir, my friend."

"No, no. No more of the duchess, no more of Langeais; I am with my dear Antoinette."

"Will you do me the pleasure to stay where you are," she said, laughing and pushing him back, gently however.

"So you have never loved me," he retorted, and anger flashed in lightning from his eyes.

"No, dear;" but the "No" was equivalent to "Yes."

"I am a great ass," he said, kissing her hands. The terrible queen was a woman once more. "Antoinette," he went on, laying his head on her feet, "you are too chastely tender to speak of our happiness to any one in this world."

"Oh!" she cried, rising to her feet with a swift, graceful spring, "you are a great simpleton." And without another word she fled into the drawing-room.

"What is it now?" wondered the general, little knowing that the touch of his burning forehead had sent a swift electric thrill through her from foot to head.

In hot wrath he followed her to the drawing-room, only to hear divinely sweet chords. The duchess was at the piano. If the man of science or the poet can at once enjoy and comprehend, bringing his intelligence to bear upon his enjoyment without loss of delight, he is conscious that the alphabet and phraseology of music are but cunning instruments for the composer, like the wood and copper wire under the hands of the executant. For the poet and the man of science there is a music existing apart, underlying the double expression of this language of the spirit and senses. *Andiamo mio ben* can draw tears of joy or pitying laughter at the will of the singer; and not infrequently one here and there in the world, some girl unable to live and bear the heavy burden of an unguessed pain, some man whose soul vibrates with the throb of passion, may take up a musical theme, and lo! heaven is opened for them, or they find a language for themselves in some sublime melody, some song lost to the world.

The general was listening now to such a song; a mysterious music unknown to all other ears, as the solitary plaint of some mateless bird dying alone in a virgin forest.

"Great heavens! what are you playing there?" he asked in an unsteady voice.

"The prelude of a ballad, called, I believe, 'Fleuve du Tage.'"

"I did not know that there was such music in a piano," he returned.

"Ah!" she said, and for the first time she looked at him as a woman looks at the man she loves, "nor do you know, my friend, that I love you, and that you cause me horrible suffering; and that I feel that I must utter my cry of pain without putting it too plainly into words. If I did not I should yield—— But you see nothing."

"And you will not make me happy!"

"Armand, I should die of sorrow the next day."

The general turned abruptly from her and went. But out in the street he brushed away the tears that he would not let fall.

The religious phase lasted for three months. At the end of that time the duchess grew weary of vain repetitions; the church, bound hand and foot, was delivered up to her lover. Possibly she may have feared that by sheer dint of talking of eternity she might perpetuate his love in this world and the next. For her own sake, it must be believed that no man had touched her heart, or her conduct would be inexcusable. She was young; the time when men and women feel that they cannot afford to lose time or to quibble over their joys was still far off. She, no doubt, was on the verge not of first love, but of her first experience of the bliss of love. And from inexperience, for want of the painful lessons which would have taught her to value the treasure poured out at her feet, she was playing with it. Knowing nothing of the glory and rapture of the light, she was fain to stay in the shadow.

Armand was just beginning to understand this strange situation; he put his hope in the first word spoken by nature. Every evening, as he came away from Mme. de Langeais', he told himself that no woman would accept the tenderest, most delicate proofs of a man's love during seven months, nor yield passively to the slighter demands of passion, only to cheat love at the last. He was waiting patiently for the sun to gain power, not doubting but that he should receive the earliest fruits. The married woman's hesitations and the religious scruples he could quite well understand. He even rejoiced over those battles. He mistook the duchess' heartless coquetry for modesty; and he would not have had her otherwise. So he had loved to see her devising obstacles; was he not gradually triumphing over them? Did not every victory won swell the meagre sum of lovers' intimacies long denied, and at last conceded with every sign of love? Still, he had had such leisure to taste the full sweetness of every small successive conquest on which a lover feeds his love, that these had come to be matters of use and wont. So far as obstacles went, there were none now save his own awe of her; nothing else left between him and his desire save the whims of her who allowed him to call her Antoinette. So he made up his mind to demand more, to demand all. Embarrassed like a young lover who cannot dare to believe that his idol can stoop so low, he hesitated for a long time. He passed through the experience of terrible reactions within himself. A set purpose was annihilated by a word, and definite resolves died within him on the threshold. He despised himself for his weakness, and still his desire remained unuttered.

Nevertheless, one evening, after sitting in gloomy melancholy, he brought out a fierce demand for his illegally legitimate rights. The duchess had not to wait for her bond-slave's request to guess his desire. When was a man's desire a secret? And have not women an intuitive knowledge of the meaning of certain changes of countenance?

"What! you wish to be my friend no longer?" she broke in at the first words, and a divine red surging like new blood under the transparent skin lent brightness to her eyes. "As a reward for my generosity, you would dishonor me? Just reflect a little. I myself have thought much over this; and I think always for us *both*. There is such a thing as a woman's loyalty, and we can no more fail in it than you can fail in honor. I cannot bind myself. If I am yours, how, in any sense, can I be Monsieur de Langeais' wife? Can you require the sacrifice of my position, my rank, my whole life, in return for a doubtful love that could not wait patiently for seven months? What! already you would rob me of my right to dispose of myself? No, no; you must not talk like this again. No, not another word. I will not, I cannot listen to you."

Mme. de Langeais raised both hands to her head to push back the tufted curls from her hot forehead; she seemed very much excited.

"You come to a weak woman with your purpose definitely planned out. You say—'For a certain length of time she will talk to me of her husband, then of God, and then of the inevitable consequences. But I will use and abuse the ascendency I shall gain over her; I will make myself indispensable; all the bonds of habit, all the misconstructions of outsiders, will make for me; and at length, when our *liaison* is taken for granted by all the world, I shall be this woman's master.' Now, be frank, these are your thoughts! Oh! you calculate, and you say that you love. Shame on you! You are enamored? Ah! that I well believe! You wish to possess me, to have me for your mistress, that is all! Very well then, No! The *Duchesse de Langeais* will not descend so far. Simple *bourgeoises* may be the victims of your treachery—I, never! Nothing gives me assurance of your love. You speak of my beauty; I may lose every trace of it in six months, like the dear princess, my neighbor. You are captivated by my wit, my grace. Great heavens! you would soon grow used to them and to the pleasures of possession. Have not the little concessions that I was weak enough to make come to be a matter of course in the last few months? Some day, when ruin comes, you will give me no reason for the change in you beyond a curt: 'I have ceased to care for you.' Then, rank and fortune and honor and all that was the Duchesse de Langeais will be swallowed up in one disappointed hope. I shall have children to bear witness to my shame, and——" With an involuntary gesture she interrupted herself, and continued: "But I am too good-natured to explain all this to you when you know it better than I. Come! let us stay as we are. I am only too fortunate in that I can still break these bonds which you think so strong. Is there anything so very heroic in coming to the Hôtel de Langeais to spend an evening with a woman whose prattle amuses you?—a woman whom you take for a plaything? Why, half-a-dozen young coxcombs come here just as regularly every afternoon between three and five. They, too, are very generous, I am to suppose? I make fun of them; they stand my petulance and insolence pretty quietly, and make me laugh; but as for you, I give all the treasures of my soul to you, and you wish to ruin me—you try my patience in endless ways. Hush, that will do, that will do," she continued, seeing that he was about to speak, "you have no heart, no soul, no delicacy. I know what you want to tell me. Very well, then—

yes. I would rather you should take me for a cold, insensible woman, with no devotion in her composition, no heart even, than be taken by everybody else for a vulgar person, and be condemned to your so-called pleasures, of which you would most certainly tire, and to everlasting punishment for it afterward. Your selfish love is not worth so many sacrifices."

The words give but a very inadequate idea of the discourse which the duchess trilled out with the quick volubility of a bird-organ. Nor, truly, was there anything to prevent her from talking on for some time to come, for poor Armand's only reply to the torrent of flute notes was a silence filled with cruelly painful thoughts. He was just beginning to see that this woman was playing with him; he divined instinctively that a devoted love, a responsive love, does not reason and count the consequences in this way. Then, as he heard her reproach him with detestable motives, he felt something like shame as he remembered that unconsciously he had made those very calculations. With angelic honesty of purpose, he looked within, and self-examination found nothing but selfishness in all his thoughts and motives, in the answers which he framed and could not utter. He was self-convicted. In his despair he longed to fling himself from the window. The egoism of it was intolerable.

What indeed can a man say when a woman will not believe in love? Let me prove how much I love you. The *I* is always there.

The heroes of the boudoir, in such circumstances, can follow the example of the primitive logician who preceded the Pyrrhonists and denied movement. Montriveau was not equal to this feat. With all his audacity, he lacked that precise kind which never deserts an adept in the formulas of feminine algebra. If so many women, and even the best of women, fall a prey to a kind of expert to whom the vulgar give a grosser name, it is perhaps because the said experts are great *provers*, and love, in spite of its delicious poetry of sentiment, requires a little more geometry than the generality of people are wont to think.

Now the duchess and Montriveau were alike in this—they were both equally unversed in love lore. The lady's knowledge of theory was but scanty; in practice she knew nothing whatever; she felt nothing, and reflected over everything. Montriveau had had but little experience, was absolutely ignorant of theory, and felt too much to reflect at all. Both therefore were enduring the consequences of the singular situation. At that supreme moment the myriad thoughts in his mind might have been reduced to the formula—"Submit to be mine——" words which seem horribly selfish to a woman for whom they awaken no memories, recall no ideas. Something nevertheless he must say. And what was more, though her barbed shafts had set his blood tingling, though the short phrases that she discharged at him one by one were very keen and sharp and cold, he must control himself lest he should lose all by an outbreak of anger.

"Madame la Duchesse, I am in despair that God should have invented no way for a woman to confirm the gift of her heart save by adding the gift of her person. The high value which you yourself put upon the gift teaches me that I cannot attach less importance to it. If you have given me your inmost self and your whole heart, as you tell me, what can the rest matter? And beside, if my happiness means so painful a sacrifice, let us say no more about it. But you must pardon a man of spirit if he feels humiliated at being taken for a spaniel."

The tone in which the last remark was uttered might perhaps have frightened another woman; but when the wearer of a petticoat has allowed herself to be addressed as a divinity, and thereby set herself above all other mortals, no power on earth can be so haughty.

"Monsieur le Marquis, I am in despair that God should not have invented some nobler way for a man to confirm the gift of his heart than by the manifestation of prodigiously vulgar desires. We become bond-slaves when we give ourselves body and soul, but a man is bound to nothing by accepting the gift. Who will assure me that love will last? The very love that I might show for you at every moment, the better to keep your love, might serve you as a reason for deserting me. I have no wish to be a second edition of Madame de Beauséant. Who can ever know what it is that keeps you beside us? Our persistent coldness of heart is the cause of an unfailing passion in some of you; other men ask for an untiring devotion, to be idolized at every moment; some for gentleness, others for tyranny. No woman in this world as yet has really read the riddle of man's heart."

There was a pause. When she spoke again it was in a different tone.

"After all, my friend, you cannot prevent a woman from trembling at the question: 'Will this love last always?' Hard though my words may be, the dread of losing you puts them into my mouth. Oh, me! it is not I who speaks, dear, it is reason; and how should any one so mad as I be reasonable? In truth, I am nothing of the sort."

The poignant irony of her answer had changed before the end into the most musical accents in which a woman could find utterance for ingenuous love. To listen to her words was to pass in a moment from martyrdom to heaven. Montriveau grew pale; and for the first time in his life he fell on his knees before a woman. He kissed the duchess' skirt hem, her knees, her feet; but for the credit of the Faubourg Saint-Germain it is necessary to respect the mysteries of its boudoirs, where many are fain to take the utmost that Love can give without giving proof of love in return.

The duchess thought herself generous when she suffered herself to be adored. But Montriveau was in a wild frenzy of joy over her complete surrender of the position.

"Dear Antoinette," he cried. "Yes, you are right; I will

not have you doubt any longer. I too am trembling at this moment—lest the angel of my life should leave me; I wish I could invent some tie that might bind us to each other irrevocably."

"Ah!" she said, under her breath, "so I was right, you see."

"Let me say all that I have to say; I will scatter all your fears with a word. Listen! if I deserted you, I should deserve to die a thousand deaths. Be wholly mine, and I will give you the right to kill me if I am false. I myself will write a letter explaining certain reasons for taking my own life; I will make my final arrangements, in short. You shall have the letter in your keeping; in the eye of the law it will be a sufficient explanation of my death. You can avenge yourself, and fear nothing from God or men."

"What good would the letter be to me? What would life be if I had lost your love? If I wished to kill you, should I not be ready to follow? No, thank you for the thought, but I do not want the letter. Should I not begin to dread that you were faithful to me through fear? And if a man knows that he must risk his life for a stolen pleasure, might it not seem more tempting? Armand, the thing I ask of you is the one hard thing to do."

"Then what is it that you wish?"

"Your obedience and my liberty."

"Ah, God!" cried he, "I am a child."

"A wayward, much-spoilt child," she said, stroking the thick hair, for his head still lay on her knee. "Ah! and loved far more than he believes, and yet he is very disobedient. Why not stay as we are? Why not sacrifice to me the desires that hurt me? Why not take what I can give, when it is all that I can honestly grant? Are you not happy, Armand?"

"Oh yes, I am happy when I have not a doubt left. Antoinette, doubt in love is a kind of death, is it not?"

In a moment he showed himself as he was, as all men are under the influence of that hot fever; he grew eloquent, insinuating. And the duchess tasted the pleasures which she reconciled with her conscience by some private, jesuitical ukase of her own; Armand's love gave her a thrill of cerebral excitement which custom made as necessary to her as society, or the opera. To feel that she was adored by this man, who rose above other men, whose character frightened her; to treat him like a child; to play with him as Poppæa played with Nero—many women, like the wives of King Henry VIII., have paid for such a perilous delight with all the blood in their veins. Grim presentiment! Even as she surrendered the delicate, pale, gold curls to his touch, and felt the close pressure of his hand, the little hand of a man whose greatness she could not mistake; even as she herself played with his dark, thick locks, in that boudoir where she reigned a queen, the duchess would say to herself—

"This man is capable of killing me if he once finds out that I am playing with him."

Armand de Montriveau stayed with her till two o'clock in the morning. From that moment this woman, whom he loved, was neither a duchess nor a Navarreins; Antoinette, in her disguises, had gone so far as to appear to be a woman. On that most blissful evening, the sweetest prelude ever played by a Parisienne to what the world calls "a slip;" in spite of all her affectations of a coyness which she did not feel, the general saw all maidenly beauty in her. He had some excuse for believing that so many storms of caprice had been but clouds covering a heavenly soul; that these must be lifted one by one like the veils that hid her divine loveliness. The duchess became, for him, the most simple and girlish mistress; she was the one woman in the world for him; and he went away quite happy in that at last he had brought her to give him such pledges of love that it seemed to him impossible but that he should be but her husband henceforth in secret, her choice sanctioned by heaven.

Armand went slowly home, turning this thought in his mind with the impartiality of a man who is conscious of all the responsibilities that love lays on him while he tastes the sweetness of its joys. He went along the quays to see the widest possible space of sky; his heart had grown in him; he would fain have had the bounds of the firmament and of earth enlarged. It seemed to him that his lungs drew an ampler breath. In the course of his self-examination, as he walked, he vowed to love this woman so devoutly that every day of her life she should find absolution for her sins against society in unfailing happiness. Sweet stirrings of life when life is at the full! The man that is strong enough to steep his soul in the color of one emotion feels infinite joy as glimpses open out for him of an ardent lifetime that knows no diminution of passion to the end; even so it is permitted to certain mystics, in ecstasy, to behold the Light of God. Love would be naught without the belief that it would last for ever; love grows great through constancy. It was thus that, wholly absorbed by his happiness, Montriveau understood passion.

"We belong to each other for ever!"

The thought was like a talisman fulfilling the wishes of his life. He did not ask whether the duchess might not change, whether her love might not last. No, for he had faith. Without that virtue there is no future for Christianity, and perhaps it is even more necessary to society. A conception of life as feeling occurred to him for the first time; hitherto he had lived by action, the most strenuous exertion of human energies, the physical devotion, as it may be called, of the soldier.

Next day M. de Montriveau went early in the direction of the Faubourg Saint-Germain. He had made an appointment at a house not far from the Hôtel de Langeais; and the business over, he went thither as if to his own home. The general's companion chanced to be a man for whom he appeared to feel a kind of repulsion whenever he met him in other houses. This was the Marquis de Ronquerolles, whose reputation had grown so great in Paris boudoirs. He was witty, clever, and what was more—courageous; he set the fashion to all the young men in Paris. As a man of gallantry, his success and experience were equally matters of envy; and neither fortune nor birth was wanting in his case, qualifications which add such lustre in Paris to a reputation as a leader of fashion.*

"Where are you going?" asked M. de Ronquerolles.

"To Madame de Langeais'."

"Ah, true. I forgot that you had allowed her to lime you. You are wasting your affections on her when they might be much better employed elsewhere. I could have told you of half-a-score of women in the financial world, any one of them a thousand times better worth your while than that titled courtesan, who does with her brains what less artificial women do with——"

"What is this, my dear fellow?" Armand broke in. "The duchess is an angel of innocence."

Ronquerolles began to laugh.

"Things being thus, dear boy," said he, "it is my duty to enlighten you. Just a word; there is no harm in it between ourselves. Has the duchess surrendered? If so, I have nothing more to say. Come, give me your confidence. There is no occasion to waste your time in grafting your great nature on that unthankful stock, when all your hopes and cultivation will come to nothing."

Armand ingenuously made a kind of general report of his position, enumerating with much minuteness the slender rights so hardly won. Ronquerolles burst into a peal of laughter

---

* Montriveau and Ronquerolles belonged to "The Thirteen." See Preface.

so heartless that it would have cost any other man his life. But from their manner of speaking and looking at each other during that colloquy beneath the wall, in a corner almost as remote from intrusion as the desert itself, it was easy to imagine the friendship between the two men knew no bounds, and that no power on earth could estrange them.

"My dear Armand, why did you not tell me that the duchess was a puzzle to you? I would have given you a little advice which might have brought your flirtation properly through. You must know, to begin with, that the women of our faubourg, like any other women, love to steep themselves in love; but they have a mind to possess and not to be possessed. They have made a sort of compromise with human nature. The code of their parish gives them a pretty wide latitude short of the last transgression. The sweets enjoyed by this fair duchess of yours are so many venial sins to be washed away in the waters of penitence. But if you had the impertinence to ask in earnest for the mortal sin to which naturally you are sure to attach the highest importance, you would see the deep disdain with which the door of the boudoir and the house would be incontinently shut upon you. The tender Antoinette would dismiss everything from her memory; you would be less than a cipher for her. She would wipe away your kisses, my dear friend, as indifferently as she would perform her ablutions. She would sponge love from her cheeks as she washes off rouge. We know women of that sort—the thoroughbred Parisienne. Have you ever noticed a grisette tripping along the street? Her face is pretty as a picture. A neat cap, fresh cheeks, trim hair, a guileful smile, and the rest of her almost neglected. Is not this true to the life? Well, that is the Parisienne. She knows that her face is all that will be seen, so she devotes all her care, finery, and vanity to her head. The duchess is the same; the head is everything with her. She can only feel through her intellect, her heart lies in her brain, she is a sort of intellectual epicure, she has a head-voice.

We call that kind of poor creature a Laïs of the intellect. You have been taken in like a boy. If you doubt it, you can have proof of it to-night, this morning, this instant. Go up to her, try the demand as an experiment, insist peremptorily if it is refused. You might set about it like the late Maréchal de Richelieu, and yet get nothing for your pains."

Armand was dumb with amazement.

"Has your desire reached the point of infatuation?"

"I want her at any cost!" Montriveau cried out despairingly.

"Very well. Now, look here. Be as inexorable as she is herself. Try to humiliate her, to sting her vanity. Do *not* try to move her heart, nor her soul, but the woman's nerves and temperament, for she is both nervous and lymphatic. If you can once awaken desire in her, you are safe. But you must drop these romantic boyish notions of yours. If when once you have her in your eagle's talons you yield a point or draw back, if you so much as stir an eyelid, if she thinks that she can regain her ascendency over you, she will slip out of your clutches like a fish, and you will never catch her again. Be inflexible as law. Show no more charity than the headsman. Hit hard, and then hit again. Strike and keep on striking as if you were giving her the knout. Duchesses are made of hard stuff, my dear Armand; there is a sort of feminine nature that is only softened by repeated blows; and as suffering develops a heart in women of that sort, so it is a work of charity not to spare the rod. Do you persevere. Ah! when pain has thoroughly relaxed those nerves and softened the fibres that you take to be so pliant and yielding; when a shriveled heart has learned to expand and contract and to beat under this discipline; when the brain has capitulated—then, perhaps, passion may enter among the steel springs of this machinery that turns out tears and affectations and languors and melting phrases; then you shall see a most magnificent conflagration (always supposing that the chimney takes fire). The steel feminine system will glow red-hot like iron in the forge; that kind of heat lasts longer than any other, and the glow of it may possibly turn to love.

"Still," he continued, "I have my doubts. And, after all, is it worth while to take so much trouble with the duchess? Between ourselves, a man of my stamp ought first to take her in hand and break her in; I would make a charming woman of her; she is a thoroughbred; whereas, you two left to yourselves will never get beyond the A B C of love. But you are in love with her, and just now you might not perhaps share my views on this subject.

"A pleasant time to you, my children," added Ronquerolles, after a pause. Then with a laugh: "I have decided myself for facile beauties; they are tender, at any rate, the natural woman appears in their love without any of your social seasonings. A woman that haggles over herself, my poor boy, and only means to inspire love! Well, have her like an extra horse—for show. The match between the lounge and confessional, black and white, queen and knight, conscientious scruples and pleasure, is an uncommonly amusing game of chess. And if a man knows the game, let him be never so little of a rake, he wins in three moves. Now, if I undertook a woman of that sort, I should start with the deliberate purpose of——" His voice sank to a whisper over the last words in Armand's ear, and he went before there was time for any reply.

As for Montriveau, he sprang at a bound across the courtyard of the Hôtel de Langeais, went unannounced up the stairs straight to the duchess' bedroom.

"This is an unheard-of thing," she said, hastily wrapping her dressing-gown about her. "Armand! this is abominable of you! Come, leave the room, I beg. Just go out of the room, and go at once. Wait for me in the drawing-room. Come, now!"

"Dear angel, has a plighted lover no privilege whatsoever?"

"But, monsieur, it is in the worst possible taste of a plighted lover or a wedded husband to break in like this upon his wife."

He came up to the duchess, took her in his arms, and held her tightly to him.

"Forgive, dear Antoinette; but a host of horrid doubts are fermenting in my heart."

"*Doubts?* Fie! Oh, fie on you!"

"Doubts all but justified. If you loved me, would you make this quarrel? Would you not be glad to see me? Would you not have felt a something stir in your heart? For I, that am not a woman, feel a thrill in my inmost self at the mere sound of your voice. Often in a ballroom a longing has come upon me to spring to your side and put my arms about your neck."

"Oh! if you have doubts of me so long as I am not ready to spring to your arms before all the world, I shall be doubted all my life long, I suppose. Why, Othello was a mere child compared with you!"

"Ah!" he cried despairingly, "you have no love for me, you——"

"Admit, at any rate, that at this moment you are not lovable."

"Then I have still to find favor in your sight?"

"Oh, I should think so. Come," added she, with a little imperious air, "go out of the room, leave me. I am not like you; I wish always to find favor in your eyes."

Never woman better understood the art of putting charm into insolence, and does not the charm double the effect? is it not enough to infuriate the coolest of men? There was a sort of untrammeled freedom about Mme. de Langeais; a something in her eyes, her voice, her attitude, which is never seen in a woman who loves when she stands face to face with him at the mere sight of whom her heart must needs begin to beat. The Marquis de Ronquerolles' counsels had cured Armand of sheepishness; and further, there came to his aid that rapid power of intuition which passion will develop at moments in the least wise among mortals, while a great man at such a time possesses it to the full. He guessed the terrible truth revealed by the duchess' nonchalance, and his heart swelled with the storm like a lake rising in flood.

"If you told me the truth yesterday, be mine, dear Antoinette," he cried; "you shall——"

"In the first place," said she composedly, thrusting him back as he came nearer—"in the first place, you are not to compromise me. My woman might overhear you. Respect me, I beg of you. Your familiarity is all very well in my boudoir in an evening; here it is quite different. Beside, what may your 'you shall' mean? 'You shall.' No one as yet has ever used that word to me. It is quite ridiculous, it seems to me, absolutely ridiculous."

"Will you surrender nothing to me on this point?"

"Oh! do you call a woman's right to dispose of herself a 'point?' A capital point, indeed; you will permit me to be entirely my own mistress on that 'point.'"

"And how if, believing in your promises to me, I should absolutely require it?"

"Oh! then you would prove that I made the greatest possible mistake when I made you a promise of any kind; and I should beg you to leave me in peace."

The general's face grew white; he was about to spring to her side, when Mme. de Langeais rang the bell, the maid appeared, and, smiling with a mocking grace, the duchess added: "Be so good as to return when I am visible."

Then Montriveau felt the hardness of a woman as cold and keen as a steel blade; she was crushing in her scorn. In one moment she had snapped the bonds which held firm only for her lover. She had read Armand's intention in his face, and held that the moment had come for teaching the Imperial soldier his lesson. He was to be made to feel that though duchesses may lend themselves to love, they do not give themselves, and that the conquest of one of them would prove a harder matter than the conquest of Europe.

"Madame," returned Armand, "I have not time to wait. I am a spoilt child, as you told me yourself. When I seriously resolve to have that of which we have been speaking, I shall have it."

"You will have it?" queried she, and there was a trace of surprise in her loftiness.

"I shall have it."

"Oh! you will do me a great pleasure by 'resolving' to have it. For curiosity's sake, I should be delighted to know how you would set about it——"

"I am delighted to put a new interest into your life," interrupted Montriveau, breaking into a laugh which dismayed the duchess. "Will you permit me to take you to the ball to-night?"

"A thousand thanks. Monsieur de Marsay has been beforehand with you. I gave him my promise."

Montriveau bowed gravely and went.

"So Ronquerolles was right," thought he, "and now for a game of chess."

Thenceforward he hid his agitation by complete composure. No man is strong enough to bear such sudden alternations from the height of happiness to the depths of wretchedness. So he had caught a glimpse of happy life the better to feel the emptiness of his previous existence? There was a terrible storm within him; but he had learned to endure, and bore the shock of tumultuous thoughts as a granite cliff stands out against the surge of an angry sea.

"I could say nothing. When I am with her my wits desert me. She does not know how vile and contemptible she is. Nobody has ventured to bring her face to face with herself.

She has played with many a man, no doubt; I will avenge them all."

For the first time, it may be, in a man's heart, revenge and love were blended so equally that Montriveau himself could not know whether love or revenge would carry all before it. That very evening he went to the ball at which he was sure of seeing the Duchesse de Langeais, and almost despaired of reaching her heart. He inclined to think that there was something diabolical about this woman, who was gracious to him and radiant with charming smiles; probably because she had no wish to allow the world to think that she had compromised herself with M. de Montriveau. Coolness on both sides is a sign of love; but so long as the duchess was the same as ever, while the marquis looked sullen and morose, was it not plain that she had conceded nothing? Onlookers know the rejected lover by various signs and tokens; they never mistake the genuine symptoms for a coolness such as some women command their adorers to feign, in the hope of concealing their love. Every one laughed at Montriveau; and he, having omitted to consult his *cornac*,* was abstracted and ill at ease. M. de Ronquerolles would very likely have bidden him compromise the duchess by responding to her show of friendliness by passionate demonstrations; but as it was, Armand de Montriveau came away from the ball, loathing human nature, and even then scarcely ready to believe in such complete depravity.

"If there is no executioner for such crimes," he said, as he looked up at the lighted windows of the ballroom where the most enchanting women in Paris were dancing, laughing, and chatting, "I will take you by the nape of the neck, Madame la Duchesse, and make you feel something that bites more deeply than the knife in the Place de la Grève. Steel against steel; we shall see which heart will leave the deeper mark."

* Lit.: Elephant driver—oracle.

For a week or so Mme. de Langeais hoped to see the Marquis de Montriveau again; but he contented himself with sending his card every morning to the Hôtel de Langeais. The duchess could not help shuddering each time that the card was brought in, and a dim foreboding crossed her mind, but the thought was vague as a presentiment of disaster. When her eyes fell on the name, it seemed to her that she felt the touch of the implacable man's strong hand in her hair; sometimes the words seemed like a prognostication of a vengeance which her lively intellect invented in the most shocking forms. She had studied him too well not to dread him. Would he murder her, she wondered? Would that bull-necked man dash out her vitals by flinging her over his head? Would he trample her body under his feet? When, where, and how would he get her into his power? Would he make her suffer very much, and what kind of pain would he inflict? She repented of her conduct. There were hours when, if he had come, she would have gone to his arms in complete self-surrender.

Every night before she slept she saw Montriveau's face; every night it wore a different aspect. Sometimes she saw his bitter smile, sometimes the Jovelike knitting of the brows; or his leonine look, or some disdainful movement of the shoulders, made him terrible for her. Next day the card seemed stained with blood. The name of Montriveau stirred her now as the presence of the fiery, stubborn, exacting lover had never done. Her apprehensions gathered strength in the silence. She was forced, without aid from without, to face the thought of a hideous duel of which she could not speak. Her proud hard nature was more responsive to thrills of hate than it had ever been to the caresses of love. Ah! if the general could but have seen her, as she sat with her forehead drawn into folds between her brows; immersed in bitter thoughts in that boudoir where he had enjoyed such happy moments, he might perhaps have conceived high hopes. Of all human passions, is not pride alone incapable of engendering anything base? Mme. de Langeais kept her thoughts to herself, but is it not permissible to suppose that M. de Montriveau was no longer indifferent to her? And has not a man gained ground immensely when a woman thinks about him? He is bound to make progress with her either one way or the other afterward.

Put any feminine creature under the feet of a furious horse or other fearsome beast; she will certainly drop on her knees and look for death; but if the brute shows a milder mood and does not utterly slay her, she will love the horse, lion, bull, or what not, and will speak of him quite at her ease. The duchess felt that she was under the lion's paws; she quaked, but she did not hate him.

The man and woman thus singularly placed with regard to each other met three times in society during the course of that week. Each time, in reply to coquettish questioning glances, the duchess received a respectful bow, and smiles tinged with such savage irony, that all her apprehensions over the card in the morning were revived at night. Our lives are simply such as our feelings shape them for us; and the feelings of these two had hollowed out a great gulf between them.

The Comtesse de Sérizy, the Marquis de Ronquerolles' sister, gave a great ball at the beginning of the following week, and Mme. de Langeais was sure to go to it. Armand was the first person whom the duchess saw when she came into the room, and this time Armand was looking out for her, or so she thought at least. The two exchanged a look, and suddenly the woman felt a cold perspiration break from every pore. She had thought all along that Montriveau was capable of taking reprisals in some unheard-of way proportioned to their condition; and now the revenge had been discovered. it was ready, heated, and boiling. Lightnings flashed from the foiled lover's eyes, his face was radiant with exultant vengeance. And the duchess? Her eyes were haggard in spite of her resolution to be cool and insolent. She went to take her place beside the Comtesse de Sérizy, who could not help exclaiming: "Dear Antoinette! what is the matter with you? You are enough to frighten one."

"I shall be all right after a quadrille," she answered, giving a hand to a young man who came up at that moment.

Mme. de Langeais waltzed that evening with a sort of excitement and transport which redoubled Montriveau's lowering looks. He stood in front of the line of spectators, who were amusing themselves by looking on. Every time that the duchess came past him, his eyes darted down upon her eddying face; he might have been a tiger with the prey in his grasp. The waltz came to an end, Mme. de Langeais went back to her place beside the countess, and the Marquis de Montriveau never took his eyes off her, talking all the while with a stranger.

"One of the things that struck me most on the journey," he was saying (and the duchess listened with all her ears), "was the remark which the man makes at Westminster when you are shown the axe with which a man in a mask cut off Charles the First's head, so they tell you. The King made it first of all to some inquisitive person, and they repeat it still in memory of him."

"What does the man say?" asked Mme. de Sérizy.

"'Do not touch the axe!'" replied Montriveau, and there was menace in the sound of his voice.

"Really, my lord marquis," said Mme. de Langeais, "you tell this old story that everybody knows if they have been to London, and look at my neck in such a melodramatic way that you seem to me to have an axe in your hand."

The duchess was in a cold sweat, but nevertheless she laughed as she spoke the last words.

"But circumstances give the story a quite new application," returned he.

"How so; pray tell me, for pity's sake?"

"In this way, madame—you have touched the axe," said Montriveau, lowering his voice.

"What an enchanting prophecy!" returned she, smiling with assumed grace. "And when is my head to fall?"

"I have no wish to see that pretty head of yours cut off. I only fear some great misfortune for you. If your head were clipped close, would you feel no regrets for the dainty golden hair that you turn to such good account?"

"There are those for whom a woman would love to make such a sacrifice; even if, as often happens, it is for the sake of a man who cannot make allowances for an outbreak of temper."

"Quite so. Well, and if some wag were to spoil your beauty on a sudden by some chemical process, and you, who are but eighteen for us, were to be a hundred years old?"

"Why, the small-pox is our battle of Waterloo, monsieur," she interrupted. "After it is over we find out those who love us sincerely."

"Would you not regret the lovely face that——?"

"Oh! indeed I should, but less for my own sake than for the sake of some one else whose delight it might have been. And, after all, if I were loved, always loved, and truly loved, what would my beauty matter to me? What do you say, Clara?"

"It is a dangerous speculation," replied Mme. de Sérizy.

"Is it permissible to ask his majesty the King of Sorcerers when I made the mistake of touching the axe, since I have not been to London as yet?——"

"*Not so*," he answered in English, with a burst of ironical laughter.

"And when will the punishment begin?"

At this Montriveau coolly took out his watch, and ascertained the hour with a truly appalling air of conviction.

"A dreadful misfortune will befall you before this day is out."

"I am not a child to be easily frightened, or rather, I am a child ignorant of danger," said the duchess. "I shall dance now without fear on the edge of the precipice."

"I am delighted to know that you have so much strength of character," he answered, as he watched her go to take her place in a square dance.

But the duchess, in spite of her apparent contempt for Armand's dark prophecies, was really frightened. Her late lover's presence weighed upon her morally and physically with a sense of oppression that scarcely ceased when he left the ballroom. And yet when she had drawn freer breath, and enjoyed the relief for a moment, she found herself regretting the sensation of dread, so greedy of extreme sensations is the feminine nature. The regret was not love, but it was certainly akin to other feelings which prepare the way for love. And then—as if the impression which Montriveau had made upon her were suddenly revived—she recollected his air of conviction as he took out his watch, and in a sudden spasm of dread she went out.

By this time it was about midnight. One of her servants, waiting with her pelisse, went down to order her carriage. On her way home she fell naturally enough to musing over M. de Montriveau's prediction. Arrived in her own courtyard, as she supposed, she entered a vestibule almost like that of her own hotel, and suddenly saw that the staircase was different. She was in a strange house. Turning to call her servants, she was attacked by several men, who rapidly flung a handkerchief over her mouth, bound her hand and foot, and carried her off. She shrieked aloud.

"Madame, our orders are to kill you if you scream," a voice said in her ear.

So great was the duchess' terror that she could never recollect how nor by whom she was transported. When she came to herself she was lying on a couch in a bachelor's lodging, her hands and feet tied with silken cords. In spite of herself, she shrieked aloud as she looked round and met Armand de Montriveau's eyes. He was sitting in his dressing-gown, quietly smoking a cigar in his armchair.

"Do not cry out, Madame la Duchesse," he said, coolly taking the cigar out of his mouth; "I have a headache. Beside, I will untie you. But listen attentively to what I have the honor to say to you."

Very carefully he untied the knots that bound her feet.

"What would be the use of calling out? Nobody can hear your cries. You are too well bred to make any unnecessary fuss. If you do not stay quietly, if you insist upon a struggle with me, I shall tie your hands and feet again. All things considered, I think that you have self-respect enough to stay on this couch as if you were lying on your own at home; cold as ever, if you will. You have made me shed many tears on this couch, tears that I hid from all other eyes."

While Montriveau was speaking, the duchess glanced about her; it was a woman's glance, a stolen look that saw all things and seemed to see nothing. She was much pleased with the room. It was rather like a monk's cell. The man's character and thoughts seemed to pervade it. No decoration of any kind broke the gray painted surface of the walls. A green carpet covered the floor. A black sofa, a table littered with papers, two big easy-chairs, a chest of drawers with an alarum clock by way of ornament, a very low bedstead with a coverlet flung over it—a red cloth with a black key border—all these things made part of a whole that told of a life reduced to its simplest terms. A triple candle-sconce of Egyptian design on the mantel recalled the vast spaces of the desert and Montriveau's long wanderings: a huge sphinx-claw stood out beneath the folds of stuff at the bedfoot; and, just beyond, a green curtain with a black and scarlet border was suspended by large rings from a spear handle above the door near one corner of the room. The other door by which the band had entered was likewise curtained, but the drapery hung from an ordinary curtain-rod. As the duchess finally noted that the pattern was the same on both, she saw that the door at the bedfoot stood open; gleams of ruddy light from the room beyond flickered below the fringed border. Naturally, the ominous light roused her curiosity; she fancied she could distinguish strange shapes in the shadows; but as it did not occur to her at the time that danger could come from that quarter, she tried to gratify a more ardent curiosity.

"Monsieur, if it is not indiscreet, may I ask what you mean to do with me?" The insolence and irony of the tone stung through the words. The duchess quite believed that she read extravagant love in Montriveau's speech. He had carried her off; was not that in itself an acknowledgment of her power?

"Nothing whatever, madame," he returned, gracefully puffing the last whiff of cigar smoke. "You will remain here for a short time. First of all, I should like to explain to you what you are, and what I am. I cannot put my thoughts into words whilst you are twisting on the couch in your boudoir; and, beside, in your own house you take offense at the slightest hint, you ring the bell, make an outcry, and turn your lover out at the door as if he were the basest of wretches. Here my mind is unfettered. Here nobody can turn me out. Here you shall be my victim for a few seconds, and you are going to be so exceedingly kind as to listen to me. You need fear nothing. I did not carry you off to insult you, nor yet to take by force what you refused to grant of your own will to my unworthiness. I could not stoop so low. You possibly think of outrage; for myself, I have no such thoughts."

He flung his cigar coolly into the fire.

"The smoke is unpleasant to you, no doubt, madame?" he said, and rising at once, he took a chafing-dish from the hearth, burnt perfumes, and purified the air. The duchess' astonishment was only equaled by her humiliation. She was in this man's power; and he would not abuse his power. The eyes in which love had once blazed like flame were now quiet and steady as stars. She trembled. Her dread of Armand was increased by a nightmare sensation of restlessness and utter inability to move; she felt as if she were turned to stone. She lay passive in the grip of fear. She thought she saw the light behind the curtains grow to a blaze, as if blown up by a pair of bellows; in another moment the gleams of flame grew brighter, and she fancied that three masked figures suddenly flashed out; but the terrible vision disappeared so swiftly that she took it for an optical delusion.

"Madame," Armand continued with cold contempt, "one minute, just one minute is enough for me, and you shall feel it afterward at every moment throughout your lifetime, the one eternity over which I have power. I am not God. Listen carefully to me," he continued, pausing to add solemnity to his words. "Love will always come at your call. You have boundless power over men: but remember that once you called love, and love came to you; love as pure and true-hearted as may be on earth, and as reverent as it was passionate; fond as a devoted woman's, as a mother's love; a love so great, indeed, that it was past the bounds of reason. You played with it, and you committed a crime. Every woman has a right to refuse herself to love which she feels she cannot share; and if a man loves and cannot win love in return, he is not to be pitied, he has no right to complain. But with a semblance of love to attract an unfortunate creature cut off from all affection; to teach him to understand happiness to the full, only to snatch it from him; to rob him of his future of felicity; to slay his happiness not merely to-day, but as long as his life lasts, by poisoning every hour of it and every thought—this I call a fearful crime!"

"Monsieur——"

"I cannot allow you to answer me yet. So listen to me still. In any case I have rights over you; but I only choose to exercise one—the right of the judge over the criminal, so that I may arouse your conscience. If you had no conscience left, I should not reproach you at all; but you are so young! You must feel some life still in your heart; or so I like to believe. While I think of you as depraved enough to do a wrong which the law does not punish, I do not think you so degraded that you cannot comprehend the full meaning of my words. I resume."

As he spoke the duchess heard the smothered sound of a pair of bellows. Those mysterious figures which she had just seen were blowing up the fire, no doubt; the glow shone through the curtain. But Montriveau's lurid face was turned upon her; she could not choose but wait with a fast-beating heart and eyes fixed in a stare. However curious she felt, the heat in Armand's words interested her even more than the crackling of the mysterious flames.

"Madame," he went on after a pause, "if some poor wretch commits a murder in Paris, it is the executioner's duty, you know, to lay hands on him and stretch him on the plank, where murderers pay for their crimes with their heads. Then the newspapers inform every one, rich and poor, so that the former are assured that they may sleep in peace, and the latter are warned that they must be on the watch if they would live. Well, you that are religious, and even a little of a bigot, may have masses said for such a man's soul. You both belong to the same family, but yours is the elder branch; and the elder branch may occupy high places in peace and live happily and without cares. Want or anger may drive your brother the convict to take a man's life; you have taken more, you have taken the joy out of a man's life, you have killed all that was best in his life—his dearest beliefs. The murderer simply lay in wait for his victim, and killed him reluctantly, and in fear of the scaffold; but *you*——! You heaped up every sin that weakness can commit against strength that suspected no evil; you tamed a passive victim, the better to gnaw his heart out; you lured him with caresses; you left nothing undone that could set him dreaming, imagining, longing for the bliss of love. You asked innumerable sacrifices of him, only to refuse to make any in return. He should see the light indeed before you put out his eyes! It is wonderful how you found the heart to do it! Such villainies demand a display of resource quite above the comprehension of those bourgeoises whom you laugh at and despise. They can give and forgive; they know how to love and suffer. The grandeur of their devotion dwarfs us. Rising higher in the social scale, one finds just as much mud as at the lower end; but with this difference, at the upper end it is hard and gilded over.

"Yes, to find baseness in perfection, you must look for a noble bringing up, a great name, a fair woman, a duchess. You cannot fall lower than the lowest unless you are set high above the rest of the world. I express my thoughts badly; the wounds you dealt me are too painful as yet, but do not think that I complain. My words are not the expression of any hope for myself; there is no trace of bitterness in them. Know this, madame, for a certainty—I forgive you. My forgiveness is so complete that you need not feel in the least sorry that you came hither to find it against your will. But you might take advantage of other hearts as childlike as my own, and it is my duty to spare them anguish. So you have inspired the thought of justice. Expiate your sin here on earth; God may perhaps forgive you; I wish that He may, but He is inexorable, and will strike."

The broken-spirited, broken-hearted woman looked up, her eyes filled with tears.

"Why do you cry? Be true to your nature. You could look on indifferently at the torture of a heart as you broke it. That will do, madame, do not cry. I cannot bear it any longer. Other men will tell you that you have given them life; as for myself, I tell you, with rapture, that you have given me blank extinction. Perhaps you guess that I am not my own, that I am bound to live for my friends, that from this time forth I must endure the cold chill of death, as well as the burden of life? Is it possible that there can be so much kindness in you? Are you like the desert tigress that licks the wounds she has inflicted?"

The duchess burst out sobbing.

"Pray spare your tears, madame. If I believed in them at all, it would merely set me on my guard. Is this another of your artifices? or is it not? You have used so many with me; how can one think that there is any truth in you? Nothing that you do or say has any power now to move me. That is all I have to say."

Mme. de Langeais rose to her feet, with a great dignity and humility in her bearing.

"You are right to treat me very hardly," she said, holding out a hand to the man who did not take it; "you have not spoken harshly enough; and I deserve this punishment."

"*I* punish you, madame! A man must love still, to punish, must he not? From me you must expect no feeling, nothing resembling it. If I chose, I might be accuser and judge in my cause, and pronounce and carry out the sentence. But I am about to fulfill a duty, not a desire of vengeance of any kind. The cruelest revenge of all, I think, is scorn of revenge when it is in our power to take it. Perhaps I shall be the minister of your pleasures; who knows? Perhaps from this time forth, as you gracefully wear the tokens of disgrace, by which society marks out the criminal, you may perforce learn something of the convict's sense of honor. And then, you will love!"

The duchess sat listening; her meekness was unfeigned; it was no coquettish device. When she spoke at last, it was after a silence.

"Armand," she began, "it seems to me that when I resisted love, I was obeying all the chaste instincts of woman's modesty; I should not have looked for such reproaches from *you*. I was weak; you have turned all my weaknesses against me, and made so many crimes of them. How could you fail to understand that the curiosity of love might have carried me further than I ought to go; and that next morning I might be angry with myself, and wretched because I had gone too far? Alas! I sinned in ignorance. I was as sincere in my wrongdoing, I swear to you, as in my remorse. There was far more love for you in my severity than in my concessions. And beside, of what do you complain? I gave you my heart; that was not enough; you demanded, brutally, that I should give my person——"

"Brutally?" repeated Montriveau. But to himself he said, "If I once allow her to dispute over words, I am lost."

"Yes. You came to me as if I were one of those women. You showed none of the respect, none of the attentions of love. Had I not reason to reflect? Very well, I reflected. The unseemliness of your conduct is not inexcusable, love lay at the source of it; let me think so, and justify you to myself. Well, Armand, this evening, even while you were prophesying evil, I felt convinced that there was happiness in store for us both. Yes, I put my faith in the noble, proud nature so often tested and proved." She bent lower. "And I was yours wholly," she murmured in his ear. "I felt a longing that I cannot express to give happiness to a man so violently tried by adversity. If I must have a master, my master should be a great man. As I felt conscious of my height, the less I cared to descend. I felt I could trust you, I saw a whole lifetime of love, while you were pointing to death. Strength and kindness always go together. My friend, you are so strong, you will not be unkind to a helpless woman who loves you. If I was wrong, is there no way of obtaining forgiveness? No way of making reparation? Repentance is the charm of love; I should like to be very charming for you. How could I, alone among women, fail to know a woman's doubts and fears, the timidity that it is so natural to feel when you bind yourself for life, and know how easily a man snaps such ties? The bourgeoises, with whom you compared me just now, give themselves, but they struggle first. Very well—I struggled; but here I am! Ah! God, he does not hear me!" she broke off, and wringing her hands, she cried out: " But I love you! I am yours!" and fell at Armand's feet.

"Yours! yours! my one and only master!"

Armand tried to raise her.

"Madame, it is too late! Antoinette cannot save the Duchesse de Langeais. I cannot believe in either. To-day you may give yourself; to-morrow you may refuse. No power in earth or heaven can insure me the sweet constancy of love. All love's pledges lay in the past; and now nothing of that past exists."

The light behind the curtain blazed up so brightly that the duchess could not help turning her head; this time she distinctly saw the three masked figures.

"Armand," she said, "I would not wish to think ill of you. Why are those men there? What are you going to do to me?"

"Those men will be as silent as I myself with regard to the thing which is about to be done. Think of them simply as my hands and my heart. One of them is a surgeon——"

"A surgeon! Armand, my friend, of all things, suspense is the hardest to bear. Just speak; tell me if you wish for my life; I will give it to you, you need not take it——"

"Then you did not understand me? Did I not speak just now of justice? To put an end to your misapprehensions," continued he, taking up a small steel object from the table, "I will now explain what I have decided with regard to you."

He held out a Lorraine cross, fastened to the tip of a steel rod.

"Two of my friends at this very moment are heating another cross, made on this pattern, red-hot. We are going to stamp it upon your forehead, here between the eyes, so that there will be no possibility of hiding the mark with diamonds, and so avoiding people's questions. In short, you shall bear on your forehead the brand of infamy which your brothers the convicts wear on their shoulders. The pain is a mere trifle, but I feared a nervous crisis of some kind, of resistance——"

"Resistance?" she cried, clapping her hands for joy. "Oh no, no! I would have the whole world here to see. Ah, my Armand, brand her quickly, this creature of yours; brand her with your mark as a poor trifle belonging to you. You asked for pledges of my love; here they are all in one. Ah! for me there is nothing but mercy and forgiveness and eternal happiness in this revenge of yours. When you have marked this woman with your mark, when you set your crimson brand on her, your slave in soul, you can never afterward abandon her, you will be mine for evermore! When you cut me off from my kind, you make yourself responsible for my happiness, or you prove yourself base; and I know that you are noble and great! Why, when a woman loves, the brand of love is burnt into her soul by her own will. Come in, gentlemen! come in and brand her, this Duchesse de Langeais. She is Monsieur de Montriveau's for ever! Ah! come quickly, all of you, my forehead burns hotter than your fire!"

Armand turned his head sharply away lest he should see the duchess kneeling, quivering with the throbbings of her heart. He said some word, and his three friends vanished.

The women of Paris salons know how one mirror reflects another. The duchess, with every motive for reading the depths of Armand's heart, was all eyes; and Armand, all unsuspicious of the mirror, brushed away two tears as they fell. Her whole future lay in those two tears. When he turned round again to help her to rise, she was standing before him, sure of love. Her pulses must have throbbed fast when he spoke with the firmness she had known so well how to use of old while she played with him.

"I spare you, madame. All that has taken place shall be as if it had never been, you may believe me. But now, let us bid each other farewell. I like to think that you were sincere in you coquetries on your couch, sincere again in this outpouring of your heart. Adieu. I feel that there is no faith in you left in me. You would torment me again; you would always be the duchess, and—— But there, farewell, we shall never understand each other.

"Now, what do you wish?" he continued, taking the tone of a master of the ceremonies—"to return home or to go back to Madame de Sérizy's ball? I have done all in my power to prevent any scandal. Neither your servants nor any one else can possibly know what has passed between us in the last quarter of an hour. Your servants have no idea that you have left the ballroom; your carriage never left Madame de Sérizy's courtyard; your carriage may likewise be found in the court of your own hôtel. Where do you wish to be?"

"What do you counsel, Armand?"

"There is no Armand now, Madame la Duchesse. We are strangers to each other."

"Then take me to the ball," she said, still curious to put Armand's power to the test. "Thrust a soul that suffered in the world, and must always suffer there, if there is no happiness for her now, down into hell again. And yet, oh my friend, I love you as your bourgeoises love; I love you so that I could come to you and fling my arms about your neck before all the world if you asked it of me. The hateful world has not corrupted me. I am young at least, and I have grown younger still. I am a child, yes, your child, your new creature. Ah! do not drive me forth out of my Eden!"

Armand shook his head.

"Ah! let me take something with me, if I go, some little thing to wear to-night on my heart," she said, taking possession of Armand's glove, which she twisted into her handkerchief.

"No, I am *not* like all those depraved women. You do

not know the world, and so you cannot know my worth. You shall know it now! There are women who sell themselves for money; there are others to be gained by gifts, it is a vile world! Oh, I wish I were a simple bourgeoise, a working-girl, if you would rather have a woman beneath you than a woman whose devotion is accompanied by high rank, as men count it. Oh, my Armand, there are noble, high, and chaste and pure natures among us; and then they are lovely indeed. I would have all nobleness that I might offer it all up to you. Misfortune willed that I should be a duchess; I would I were a royal princess, that my offering might be complete. I would be a grisette for you, and a queen for every one beside."

He listened, damping his cigarettes with his lips.

"You will let me know when you wish to go," he said.

"But I should like to stay——"

"That is another matter!"

"Stay, that was badly rolled," she cried, seizing on a cigarette and grasping all that Armand's lips had touched.

"Do you smoke?"

"Oh, what would I not do to please you?"

"Very well. Go, madame."

"I will obey you," she answered, with tears in her eyes.

"You must be blindfolded; you must not see a glimpse of the way."

"I am ready, Armand," she said, bandaging her eyes.

"Can you see?"

"No."

Noiselessly he knelt before her.

"Ah! I can hear you!" she cried, with a little fond gesture, thinking that the pretense of harshness was over.

He made as if he would kiss her lips; she held up her face.

"You can see, madame."

"I am just a little bit curious."

"So you always deceive me?"

"Ah! take off this handkerchief, sir," she cried out, with the passion of a great generosity repelled with scorn, "lead me; I will not open my eyes."

Armand felt sure of her after that cry. He led the way; the duchess, nobly true to her word, was blind. But while Montriveau held her hand as a father might, and led her up and down flights of stairs, he was studying the throbbing pulses of this woman's heart so suddenly invaded by Love. Mme. de Langeais, rejoicing in this power of speech, was glad to let him know all; but he was inflexible; his hand was passive in reply to the questionings of her hand.

At length, after some journey made together, Armand bade her go forward; the opening was doubtless narrow, for as she went she felt that his hand protected her dress. His care touched her; it was a revelation surely that there was a little love still left; yet it was in some sort a farewell, for Montriveau left her without a word. The air was warm; the duchess, feeling the heat, opened her eyes, and found herself standing by the fire in the Comtesse de Sérizy's boudoir. She was alone. Her first thought was for her disordered toilette; in a moment she had adjusted her dress and restored her picturesque coiffure.

"Well, dear Antoinette, we have been looking for you everywhere." It was the Comtesse de Sérizy who spoke as she opened the door.

"I came here to breathe," said the duchess; "it is unbearably hot in the rooms."

"People thought that you had gone; but my brother Ronquerolles told me that your servants were waiting for you."

"I am tired out, dear, let me stay and rest here for a minute," and the duchess sat down on the sofa.

"Why, what is the matter with you? You are shaking from head to foot!"

The Marquis de Ronquerolles came in.

"Madame la Duchesse, I was afraid that something might have happened. I have just come across your coachman, the man is as tipsy as all the Swiss in the whole of the twenty-two cantons."

The duchess made no answer; she was looking round the room, at the mantel and the tall mirrors, seeking the trace of an opening. Then with an extraordinary sensation she recollected that she was again in the midst of the gayety of the ballroom after that terrific scene which had changed the whole course of her life. She began to shiver violently.

"Monsieur de Montriveau's prophecy has shaken my nerves," she said. "It was a joke, but still I will see whether his axe from London will haunt me even in my sleep. So farewell, dear. Adieu, Monsieur le Marquis."

As she went through the rooms she was beset with inquiries and regrets. Her world seemed to have dwindled now that she, its queen, had fallen so low, was so diminished. And what, moreover, were these men compared with him whom she loved with all her heart; with the man grown great by all that she had lost in stature? The giant had regained the height that he had lost for a while, and she exaggerated it perhaps beyond measure. She looked, in spite of herself, at the servant who had attended her to the ball. He was fast asleep.

"Have you been here all the time?" she asked.

"Yes, madame."

As she took her seat in her carriage she saw, in fact, that her coachman was drunk—so drunk, that at any other time she would have been afraid; but after a great crisis in life, fear loses its appetite for common food. She reached home, at any rate, without accident; but even there she felt a change in herself, a new feeling that she could not shake off. For her, there was now but one man in the world; which is to say, that henceforth she cared to shine for his sake alone.

While the philosopher can define love promptly by following out natural laws, the moralist finds a far more perplexing problem before him if he attempts to consider love in all its developments due to social conditions. Still, in spite of the heresies of the endless sects that divide the church of Love, there is one broad and trenchant line of difference in doctrine, a line that all the discussion in the world can never deflect. A rigid application of this line explains the nature of the crisis through which the duchess, like most women, was to pass. Passion she knew, but she did not love as yet.

Love and passion are two different conditions which poets and men of the world; philosophers and fools alike, continually confound. Love implies a give and take, a certainty of bliss that nothing can change; it means so close a clinging of the heart, and an exchange of happiness so constant, that there is no room left for jealousy. Then possession is a means and not an end; unfaithfulness may give pain, but the bond is not the less close; the soul is neither more nor less ardent or troubled, but happy at every moment; in short, the divine breath of desire spreading from end to end of the immensity of Time steeps it all for us in the selfsame hue; life takes the tint of the unclouded heaven. But Passion is the foreshadowing of Love, and of that Infinite to which all suffering souls aspire. Passion is a hope that may be cheated. Passion means both suffering and transition. Passion dies out when hope is dead. Men and women may pass through this experience many times without dishonor, for it is so natural to spring toward happiness; but there is only one love in a lifetime. All discussions of sentiment ever conducted on paper or by word of mouth may, therefore, be resumed by two questions—"Is it passion? Is it love?" So, since love comes into existence only through the intimate experience of the bliss which gives it lasting life, the duchess was beneath the yoke of passion as yet; and as she knew the fierce tumult, the unconscious calculations, the fevered cravings, and all that is meant by that word *passion*—she suffered. Through all the trouble of her soul there rose eddying gusts of tempest, raised by vanity or self-love, or pride or a high spirit; for all these forms of egoism make common cause together.

She had said to this man: "I love you; I am yours!" Was it possible that the Duchesse de Langeais should have uttered those words—in vain? She must either be loved now or play her part of queen no longer. And then she felt the loneliness of the luxurious couch where pleasure had never yet set his glowing feet; and over and over again, while she tossed and writhed there, she said: "I want to be loved."

But the belief that she still had in herself gave her hope of success. The duchess might be piqued, the vain Parisienne might be humiliated; but the woman saw glimpses of wedded happiness, and imagination, avenging the time lost for nature, took a delight in kindling the inextinguishable fire in her veins. She all but attained to the sensations of love; for amid her poignant doubt whether she was loved in return, she felt glad at heart to say to herself: "I love him!" As for her scruples, religion, and the world, she could trample them under foot! Montriveau was her religion now. She spent the next day in a state of moral torpor, troubled by a physical unrest, which no words could express. She wrote letters and tore them all up in turn, and invented a thousand and one impossible fancies.

When M. de Montriveau's usual hour arrived, she tried to think that he would come, and enjoyed the feeling of expectation. Her whole life was concentrated in the single sense of hearing. Sometimes she shut her eyes, straining her ears to listen through space, wishing that she could annihilate everything that lay between her and her lover, and so establish that perfect silence which sounds may traverse from afar. In her tense self-concentration, the ticking of the clock grew hateful to her; she stopped its ill-omened garrulity. The twelve strokes of midnight sounded from the drawing-room.

"Ah, God!" she cried, "to see him here would be happiness. And yet, it is not so very long since he came here, brought by desire, and the tones of his voice filled this boudoir. And now there is nothing."

She remembered the times that she had played the coquette with him, and how that her coquetry had cost her her lover, and the despairing tears flowed for long.

Her woman came at length with, "Madame la Duchesse does not know, perhaps, that it is two o'clock in the morning; I thought that madame was not feeling well."

"Yes, I am going to bed," said the duchess, drying her eyes. "But remember, Suzanne, never to come in again without orders; I tell you this for the last time."

For a week, Mme. de Langeais went to every house where there was a hope of meeting M. de Montriveau. Contrary to her usual habits, she came early and went late; gave up dancing, and went to the card-tables. Her experiments were fruitless. She did not succeed in getting a glimpse of Armand. She did not dare to utter his name now. One evening, however, in a fit of despair, she spoke to Mme. de Sérizy, and asked as carelessly as she could: "You must have quarreled with Monsieur de Montriveau? He is not to be seen at your house now."

The countess laughed. "So he does not come here either?" she returned. "He is not to be seen anywhere, for that matter. He is interested in some woman, no doubt."

"I used to think that the Marquis de Ronquerolles was one of his friends——" the duchess began sweetly.

"I have never heard my brother say that he was acquainted with him."

Mme. de Langeais did not reply. Mme. de Sérizy concluded from the duchess' silence that she might apply the scourge with impunity to a discreet friendship which she had all too plainly seen, with much bitterness of soul, for a long time past.

"So you miss that melancholy personage, do you? I have heard most extraordinary things of him. Wound his feelings, he never comes back, he forgives nothing; and, if you love him, he keeps you in chains. To everything that I said of him, one of those that praise him sky-high would always answer: 'He knows how to love!' People are always telling me that Montriveau would give up all for his friend; that his is a great nature. Pooh! society does not want such tremendous natures. Men of that stamp are all very well at home; let them stay there and leave us to our pleasant littlenesses. What do you say, Antoinette?"

Woman of the world though she was, the duchess seemed agitated, yet she replied in a natural voice that deceived her fair friend:

"I am sorry to miss him. I took a great interest in him, and promised to myself to be his sincere friend. I like great natures, dear friend, ridiculous though you may think it. To give one's self to a fool is a clear confession, is it not, that one is governed wholly by one's senses?"

Mme. de Sérizy's "preferences" had always been for commonplace men; her lover at the moment, the Marquis d'Aiglemont, was a fine, tall man.

After this, the countess soon took her departure, you may be sure. Mme. de Langeais saw hope in Armand's withdrawal from the world; she wrote to him at once; it was a humble, gentle letter, surely it would bring him if he loved her still. She sent her footman with it next day. On the servant's return, she asked whether he had given the letter to M. de Montriveau himself, and could not restrain the movement of joy at the affirmative answer. Armand was in Paris! He stayed alone in his house; he did not go out into society! So she was loved! All day long she waited for an answer that never came. Again and again, when impatience grew unbearable, Antoinette found reasons for his delay. Armand felt embarrassed; the reply would come by mail; but night came, and she could not deceive herself any longer. It was a dreadful day, a day of pain grown sweet, of intolerable heart-throbs, a day when the heart squanders the very forces of life in riot.

Next day she sent for an answer.

"Monsieur le Marquis sent word that he would call on Madame la Duchesse," reported Julien.

She fled lest her happiness should be seen in her face, and flung herself on her couch to devour her first sensations.

"He is coming!"

The thought rent her soul. And, in truth, woe unto those for whom suspense is not the most horrible time of tempest, while it increases and multiplies the sweetest joys; for they have nothing in them of that flame which quickens the images of things, giving to them a second existence, so that we cling as closely to the pure essence as to its outward and visible manifestation. What is suspense in love but a constant drawing upon an unfailing hope?—a submission to the terrible scourgings of passion, while passion is yet happy, and the disenchantment of reality has not set in. The constant putting forth of strength and longing, called suspense, is surely, to the human soul, as fragrance to the flower that breathes it forth. We soon leave the brilliant, unsatisfying colors of tulips and coreopsis, but we turn again and again to drink in the sweetness of orange-blossoms or volkameria—flowers compared separately, each in its own land, to a betrothed bride, full of love, made fair by the past and future.

The duchess learned the joys of this new life of hers through the rapture with which she received the scourgings of love. As this change wrought in her, she saw other destinies before her, and a better meaning in the things of life. As she hurried to her dressing-room, she understood what studied adornment and the most minute attention to her toilet mean when these are undertaken for love's sake and not for vanity. Even now this making ready helped her to bear the long time of waiting. A relapse of intense agitation set in when she was dressed; she passed through nervous paroxysms brought on by the dreadful power which sets the whole mind in ferment. Perhaps that power is only a disease, though the pain of it is sweet. The duchess was dressed and waiting at two o'clock in the afternoon. At half-past eleven that night M. de Montriveau had not arrived. To try to give an idea of the anguish endured by a woman who might be said to be the spoilt child of civilization would be to attempt to say how many imaginings the heart can condense into one thought. As well endeavor to measure the forces expended by the soul in a sigh whenever the bell rang; to estimate the drain of life when a carriage rolled past without stopping, and left her prostrate.

"Can he be playing with me?" she said, as the clock struck midnight.

She grew white; her teeth chattered; she struck her hands together and leapt up and crossed the boudoir, recollecting as she did so how often he had come thither without a summons. But she resigned herself. Had she not seen him grow pale, and start up under the stinging barbs of her irony? Then Mme. de Langeais felt the horror of the woman's appointed lot; a man's is the active part, a woman must wait passively when she loves. If a woman goes beyond her beloved, she makes a mistake which few men can forgive; a'most every man would feel that a woman lowers herself by this piece of angelic flattery. But Armand's was a great nature; he surely must be one of the very few who can repay such exceeding love by love that lasts for ever.

"Well, I will make the advance," she told herself, as she tossed on her bed and found no sleep there; "I will go to him. I will not weary myself with holding out a hand to him, but I will hold it out. A man of a thousand will see a promise of love and constancy in every step that a woman takes toward him. Yes, the angels must come down from heaven to reach men; and I wish to be an angel for him."

Next day she wrote. It was a billet of the kind in which the intellects of the ten thousand Sévignés that Paris now can number particularly excel. And yet only a Duchesse de Langeais, brought up by Mme. la Princesse de Blamont-Chauvry, could have written that delicious note; no other woman could complain without lowering herself; could spread wings in such a flight without draggling her pinions in humiliation; rise gracefully in revolt; scold without giving offense; and pardon without compromising her personal dignity.

Julien went with the note. Julien, like his kind, was the victim of love's marches and countermarches.

"What did Monsieur de Montriveau reply?" she asked, as indifferently as she could, when the man came back to report himself.

"Monsieur le Marquis requested me to tell Madame la Duchesse that it was all right."

Oh the dreadful reaction of the soul upon herself! To have her heart stretched on the rack before curious witnesses; yet not to utter a sound, to be forced to keep silence! One of the countless miseries of the rich!

More than three weeks went by. Mme. de Langeais wrote again and again, and no answer came from Montriveau. At last she gave out that she was ill, to gain a dispensation from attendance on the princess and from social duties. She was only at home to her father the Duc de Navarreins, her aunt the Princesse de Blamont-Chauvry, the old Vidame de Pamiers (her maternal great-uncle), and to her husband's uncle, the Duc de Grandlieu. These persons found no difficulty in believing that the duchess was ill, seeing that she grew thinner and paler and more dejected every day. The vague ardor of love, the smart of wounded pride, the continual prick of the only scorn that could touch her, the yearnings toward joys that she craved with a vain continual longing—all these things told upon her, mind and body; all the forces of her nature were stimulated to no purpose. She was paying the arrears of her life of make-believe.

She went out at last to a review. M. de Montriveau was to

be there. For the duchess, on the balcony of the Tuileries with the royal family, it was one of those festival days that are long remembered. She looked supremely beautiful in her languor; she was greeted with admiration in all eyes. It was Montriveau's presence that made her so fair. Once or twice they exchanged glances. The general came almost to her feet in all the glory of that soldier's uniform, which produces an effect upon the feminine imagination to which the most prudish will confess. When a woman is very much in love, and has not seen her lover for two months, such a swift moment must be something like the phase of a dream when the eyes embrace a world that stretches away forever. Only women or young men can imagine the dull, frenzied hunger in the duchess' eyes. As for older men, if during the paroxysms of early passion in youth they had experience of such phenomena of nervous power; at a later day it is so completely forgotten that they deny the very existence of the luxuriant ecstasy—the only name that can be given to these wonderful intuitions. Religious ecstasy is the aberration of a soul that has shaken off its bonds of flesh; whereas in amorous ecstasy all the forces of soul and body are embraced and blended in one. If a woman falls a victim to the tyrannous frenzy before which Mme. de Langeais was forced to bend, she will take one decisive resolution after another so swifty that it is impossible to give account of them. Thought after thought rises and flits across her brain, as clouds are whirled by the wind across the gray veil of mist that shuts out the sun. Thenceforth the facts reveal all. And the facts are these:

The day after the review, Mme. de Langeais sent her carriage and liveried servants to wait at the Marquis de Montriveau's door from eight o'clock in the morning till three in the afternoon. Armand lived in the Rue de Tournon, a few steps away from the Chamber of Peers, and that very day the House was sitting; but long before the peers returned to their palaces, several people had recognized the duchess' carriage and liveries. The first of these was the Baron de Maulincour. That young officer had met with disdain from Mme. de Langeais and a better reception from Mme. de Sérizy; he betook himself at once therefore to his mistress, and under seal of secrecy told her of this strange freak.

In a moment the news was spread with telegraphic speed through all the coteries in the Faubourg Saint-Germain; it reached the Tuileries and the Élysée-Bourbon; it was the sensation of the day, the matter of all the talk from noon till night. Almost everywhere the women denied the facts, but in such a manner that the report was confirmed; the men one and all believed it, and manifested a most indulgent interest in Mme. de Langeais. Some among them threw the blame on Armand.

"That savage of a Montriveau is a man of bronze," said they; "he insisted on making this scandal, no doubt."

"Very well, then," others replied, "Madame de Langeais has been guilty of a most generous piece of imprudence. To renounce the world, and rank, and fortune, and consideration for her lover's sake, and that in the face of all Paris, is as fine a *coup d'état* for a woman as that barber's knife-thrust, which so affected Canning in a court of assize. Not one of the women who blame the duchess would make a declaration worthy of ancient times. It is heroic of Madame de Langeais to proclaim herself so frankly. Now there is nothing left to her but to love Montriveau. There must be something great about a woman if she says: 'I will have but one passion.'"

"But what is to become of society, monsieur, if you honor vice in this way without respect for virtue?" asked the Comtesse de Granville, the attorney-general's wife.

While the château, the faubourg, and the Chaussée d'Antin were discussing the shipwreck of aristocratic virtue; while excited young men rushed about on horseback to make sure that the carriage was standing in the Rue de Tournon, and the duchess in consequence was beyond a doubt in M. de

Montriveau's rooms, Mme. de Langeais, with heavy throbbing pulses, was lying hidden away in her boudoir. And Armand? he had been out all night, and at that moment was walking with M. de Marsay in the gardens of the Tuileries. The elder members of Mme. de Langeais' family were engaged in calling upon one another, arranging to read her a homily and to hold a consultation as to the best way of putting a stop to the scandal.

At three o'clock, therefore, M. le Duc de Navarreins, the Vidame de Pamiers, the old Princesse de Blamont-Chauvry, and the Duc de Grandlieu were assembled in Mme. la Duchesse de Langeais' drawing-room. To them, as to all curious inquirers, the servants said that their mistress was not at home; the duchess had made no exceptions to her orders. But these four personages shone conspicuous in that lofty sphere, of which the revolutions and hereditary pretensions are solemnly recorded year by year in the "Almanach de Gotha," wherefore without some slight sketch of each of them this picture of society were incomplete.

The Princesse de Blamont-Chauvry, in the feminine world, was a most poetic wreck of the reign of Louis Quinze. In her beautiful prime, so it was said, she had done her part to win for that monarch his appellation of *le Bien-aimé* (the well-beloved). Of her past charms of feature, little remained save a remarkably prominent slender nose, curved like a Turkish scimitar, now the principal ornament of a countenance that put you in mind of an old white glove. Add a few powdered curls, high-heeled pantoufles, a cap with upstanding loops of lace, black mittens, and a decided taste for *ombre*. But to do full justice to the lady, it must be said that she appeared in low-necked gowns of an evening (so high an opinion of her ruins had she), wore long gloves, and reddened her cheeks with Martin's classic rouge. An appalling amiability in her wrinkles, a prodigious brightness in the old lady's eyes, a profound dignity in her whole person, together with the triple barbed wit of her tongue, and an infallible memory in her head, made of her a real power in the land. The whole Cabinet des Chartes was entered in duplicate on the parchment of her brain. She knew all the genealogies of every noble house in Europe—princes, dukes, and counts—and could put her hand on the last descendants of Charlemagne in the direct line. No usurpation of title could escape the Princesse de Blamont-Chauvry.

Young men who wished to stand well at Court, ambitious men, and young married women paid her assiduous homage. Her salon set the tone of the Faubourg Saint-Germain. The words of this Talleyrand in petticoats were taken as final decrees. People came to consult her on questions of etiquette or usages, or to take lessons in good taste. And, in truth, no other old woman could put back her snuff-box in her pocket as the princess could; while there was a precision and a grace about the movements of her skirts, when she sat down or crossed her feet, which drove the finest ladies of the young generation to despair. Her voice had remained in her head during one-third of her lifetime; but she could not prevent a descent into the membranes of the nose, which lent to it a peculiar expressiveness. She still retained a hundred and fifty thousand francs of her great fortune, for Napoleon had generously returned her woods to her; so that personally and in the matter of possessions she was a woman of no little consequence.

This curious antique, seated in a low chair by the fireside, was chatting with the Vidame de Pamiers, a contemporary ruin. The vidame* was a big, tall, and spare man, a lord of the old school, and had been a commander of the order of Malta. His neck had always been so tightly compressed by a strangulation stock that his cheeks pouched over it a little, and he held his head high; to many people this would have

---

* A feudal title of those holding the estates of a bishopric on condition of defending them.

given an air of self-sufficiency, but in the vidame it was justified by a Voltairean wit. His wide prominent eyes seemed to see everything, and as a matter of fact there was not much that they had not seen. Altogether, his person was a perfect model of aristocratic outline, slim and slender, supple and agreeable. He seemed as if he could be pliant or rigid at will, and twist and bend, or rear his head like a snake.

The Duc de Navarreins was pacing up and down the room with the Duc de Grandlieu. Both were men of fifty-six or thereabout, and still hale; both were short, corpulent, flourishing, somewhat florid-complexioned men with jaded eyes, and lower lips that had begun to hang already. But for an exquisite refinement of accent, an urbane courtesy, and an ease of manner that could change in a moment to insolence, a superficial observer might have taken them for a couple of bankers. Any such mistake would have been impossible, however, if the listener could have heard them converse, and seen them on their guard with men whom they feared, vapid and commonplace with their equals, slippery with their inferiors, whom courtiers and statesmen know how to tame by a tactful word or to humiliate with an unexpected phrase.

Such were the representatives of the great noblesse that determined to perish rather than submit to any change. It was a noblesse that deserved praise and blame in equal measure; a noblesse that will never be judged impartially until some poet shall arise to tell how joyfully the nobles obeyed the King though their heads fell under a Richelieu's axe, and how deeply they scorned the guillotine of '89 as a foul revenge.

Another noticeable trait in all the four was a thin voice that agreed peculiarly well with their ideas and bearing. Among themselves, at any rate, they were on terms of perfect equality. None of them betrayed any sign of annoyance over the duchess' escapade, but all of them had learned at Court to hide their feelings.

And here, lest critics should condemn the puerility of the opening of the forthcoming scene, it is perhaps as well to remind the reader that Locke, once happening to be in the company of several great lords, renowned no less for their wit than for their breeding and political consistency, wickedly amused himself by taking down their conversation by some shorthand process of his own; and afterward, when he read it over to them to see what they could make of it, they all burst out laughing. And, in truth, the tinsel jargon which circulates among the upper ranks in every country yields mighty little gold to the crucible when washed in the ashes of literature or philosophy. In every rank of society (some few Parisian salons excepted) the curious observer finds folly a constant quantity beneath a more or less transparent varnish. Conversation with any substance in it is a rare exception, and bœotianism is current coin in every zone. In the higher regions they must perforce talk more, but to make up for it they think the less. Thinking is a tiring exercise, and the rich like their lives to flow by easily and without effort. It is by comparing the fundamental matter of jests, as you rise in the social scale from the street-boy to the peer of France, that the observer arrives at a true comprehension of M. de Talleyrand's maxim: "The manner is everything;" an elegant rendering of the legal axiom: "The form is of more consequence than the matter." In the eyes of the poet the advantage rests with the lower classes, for they seldom fail to give a certain character of rude poetry to their thoughts. Perhaps also this same observation may explain the sterility of the salons, their emptiness, their shallowness, and the repugnance felt by men of ability for bartering their ideas for such pitiful small change.

The duke suddenly stopped as if some bright idea occurred to him, and remarked to his neighbor—

"So you have sold Tornthon?"

"No, he is ill. I am very much afraid I shall lose him,

and I should be uncommonly sorry. He is a very good hunter. Do you know how the Duchesse de Marigny is?"

"No. I did not go this morning. I was just going out to call when you came in to speak about Antoinette. But yesterday she was very ill indeed; they had given her up, she took the sacrament."

"Her death will make a change in your cousin's position."

"Not at all. She gave away her property in her lifetime, only keeping an annuity. She made over the Guébriant estate to her niece, Madame de Soulanges, subject to a yearly charge."

"It will be a great loss for society. She was a kind woman. Her family will miss her; her experience and advice carried weight. Her son Marigny is an amiable man; he has a sharp wit; he can talk. He is pleasant, very pleasant. Pleasant? oh, that no one can deny, but—ill regulated to the last degree. Well, and yet it is an extraordinary thing, he is very acute. He was dining at the club the other day with that moneyed Chaussée-d'Antin set. Your uncle (he always goes there for his game of cards) found him there to his astonishment, and asked if he was a member. 'Yes,' said he, 'I don't go into society now; I am living among the bankers.' You know why?" added the marquis, with a meaning smile.

"No," said the duke.

"He is smitten with that little Madame Keller, Gondreville's daughter; she is only lately married, and has a great vogue, they say, in that set."

"Well, Antoinette does not find time heavy on her hands, it seems," remarked the vidame.

"My affection for that little woman has driven me to find a singular pastime," replied the princess, as she returned her snuff-box to her pocket.

"Dear aunt, I am extremely vexed," said the duke, stopping short in his walk. "Nobody but one of Bonaparte's men could ask such an indecorous thing of a woman of fashion. Between ourselves, Antoinette might have made a better choice."

"The Montriveaus are a very old family and very well connected, my dear," replied the princess; "they are related to all the noblest houses of Burgundy. If the Dulmen branch of the Arschoot-Rivaudoults should come to an end in Galicia, the Montriveaus would succeed to the Arschoot title and estates. They inherit through their great-grandfather."

"Are you sure?"

"I know it better than this Montriveau's father did. I told him about it, I used to see a good deal of him; and, chevalier of several orders though he was, he only laughed; he was an encyclopædist. But his brother turned the relationship to good account during the emigration. I have heard it said that his northern kinsfolk were most kind in every way——"

"Yes, to be sure. The Comte de Montriveau died at St. Petersburg," said the vidame. "I met him there. He was a big man with an incredible passion for oysters."

"How many did he ever eat?" asked the Duc de Grandlieu.

"Ten dozen every day."

"And did they not disagree with him?"

"Not the least bit in the world."

"Why, that is extraordinary! Had he neither the stone nor gout, nor any other complaint, in consequence?"

"No; his health was perfectly good, and he died through an accident."

"By accident! Nature prompted him to eat oysters, so probably he required them; for up to a certain point our predominant tastes are conditions of our existence."

"I am of your opinion," said the princess, with a smile.

"Madame, you always put a malicious construction on things," returned the marquis.

"I only want you to understand that these remarks might

leave a wrong impression on a young woman's mind," said
she, and interrupted herself to exclaim, "But this niece, this
niece of mine!"

"Dear aunt, I still refuse to believe that she can have gone
to Monsieur de Montriveau," said the Duc de Navarreins.

"Bah!" returned the princess.

"What do you think, vidame!" asked the marquis.

"If the duchess were an artless simpleton I should think
that——."

"But when a woman is in love she becomes an artless
simpleton," retorted the princess. "Really, my poor vidame,
you must be getting older."

"After all, what is to be done?" asked the duke.

"If my dear niece is wise," said the princess, "she will go
to Court this evening—fortunately, to-day is Monday, and
reception day—and you must see that we all rally round her
and give the lie to this absurd rumor. There are hundreds of
ways of explaining things; and if the Marquis de Montriveau
is a gentleman, he will come to our assistance. We will bring
these children to listen to reason——."

"But, dear aunt, it is not easy to tell Monsieur de Montriveau
the truth to his face. He is one of Bonaparte's pupils, and
he has a position. Why, he is one of the great men of the day;
he is high up in the Guards, and very useful there. He has
not a spark of ambition. He is just the man to say: 'Here is
my commission, leave me in peace,' if the King should say a
word that he did not like."

"Then, pray, what are his opinions?"

"Very unsound."

"Really," sighed the princess, "the King is, as he always
has been, a Jacobin under the lilies of France."

"Oh! not quite so bad," said the vidame.

"Yes; I have known him for a long while. The man that
pointed out the Court to his wife on the occasion of her first
State dinner in public with: 'These are our people,' could

only be a black-hearted scoundrel. I can see monsieur exactly the same as ever in the King. The bad brother who voted so wrongly in his department of the Constituent Assembly was sure to compound with the Liberals and allow them to argue and talk. This philosophical cant will be just as dangerous now for the younger brother as it used to be for the elder; this fat man with the little mind is amusing himself by creating difficulties, and how his successor is to get out of them I do not know; he holds his younger brother in abhorrence; he would be glad to think as he lay dying: 'He will not reign very long——' "

"Aunt, he is the King, and I have the honor to be in his service——"

" But does your post take away your right of free speech, my dear? You come of quite as good a house as the Bourbons. If the Guises had shown a little more resolution, his majesty would be a nobody at this day. It is time I went out of this world, the noblesse is dead. Yes, it is all over with you, my children," she continued, looking as she spoke at the vidame. " What has my niece done that the whole town should be talking about her? She is in the wrong; I disapprove of her conduct, a useless scandal is a blunder; that is why I still have my doubts about this want of regard for appearances; I brought her up, and I know that——"

Just at that moment the duchess came out of her boudoir. She had recognized her aunt's voice and heard the name of Montriveau. She was still in her loose morning-wrapper; and even as she came in, M. de Grandlieu, looking carelessly out of the window, saw his niece's carriage driving back along the street. The duke took his daughter's face in both hands and kissed her on the forehead. " So, dear girl," he said, "you do not know what is going on?"

" Has anything extraordinary happened, father dear?"

"Why, all Paris believes that you are with Monsieur de Montriveau."

"My dear Antoinette, you were at home all the time, were you not?" said the princess, holding out a hand, which the duchess kissed with affectionate respect.

"Yes, dear mother; I was at home all the time. And," she added, as she turned to greet the vidame and the marquis, "I wished that all Paris should think that I was with Monsieur de Montriveau."

The duke flung up his hands, struck them together in despair, and folded his arms.

"Then, cannot you see what will come of this mad freak?" he asked at last.

But the aged princess had suddenly risen and stood looking steadily at the duchess; the younger woman flushed and her eyes fell. Mme. de Chauvry gently drew her closer, and said: "My little angel, let me kiss you!"

She kissed her niece very affectionately on the forehead, and continued smiling, while she held her hand in a tight clasp.

"We are not under the Valois now, dear child. You have compromised your husband and your position. Still, we will arrange to make everything right."

"But, dear aunt, I do not wish to make it right at all. It is my wish that all Paris should say that I was with Monsieur de Montriveau this morning. If you destroy that belief, however ill-grounded it may be, you will do me a singular disservice."

"Do you really wish to ruin yourself, child, and to grieve your family?"

"My family, father, unintentionally condemned me to irreparable misfortune when they sacrificed me to family considerations. You may, perhaps, blame me for seeking alleviations, but you will certainly feel for me."

"After all the endless pains you take to settle your daughters suitably!" muttered M. de Navarreins, addressing the vidame.

The princess shook a stray grain of snuff from her skirts. "My dear little girl," she said, "be happy, if you can. We are not talking of troubling your felicity, but of reconciling it with social usages. We all of us here assembled know that marriage is a defective institution tempered by love. But when you take a lover, is there any need to make your bed in the Place du Carrousel? See now, just be a bit reasonable, and hear what we have to say."

"I am listening."

"Madame la Duchesse," began the Duc de Grandlieu, "if it were any part of an uncle's duty to look after his nieces, he ought to have a position; society would owe him honors and rewards and a salary, exactly as if he were in the King's service. So I am not here to talk about my nephew, but of your own interests. Let us look ahead a little. If you persist in making a scandal—I have seen the animal before, and I own that I have no great liking for him—Langeais is stingy enough, and he does not care a rap for any one but himself; he will have a separation; he will stick to your money, and leave you poor, and consequently you will be a nobody. The income of a hundred thousand francs that you have just inherited from your maternal great-aunt will go to pay for his mistresses' amusements. You will be bound and gagged by the law; you will have to say Amen to all these arrangements. Suppose Monsieur de Montriveau leaves you—— dear me! do not let us put ourselves in a passion, my dear niece; a man does not leave a woman while she is young and pretty; still, we have seen so many pretty women left disconsolate, even among princesses, that you will permit the supposition, an all but impossible supposition I quite wish to believe—— Well, suppose that he goes, what will become of you without a husband? Keep well with your husband as you take care of your beauty; for beauty, after all, is a woman's paraclete, and a husband also stands between you and worse. I am supposing that you are happy and loved to the end, and I am leaving unpleasant or unfortunate events altogether out of the reckoning. This being so, fortunately or unfortunately, you may have children. What are they to be? Montriveaus? Very well; they certainly will not succeed to their father's whole fortune. You will want to give them all that you have; he will wish to do the same. Nothing more natural, dear me! And you will find the law against you. How many times have we seen heirs-at-law bringing a lawsuit to recover the property from illegitimate children? Every court of law rings with such actions all over the world. You will create a *fidei commissum* perhaps; and if the trustee betrays your confidence, your children have no remedy against him; and they are ruined. So choose carefully. You see the perplexities of the position. In every possible way your children will be sacrificed of necessity to the fancies of your heart; they will have no recognized status. While they are little they will be charming; but, Lord! some day they will reproach you for thinking of no one but your two selves. We old gentlemen know all about it. Little boys grow up into men, and men are ungrateful beings. When I was in Germany, did I not hear young de Horn say, after supper: 'If my mother had been an honest woman, I should be prince-regnant!' 'IF?' We have spent our lives in hearing plebeians say *if*. *If* brought about the Revolution. When a man cannot lay the blame on his father or mother, he holds God responsible for his hard lot. In short, dear child, we are here to open your eyes. I will say all I have to say in a few words, on which you had better meditate: A woman ought never to put her husband in the right."

"Uncle, so long as I cared for nobody, I could calculate; I looked at interests then, as you do; now, I can only feel."

"But, my dear little girl," remonstrated the vidame, "life is simply a complication of interests and feelings; to be happy, more particularly in your position, one must try to reconcile one's feelings with one's interests. A grisette may love according to her fancy, that is intelligible enough, but you have a pretty fortune, a family, a name and a place at Court, and you ought not to fling them out of the window. And what have we been asking you to do to keep them all? To manœuvre carefully instead of falling foul of social conventions. Lord! I shall very soon be eighty years old, and I cannot recollect, under any régime, a love worth the price that you are willing to pay for the love of this lucky young man."

The duchess silenced the vidame with a look; if Montriveau could have seen that glance, he would have forgiven all.

"It would be very effective on the stage," remarked the Duc de Grandlieu, " but it all amounts to nothing when your jointure and position and independence are concerned. You are not grateful, my dear niece. You will not find many families where the relatives have courage enough to teach the wisdom gained by experience, and to make rash young heads listen to reason. Renounce your salvation in two minutes, if it pleases you to damn yourself; well and good; but reflect well beforehand when it comes to renouncing your income. I know of no confessor who remits the pains of poverty. I have a right, I think, to speak in this way to you; for if you are ruined, I am the one person who can offer you a refuge. I am almost an uncle to Langeais, and I alone have the right to put him in the wrong."

The Duc de Navarreins roused himself from painful reflections.

"Since you speak of feeling, my child," he said, "let me remind you that a woman who bears your name ought to be moved by sentiments which do not touch ordinary people. Can you wish to give an advantage to the Liberals, to those jesuits of Robespierre's that are doing all they can to vilify the noblesse? Some things a Navarreins cannot do without failing in duty to his house. You would not be alone in your dishonor——"

"Come, come!" said the princess. "Dishonor? Do not

make such a fuss about the journey of an empty carriage, children, and leave me alone with Antoinette. All three of you come and dine with me. I will undertake to properly arrange matters. You men understand nothing; you are beginning to talk sourly already, and I have no wish to see a quarrel between you and my dear child. Do me the pleasure of going."

The three gentlemen probably guessed the princess' intentions; they took their leave. M. de Navarreins kissed his daughter on the forehead with: "Come, be good, dear child. It is not too late yet if you choose."

"Couldn't we find some good fellow in the family to pick a quarrel with this Montriveau?" said the vidame, as they went downstairs.

When the two women were alone, the princess beckoned her niece to a little low chair by her side.

"My pearl," said she, "in this world below, I know nothing worse calumniated than God and the Eighteenth Century; for as I look back over my own young days, I do not recollect that a single duchess trampled the proprieties under foot as you have just done. Novelists and scribblers brought the reign of Louis XV. into disrepute. Do not believe them. The du Barry, my dear, was quite as good as the Widow Scarron, and the more agreeable woman of the two. In my time a woman could keep her dignity among her gallantries. Indiscretion was the ruin of us, and the beginning of all the mischief. The philosophists—the nobodies whom we admitted into our salons—had no more gratitude or sense of decency than to make an inventory of our hearts, to traduce us one and all, and to rail against the age by way of a return for our kindness. The people are not in a position to judge of anything whatsoever; they looked at the facts, not at the form. But the men and women of those times, my heart, were quite as remarkable as at any other period of the Monarchy. Not one of your Werthers, none of your notabilities, as they are called, never a one of your men in yellow kid gloves and trousers that disguise the poverty of their legs, would cross Europe in the dress of a traveling hawker to brave the daggers of a Duke of Modena, and to shut himself up in the dressing-room of the Regent's daughter at the risk of his life. Not one of your little consumptive patients with their tortoise-shell eyeglasses would hide himself in a closet for six weeks, like Lauzun, to keep up his mistress' courage while she was lying-in of her child. There was more passion in Monsieur de Jaucourt's little finger than in your whole race of higglers that leave a woman to better themselves elsewhere! Just tell me where to find the page that would be cut in pieces and buried under the floor boards for one kiss on the Königsmark's gloved finger.

"Really, it would seem to-day that the roles are exchanged, and women are expected to show their devotion for men. These modern gentlemen are worth less, yet think more of themselves. Believe me, my dear, all these adventures that have been made public, and now are turned against our good Louis XV., were kept quite secret at first. If it had not been for a pack of poetasters, scribblers, and moralists, who hung about our waiting-women, and penned their slanders, our epoch would have appeared in literature as a well-conducted age. I am justifying the century and not its fringe. Perhaps a hundred women of quality were lost : but for every one, the rogues set down ten, like the gazettes after a battle when they count up the losses of the beaten side. And in any case I do not know that the Revolution and the Empire can reproach us ; they were coarse, dull, licentious times. Faugh ! it is revolting.

"Those are the brothels of French history.

"This preamble, my dear child," she continued after a pause, "brings me to the thing that I have to say. If you care for Montriveau, you are quite at liberty to love him at your ease, and as much as you can. I know by experience that, unless you are locked up (but locking people up is out of fashion now), you will do as you please; I should have done the same at your age. Only, sweet heart, I should not have given up my right to be the mother of future Ducs de Langeais. So mind appearances. The vidame is right. No man is worth a single one of the sacrifices which we are foolish enough to make for their love. Put yourself in such a position that you may still be Monsieur de Langeais' wife, in case you should have the misfortune to repent. When you are an old woman, you will be very glad to hear mass said at Court, and not in some provincial convent. Therein lies the whole question. A single imprudence means an allowance and a wandering life; it means that you are at the mercy of your lover; it means that you must put up with insolence from women that are not so honest, precisely because they have been very vulgarly sharp-witted. It would be a hundred times better to go to Montriveau's at night in a cab, and disguised, instead of sending your carriage in broad daylight. You are a little simpleton, my dear child! Your carriage flattered his vanity; your person would have ensnared his heart. All this that I have said is just and true; but, for my own part, I do not blame you. You are two centuries behind the times with your false ideas of greatness. There, leave us to arrange your affairs, and say that Montriveau made your servants drunk to gratify his vanity and to compromise you——"

The duchess rose to her feet with a spring. "In heaven's name, aunt, do not slander him!"

The old princess' eyes flashed.

"My dear child," she said, "I should have liked to spare such of your illusions as were not fatal. But there must be an end of all illusions now. You would soften me if I were not so old. Come, now, do not vex him, or us, or any one else. I will undertake to satisfy everybody; but promise me not to permit yourself a single step henceforth until you have consulted me. Tell me all, and perhaps I may bring it all right again."

"Aunt, I promise——"

"To tell me everything?"

"Yes, everything. Everything that can be told."

"But, my sweet heart, it is precisely what cannot be told that I want to know. Let us understand each other thoroughly. Come, let me put my withered old lips on your beautiful forehead. No; let me do as I wish. I forbid you to kiss my bones. Old people have a courtesy of their own. There, take me down to my carriage," she added, when she had kissed her niece.

"Then may I go to him in disguise, dear aunt?"

"Why—yes. The story can always be denied," said the old princess.

This was the one idea which the duchess had clearly grasped in the sermon. When Mme. de Chauvry was seated in the corner of her carriage, Mme. de Langeais bade her a graceful adieu and went up to her room. She was quite happy again.

"My person would have snared his heart; my aunt is right; a man cannot surely refuse a pretty woman when she understands how to offer herself."

That evening, at the Élysée-Bourbon, the Duc de Navarreins, M. de Pamiers, M. de Marsay, M. de Grandlieu, and the Duc de Maufrigneuse triumphantly refuted the scandals that were circulating with regard to the Duchess de Langeais. So many officers and other persons had seen Montriveau walking in the Tuileries that morning, that the silly story was set down to chance, which takes all that is offered. And so, in spite of the fact that the duchess' carriage had waited before Montriveau's door, her character became as clear and as spotless as Mambrino's sword after Sancho had polished it up.

But, at two o'clock, M. de Ronquerolles passed Montriveau in a deserted alley, and said with a smile: "She is coming on, is your duchess. Go on, keep it up!" he added, and gave a significant cut of the riding-whip to his mare, who sped off like a bullet down the avenue.

Two days after the fruitless scandal, Mme. de Langeais wrote to M. de Montriveau. That letter, like the preceding ones, remained unanswered. This time she took her own measures, and bribed M. de Montriveau's man, Auguste. And so at eight o'clock that evening she was introduced into Armand's apartment. It was not the room in which that secret scene had passed; it was entirely different. The duchess was told that the general would not be at home that night. Had he two houses? The man would give no answer. Mme. de Langeais had bought the key of the room, but not the man's whole loyalty.

When she was left alone she saw her fourteen letters lying on an old-fashioned stand, all of them uncreased and unopened. He had not read them. She sank into an easy-chair, and for a while she lost consciousness. When she came to herself, Auguste was holding toilet vinegar for her to inhale.

"A carriage; quick!" she ordered.

The carriage came. She hastened downstairs with convulsive speed, returned home, and left orders that no one was to be admitted. For twenty-four hours she lay in bed, and would have no one near her but her woman, who brought her a cup of orange-flower water from time to time. Suzette heard her mistress moan once or twice, and caught a glimpse of tears in the brilliant eyes, now circled with dark shadows.

The next day, amid despairing tears, Mme. de Langeais took her resolution. Her man of business came for an interview, and no doubt received instructions of some kind. Afterward she sent for the Vidame de Pamiers; and while she waited, she wrote a letter to M. de Montriveau. The vidame punctually came toward two o'clock that afternoon, to find his young cousin looking white and worn, but resigned; never had her divine loveliness been more poetic than now in the languor of her agony.

"You owe this assignation to your eighty-four years, dear cousin," she said. "Ah! do not smile, I beg of you, when an unhappy woman has reached the lowest depths of wretchedness. You are a gentleman, and after the adventures of your youth you must feel some indulgence for women."

"None whatever," said he.

"Indeed!"

"Everything is in their favor."

"Ah! Well, you are one of the inner family circle; possibly you will be the last relative, the last friend, whose hand I shall press, so I can ask your good offices. Will you, dear vidame, do me a service which I could not ask of my own father, nor of my Uncle Grandlieu, nor of any woman? You cannot fail to understand. I beg of you to do my bidding, and then to forget what you have done, whatever may come of it. It is this: Will you take this letter and go to Monsieur de Montriveau? will you see him yourself, give it into his hands, and ask him, as you men can ask things between yourselves—for you have a code of honor between man and man which you do not use with us, and a different way of regarding things between yourselves—ask him if he will read this letter? Not in your presence. Certain feelings men hide from each other. I give you authority to say, if you think it necessary to bring him, that it is a question of life or death for me. If he deigns——"

"*Deigns!*" repeated the vidame,

"If he deigns to read it," the duchess continued with dignity, "say one thing more. You will go to see him about five o'clock, for I know that he will dine at home to-day at that time. Very good. By way of answer he must come to see me. If, three hours afterward, by eight o'clock, he does not leave his house, all will be over. The Duchesse de Langeais will have vanished from the world. I shall not be dead, dear friend, no, but no human power will ever find me again on this earth. Come and dine with me; I shall at least have one friend with me in the last agony. Yes, dear cousin, to-night will decide my fate; and whatever happens to me, I pass through an ordeal by fire. There! not a word. I will hear nothing of the nature of comment or advice—— Let us chat and laugh together," she added, holding out a hand, which he kissed. "We will be like two gray-headed philosophers who have learned to enjoy life to the last moment. I will look my best; I will be very enchanting for you. You perhaps will be the last man to set eyes on the Duchesse de Langeais."

The vicomte bowed, took the letter, and went without a word. At five o'clock he returned. His cousin had studied to please him, and she looked lovely indeed. The room was gay with flowers as if for a festivity; the dinner was exquisite. For the gray-headed vidame the duchess displayed all the brilliancy of her wit; she was more charming than she had ever been before. At first the vidame tried to look on all these preparations as a young woman's jest; but now and again the attempted illusion faded, the spell of his fair cousin's charm was broken. He detected a shudder caused by some kind of sudden dread, and once she seemed to listen during a pause.

"What is the matter?" he asked.

"Hush!" she said.

At seven o'clock the duchess left him for a few minutes. When she came back again she was dressed as her maid might have dressed her for a journey. She asked her guest to be her escort, took his arm, sprang into a hackney-coach, and by a quarter to eight they stood outside M. de Montriveau's door.

Armand meantime had been reading the following letter:

"MY FRIEND:—I went to your rooms for a few minutes without your knowledge; I found my letters there, and took them away. This cannot be indifference, Armand, between us; and hatred would show itself quite differently. If you love me, make an end of this cruel play, or you will kill me, and afterward, learning how much you were loved, you might be in despair. If I have not rightly understood you, if you have no feeling toward me but aversion, which implies both contempt and disgust, then I give up all hope. A man never recovers from those feelings. You will have no regrets. Dreadful though that thought may be, it will comfort me in my long sorrow. Regrets? Oh! my Armand, may I never know of them; if I thought I had caused you but a single regret—— But, no, I will not tell you what desolation I should feel. I should be living still, and I could not be your wife; it would be too late!

"Now that I have given myself wholly to you in thought, to whom else should I give myself?—to God. The eyes that you loved for a little while shall never look on another man's face; and may the glory of God blind them to all beside. I shall never hear human voices more since I heard yours—so gentle at the first, so terrible yesterday; for it seems to me that I am still only on the morrow of your vengeance. And now may the will of God consume me. Between His wrath and yours, my friend, there will be nothing left for me but a little space for tears and prayers.

"Perhaps you wonder why I write you? Ah! do not think ill of me if I keep a gleam of hope, and give one last sigh to happy life before I take leave of it forever. I am in a hideous position. I feel all the inward serenity that comes when a great resolution has been taken, even while I hear the last growlings of the storm. When you went out on that terrible adventure which so drew me to you, Armand, you went from the desert to the oasis with a good guide to show you the way. Well, I am going out of the oasis into the desert, and you are a pitiless guide to me. And yet you only, my friend, can understand how melancholy it is to look back for the last time on happiness—to you, and you only, I can make moan without a blush. If you grant my entreaty, I shall be happy;

if you are inexorable, I shall expiate the wrong that I have done. After all, it is natural, is it not, that a woman should wish to live, invested with all noble feelings, in her friend's memory? Oh! my love and only love, let her to whom you gave life go down into the tomb in the belief that she is great in your eyes. Your harshness led me to reflect; and now that I love you so, it seems to me that I am less guilty than you think. Listen to my justification, I owe it to you; and you, that are all the world to me, owe me at least a moment's justice.

"I have learned by my own anguish all that I made you suffer by my coquetry; but in those days I was utterly ignorant of love. *You*, knowing what the torture is, *you* mete it out to me! During those first eight months that you gave me you never roused any feeling of love in me. Do you ask why this was so, my friend? I can no more explain it than I can tell you why I love you now. Oh! certainly it flattered my vanity that I should be the subject of your passionate talk, and receive those burning glances of yours; but you left me cold. No, I was not a woman; I had no conception of womanly devotion and happiness. Who was to blame? You would have despised me, would you not, if I had given myself without the impulse of passion? Perhaps it is the highest height to which we can rise—to give all and receive no joy; perhaps there is no merit in yielding one's self to bliss that is foreseen and ardently desired. Alas, my friend, I can say this now; these thoughts came to me when I played with you; and you seemed to me so great even then that I would not have you owe the gift to pity—— What is this that I have written?

"I have taken back all my letters; I am flinging them one by one on the fire; they are burning. You will never know what they confessed—all the love and the passion and the madness——

"I will say no more. Armand: I will stop. I will not say another word of my feelings. If my prayers have not echoed from my soul through yours, I also, woman that I am, decline to owe your love to your pity. It is my wish to be loved, because you cannot choose but love me, or else to be left without mercy. If you refuse to read this letter, it shall be burnt. If, after you have read it, you do not come to me within three hours, to be henceforth for ever my husband, the one man in the world for me; then I shall never blush to know that this letter is in your hands, the pride of my despair will protect my memory from all insult, and my end shall be worthy of my love. When you see me no more on earth, albeit I shall still be alive, you yourself will not think without a shudder of the woman who, in three hours' time, will live only to overwhelm you with her tenderness; a woman consumed by a hopeless love, and faithful—not to memories of past joys—but to a love that was slighted.

"The Duchesse de la Vallière wept for lost happiness and vanished power; but the Duchesse de Langeais will be happy that she may weep and be a power for you still. Yes, you will regret me. I see clearly that I was not of this world, and I thank you for making it clear to me.

"Farewell; you will never touch *my* axe. Yours was the executioner's axe, mine is God's; yours kills, mine saves. Your love was but mortal, it could not endure disdain or ridicule; mine can endure all things without growing weaker, it will last eternally. Ah! I feel a sombre joy in crushing you that believe yourself so great; in humbling you with the calm, indulgent smile of one of the least among the angels that lie at the feet of God, for to them is given the right and the power to protect and watch over men in His name. You have but felt fleeting desires, while the poor nun will shed the light of her ceaseless and ardent prayer about you, she will shelter you all your life long beneath the wings of a love that has nothing of earth in it.

"I have a presentiment of your answer: our trysting-place will be—in heaven. Strength and weakness can both enter there, dear Armand; the strong and the weak are bound to suffer. This thought soothes the anguish of my final ordeal. So calm am I that I should fear that I had ceased to love you if I were not about to leave the world for your sake.

"ANTOINETTE."

"Dear vidame," said the duchess as they reached Montriveau's house, "do me the kindness to ask at the door whether he is at home."

The vidame, obedient after the manner of the eighteenth century to a woman's wish, got out, and came back to bring his cousin an affirmative answer that sent a shudder through her. She grasped his hand tightly in hers, suffered him to kiss her on either cheek, and begged him to go at once. He must not watch her movements nor try to protect her.

"But the people passing in the street," he objected.

"No one can fail in respect to me," she said. It was the last word spoken by the duchess and the woman of fashion.

The vidame went. Mme. de Langeais wrapped herself about in her cloak, and stood on the doorstep until the clocks struck eight. The last stroke died away. The unhappy woman waited ten, fifteen minutes; to the last she tried to see a fresh humiliation in the delay, then her faith ebbed. She turned to leave the fatal threshold.

"Oh, God!" the cry broke from her in spite of herself; it was the first word spoken by the Carmelite.

Montriveau and some of his friends were talking together. He tried to hasten them to a conclusion, but his clock was slow, and by the time he started out for the Hôtel de Langeais the duchess was hurrying on foot through the streets of Paris, goaded by the dull rage in her heart. She reached the Boulevard d'Enfer, and looked out for the last time through falling tears on the noisy, smoky city that lay below in a red mist.

lighted up by its own lamps. Then she hailed a coach, and drove away, never to return.

When the Marquis de Montriveau reached the Hôtel de Langeais, and found no trace of his mistress, he thought that he had been duped. He hurried away at once to the vidame, and found that worthy gentleman in the act of slipping on his flowered dressing-gown, thinking the while of his fair cousin's happiness. Montriveau gave him one of the terrific glances that produced the effect of an electric shock on men and women alike.

"Is it possible that you have lent yourself to some cruel hoax, monsieur?" Montriveau exclaimed. "I have just come from Madame de Langeais' house; the servants say that she is out."

"Then a great misfortune has happened, no doubt," returned the vidame, "and through your fault. I left the duchess at your door——"

"When?"

"At a quarter to eight."

"Good-evening," returned Montriveau, and he hurried home to ask the porter whether he had seen a lady standing on the door-step that evening.

"Yes, my lord marquis, a handsome woman, who seemed very much put out. She was crying like a Magdalen, but she never made a sound, and stood as upright as a post. Then at last she went, and my wife and I that were watching her, while she could not see us, heard her say, 'Oh, God!' so that it went to our hearts, asking your pardon, to hear her say it."

Montriveau, in spite of all his firmness, turned pale at those few words. He wrote a few lines to Ronquerolles, sent off the message at once, and went up to his rooms. Ronquerolles came just about midnight.

Armand gave him the duchess' letter to read.

"Well?" asked Ronquerolles.

"She was here at my door at eight o'clock; at a quarter-past eight she had gone. I have lost her, and I love her. Oh! if my life were altogether my own, I could blow my brains out."

"Pooh, pooh! Keep cool," said Ronquerolles. "Duchesses do not fly off like wagtails. She cannot travel faster than three leagues an hour, and to-morrow we will ride six. Confound it! Madame de Langeais is no ordinary woman," he continued. "To-morrow we will all of us mount and ride. The police will put us on her track during the day. She must have a carriage; angels of that sort have no wings. We shall find her whether she is on the road or hidden in Paris. There is the semaphore. We can stop her. You shall be happy. But, my dear fellow, you have made a blunder, of which men of your energy are very often guilty. They judge others by themselves, and do not know the point when human nature gives way if you strain the cords too tightly. Why did you not say a word to me sooner? I would have told you to be punctual. Adieu till to-morrow," he added, as Montriveau said nothing. "Sleep if you can," he added, with a grasp of the hand.

But the greatest resources which society has ever placed at the disposal of statesmen, kings, ministers, bankers, or any human power, in fact, were all exhausted in vain. Neither Montriveau nor his friends could find any trace of the duchess. It was clear that she had entered a convent. Montriveau determined to search, or to institute a search, for her through every convent in the world. He must have her, even at the cost of all the lives in a town. And in justice to this extraordinary man, it must be said that his frenzied passion awoke to the same ardor daily and lasted through five years. Only in 1829 did the Duc de Navarreins hear by chance that his daughter had traveled to Spain as Lady Julia Hopwood's maid, that she had left her service at Cadiz, and that Lady Julia never discovered that Mlle. Caroline was the illustrious duchess whose sudden disappearance wagged the tongues of the highest society of Paris.

The feelings of the two lovers when they met again on either side of the grating in the Carmelite convent should now be comprehended to the full, and the violence of the passion awakened in either soul will doubtless explain the catastrophe of the story.

In 1823 the Duc de Langeais was dead, and his wife was free. Antoinette de Navarreins was living, consumed by love, on a ledge of rock in the Mediterranean; but it was in the pope's power to dissolve Sister Theresa's vows. The happiness bought by so much love might yet bloom for the two lovers. These thoughts sent Montriveau flying from Cadiz to Marseilles, and from Marseilles to Paris.

A few months after his return to France, a merchant brig, fitted out and munitioned for active service, set sail from the port of Marseilles for Spain. The vessel had been chartered by several distinguished men, most of them Frenchmen, who, smitten with a romantic passion for the East, wished to make a journey to those lands. Montriveau's familiar knowledge of Eastern customs made him an invaluable traveling companion, and at the entreaty of the rest he had joined the expedition; the Minister of War appointed him lieutenant-general, and put him on the Artillery Commission to facilitate his departure.

Twenty-four hours later the brig lay to off the northwest shore of an island within sight of the Spanish coast. She had been specially chosen for her shallow keel and light mastage, so that she might lie at anchor in safety half a league away from the reefs that secure the island from approach in this direction. If fishing vessels or the people on the island caught sight of the brig, they were scarcely likely to feel suspicious of her at once; and beside, it was easy to give a reason for her presence without delay. Montriveau hoisted the flag of the

United States before they came in sight of the island, and the crew of the vessel were all American sailors, who spoke nothing but English. One of M. de Montriveau's companions took the men ashore in the ship's long boat, and made them so drunk at an inn in the little town that they could not talk. Then he gave out that the brig was manned by treasure-seekers, a gang of men whose hobby was well known in the United States; indeed, some Spanish writer had written a history of them. The presence of the brig among the reefs was now sufficiently explained. The owners of the vessel, according to the self-styled boatswain's mate, were looking for the wreck of a galleon which foundered thereabout in 1778 with a cargo of treasure from Mexico. The people at the inn and the authorities asked no more questions.

Armand and the devoted friends who were helping him in his difficult enterprise were all from the first of the opinion that there was no hope of rescuing or carrying off Sister Theresa by force or stratagem from the side of the little town. Wherefore these bold spirits, with one accord, determined to take the bull by the horns. They would make a way to the convent at the most seemingly inaccessible point; like General Lamarque, at the storming of Capri, they would conquer Nature. The cliff at the end of the island, a sheer block of granite, afforded even less hold than the rock of Capri. So it seemed at least to Montriveau, who had taken part in that incredible exploit, while the nuns in his eyes were much more redoubtable than Sir Hudson Lowe. To raise a hubbub over carrying off the duchess would cover them with confusion. They might as well set siege to the town and convent, like pirates, and leave not a single soul to tell of their victory. So for them their expedition wore but two aspects. There should be a conflagration and a feat of arms that should dismay all Europe, while the motives of the crime remained unknown; or, on the other hand, a mysterious, aerial descent which should persuade the nuns that the devil himself had paid them a visit. They had decided upon the latter course in the secret council held before they left Paris, and subsequently everything had been done to insure the success of an expedition which promised some real excitement to jaded spirits weary of Paris and its pleasures.

An extremely light pirogue, made at Marseilles on a Malayan model, enabled them to cross the reef, until the rocks rose from out the water. Then two cables of iron-wire were fastened several feet apart between one rock and another. These wire-ropes slanted upward and downward in opposite directions, so that baskets of iron-wire could travel to and fro along them; and in this manner the rocks were covered with a system of baskets and wire-cables, not unlike the filaments which a certain species of spider weaves about a tree. The Chinese, an essentially imitative people, were the first to take a lesson from the work of instinct. Fragile as these bridges were, they were always ready for use; high waves and the caprices of the sea could not throw them out of working order; the ropes hung just sufficiently slack, so as to present to the breakers that particular curve discovered by Cachin, the immortal creator of the harbor at Cherbourg. Against this cunningly devised line the angry surge is powerless; the law of that curve was a secret wrested from Nature by that faculty of observation in which nearly all human genius consists.

M. de Montriveau's companions were alone on board the vessel, and out of sight of every human eye. No one from the deck of a passing vessel could have discovered either the brig hidden among the reefs, or the men at work among the rocks; they lay below the ordinary range of the most powerful telescope. Eleven days were spent in preparation before the Thirteen, with all their infernal power, could reach the foot of the cliffs. The body of the rock rose up straight from the sea to a height of one hundred and eighty feet. Any attempt to climb the sheer wall of granite seemed impossible; a mouse

might as well try to creep up the slippery sides of a plain
china vase. Still there was a cleft, a straight line of fissure so
fortunately placed that large blocks of wood could be wedged
firmly into it at a distance of about a foot apart. Into these
blocks the daring workers drove iron clamps, specially made
for the purpose, with a broad iron bracket at the outer end,
through which a hole had been drilled. Each bracket carried
a light pine board which corresponded with a notch made in
a pole that reached to the top of the cliffs, and was firmly
planted in the beach at their feet. With ingenuity worthy of
these men who found nothing impossible, one of their number,
a skilled mathematician, had calculated the angle from which
the steps must start; so that from the middle they rose gradually, like the sticks of a fan, to the top of the cliff, and descended in the same fashion to its base. That miraculously
light, yet perfectly firm, staircase cost them twenty-two days
of toil. A little tinder and the surf of the sea would destroy
all trace of it for ever in a single night. A betrayal of the
secret was impossible; and all search for the violators of the
convent would be doomed to failure.

At the top of the rock there was a platform with sheer precipice on all sides. The Thirteen, reconnoitring the ground
with their glasses from the masthead, made certain that,
though the ascent was steep and rough, there would be no
difficulty in gaining the convent garden, where the trees were
thick enough for a hiding-place. After such great efforts
they would not risk the success of their enterprise, and were
compelled to wait till the moon passed out of her last quarter.

For two nights Montriveau, wrapped in his cloak, lay out
on the rock platform. The singing at vespers and matins
filled him with unutterable joy. He stood under the wall to
hear the music of the organ, listening intently for one voice
among the rest. But in spite of the silence, the confused
effect of music was all that reached his ears. In those sweet
harmonies defects of execution are lost; the pure spirit of art

comes into direct communication with the spirit of the hearer, making no demand on the attention, no strain on the power of listening. Intolerable memories awoke. All the love within him seemed to break into blossom again at the breath of that music; he tried to find auguries of happiness in the air. During the last night he sat with his eyes fixed upon an ungrated window, for bars were not needed on the side of the precipice. A light shone there all through the hours; and that instinct of the heart, which is sometimes true, and as often false, cried within him: "She is there!"

"She is certainly there! To-morrow she will be mine," he said to himself, and joy blended with the slow tinkling of a bell that began to ring.

Strange unaccountable workings of the heart! The nun, wasted by yearning love, worn out with tears and fasting, prayer and vigils; the woman of nine-and-twenty, who had passed through heavy trials, was loved more passionately than the light-hearted girl, the woman of four-and-twenty, the sylphide, had ever been. But is there not, for men of vigorous character, something attractive in the sublime expression engraven on women's faces by the impetuous stirrings of thought and misfortunes of no ignoble kind? Is there not a beauty of suffering which is the most interesting of all beauty to those men who feel that within them there is an inexhaustible wealth of tenderness and consoling pity for a creature so gracious in weakness, so strong in love? It is the ordinary nature that is attracted by young, smooth, pink-and-white beauty, or, in one word, by prettiness. In some faces love awakens amid the wrinkles carved by sorrow and the ruin made by melancholy: Montriveau could not but feel drawn to these. For cannot a lover, with the voice of a great longing, call forth a wholly new creature? a creature athrob with the life but just begun breaks forth for him alone, from the outward form that is fair for him, and faded for all the world beside. Does he not love two women? One of them, as others see her, is pale and wan and sad; but the other, the unseen love that his heart knows, is an angel who understands life through feeling, and is adorned in all her glory only for love's high festivals.

The general left his post before sunrise, but not before he had heard voices singing together, sweet voices full of tenderness sounding faintly from the cell. When he came down to the foot of the cliffs where his friends were waiting, he told them that never in his life had he felt such inthralling bliss, and in the few words there was that unmistakable thrill of repressed strong feeling, that magnificent utterance which all men respect.

That night eleven of his devoted comrades made the ascent in the darkness. Each man carried a poinard, a provision of chocolate, and a set of house-breaking tools. They climbed the outer walls with scaling-ladders, and crossed the cemetery of the convent. Montriveau recognized the long, vaulted gallery through which he went to the parlor, and remembered the windows of the room. His plans were made and adopted in a moment. They would effect an entrance through one of the windows in the Carmelite's half of the parlor, find their way along the corridors, ascertain whether the sisters' names were written on the doors, find Sister Theresa's cell, surprise her as she slept, and carry her off, bound and gagged. The programme presented no difficulties to men who combined boldness and a convict's dexterity with the knowledge peculiar to men of the world, especially as they would not scruple to give a stab to insure silence.

In two hours the bars were sawn through. Three men stood on guard outside, and two inside the parlor. The rest, barefooted, took up their posts along the corridor. Young Henri de Marsay, the most dexterous man among them, disguised by way of precaution in a Carmelite's robe, exactly like the costume of the convent, led the way, and Montriveau came immediately behind him. The clock struck three just as the two men reached the dormitory cells. They soon saw the position. Everything was perfectly quiet. With the help of a dark lantern they read the names luckily written on every door, together with the picture of a saint or saints and the mystical words which every nun takes as a kind of motto for the beginning of her new life and the revelation of her last thought. Montriveau reached Sister Theresa's door and read the inscription: *Sub invocatione sanctæ matris Theresæ*, and her motto: *Adoremus in æternum*. Suddenly his companion laid a hand on his shoulder. A bright light was streaming through the chinks of the door. M. de Ronquerolles came up at that moment.

"All the nuns are in the church," he said; "they are beginning the Office for the Dead."

"I will stay here," said Montriveau. "Go back into the parlor, and shut the door at the end of the passage."

He threw open the door and rushed in, preceded by his disguised companion, who let down the veil over his face.

There before them lay the duchess—dead; her plank bed had been laid on the floor of the outer room of her cell, between two lighted candles. Neither Montriveau nor de Marsay spoke a word or uttered a cry; but they looked into each other's faces. The general's dumb gesture seemed to say: "Let us carry her away!"

"Quick!" shouted Ronquerolles, "the procession of nuns is leaving the church. You will be caught!"

With magical swiftness of movement, prompted by an intense desire, the dead woman was carried into the convent parlor, passed through the window, and lowered from the walls before the abbess, followed by the nuns, returned to take up Sister Theresa's body. The sister left in charge had imprudently left her post; there were secrets that she longed to know; and so busy was she ransacking the inner room that she heard nothing, and was horrified when she came back to find that the body was gone. Before the women, in their blank amazement, could think of making a search, the duchess had been lowered by a cord to the foot of the crags, and Montriveau's companions had destroyed all traces of their work. By nine o'clock that morning there was not a sign to show that either staircase or wire-cables had ever existed, and Sister Theresa's body had been taken on board. The brig came into the port to ship her crew, and sailed that day.

Montriveau, down in the cabin, was left alone with Antoinette de Navarreins. For some hours it seemed as if her dead face was transfigured for him by that unearthly beauty which the calm of death gives to the body before it perishes.

"Look here!" said Ronquerolles when Montriveau reappeared on deck, "*that* was a woman once, now it is nothing. Let us tie a cannon-ball to both feet and throw the body overboard; and if you ever think of her again, think of her as of some book that you read as a boy."

"Yes," assented Montriveau, "it is nothing now but a dream."

"That is sensible of you. Now, after this, have passions; but as for love, a man ought to know how to place it wisely. It is only the last love of a woman that can satisfy the first love of a man."

Pré-Lévêque, Geneva, *January* 26, 1834.

MAÎTRE CORNÉLIUS.

TRANSLATED BY JNO. RUDD, B. A.

To Monsieur Le Compte George Mniszech.

Some envious beings may imagine on seeing this page adorned by one of the most illustrious of Samartian names that I am trying, as the goldsmiths do, to enhance a modern work with an ancient jewel—one of the fashions of the day. But you, my dear count, and a few others will know that I am only aiming at paying the debt I owe to Talent, Memory, and Friendship.

In 1479, on All-Saints' Day, the time at which this history commences, vespers were just ending in the cathedral of Tours. The Archbishop Hélie de Bourdeilles arose from his throne to himself give the benediction to the faithful. The sermon had been long, and darkness had fallen before its conclusion; and in some portions of the great church, the towers of which were not finished at that time, the densest obscurity prevailed.

However, a goodly number of tapers were burning in honor of the saints, on the triangular frames destined to receive these so pious offerings, the merit and significance of which have never been properly explained. The lights on each altar and the candles of the candelabra in the chancel were all flaming. Most irregularly shed among the forest of columns and arches which support the roof of the main aisles of the cathedral, the gleam of those masses of candles scarcely illumined the vast building; for, by the strong shadows cast by the pillars and projected upward among the galleries, they caused a myriad fantastic effects and increased the gloom that enveloped the arches, the vaulted ceilings, and the lateral chapels—which, even at mid-day, were always gloomy.

The immense congregation presented no less picturesque effects. Some figures were so vaguely seen in the uncertain light that they seemed like phantoms; while others, lit up by some chance side-light, drew the attention like the principal heads in a picture. Some statues were animate, some of the men were stone. Here and there eyes might be seen sparkling among the columns; the marble saw, the stone spake, the vaulted groins reëchoed sighs, the whole edifice was instinct with life.

The existence of nations can present no more solemn scenes, no moment more majestic. Mankind in the mass needs motion to make it poetical; but in these resorts of religious thought, when mundane wealth unites itself with celestial splendor, an incredible sublimity is experienced in the silence; there is awe in the bent knees, hope in the upraised hands. The concert of feeling which is ascending heavenward from each soul produces an inexplicable phenomenon of spiritual effect.

The mystical exaltation of the true worshipers reacts upon each individual; the feebler are doubtless upborne upon this flood-tide of faith and love. Prayer, an electric force, draws our nature higher than itself. This involuntary unison of all wills, each equally humbled to earth, equally risen to heaven, contains, doubtless, the secret of the magic influence wielded by the intonations of the priests, the music of the organs, the perfumes and pomps of the altar, the voices of the crowd, its silent meditations.

Therefore we need not be astonished to see in the Middle Ages that so many affairs of the heart began in churches after long ecstatic hours—passions not always ending in sanctity, and for which, as is usually the case, woman did the penance.

In those days religious sentiment certainly was in close affinity to love; either it was the motive or the end of it. Love was but a second religion; it had its fine frenzies, its innocent superstitions, its sublime emotions, all in sympathy with Christianity.

The manners of that period will also serve to explain the alliance existing between religion and love. First, then, social life had no place of meeting but before the altar. Lords, vassals, men, women were never equals elsewhere. In the church alone could lovers meet and exchange their vows. The festivals of the church formed our predecessors' theatres; woman's soul was more deeply stirred than to-day it is at an opera or a ball; and does not every strong emotion invariably bring woman around to love?

So, by dint of mingling with life and seizing it in all its acts and interests, religion had become the sharer of every virtue, the accomplice of every vice. Religion had become a science; it was mixed up with politics, eloquence, crime; it entered the skin of the sick man and the poor; it sat on thrones—it was all-pervading. These semi-learned observations may, perhaps, serve to vindicate the veracity of this Study, though certain details may scandalize the more perfect morals of our age, which are, as is known of all, a trifle too strait-laced.

At that moment when the priests stopped their chanting, and the notes of the organ mingled with the vibrant voices of the loud "Amen" as it issued from the deep chests of the choir-men, and sent a murmuring echo through the farther arches, the while the devout assembly awaited the archbishop's benediction, a burgher, impatient to get home or trembling for the safety of his purse in the crowd when the congregation should disperse, quietly slipped out, taking the risk of being called a bad Catholic. On this, a gentleman, who was leaning on one of the enormous columns that surround the choir, where he was enshrouded in the shadows, hastened to

take the place so recently vacated by the worthy Tourangeau.
Which done, he quickly hid his face behind the tall plumes
of his tall, gray cap, and knelt down before his chair with so
deep an air of contrition that it might even have deceived an
inquisitor.

His immediate neighbors, after observing him closely,
seemed to recognize him; after which as with one accord they
returned to their devotions with a significant shrug expressive
of all their thoughts—a caustic, jeering, mocking scandal.
Two old women nodded their heads expressively, exchanging
glances which seemed to penetrate the future.

The chair into which this young man had glided was near
by a chapel built in between two columns, inclosed by an
iron railing. It was a custom for the dean and chapter of the
cathedral to rent at a high figure to seignorial families, and
even to rich burgesses, the right to be present at the services,
themselves and their household exclusively, in the various
lateral chapels situated along the side-aisles of the cathedral.
This simony is practiced even now. Then a woman had her
chapel as she now has her box at the opera. The tenants of
these privileged places were expected to decorate and keep up
the altars therein; and each made it a pride to adorn theirs
most sumptuously—a vanity which, needless to say, was not
rebuked by the church.

In this particular chapel a lady was kneeling close to the
railing on a handsome rug of red velvet trimmed with gold
tassels, and close to the spot but now vacated by the worthy
citizen. A silver-gilt lamp hung from the vaulted ceiling of
the chapel before the magnificently decorated altar and cast
its mild light on the Book of Hours* held by the lady. The
book trembled violently in her hand as the young man approached her.

"Amen!"

To that response, chanted with a low, sweet, agitated voice,

* Prayer Book.

happily submerged in the now general clamor, she rapidly added in a whisper:

"You will ruin me!"

The words were spoken with an innocence to which any man of delicacy would at once have submitted; they reached and pierced the heart. But the stranger, carried away perhaps by one of those paroxysms of passion which stifle conscience, remained in his chair, and slightly raised his head that he might peer into the chapel.

"He sleeps!" he replied in a voice so low that the words could only be heard by the young woman as sound is heard in its own echo.

The lady turned pale; her furtive glance left for an instant the vellum page of the missal and turned on the old man whom the youthful one had designated. What terrible complicity was in that look? When the young woman had cautiously examined the old man, she drew a deep breath and raised her brow, adorned with a precious jewel, to a picture of the Virgin; this simple movement, her attitude, the glistening eye, disclosed her life with ingenuous candor; had she been wicked she would have exercised more dissimulation.

The person who thus inspired these two with terror was a little old hunchback, nearly bald, with a savage expression, and who wore a long, dingy-colored gray beard cut into the shape of a broad fan. On his breast glittered the cross of St. Michael. His coarse, thick hands were covered with rough gray hairs and had been clasped together, but they had now dropped slightly asunder in the slumber to which he had so imprudently yielded himself. The right hand seemed ready to grasp the dagger, the handle guard of which was of iron in shape like a shell. In the manner in which he had disposed this weapon the hilt was immediately under his hand; if by ill-luck he should touch it he would, beyond doubt, awaken instantly and look at his wife.

His sardonic mouth, the peaked chin, aggressively pushed

forward, showed all the characteristics of malignancy, of a coldly cruel sagacity, which would surely enable him to divine all because he suspected all. His yellow forehead was puckered like to those of men who believe nothing, weigh everything, who test the exact meaning of every human act and the meaning thereof. His bodily frame, though deformed, was bony and sinewy; it looked to be both vigorous and irritable; he was, in short, an ogre who had been spoiled in the making.

When this terrible being should awake the young lady was evidently in much danger. That jealous husband would certainly not fail to at once detect the difference between the worthy old burgher, who gave him no umbrage, and the newcomer, a young courtier, slender and elegant.

"*Libera nos a malo*" [deliver us from evil], said she, trying to impart her fears to the young cavalier.

The latter raised his eyes and looked at her. Tears were in his eyes; the tears of love and despair. When the young lady saw them she trembled and thus betrayed herself. Perhaps both had long resisted and were no longer able to further hold out against a love which increased with each recurring day through invincible obstacles, brooded over by fear, strengthened by youth.

The lady was fairly handsome; but her pallor told of sufferings endured in secret, which made her interesting. Moreover, she had an elegant figure and her hair was the most lovely in the world. Watched over by a tiger, her life was the forfeit if discovered whispering a word, accepting a glance, or in permitting a mere pressure of the hand.

It is possible that love may have been more deeply felt than by those hearts, if never more rapturously confessed, never more enjoyed, but certes it is that never was passion so perilously circumstanced. It is easy to understand that to these two beings the air, the sounds about them, the foot-falls and so forth, things of utter indifference to other people, presented hidden qualities, perceptible peculiarities which only they could distinguish. It may be that their love caused them to become faithful interpreters of the touch of the icy hands of the old priest to whom they made their auricular confessions of their sins, and from whose hands they received the Host as they knelt at the holy altar of God. It was a deep love, love gashed into the soul like as a scar is hewn upon the body and which remains during the whole of our life! As these two young people regarded each other, the woman seemed to say to her lover: "Let us perish, but as one." And the young knight made answer: "We are one, but we will not die!"

For her response she made him a sign, indicating the presence of her elderly duenna and two pages.

The duenna slept; the pages were but youthful ones and seemingly careless of what might happen, of good or evil, to their master.

"Do not be alarmed as you leave the church; go and be managed as you may be led."

The young noble had but murmured these words, when the hand of the old seigneur slipped down upon the handle of his dagger. Feeling the cold touch of the iron he instantly awoke, and his tawny eyes at once fixed themselves upon his wife. By a peculiarity, seldom granted even to men of genius, he awoke with an alert brain and as vivid ideas as though he had never slept.

He was jealous.

The lover, one eye on his mistress, the other on her husband, whom he closely watched, now rose and vanished behind a column at the first movement he had detected in the old man's hands; then he effaced himself swiftly as a bird. The lady's eyes were engaged on her book and she appeared to be quite calm. But try how she might, she could not prevent the flushing of her face nor the unwonted violence of the beating of her heart. The old lord saw the unusual crimson of her cheeks, forehead, and even of her eyelids. He could also hear the vehement throbs of her heart, which were distinctly audible in the chapel. He looked inquisitively around, but not seeing any one whom he could distrust, said to his wife:

"What troubles you, my dear?"

"The scent of the incense sickens me," she replied.

"Is it particularly unpleasant to-day?" he asked.

Despite this sarcastic query, the wily old man pretended to accept this excuse; but still he suspected some treachery and resolved to watch his treasure more carefully even than he had hitherto done.

The benediction was pronounced. Without waiting for the *Sæcula sæculorum*, the crowd rushed like a heaving torrent to the doors of the church. Following his usual custom, the old lord waited until the general hurry was over; then issued forth, the duenna in front with the youngest page, who carried a lantern on a pole; himself, his wife on arm, being followed by the other page.

As he made his way to the side-door opening on the west nave of the cloister, by which he generally went out, a stream of people detached itself from the flood which obstructed the great portals and surged through the aisle around the old noble and his people. The mass was impacted too solidly to allow of his retracing his steps; and the gentleman and his wife were therefore pushed onward to the door by the tremendous pressure of the crowd behind them.

The husband tried to pass out first, dragging the lady by her arm, but just then he was jerked vigorously into the street and his wife snatched from him by a stranger. The sinister hunchback at once saw that he had fallen into a trap, and one that had been cleverly arranged.

It was now he repented himself that he had slept; but he collected his whole strength, seized his wife once more by the sleeve of her gown and with his other tried to cling fast to the door-post of the church; but love's ardor carried the day against jealous rage. The young man clasped his mistress round the waist and tore her away with the strength of despair; so violent was the disruption that the stuff of silk and gold was rent noisily apart, the brocade and whalebone gave way, and the old man remained standing with naught save the sleeve in his clutch.

A roar like that of a lion rose above the tumult of the multitude, and a terrible voice was heard bawling out the words:

"To me, Poitiers! Help; here to the door! The Comte de Saint-Vallier's retainers, here, help!"

And the Comte Aymar de Poitiers, Sire de Saint-Vallier, attempted to draw his sword and clear a space around him. But he found himself pressed upon and surrounded by forty or fifty gentlemen whom it were most dangerous to wound. Several of these, especially of the highest rank, replied gibingly to him as they dragged him along the cloisters.

With a lightning-like celerity the abductor carried the countess to an open chapel, seating her on a wooden bench behind a confessional box. By the light of the candles burning before the saint to whom the chapel was dedicated they gazed upon each other for a silent moment, clasped hands, and amazed at their audacity. The countess could not summon the cruel courage to blame the young man for the boldness to which they owed this first and only instant of happiness.

"Will you fly with me into the adjacent States?" asked the young man eagerly. "Two English horses are awaiting us near-by which are able to do thirty leagues at a stretch."

"Ah!" she cried softly, " in what corner of the world could you find a hiding-place for a daughter of King Louis the Eleventh?"

"True," answered the young man, silenced by a difficulty he had not anticipated.

"Why, then, did you tear me from my husband?" she asked in a voice of terror.

"Alas!" replied the young lover, "I did not guess at the agitation I should experience in finding myself by your side, in hearing your voice as you spoke to me. I had arranged plans, two or three schemes, and now that I see you, I feel as if all were accomplished."

"But I am lost!" said the countess.

"We are saved!" the young man cried in the blind enthusiasm of love. "Listen carefully to me."

"This will cost me my life!" said she, letting the tears that filled her eyes go rolling down her cheeks. "The count will kill me—perhaps this very night! But go you to the King; tell him all the tortures his daughter has endured these five years. He loved me well when I was a child; he used to laugh and call me 'Marie-full-of-grace,' because I was so ugly. Ah! could he only know to what a man he gave me, his anger would be terrible. I have never dared complain out of a sense of pity for the count. Beside, how could my plaint reach the ears of the King? Even my confessor is but a spy of Saint-Vallier. That is why I consented to this criminal meeting, hoping to find a champion—some one who will declare the truth to the King. But—may I dare trust? Oh!" she cried, turning pale and interrupting herself, "here comes the page."

The distraught countess put her hands before her face and tried to veil it.

"Fear nothing," said the young lord, "he is ours! You may safely trust him; he belongs to me. When the count contrives to return to you, he will give us timely warning. In the confessional," he added in a muttered tone, "is a priest, a friend of mine; he will say that he rescued you from the turmoil, and drew you here for safety out of the crowd, and gave you his protection in this chapel. Thus all is arranged to deceive him."

At these words the countess dried her tears, but a saddened expression clouded her face.

"He cannot be deceived," said she. "To-night he will know all. Beware his revenge. Save me from his blows. At once to le Plessis, see the King, tell him——;" here she hesitated; but some dreadful memory gave her courage to disclose some secrets of her married life, so she continued:

"Yes, tell him that to obtain the mastery over me the count has me bled in both arms—to exhaust me. Tell him that my husband drags me around by my hair; tell him that I am a prisoner; say that——"

Her heart was bursting, sobs choked her throat, tears rained from her eyes. In her agitation she allowed the young man to kiss her hand, the while he muttered broken, inconsecutive words.

"Poor love! No one may speak to the King. Although my uncle is chief master of his bowmen. I cannot obtain admission to le Plessis. My darling lady! my most beautiful queen! Oh! but what has she not suffered? Marie, at least let me say two words to you, or we are assuredly lost."

"What will become of us?" she murmured. Then, discerning on the dark wall a picture of the Virgin on which the light fell from the lamp, she cried out:

"Holy Mother of God, give us counsel!"

"To-night," said the young man, "I shall be in your room with you."

"How?" was her naïve question.

"This evening I go to propose myself as an apprentice to Maître Cornélius, the King's silversmith. To him I bear a letter of introduction which will compel him to receive me. His house is next to yours. Once under the roof of that old scoundrel I can, by the aid of a silken ladder, soon find my way to your suite of rooms."

"Oh!" said she, petrified with horror, "if you love me, do not go to Maître Cornélius."

"Ah!" cried he, pressing her to his heart with all the energy of youth, "then, indeed, you do love me!"

"Yes," said she. "Are you not my sole hope? Beside," she added, regarding him with dignity, "you are a gentleman, I confide myself to your honor. So unhappy am I that you will never betray my trust. But to what end is all this? Go, the rather let me die than that you should abide in the house of Maître Cornélius. Do you not know that all his apprentices——"

"Have been hanged?" said the young noble, laughing.

"But do not go; you will become the victim of some sorcery."

"I cannot pay a too high price for the great honor of serving you," said he, with a look of such ardor that her eyes drooped under it.

"And my husband?" said she.

"Here is that will cause him to sleep," answered the young man, drawing a small phial from his belt.

"Not for ever?" queried the countess tremblingly.

For all reply the young seigneur made a gesture of horror.

"I would long ago have defied him to mortal combat if it were not for his great age," said he. "But God preserve me from ridding his life by a philter."

"Forgive me," said the countess blushing. "My sins have cruelly punished me. In a moment of despair I have thought of killing the count—I feared you might have the same desire. So great has my sorrow been that as yet I have never been able to confess the so wicked thought; I believed it would be repeated to him, and then he would be avenged on me. I have shamed you," she went on, distressed by his silence. "Well, I deserve your blame!"

She flung the phial with great violence to the ground and it was broken.

"Do not come," said she, "it is that my husband sleeps lightly; my duty demands that I await the help of heaven—that will I do."

She arose to leave the chapel. "Ah!" cried the young man, "but bid me kill him and I will do it. You will see me this evening, madame."

"I showed wisdom in destroying that drug," she murmured

in a voice husky with joy at finding herself so ardently loved. "The dread of arousing my husband will save us from ourselves."

"I pledge you my life," said the young man, pressing her hand.

"Should the King be willing the pope can annul my marriage; then we may be united," she cried, giving him a look full of delicious hopes.

"Monseigneur comes!" exclaimed the page bustling in.

Instantly the young noble, surprised at the short time he had gained with his mistress and greatly wondering at the count's celerity, snatched a kiss which the countess could not refuse.

"To-night," said he, as he hastily slipped out of the chapel.

Thanks to the darkness, the lover made his way to the great portal in safety, gliding from pillar to pillar in the long shadows which they cast across the nave. An old canon suddenly issued from the confessional, came to the side of the countess and gently closed the railing, while the page gravely marched up and down with the manner of a sentry.

A blaze of light heralded the coming of the count. He was accompanied by a number of his friends and by servants bearing torches; himself advanced, drawn sword in hand. His gloomy gaze seemed to pierce the dense cathedral shadows and to rake the remotest depths.

"Monseigneur, madame is there," said the page to him.

The Count de Saint-Vallier found his wife kneeling on the steps before the altar, the canon standing alongside reading his breviary. At the sight the count violently shook the railing as if to give vent to his fury.

"What want you here in church, with a drawn sword?" asked the old priest.

"Father, this is my husband," said the countess.

The priest took a key out of his sleeve and unlocked the

railed gate of the chapel. The count, almost against his will, cast an eye into the confessional, then entered the chapel, and seemed to be listening to the silence of the place.

"Monsieur," said his wife, "you owe your thanks to this venerable canon for giving me a refuge here."

The Count de Saint-Vallier turned pale with anger; he dared not look at his friends, who had come less with the intention of assisting than of laughing at him. Then he curtly answered:

"Thank the Lord, my father, for I will surely find some way to repay you."

He took his wife by the arm, and, without giving her an opportunity to finish the curtsey she was making to the canon, he signed to his retainers and left the church without uttering a word to those who had accompanied him. His silence was ominous.

Impatient to reach his castle and occupied as he was in an effort to get at the truth, he made his way through the tortuous street which at that time separated the cathedral from the chancellerie, a fine building but recently erected by the Chancellor Juvénal des Ursins, on the site of an old fortress given by Charles VII. to that faithful servant as a guerdon for his splendid services. This street, the Rue de la Scellerie, so named in honor of the office of the Great Seal which long stood there, connected old Tours with Châteauneuf, where was the noted abbey of Saint-Martin, of which many Kings had been glad to be elected canons. After long discussions this borough had been incorporated with the city; this had been so now for nearly a hundred years.

At last the count reached the Rue du Mûrier in which his dwelling, the Hôtel de Poitiers, was situated. When the escort had passed the gates into the courtyard, and they had been closed after them, a profound silence pervaded the narrow street where a few high seigneurs at that time had residences; for this new suburb of the town was near to le Plessis, the King's usual place of abode, and where the courtiers when summoned could instantly go. The last house in the street was also the last in the town. It belonged to Maître Cornélius Hoogworst, an old merchant of Brabant, to whom Louis the Eleventh gave his closest confidences in the various financial dealings which his cunning policy required done outside his own kingdom. For the favorable opportunity it gave to his tyranny over his wife, the Comte de Saint-Vallier had taken the mansion next to the house of Maître Cornélius.

An explanation of the houses will show the advantages offered the jealous husband. It was easy to be seen that the same architect had built both of them, and that they were destined as the abodes of tyrants. The count's house had been built near the old boundary of the city, and was inclosed in a garden. On the side next the embankment, lately constructed by Louis XI. between Tours and le Plessis, dogs defended the entrance to the premises; while on the east they were divided from the nearest houses by a large courtyard; on the west backed up the house occupied by Maître Cornélius.

Each was of sinister aspect and resembled a small fort, which could be well defended against a turbulent populace. The riots and civil wars of this period amply justified these precautions. The windows looking on the street were strongly barred with iron, and shutters of the same material. A stone block used for mounting horseback stood close to the porch.

As six o'clock was striking from the great tower of the abbey Saint-Martin, the lover of the hapless countess walked past the de Poitiers hôtel and paused there for a moment to listen for any sound made by the servants in the lower hall, who were taking their suppers. Casting a glance at the window of the room he supposed to be his mistress', he went on his way to the next house. Everywhere on his way the young man had heard the roistering of the jolly holiday-makers, in honor of the day. The badly-joined blinds let out beams of light, the chimneys smoked, the pleasant savor of roasting meats pervaded the town. Religious services being over, the inhabitants were regaling themselves with confused mutterings of satisfaction, more readily imagined than described. But here deep silence reigned, for in those two dwellings lived two passions which can never rejoice.

Beyond them stretched the silent country. While these two dwellings standing beneath the towers of Saint-Martin, standing apart from the others in the street, at the crooked end of it, seemed afflicted with leprosy. The opposite building was the property of some State criminal and was under the ban of the law. No young man but would have been struck by the great contrast. About, as he was, to fling himself into a horribly hazardous enterprise, it is not to be wondered at that the daring young noble stopped short before the door of the silversmith-treasurer, and called to mind the many uncanny tales he had heard of the life of Maître Cornélius— tales which had caused such untoward terror to the countess.

In this time a man of war, a lover even, every man trembled at the word "magic." Few indeed were the minds whose imaginations were incredulous of occult forces and tales of the marvelous. This lover of the Comtesse de Saint-Vallier, one of the daughters of Louis XI. by Madame de Sassenage, and born in Dauphiné, courageous as he was in other respects, was apt to think twice before entering the house of a sorcerer.

The history of Maître Cornélius Hoogworst will fully explain the confidence he had inspired in the count, the terrible fear of the countess, and the hesitation to which the lover now made pause. To enable the nineteenth-century reader to clearly understand how such seeming commonplace events could be turned into something supernatural, and to cause them to share the dread of that olden time, it is necessary to interrupt the course of the narrative and cast a glance at the preceding life and career of Maître Cornélius.

Cornélius Hoogworst, one of the richest merchants of

Ghent, having drawn upon himself the resentment of Charles, Duke of Burgundy, had found a refuge and protection at the Court of Louis XI. The King was well aware of the advantages he could gain from a man connected with all the principal houses of commerce of Flanders, Venice, and the East; he naturalized and ennobled—by royal letters—and, more, flattered Maître Cornelius; a most rare thing with that monarch. Louis XI. pleased the Fleming as much as the Fleming pleased the King. Wily, suspicious, avaricious; equally politic, equally well informed; both superior to their time; each understanding the other marvelously; they discarded and resumed with equal facility, the one his conscience, the other his religion; they worshiped the same Virgin—one from conviction, the other from policy; in short, if we may trust the jealous statements of Olivier le Daim and Tristan, the King resorted to the Fleming's house for those diversions with which King Louis XI. amused himself.* History has been at the pains to preserve to the knowledge of posterity the licentious tastes of this monarch who was certainly not averse to debauchery. No doubt the Fleming derived both pleasure and profit in lending himself to the caprices and indulgences of his royal client.

Cornélius at this time had lived for nine years in the city of Tours. During these nine years extraordinary events had occurred in his house, which had made him the object of universal execration. On his arrival he had spent immense sums in order to safely guard his treasures. The curious inventions secretly made for him by the locksmiths of the town, the singular precautions he took to bring them to his house in a way to compel their silence, were for a long time the subject of countless tales, which furnished the evening gossip of the Tourangeaux. These peculiar devices on the part of the old man caused every one to believe him the possessor of Oriental wealth. Consequently the story-tellers of that district—the

* See "Droll Stories."

birthplace of French romance—built rooms full of gold and precious stones in the Fleming's house, not omitting to ascribe this fabulous wealth to compacts with unholy genii.

Maître Cornélius had brought with him from Ghent two Flemish servants, an old woman and a young apprentice; the latter, youthful, with a gentle, attractive appearance, served as his secretary, cashier, factotum, and messenger. During the first year of his settlement in Tours a considerable robbery was effected on his premises; judicial inquiry showed that the crime must have been committed by one of its inmates. The old man had his two menservants and apprentice put in prison. The young lad was weakly and he died under the sufferings of the "question,"* still protesting his innocence. The two men confessed the crime to escape torture; but when asked by the judge where the stolen property could be found, they kept silence; so, after renewed tortures, they were tried, condemned, and hung. On their way to the gallows they declared themselves innocent, as is the custom of all men when about to be executed.

For many a day the town of Tours talked over this singular business; but the criminals were Flemish, and the interest in their unhappy fate, and that of the young clerk, soon evaporated. In those days, wars and seditions supplied continual excitement, and each day's new drama eclipsed that of the preceding night.

More affected by the loss of his pelf than by the death of his three servants, Maître Cornélius lived alone in the house with the old Flemish woman, his sister. From the King he obtained the privilege to use the royal couriers for his private affairs; sold his mules to a muleteer in the neighborhood, and lived thenceforward in the deepest solitude, seeing no one but the King, and transacting his business through the medium of Jews, who, shrewd arithmeticians, served him faithfully and well for the sake of his so-powerful interest.

* Torture to induce confession.

Some time after this affair, the King himself placed with his old *torçonnoir* a young orphan in whom he took much interest. Louis XI. called Maître Cornélius by that obsolete term, familiarly, which under the reign of Saint-Louis meant a usurer, a collector of taxes, a man who squeezed money out of folk by extortion. The term *tortionnaire*, which is a legal term still extant, explains the old French word *torçonnier*, and which is often spelled *tortionneur*. The poor young boy devoted himself to the interest of his master, the old Fleming, and succeeded in winning his encomiums and getting into his good graces. One winter's night the diamonds placed in Cornélius' keeping by the King of England as security for a hundred thousand crowns were stolen; suspicion naturally fell on the poor orphan. Louis XI. was the more severe with him because he had vouched for the boy's fidelity. So, after a very brief examination by the grand provost, the unfortunate youth was taken out and hanged. After that it was a long time before any one dared to go to learn the art of banking and exchange from Maître Cornélius.

In the course of time, however, it came that two young men of the town, Tourangeaux, men of honor, eager to make their fortunes, took service with the silversmith. Large robberies coincided with the admission of the two youths into the house. The circumstances of these crimes, the manner of the perpetration, plainly enough showed some collusion between the thieves and the inmates of the house; how was it possible that the new-comers should escape accusation? Become by this time more than ever suspicious and vindictive, the old Fleming laid the matter before the King, who placed the case in the hands of his grand provost. A trial was promptly had, and more quickly finished. Each was more promptly executed.

But the inhabitants of Tours, in their patriotism, secretly blamed Tristan l'Hermite for unseemly haste. Guilty or not guilty, the young fellow-townsmen were looked upon as victims, and Cornélius as an executioner. The two families thus thrown into mourning were of much esteem; their complaints secured much sympathy, and, little by little, they succeeded in making it come to be common belief that all the victims sent to the scaffold by the King's silversmith were innocent. Some went so far as to say that the cruel miser imitated the King and sought to put terror and the gibbet between himself and the world of men; others there were who declared he had never been robbed at all—that these terrible executions were brought about as the result of cold calculation; that all he cared about was to be relieved of all care for his treasure.

The first effect of these rumors was to effectually isolate Maître Cornélius. The good people of Tours treated him as they would have done a leper; called him the "tortionnaire," and named his house Malemaison—House of Evil. Even if the Fleming could have found strangers to the town bold enough to enter his service, the inhabitants of the town would have prevented by their warnings. The most favorable impression had of Maître Cornélius was that of those who considered him as being merely baneful and sinister. Some he inspired with instinctive dread; others were impressed with the power that is always paid to great wealth and influence; to some he had the fascination of mystery. His mode of life, his countenance, and the favor of the King seemed to justify all the rumors of which he was the subject.

After the death of his persecutor, the Duke of Burgundy, Cornélius traveled much in foreign lands; during his absence the King caused his house to be patrolled by a company of his Scottish Guard. This royal solicitude it was that made the courtiers believe that Maître Cornélius had bequeathed his property to Louis XI. When he was home it was but rarely that he left his premises; the gentlemen of the Court frequently visited him, and he loaned them money rather liberally, though he was very capricious about so doing. On certain days he refused them a sou; the next day he would offer large sums always, though, at high interest and on undoubtedly good security. He was a good Catholic, went regularly to the services, and always attended the earliest mass at Saint-Martin's; and as he had purchased there a chapel in perpetuity, as elsewhere, he was separated even in church from other Christians. A popular proverb of that day, and was long remembered, was the saying: "You passed in front of the usurer; evil will befall you." To pass in front of the Fleming explained every misfortune; it explained all sudden pains and evil, involuntary depression, bad turns of fortune among the people of Tours. Even at Court the people most oftener than not attributed to Cornélius that fatal influence which Italian, Spanish, and Asiatic superstition has termed the "Evil Eye."

Only for the terrible power of Louis XI., which overspread his house like a mantle, the populace on the least pretext would have utterly demolished la Malemaison—that "evil house" in the Rue du Mûrier. And yet it was Cornélius that was the first to plant mulberry trees in Tours, and at that time the Tourangeaux looked upon him as their good genie. Who may depend on popular favor?

A few seigneurs having met Maître Cornélius on his journeys out of France had been astonished at his friendliness and good-humor. At Tours he was always gloomy and absent-minded, but yet he returned there. Some inexplicable attraction brought him back to his dismal house in the Rue du Mûrier. Like a snail, whose life is so strongly a part of its shell, he admitted to the King that he was not at his ease elsewhere; he only found it under the bolts and time-worn stone of his little bastille; and yet he was well aware that should the King die it would be the most dangerous spot on earth for him.

"The devil is amusing himself at the expense of our crony the *torçonnier*," said Louis XI. to his barber, a few days before the festival of All-Saints. "He says he has been robbed again, but he can't hang anybody this time, unless he hangs himself. The old vagabond came and asked me if I had not chanced to carry off a string of rubies that he had intended selling to me. 'Pasques-Dieu! I don't steal what I have only to take,' said I."

"And was he afraid?" asked the barber.

"Misers are only afraid of one thing," responded the King. "My chum the *torçonnier* knows very well that I shall not plunder him for nothing; otherwise I were unjust, and I have never yet done anything but what is just and necessary."

"And yet that old bandit overcharges you," replied the barber.

"You only wish he did, don't you?" answered the King, with a sinister look at the barber.

"By Mahomet's belly, Sire, the inheritance would be a noble one, between you, me, and the devil."

"There, there!" said the King. "Don't put bad ideas into my head. My crony is a more faithful man than many whose fortunes I have made—it may be it is because he owes me nothing."

For the two last years, Maitre Cornélius had lived entirely alone with his old sister, who was believed to be a witch. A tailor who lived hard by declared that he had frequently seen her at night, on the roof the house, looking out for the witches' Sabbath. This seemed the more extraordinary, as it was known to be the miser's custom to lock up his sister in her bedroom when night came, the windows of which were barred with iron.

As he grew older, Cornélius, always afraid of being robbed or duped by men, came to hate everybody but the King, whom he highly esteemed. He had sunk into a state of abject misanthropy; but, like most misers, his passion for gold, the assimilation, as it were, of that metal with his very substance, became more and more complete, while age but intensified it. He was even suspicious of his sister, though she was a shade the more miserly and rapacious than her brother, and really surpassed him in penurious inventiveness. Their way of life was a mysterious enigma. The old woman rarely took bread of the baker; so seldom she appeared in the market, that the least credulous of the townsfolk at last attributed to her some diabolical knowledge of a secret for maintaining life. Others there were who dabbled in alchemy that declared that Maître Cornélius possessed the power of making gold. Men of science stated that he had discovered the Universal Panacea. According to most of the country people, when they spoke of him, Cornélius was a chimerical being, and a number came to view his house out of mere curiosity.

The young seigneur, whom we left in front of that house, looked about him, first at the Hôtel de Poitiers, the home of his mistress, and then at the Malemaison. The moonbeams shed their light on the prominent parts, giving a tint of light and shadow in the carvings and reliefs. The caprices of this white light gave a sinister expression to both edifices; it seemed as if Nature had tried to encourage the superstitious dread that hung around the place.

The young man called to mind the many traditions which made Cornélius such a strange and formidable person. Though the violence of his passion still held him to the decision of entering that house, and to stay there long enough to accomplish his purpose, he yet hesitated at taking the final step, all the time aware that he would at last do this. But what man is there who, in a crisis of his life, does not willingly pay heed to presentiments, and gyrate, as it were, over the precipice of uncertainty? A lover worthy of his love, the young man feared he might perish before the love of the countess should crown his life.

His mental deliberation was so painfully absorbing that he did not feel the cold wind that whistled round his legs and against the buildings. On entering that house he must lay aside his name, as he already had laid aside the handsome garb of a noble. In case of disaster he would be unable to claim the privileges of his rank or the protection of his friends without destroying the Countess of Saint-Vallier. If her old husband suspected her of having a lover paying nocturnal visits, he was quite capable of roasting her alive in an iron cage by a slow fire, or of killing her by degrees in the depths of some dank dungeon.

Looking over his shabby clothes in which he was disguised, the young man felt ashamed of his appearance. His black leather belt, his heavy shoes, ribbed hose, frieze breeches, and his gray woolen doublet made him look like the clerk of some poor devil of a justice. To a nobleman of the fifteenth century it was like to death itself to play the part of a mean burgher, and renounce the privileges of his rank. But yet, to climb the roof of the house where his mistress was weeping; to descend the chimney or crawl along the cornice from gutter to gutter to the window of her room; to risk his life if haply he might sit by her side before a glowing fire, during the slumber of a dangerous husband, whose every snore would add to their rapture; to defy both heaven and earth in exchanging the most audacious embrace; to say no word which would not be the certainty of death, or at least of bloody combat, if overheard—these all-entrancing visions, with the romantic perils of the adventure, made the decision of the young man.

However slight the guerdon of his endeavor might be, could he but once more kiss the hand of his lady, he would venture all, urged on by the peril-loving, passionate spirit of his age. Never for one moment did he think that the countess would refuse him the sweetest reward of love in the midst of such mortal danger. The adventure was too perilous, too impossible, not to be attempted to carry out.

Suddenly every bell in the town rang out the curfew—a custom elsewhere fallen into desuetude, but was still observed in the country—for in the provinces customs die slowly. Though the lights were not extinguished, the watchman placed the chains across the streets. Many doors were barred and bolted; the steps of a few belated citizens were heard in the distance, attended by their servants, armed to the teeth and bearing lanterns. Soon the town, garroted, as it were, seemed to be slumbering, fearing naught of robbers and malefactors except by the roofs. At that time the roofs of houses were like a highway, so thronged were they at night.

The streets were so narrow in the country towns, and even in Paris, that robbers could jump from the roofs on one side on to those of the other. This perilous game was once the delight of King Charles IX. in his youth, if we may put faith in the chronicles of his day.

Fearing that he might be too late in presenting himself to the old Maître Cornélius, the young noble now went up to the Malemaison, intending to knock at the door, when, on looking at it, his attention was excited by a kind of vision, which the writers of that day would have termed devilish (*cornue*), perhaps with reference to horns and hoofs. He rubbed his eyes to clear them, a thousand diverse ideas coursing through his mind the while at the spectacle before him. On each side of the door was a face framed between the bars in a kind of loophole. At first he took these faces to be grotesque gargoyles carved in stone, so angular, so distorted, exaggerated, motionless, and discolored were they; but presently the cold wind and the moonlight enabled him to detect the thin white mist which living breath sent out from two blue noses; at last he could make out in each hollow face, beneath the shadow of the eyebrows, a pair of blue china eyes casting fire like those of a wolf crouching in the brushwood when it hears the bay of the hounds in full cry. The uneasy gleam of those eyes was turned on him so fixedly that for quite a minute's space he felt like a bird put up by a pointer-dog; a fever-spasm struck his soul, but it was at once repressed. The two faces, strained and suspicious, were beyond a doubt those of Cornélius and his sister.

The young man pretended to be gazing around him, as if

in uncertainty as to his whereabouts, and to be searching for a dwelling the address of which might be on the card he took from his pocket and was trying to read by the moonlight; then straight to the door he walked and struck three blows upon it, which echoed within as though it had been the entrance to a cavern. A faint light became visible beneath the door, and an eye was seen at a small and strongly barred wicket-gate.

"Who is there?"

"A friend, sent by Oosterlinck, of Brussels."

"What do you want?"

"To come in."

"Your name?"

"Philippe Goulenoire."

"Have you credentials?"

"Here they are."

"Put them in through the box."

"Where is it?"

"To your left."

Philippe Goulenoire put the letter through the slit of an iron box above which was a loophole.

"The devil!" thought he. "It is very evident that the King comes here, as they say he does; he could not take more precautions at le Plessis."

For over a quarter of an hour he waited on the street. At the end of that time he heard the old man say to his sister:

"Close the traps of the door."

A clanging of chains sounded from within. Philippe heard the bolts slide, the locks creak, and finally a small, low door, iron-bound, opened just the smallest chink through which a man could press. At the risk of tearing his clothes, Philippe squeezed rather than walked himself into la Malemaison. A toothless old woman with a hatchet face, eyebrows like the handle of a caldron, who could not have put a nut between her nose and chin so near were they together—a pallid, haggard creature, her hollow temples made up only, or so it seemed, of bones and sinews—silently preceded the stranger into a lower chamber, Cornélius prudently following him.

"Seat yourself there," said she to Philippe, pointing out a three-legged stool, standing beside a huge, carved fireplace of stone; the hearth though was fireless.

On the other side of the fireplace was a walnut-wood table with twisted legs, on which were an egg on a plate and ten or a dozen of little bread-sops, hard and dry, each cut with parsimonious exactitude. Two stools placed beside the table, on one of which the old woman seated herself, showed that the miserly pair were about supping.

Cornélius went to the door and closed two iron shutters, thus most likely securing the looped windows through which they had been gazing out on the street; then he returned to his seat. Philippe Goulenoire, as he called himself, next saw the brother and sister dipping each their sops in turns into the egg, and with the perfect gravity and precision that soldiers use in dipping their spoons in regular rotation into the mess-pan. This performance was gone through in perfect silence. But as he ate Cornélius studied the mock apprentice with as much carefulness and shrewdness as if he had been gold coin in the balance.

Philippe felt, as it might be, an icy cloak had fallen on his shoulders, he was tempted to look around; but with the circumspection born of an amorous adventure he was careful not to glance, even furtively, at the walls, for he was well aware that so suspicious a person as Cornélius would not house an inquisitive inmate. He restricted himself to the modest contemplation of first the egg, then the old woman, and anon his future master.

Louis XI.'s silversmith-treasurer resembled that monarch. He had even caught the same tricks of expression, as often happens where persons dwell in a kind of quasi intimacy. The thick eyebrows of the Fleming almost concealed his eyes, but by raising them a little he could flash out a glance that was bright, penetrating, and full of power, the look of men habituated to silence, and to whom concentration of thought is familiar. His thin lips, finely furrowed with vertical lines, gave him an air of keen subtlety. The lower part of the face bore a vague resemblance to a fox; but a lofty, prominent forehead, deeply indented with wrinkles, bespoke great and noble qualities and nobility of soul—one whose flights had been degraded by experience and whence the cruel lessons of life had driven it back into the farthest recesses of his strange humanity. Most certainly he was no ordinary miser; his passion covered, no doubt, the highest pleasures and secret conceptions.

"At what rate are Venetian sequins going?" he abruptly asked his to be apprentice.

"Three-fourths at Brussels; one at Ghent."

"What is the freight on the Scheldt?"

"Three sous parisis."

"Anything new in Ghent?"

"The brother of Liéven d'Herde is ruined."

"Ah!"

After giving vent to this exclamation, the old man spread the skirts of his dalmation over his knees—this was a sort of robe made of black velvet, open in front, wide sleeves, no collar, the sumptuous material being much worn and shiny. This corpse of a magnificent costume he had formerly worn as president of the tribunal of the Parchons—a position which had earned him the enmity of the Duke of Burgundy—was now but a mere rag.

Philippe was not cold, he perspired in the harness he had assumed, dreading further questioning. Thus far the brief information he had extracted the day before, from a Jew whose life he had saved, had been enough—thanks to his good memory and to the Jew's perfect understanding of the customs of Maître Cornélius and his habits and manners.

But the young man, who in his first flush of enthusiasm had feared nothing, now began to perceive the difficulties of his undertaking. The solemn, grave manner of the Fleming reacted upon himself; he felt himself under lock and key and remembered that the urbane Grand Provost Tristan and his rope obeyed the behest of Maître Cornélius.

"Have you supped?" asked the miser in a tone which implied an affirmative answer.

The old maid, despite her brother's tone, trembled as she looked at the new inmate, as if gauging the capacity of the stomach she might have to fill, then said with a specious grin:

"You do not belie your name; your hair and mustache are both black as the devil's tail."

"I have supped," said he.

"Well, then," replied the usurer, "you can come and see me again to-morrow. I have had no apprentice for a number years. Beside, in the night comes wisdom."

"Hey! by Saint-Bavon, monsieur, I am from Flanders; I know not one soul in this place; the chains are up in the streets; I shall be thrown into prison. However," he went on, alarmed at his own temerity, "if it suits your good pleasure, of course I will go."

The oath had a singular effect on the old man.

"Come, then, by Saint-Bavon! You shall sleep here."

"But——" began his sister.

"Silence," said Cornélius. "In his letter Oosterlinck says that he will be answerable for this young man. You well know," he whispered in his sister's ear, "that we have a hundred thousand livres here belonging to Oosterlinck. Is that not security enough?"

"And suppose he steals the Bavarian jewels? He looks more like a thief than a Fleming."

"Hark!" said the old man listening attentively.

The two misers listened. An instant after the "hark"

uttered by Cornélius, a noise caused by men's footsteps echoed in the distance on the other side of the town moat.

"The guard of le Plessis is on its rounds," said the sister.

"Give me the key to the apprentices' room," Cornélius continued.

The old woman was about to take up the lamp.

"What, do you mean to leave us alone together without a light?" exclaimed Cornélius in a voice eloquent with some hidden meaning. "Old as you are you ought to be able to see in the dark. It is not so difficult to find a key."

The sister evidently understood the meaning hidden in these words and left the room. As he looked at this singular creature, as she made her way toward the door, Philippe was able to hide the glance from Cornélius that he cast around the room. It was wainscoted half-way up with oak, the walls were hung with yellow leather stamped out with black arabesques; but what most struck the young man was a match-lock musket with its long spring dagger attached. This then new and terrible weapon lay close to Cornélius.

"How do you expect to earn your living with me?" asked the miser.

"I have but little money," said Philippe, "but I know some good business schemes. If you give me but one sou on every mark I make you, I shall be satisfied."

"A sou! a sou." spoke out the miser, "why that's a great deal!"

At this time reëntered the old hag with the key.

"Come." said Cornélius to Philippe.

The pair went out beneath the portico and mounted a spiral stairway of stone the circular well of which rose through a turret by the side of the room they had occupied. On the second floor the young man came to a stand.

"Nay, nay," cried Cornélius, "the devil! why, this is the cranny in which the King enjoys himself."

The architect had constructed the room used for the apprentices' lodging under the pointed roof of the turret up which the stairs wound. It was a little circular room, the walls of stone, cold and bare of ornament. The tower stood in the centre of the facade on the courtyard, which was like all country courtyards—narrow and dark. At the farther end, through an iron grating, could be seen a wretched garden, in which only the mulberries grew that Cornélius had introduced. The young noble could take in these details through the loop-holes of the turret, the moon, luckily, casting a brilliant light.

A cot, a stool, an unmatched pitcher and basin, and a flimsy chest comprised the furniture in the room. The light could only enter through little square slits, placed at intervals in the wall of the tower, corresponding, no doubt, to the ornamentation of the outside.

"Here is your lodging," said Cornélius; "it is plain and substantial, and contains all that is needed for sleep. Goodnight! Do not leave this room as the others did."

After giving his apprentice a last look fraught with divers meanings, Cornélius double-locked the door, took away the key and went down the stairs, leaving the young fellow as much befooled as a bell-founder who on opening his mould finds it empty. Alone, without a light, seated on a stool in this small garret-room from which so many of his predecessors had gone to the gallows, the young noble felt like a wild beast caught in a trap. He jumped on to the stool and stood on tip-toe to peer out of one of the little slits through which shone a faint glimmer of light. From thence he could see the Loire, the lovely slopes of Saint-Cyr, the sombre splendeur of le Plessis, where a few lights were gleaming in the deep recesses of the windows. Farther away lay the beautiful meadows of Touraine and the silvery stream of the great river. Every point of this lovely landscape wore, just then, a mysterious charm; the windows, the waters, the roofs of the houses glistened like diamonds in the trembling rays of the moon.

The soul of the young noble could not altogether repress some tender, sweet and sad emotions.

"Suppose this is my last farewell!" said he to himself.

As he stood there, he already felt the terrible emotion his adventure promised him; he yielded to the fears of a prisoner who still retains a gleam of hope. His mistress brightened each difficulty. To him she was no more a woman, she became a supernatural being seen in the incense vapors of his hot desire. A feeble cry, which seemed to come from the Hôtel de Poitiers, restored him to reason and to a realization of his situation. He threw himself on his bed to meditate on his course; soon he heard a slight rustling sound which came from the spiral staircase. He listened with all his ears, when the whispered words: "He is in bed," uttered by the old woman, came to his ear.

By an accident of which the architect was ignorant, the lightest sound on the stairway was echoed in the room of the apprentices, so the ostensible apprentice did not miss a single movement of the old miser and his sister, who were spying upon him. He undressed, got into bed, and pretended to sleep; during the time the couple remained on the stairs he was employed in devising means to escape his prison and his entry of the Hôtel de Poitiers.

About ten o'clock Cornélius and his sister, convinced that the new inmate was asleep, retired to their own rooms.

The young man paid careful attention to the sound they made in thus doing, and thought he could guess as to the rooms they each occupied; they must, he thought, occupy the whole of the second floor.

Like all the houses of that date, this floor was next below the roof, from which its dormer windows projected, which were adorned with tops of richly sculptured stone. The roof was bordered with a kind of balustrade, which concealed the gutters for the descent of the rain-water which gargoyles, like crocodiles' heads, discharged into the street. The youth, who had so carefully studied his bearings like as a cat might cunningly have done, believed he could make his way from the tower to the roof, thence to Madame de Vallier's room by the waterspouts and gargoyles; but he had not counted on the narrowness of the windows in the turret; it was a manifest impossibility that he could pass through them. He now made up his mind to get upon the roof of the house through the window of the staircase on the second story. To accomplish this bold project he must have egress from his room—— and Cornélius had carried off the key!

The young noble had taken the precaution of bringing with him, concealed under his clothes, one of those poinards used at that time for dealing the *coup-de-grâce* in a duel, when the vanquished adversary begged the victor to dispatch him. This horrible weapon had one edge sharpened like a razor, and the other one was toothed like a saw, but the teeth running in the reverse direction to that by which it would enter the body in the thrust. The youth purposed to use this latter edge as a saw to cut the wood through around the lock. Happily for him the staple of the lock was attached to the outside of the door by four stout screws. By the help of his dagger he contrived, not without much difficulty, to unscrew and remove this altogether; he carefully laid aside the staple and the four screws, and proceeded down the stairs without his shoes to reconnoitre the locality. It was midnight when he was free.

He was quite astonished to discover a wide-open door to a corridor leading to several chambers, at the end of which passage was a window opening on to the V-shaped roof connecting the roofs of the Hôtel de Poitiers and the "evil house," which there met. Nothing could express his joy, unless it be the vow which he forthwith made to the Blessed Virgin to found a mass in her honor at the noted parish church of the Escrignoles, at Tours.

After examining the vast, tall chimneys of the Hôtel de

Poitiers, he retraced his steps to fetch his poinard; he saw, to his terror, a bright light upon the stairs, and Maître Cornélius himself in his dalmation, carrying a lamp, holding it out as far as possible, his eyes open to their fullest extent and fixed upon the corridor, at the entrance of which he stood still as a spectre.

"If I open the window and jump out upon the roof, he will hear me," thought the young man.

But the terrible old man was coming on—coming like the hour of death stealing upon the criminal. In this extremity Philippe, his wits quickened by love, recovered his presence of mind; he slipped into a doorway, squeezing himself into the angle of it, and awaited the old man's passing him. As soon as Cornélius, holding his lamp in advance, came into line with the current of air which the young man ejected from his lungs, the light was blown out.

Cornélius uttered a Dutch oath and muttered some vague phrases; but he turned around and retraced his footsteps. Then the noble hurriedly sought his room and the poinard, returned with the latter to his so blessed window, softly opened it, and sprang out upon the roof.

Once free and under the open sky, he felt weak, so deliriously happy was he. The excitement of the danger, or the audacity of his enterprise, caused his emotion; victory is to the full as perilous as the battle. He leaned against the parapet, quivering in his satisfaction, and said to himself:

"By which of these chimneys, now, can I get into her room?"

He looked at them all. With the instinct of a lover, he touched each in turn to judge by the feel in which there had been a fire. When his mind was made up on this point, the daring young man securely stuck his poinard in the joint between two stones, attached to it a silken ladder, threw the latter down the chimney, and then, trusting to his good blade and the chance of having selected the route to his mistress' room, without a tremor descended. He knew not whether Saint-Vallier was asleep or awake; but one thing he did know, and that was that he would embrace the countess, even if it should be at the price of two men's lives.

Presently his feet touched warm embers; he gently trod them; more gently yet he stooped down and saw the countess seated in an armchair.

And she saw him.

By the light of the lamp, the timid being, pale and palpitating with pleasurable emotions, pointed to the Comte de Saint-Vallier lying in bed, about ten feet away from her. You may suppose that their burning, silent kisses echoed only in their hearts.

The next day, about nine in the morning, as Louis XI. was leaving his chapel after attending mass, he found Maître Cornélius in his path.

"Good-luck, crony," said he, straightening his cap in his usual jerky manner.

"Sire, I would willingly pay you a thousand gold crowns if I could have a moment's speech with your majesty; I have discovered the thief who stole the rubies and all the jewels of the Duke——"

"Let us hear about this," said Louis XI., going into the courtyard of le Plessis, followed by his silversmith, Coyctier his physician, Olivier le Daim, and the captain of the Scottish Guard. "Tell me this business. Another man to hang for you! Halloo, Tristan!"

The grand provost, who was marching up and down the courtyard, came with slow steps, like a dog proud of his fidelity. The group paused under a tree. The King seated himself on a bench and the courtiers formed a circle around him.

"Sire, a man pretending to be a Fleming has entrapped and got the better of me——" began Cornélius.

"Indeed, then he must be crafty," said the King, wagging his head.

"Yes, truly," answered the silversmith. "But methinks he would have snared even yourself. How should I distrust a poor beggar recommended to me by Oosterlinck, a man for whom I hold a hundred thousand livres? Nay, I will wager that the Jew's letter and seal were forged! In short, Sire, I found myself this morning robbed of those jewels you praised so admiringly. They have been ravished from me, Sire! To steal the jewels of the Elector of Bavaria! The scoundrels will stop at nothing! They'll steal your kingdom if you don't look out. They respect no one!

"As soon as I missed the jewels I went up to the room of that apprentice, who is certainly a pastmaster in thievery. This time proof is not lacking. He had forced the lock of his door. The moon was down when he returned to his room, so he couldn't find all the screws. By good chance I trod upon one as I entered his room. He was sound asleep, the wretch, tired out. Just fancy, gentlemen, he climbed into my strong room by way of the chimney. To-morrow, or perhaps to-night, I'll make it hot for him though. We can always learn something from these villains. He had a silk ladder about him, and his clothes were marked with the dust of the roofs over which he had clambered, and the soot of the chimney down which he had descended. He intended remaining with me and robbing me night after night, the bold villain! But where has he hid the jewels? The countryfolk coming early into town saw him on the roof. He must have had accomplices, who waited for him on that dyke you made. Ah! Sire, you are the accomplice of fellows who come in boats; when, crack! they carry off everything and leave never a trace! But we hold this fellow, this leader, as a key, the horrid miscreant, the daring scapegrace. Ah! but he'll be a dainty morsel for the gibbet; with a screw or two of *questioning* beforehand, he will tell all. And the honor of your reign is concerned in it—is it not? There ought not to be robbers in the realm of so great a King."

But for long the King had ceased to listen. He had fallen into one of those gloomy meditations which became so frequent and ominous in the latter period of his life. A deep silence reigned.

"This is your business," said he at length to Tristan. "Search ye it out."

He rose, walked a few steps, and the courtiers left him alone. He then perceived Cornélius, who, mounted on his mule, was riding away in the company of the grand provost.

"And the thousand gold crowns?" shouted the King after him.

"Ah! Sire, you are too great a King! No sum can pay for your justice!"

Louis XI. smiled. The courtiers envied the old Fleming his bold speech and privileges, as he passed off at a good pace down the avenue of young mulberry trees leading from Tours to le Plessis.

Exhausted with fatigue, the young siegneur was sleeping soundly. When he returned from his gallant adventure the spirit which had carried him through ceased to act in giving him the ability to defend himself against distant or imaginary dangers; he was no longer rashly pursuing anticipated joys. He postponed until the morrow the cleansing of his soiled garb; a great blunder, to which all else conspired. It is true that the moon had failed him; through this he was unable to find all the screws belonging to the cursed lock, he was impatient. Then with the happy-go-lucky indifference of a tired man he trusted to chance which had served him so well. He did, indeed, make a bargain with himself to awake at the dawn, but the events of the day and the tumults of the night prevented his keeping the promise. Happiness is forgetful. Cornélius was no longer, so it seemed, formidable to him, as he flung himself down on the truckle-bed where so many poor wretches had awoke to their doom. This recklessness was his ruin.

While the King's silversmith was returning from le Plessis, in the company of the grand provost and his redoubtable bowmen, the pretended Goulenoire was being watched by the old sister, who was seated on the spiral stairs, knitting stockings and paying no heed to the cold.

The young man continued to dream of the ravishing enchantments of the charming night, in full ignorance of that danger which was rushing upon him at a hand-gallop. He saw himself on a cushion at the feet of the countess, his head on her knees warm with affection's fire.

He was dreaming.

He listened to the story of her persecutions and the full details of the count's petty tyranny; he wept over the lot of the unhappy lady, who was, in truth, the one natural daughter of Louis XI., who was best beloved by him. He promised her that to-morrow he would go to the King and reveal her wrongs to that terrible father; everything, he assured her, should be satisfactorily arranged as she might wish, the marriage annulled, the husband banished—while they themselves might be the victims of his sword, so perilously near, if the slightest noise should awaken him. But in his dreams, the gleam of the lamp, the flame of their eyes, the colors of the stuffs and draperies were more vivid, brighter than in reality; a more delightful perfume exhaled from their night-dresses; there was more of love in the air, more fire in the atmosphere than there had really been. The Marie of his dream did not so strongly resist his advances as the living Marie had done. The adoring glances, those tender entreaties, those adroit silences, those voluptuous solicitations, the affected generosity, which render the first moments of a passion so fiercely ardent, which arouse a fresh delirium at each new step toward love, were less objected to.

In obedience to the amorous jurisprudence of the period,

Marie de Saint-Vallier granted her lover all the superficial privileges of the tender passion, *la petite oie*.* She willingly allowed him to kiss her feet, her robe, her hands, her throat; she avowed her love; she accepted his vows and attentions; she consented for him to die for her; she yielded to an intoxication which the rigor of her half-chasteness intensified; further than that she could not be induced to go—she made her deliverance the guerdon of the highest surrender to his love.

In order to have a marriage annulled, in those days, it was necessary to apply to Rome; to obtain the help of certain cardinals, and to personally appear before the sovereign pontiff armed with the approval of the King. Marie was firm in desiring to be free to love, that she might freely give it to the one she loved.

Almost every woman in those days had enough of power to establish her empire in the heart of a man in such manner as to make that passion the history of his life, the principle of his noblest resolves. Women were then a power in France, they were sovereigns; they had noble pride; their lovers far more belonged to them than they to their lovers; their love was often the cause of bloodshed, but this must be faced to become a lover. But this Marie of his dream was gracious; she was deeply moved by her lover's devotion; she made but small defense against his vehement onslaught.

Which one was true? Did the false apprentice see the real woman in his dream? Was the lady he saw in the Hôtel de Poitiers only assuming virtue's mask? This question it is difficult to decide; it is too delicate; woman's honor demands, as it were, that it should remain unanswered.

At the instant that the Marie of the dream may have been about to forget her high dignity as his mistress, the lover found himself in the grasp of an iron hand, and the sharp tones of the grand provost, as he thus addressed him:

* Lit.: the little goose.

"Come, you Christian of midnight, who feel around the roofs for God, wake up, come!"

The young man saw the black face of Tristan d'Hermite above him; he recognized his sardonic leer; then on the steps of the corkscrew stairway he saw Cornélius and his sister, while beyond them were the provost guards. At that sight and noticing the diabolical visages, expressive of either hatred or curiosity of persons accustomed to hanging people, the whilom Philippe Goulenoire sat up on his bed and rubbed his eyes.

"'Sdeath!" he exclaimed, seizing the poinard which was under his pillow. "Now is the time for our knives to play."

"Ho, ho!" cried Tristan, "that's the speech of a noble. It seemeth me that here is Georges de Estouteville, nephew of the grandmaster of bowmen."

Hearing his real name uttered by Tristan, young d'Estouteville thought less of himself than of the danger his recognition would cause his unhappy mistress. To avert suspicion he cried out:

"By Mahomet's belly! help, help, comrades, help!"

After this terrible outcry, and made really in despair, the young courtier gave a bound, poinard in hand, and reached the landing on the stairs. But the myrmidons of the grand provost were well up in such games. As Georges d'Estouteville reached the stairs they most dexterously seized him, not at all alarmed at the vigorous lunges he made at them with his dagger, which, fortunately for the man at whom it was aimed, slipped on his corslet. He was disarmed, his arms tied, and he was thrown on the bed before the provost, who stood motionless, thinking.

Tristan looked for a moment, without speaking, at the prisoner's hands; he scratched his chin and pointed Cornélius to them, and said:

"Those are no vagabond's hands, neither are they those of an apprentice. He is a noble."

"Say a thief, rather!" retorted the Fleming. "My good Tristan, whether noble or serf, he has undone me, the villain. I would that this moment I could see his feet warming in your pretty boots. Beyond any doubt he is the chief of that gang of invisible devils who know all my secrets, open my locks, rob me, kill me by inches. They are rich with my wealth, Tristan. Ah! this time, though, we will recover the treasure, for this fellow has the face of the King of Egypt. I shall recover my so precious rubies, all the sums I have lost; our good King shall have his division of the spoil."

"Oh, our hiding-places are more secret than yours," said Georges, smiling.

"Ah, the damned villain, he confesses!" cried the miser.

The provost during this time had been carefully examining Georges' clothing and the lock of the door.

"How did you remove those screws?" asked Tristan.

Georges kept silent.

"Oh, all right; hold your tongue if you wish. You will soon confess to Saint Rackbones," said the provost.

"Now you talk business!" cried Cornélius.

"Away with him," said the grand provost.

Georges d'Estouteville asked permission to dress himself. On a sign from their chief the guard put on his clothing with the deft rapidity of a nurse who is changing a baby's dress during a moment's quietude.

An immense throng had assembled in the Rue du Mûrier. The growling increased with every moment, and had the sound of an incipient riot. Rumors of the theft had been prevalent since early morning. On all sides popular favor was aroused on behalf of the apprentice, who was said to be young and handsome; while the hatred against Cornélius had revived afresh. There was not a young woman with fresh cheeks and pretty feet to exhibit, nor a mother's son in all the town, but was determined on seeing the victim. When Georges issued from the house there was a frightful uproar in the street, as he was seen led by one of the guard, who, after he had mounted his horse, kept the twisted end of the strong leathern thong that bound his prisoner's arms.

Whether it was that the mob merely wished to see this new victim, or whether rescue was intended, the people behind pushed those in front close upon the little squad of cavalry posted outside the Malemaison. At this time, Cornélius and his sister slammed the door and banged the shutters to with the violence of panic-terror. Tristan was not accustomed to respect the populace, as in those days they were not yet the "sovereign people," and cared but little for a probable riot.

"Push on! Push on!" he cried to his men.

At his voice the bowmen spurred their horses toward the end of the street. The crowd seeing a few persons knocked down and trampled by the horses, and others crushed up against the walls of the houses and nearly suffocated, took the wise course of returning to their homes.

"Make way for the King's justice!" cried Tristan. "What are you doing here? Do some of you want hanging, too? Go home, good people; your dinner is being burned. Here, my good dame, your husband's hose need mending, get off home and darn them, get back to your needles."

Though this jocular speech showed that the grand provost was in a good humor, the most obstreperous fled before them as if he were the Black Plague itself.

At the time the crowd began to give somewhat, Georges de Estouteville was astounded to see at one of the windows of the Hôtel de Poitiers his beloved Marie de Saint-Vallier, laughing with the count. She was mocking at *him*, the poor devoted lover, who was going to his death for her. But, perhaps, she was only amused by seeing the caps of the populace knocked off by the spears of the bowmen.

One must be twenty-three years old, rich in illusions, fully able to believe in a woman's love, must love with all the power of our life, risking it with pleasure on the handsel of a kiss, and then be betrayed to comprehend the fury of hatred and despair which shook Georges de Estouteville's heart at the sight of his laughing mistress, who only vouchsafed him a cold, indifferent glance. Without a doubt she had been there some time, for her arms rested on a cushion; she was quite at her ease and her old mountebank seemed content. He, too, was laughing—all curses on the hunchback!

A few tears ran from the young man's eyes; but when Marie saw them she hastily drew back. The tears, though, were suddenly dried when Georges beheld the red and white plumes of the page who was in his interest. The count did not notice the movements of this cautious page, for he advanced to his mistress on tip-toe. After he had spoken a few words in her ear, Marie returned to the window. She managed to elude the watchful eye of her tyrant for a moment and cast upon Georges a look that was bright with the fires of love—and the triumph of having so skillfully deceived her Argus—a glance that seemed to say:

"I am watching over you."

Had she cried aloud these words to him, she could not more have impressed them upon his hearing; that glance was full of a thousand thoughts, it was charged with the terrors, hopes, pleasure, of their situation. He had passed in that one second from heaven to martyrdom, from martyrdom back to heaven! So, then, this brave young man, light-hearted and content, walked gayly to his doom; he adjudged the horrors of the grim "question" but a small price for the rapture of his love.

As Tristan was turning off the Rue du Mûrier, his men halted as an officer of the Scottish Guard rode toward them at full tilt.

"What is to do?" asked the provost.

"Naught concerning you," replied the officer, scornfully. "The King sends me to summon the Comte and Comtesse de Saint-Vallier, whom he bids dine with him."

The grand provost had barely reached the quay of le Plessis

when the count and countess, both riding, he on his horse, she on a white mule, and followed by their pages, joined the bowmen, intending to enter Plessis-le-Tours in their company. All were moving slowly. Georges was on foot between two mounted guards, one of whom still held him by the leathern thong.

Tristan, the count, and his wife naturally led the van; the criminal followed them. The young page mingled with the bowmen and questioned them, at times addressing the prisoner; he contrived with some cunning to say to him in a low voice:

"I got over the garden-wall of le Plessis and took a missive to the King from madame. She was nearly dying when she learned of your arrest for theft. Be of good courage. She now goes to the King to speak for you."

Already had love given wiliness and courage to the countess. The laughter she had forced was part of the heroism women can display in the great crises of life.

Despite the singular fancy which possessed the author of "Quentin Durward" to place the royal château of Plessis-le-Tours on an eminence, we must content ourselves in leaving it where it really was situated, that is, on the low land, protected on either side by the Cher and the Loire; also by the Canal Sainte-Anne, so named in honor of his well-loved daughter, Madame du Beaujeu. By uniting the two rivers between Tours and le Plessis, this canal served as a formidable further protection to the castle, and was also valuable as a highway for commerce. On that side toward Bréhémont, a broad, fertile plain, the park was inclosed by a moat, the remains of which still show its extent and depth.

At a period when the power of artillery was still in embryo, the position of le Plessis, long the favorite retreat of Louis XI., might be considered impregnable. The château, built of brick and stone, was in no way remarkable; but surrounding it were noble trees, and from its windows could be seen through the well-arranged vistas* the loveliest views imaginable. No rival place was to be found near this solitary castle, which stood in the very centre of the little plain reserved for the King and guarded by four streams of water.

If tradition may be relied upon, Louis XI. occupied the West wing, and from his chamber could see at one glance the course of the Loire, the pretty valley watered by the Croisville, and some part of the slopes of Saint-Cyr. From the windows opening on the courtyard he could see the entrance to his fortress and the dyke by which he had connected his favorite residence with the city of Tours. The suspicious disposition of the King gives much weight to this tradition. It is certain that had Louis XI. bestowed upon the building of his castle the luxury of architecture which François I. afterward displayed at Chambord, the royal residence of France would always have remained in Touraine. This lovely spot and exquisite scenery need only to be seen to at once establish its superiority over all other royal residences in the fair realm of France.

Louis XI., now in his fifty-seventh year, had scarcely more than three years of life before him; already he began to feel death's approach by many attacks of that illness which was to prove mortal; delivered from his enemies; on the point of adding to his territories by absorbing the possessions of the duchy of Burgundy, through the marriage of the dauphin and Marguerite, the sole heiress of that dukedom—which marriage was arranged by Desquerdes, the captain-general of his army in Flanders; having established his authority throughout his realm; now meditating ameliorations and improvements of every description in the kingdom, he found time slipping from his grasp, no troubles remaining to him save those of old age. Deceived by every one, even by the minions nearest him, experience had increased his natural distrust. The desire to live had become in him the egotism of a king who has be-

---

¹ *Plexitium.*

come incarnate in his subjects; he craved long life in which to carry out vast designs.

Everything that the commonsense of statesmen of spirit or the genius of revolution has since introduced of change in the monarchy, Louis XI. had devised. Equality of taxation, and of people before the law—the Sovereign being then the Law— were the objects for which he endeavored. On the eve of All-Saints he had gathered together the learned goldsmiths of France for the purpose of establishing in his kingdom a system of uniform weights and measures. He had already established a uniform power. Thus his great spirit soared like an eagle above his realm, joining, singular but true, the prudence of a king to the idiosyncrasies of a man of genius.

At no period of our history has Monarchy's figure been greater or more majestic. Amazing contrast! A great mind in a frail body; an unbelieving spirit as concerned the mundane, a devout believer in all the practices of religion; a man struggling against two powers greater than his own—the present, the future; the future in which he dreaded eternal torment, a fear causing him to sacrifice largely to the church; the present, his own life, for the saving of which he was the slave of Coyctier. This King, who could crush all about him, was himself crushed by remorse, by disease, in the midst of that mysterious poem—the combat of Man in his highest manifestations of power tilting against nature.

It was stupendous, it was impressive.

While awaiting his dinner, which, in those days, was partaken between eleven o'clock and noon, Louis XI., after a short walk, sat down in a large, tapestried chair near the fire in his private chamber. Olivier le Daim and Coyctier, the leech, looked at each other without a word, standing in a window recess and watching their master, who was sleeping. The only sound to be heard was the steps of the two chamberlains as they paced back and forth in the anteroom, the Sire de Montrésor and Jean Dufou, Sire de Montbazon. These two seigneurs of Touraine kept an eye on the captain of the Scottish Guard, who, according to his usual custom, was sleeping in his chair.

The King seemed to be dozing. His head drooped upon his breast; his cap, pulled forward over his forehead, hid his eyes. Thus, seated on his high chair of State, which was surmounted by a crown, he seemed, huddled up as he was, like a man who had fallen asleep while engaged in some profound meditation.

At this moment Tristan and his followers crossed the bridge of Sainte-Anne over the canal, about two hundred feet from the entrance to le Plessis.

"Who goes there?" asked the King.

The courtiers, in surprise, looked at each other inquiringly.

"He is dreaming," said Coyctier in a low voice.

"*Pasques-Dieu!*" cried Louis XI. "Do you think I'm a fool? People are now crossing the bridge. To be sure I am sitting near the chimney, and I may hear more clearly than you. This effect of nature might be made useful," he thoughtfully added.

"What a man!" said le Daim.

Louis XI. arose and walked toward one of the windows looking over the town. He saw the grand provost and exclaimed:

"Ha, ha! here come my old crony and his thief. And there, too, is my little Marie de Saint-Vallier; I had forgotten all about that. Olivier," he continued to the barber, "go at once and tell Monsieur de Montbazon to serve us some good Bourgueil wine at dinner, and mind the cook forgets not the lampreys. Madame la Comtesse likes those of all things. May I eat lampreys?" he added after a pause, glaring uneasily at Coyctier.

For all answer the physician commenced to examine his master's face. The two men were a picture.

Historians and romancists have consecrated the brown camlet large coat, with breeches of the same material, worn by Louis XI. His cap, decorated with pewter medallions, his collar of the order of Saint-Michael are not less known; but no writer, no painter, has ever depicted the visage of that terrible monarch in his last years; sickly, hollow, yellow, brown, every feature of which was expressive of sour cunning and cold sarcasm. This mask had the brow of a noble man, a forehead furrowed with wrinkles, weighty with deep thoughts; but on his lips and cheeks was a something indescribably low and vulgar. Looking at certain details of that countenance you might have thought him a debauched vine-grower or a miserly tradesman; but then, above these resemblances and the decrepitude of a dying old man, could vaguely be seen the King, the man of power, the man of action, arising supreme. His pale yellow eyes seemed extinct of sight; but a spark of courage and wrath lurked within; at the slightest friction it could burst into flame and cast about consuming fires.

The physician was a stout burgher with a florid face, dressed in black, peremptory, greedy of gain, of much self-importance.

These two personages were framed, so to say, in that paneled chamber of walnut-wood, hung about with tapestry of Flanders; the ceiling was of carved beams and dingy with smoke.

The furniture, the bed, all inlaid with arabesques of polished pewter, would to-day seem more valuable than they were at that time when the arts were just exploiting their numberless masterpieces.

"Lampreys are not good for you," replied the physician.

(This title, *le physicien*, but recently substituted for the former term *maître myrrhe*, is still applied to the faculty in England. The name was at that time almost universally used in France.)

"What then may I eat?" asked the King humbly.

"Widgeon in salt. Otherwise, you have so much bile moving that you might die on All-Souls' Day."

"To-day!" cried the King, terrified.

"Be composed, Sire," answered Coyctier. "Do not fret your mind; try and amuse yourself some."

"Ah!" said the King, "my daughter Marie used to succeed in that difficult business."

As he spoke, Imbert de Basternay, Sire de Montrésor, and de Bridoré, softly knocked on the royal door. By the King's permission he entered and announced the Comte and Comtesse de Saint-Vallier. Louis nodded a sign. Marie appeared, followed by her aged husband, who had to allow her to precede him.

"Good-day, my children," said the King.

"Sire," replied the lady in a whisper, as she embraced him, "I would speak secretly with you."

Louis made as though he had not heard her.

"Dufou, Holà!" he cried in a hollow voice, turning to the door.

Dufou, Lord of Montbazon, grand cupbearer of France, entered in haste.

"Go to the steward; tell him I must have widgeon salted for dinner. Then to Madame de Beaujeu, inform her that I dine alone to-day. Do you know, madame," continued the King, pretending to some feeling, "that you neglect me. It is nearly three years since I saw you. Come, come hither, pretty one," he added, sitting down and holding out his arms to her. "How thin you have become! Why have you allowed her to get so thin? Eh?" he ejaculated, turning to the Count de Poitiers.

The jealous husband cast so frightened a look at his wife that she almost pitied him.

"It's happiness, Sire," replied he.

"Ah! you love each other too much, do you?" said the King, holding his daughter between his knees. "I was right in calling you Marie-pleine-de-Grace. Coyctier, leave us! Now, what do you want of me?" he asked his daughter, as soon as he saw the physician was gone. "After sending me your——"

In this so great danger Marie audaciously placed her hand on the King's lips and whispered in his ear:

"I always thought you cautious and quick-witted——"

"Saint-Vallier," said the King, laughing, "I think Bridoré has something he wishes to say to you."

The count left the room; but he made a gesture with his shoulder, well known to his wife, who could guess the thoughts of this jealous man, and realized that she must guard against his malignancy.

"Tell me, child, how you think I am looking? Have I changed much, eh?"

"Do you want the truth, my lord? Or must I only speak you fair?"

"No," said he in a husky tone of voice, "I want to know where I am."

"In that case you look but poorly to-day. I trust, though, that my veracity mars not my cause's success."

"What is your cause?" asked the King, frowning and passing one hand over his forehead.

"Ah! Sire," she replied, "the young man that you have had arrested in the house of your silversmith, Maître Cornélius, and who is now a prisoner to the grand provost, is innocent of theft."

"How know you this?" asked the King.

Marie hung her head and blushed.

"I need not ask if there is love at the bottom of this business," said the King gently, and stroking his chin, while he raised his daughter's face. "If you do not confess every morning, child, you will go to hell."

"Cannot you oblige me without questioning my secret thoughts?"

"Where were the pleasure in that?" exclaimed the King, seeing a chance of some amusement in this affair.

"Ah! but would you have pleasure at the cost of my sorrow?"

"Oh! you sly puss, you; won't you give me your confidence, then?"

"So, then, my lord, set that young noble free."

"Oh, oh! he is a nobleman, is he?" cried the King. "Then he is not an apprentice?"

"He is certainly innocent," said she.

"I do not so see it," replied the King coldly. "I am the supreme judge in my kingdom; it is my duty to punish malefactors."

"Come, put not on that solemn face of yours! Grant to me the life of that young man."

"Would not that be giving back your own?"

"Sire," said she, "I am pure and virtuous. You do but jest——"

"Then," said Louis XI., interrupting her, "if you cannot show me my way, I must get the light of Tristan upon it."

Marie de Sassenage turned pale; she made a violent effort; she said:

"Sire, let me assure you that should you do this, you will afterward regret it. The so-called thief has stolen nothing. If you will but grant me his pardon, I will tell you all, even though you should visit it on me."

"Oh, ho! this is becoming serious," exclaimed the King as he pushed up his cap. "Speak, child."

"Well," said she in a low voice in her father's ear, "he was in my room all night."

"He may have been there and yet robbed Cornélius; a double larceny."

"Sire, I have your blood in my veins—I was not born to love a scoundrel. That young noble is the nephew of the captain-general of your bowmen."

"Well, well!" cried the King, "you are hard to confess."

At these words the King pushed his daughter off his knee, hurried to the door of the room, but softly and on tiptoe, making no sound. A moment ago the light from the window in the outer room, shining in the space beneath the door, had traced the shadow of a listener's foot projected slightly on the floor of his room. He abruptly opened the iron-bound door and surprised the Comte de Saint-Vallier eavesdropping. "*Pasques-Dieu!*" he exclaimed, "such insolence deserves the axe."

"My liege," said Saint-Vallier boldly, "I would rather the axe were at my neck than that the ornament of the married were on my head."

"You may yet have both," said Louis XI. "Not a man of the lot of you is safe from such a misfortune, my lords, all. Go into the outer hall. Conyngham," continued the King, addressing the Scottish captain, "you were asleep, eh? Where, then, is Monsieur de Bridoré? Why do you thus allow me to be invaded? *Pasques-Dieu*, the meanest burgher in Tours is better served than his King."

After venting his anger Louis reëntered the room; but he was careful to draw the tapestry curtains, which formed a second door, intended less for the stoppage of the whistling, harsh winds than for the stifling of the King's words.

"So, my daughter," said he, amusing himself with teasing her as a cat does with a mouse, "Georges de Estouteville was your lover last night?"

"Oh, no, Sire!"

"No? Ah! by Saint-Carpion! he deserves death. Did the villain then not think my daughter fair enough?"

"Oh! that's not the way of it," said she. "He kissed my feet and hands with such ardor as might have melted the most virtuous wife. He loves me truly and in all honor," she added.

"Then do you mistake me for Saint-Louis, that I should believe such nonsense? A young fellow made like he is, to risk his life just to kiss your little slippers or your sleeve? Tell that to some one else."

"But aye, my lord, it is true! Still he came for another reason."

Having uttered these words, Marie felt that she had endangered her husband's life, for Louis eagerly asked:

"For what?"

The adventure amused him muchly. He certainly did not anticipate the strange confidences his daughter now made him after she had stipulated for her husband's pardon.

"Oh, ho! Monsieur de Saint-Vallier. So you would even dare to shed the royal blood!" cried the King, his eyes blazing with fury.

At this moment the bell of le Plessis rang the hour of dinner and the escort of the King to arms. Leaning on his daughter's arm, Louis XI. appeared with lowering brow on the threshold of his Chamber, and there found his guard in attendance. He glanced ambiguously at the Comte de Saint-Vallier, as he was thinking up the sentence he meant to pronounce on him.

The deep silence which reigned was presently broken by Tristan's footsteps as he ascended the grand stairway. The grand provost entered the hall, and, advancing toward the King, said:

"Sire, the affair is settled."

"What, is it all over?" said the King.

"Our man is in the hands of the monks. He confessed the theft after a screw of the 'question.'"

The countess sighed and turned pale; she was unable to utter a word, she could only gaze at the King. That look was observed by Saint-Vallier, who muttered in an undertone:

"I am betrayed! The thief is acquainted with my wife."

"Silence!" commanded the King. "Some one there is here who tires my patience. At once, and stop the execution," he added, addressing the grand provost. "Your own body will answer for that of the criminal, my too prompt friend! This affair must be thoroughly sifted, I purpose the doing of it myself. Set the prisoner at large provisionally; I can always recover him; these robbers have hiding-places that they love, lairs where they lurk. Let it be made known to Cornélius that to-night I go to his house to conduct the inquiry. Monsieur de Saint-Vallier," said the King, fixing his eyes on the count, "I know of your doings. All the blood in your body could not pay for one drop of mine; do'st understand? By our Lady of Cléry! You have committed *lèse-majesté*. Did I give you so sweet a wife that you should make her pale and haggard? To your house at once, there make ready preparations for a long journey."

The mere habit of cruelty made the King pause at these words; then he added:

"To-night you set forth to Venice to attend to my business with that government. You need have no anxiety about your wife; she will abide with me at le Plessis; she certainly should be safe here. From this on I shall watch over her with greater care than I have done since I married her to you."

When she heard these words, Marie silently pressed her father's arm as though thanking him for his clemency and good grace. As for Louis XI., he was laughing in his sleeve.

Louis XI. was particularly fond of interfering in the domestic concerns of his subjects, and he was every ready to mingle his royal majesty in bourgeoisie life. This taste, sincerely blamed by some historians, was really but a passion for the *incognito*, one of the greatest relaxations of princes—a kind of temporary abdication, enabling them to put a dash of spice into their existence which becomes insipid for the lack of opposition. Louis XI., however, played his *incognito* without disguise. On such occasions he was always the "good-fellow," endeavoring to please the middle-class whom he thus made his allies against grim feudality. It was some time now since he had found an opportunity of "making himself popular," or taking up the defense of some person *engarrié*, an old term still surviving in Tours and meaning petty litigation, so that he vehemently entered into the secret sorrows of Maître Cornélius, as also into his anxieties.

Several times during dinner he said to his daughter:

"Who, think you, can have robbed my old crony? His losses from theft now amount to over twelve hundred thousand crowns' worth of jewels, this in eight years. Twelve hundred thousand crowns, my lords!" he went on, looking round at the gentlemen-in-waiting. "By our lady! with such a sum a great many absolutions may be bought at Rome. *Pasques-Dieu*, with such a sum of money I could have built the bank along the Loire, or, still better, have conquered Piedmont; a fine buffer all ready constructed for our kingdom."

When dinner was ended, Louis XI. led away his daughter, the physician, and the grand provost, with an escort of men-at-arms, to the Hôtel de Poitiers, where he found, as he expected, the Comte de Saint-Vallier awaiting his wife, most likely to make away with her.

"Monsieur," said the King, "my instructions were for your immediate departure. Bid farewell to your wife, and at once proceed to the frontier; you will be accompanied by an escort of honor. As to your instructions and credentials, they will be in Venice before yourself."

Louis issued his orders, not forgetting to add certain secret instructions to a lieutenant of the Scottish Guard, to take a squad of men and attend the King's envoy to Venice. Saint-Vallier departed in haste, after giving a cold kiss to his wife, which he would have been pleased had it been fatal to her.

When the countess had retired to her chamber, Louis XI. crossed over to the Malemaison, eager to begin the unraveling of the dismal farce, lasting, as it had done, for eight years, in the house of his silversmith. He flattered himself that being the King he could exercise enough penetration to discover the mystery of the robberies. Cornélius did not look upon the advent of this numerous retinue without forebodings of woe.

"And are all these people to take part in the inquiry?" he asked the King.

Louis could not refrain from smiling at the evident fright of the old miser and his sister.

"No, crony," said he; "don't worry yourself, they will sup with us at le Plessis; you and I will alone go into the matter. I am so excellent an investigator that I will wager ten thousand crowns with you that I can find the criminal."

"Never mind the wager, Sire; just find him."

They went at once into the strong-room in which the Fleming kept his treasures. There King Louis, who first asked to see the casket whence the Duke of Burgundy's jewels had been abstracted, and then the chimney down which the robber was supposed to have come, easily proved to the silversmith the falseness of the latter supposition, inasmuch as there was no sign of soot upon the hearth—where, of a truth, a fire was but seldom kindled—and no trace of anything having descended the flue. Moreover, that the chimney issued at a portion of the roof that was practically inaccessible.

After two hours of close investigation, marked with that sagacity which distinguished the suspicious nature of Louis XI., it was proved to a demonstration that no one had forced an entrance into the treasury. No marks of violence showed upon the locks, inside or out, nor on the iron coffers used to contain the gold, silver, and jewels hypothecated by wealthy debtors.

"If the thief opened this box," said the King, "why did he take nothing more than the Bavarian jewels? What reason had he for leaving this pearl necklace laying beside them? A queer robber!"

At this remark the wretched miser turned deathly pale; the King and he eyed each other for a moment.

"Then, my liege, for what did that robber come here whom you have taken under your protection? And, also, why was he prowling around at night?"

"If you have not guessed, oh! my crony, I command you to remain in ignorance. That is a secret of my own."

"Then I am haunted of the devil!" cried the usurer lamentably.

Under any other circumstances the King would have laughed at his silversmith's cry; but in place of this he was studious and thoughtful; he was now casting on the Fleming a scrutiny peculiar to men of genius and force, penetrating to the brain. Cornélius was alarmed; he thought he must have, in some way, offended his dangerous master.

"Be it devil or angel, I'll have him, the criminal," the King abruptly exclaimed. "Should you be robbed to-night, to-morrow I will know who did it. Summon that old hag, your sister," he added.

Cornélius slightly hesitated at leaving the King alone in his treasure chamber; but the stern smile that curled Louis' withered lips compelled him. He, nevertheless, hastened to return, followed by the old woman.

"Have you any flour?" demanded the King.

"Oh, yes; we have laid in our winter supply," she answered.

"Well, go and fetch some," said the King.

"What then would you be doing with our flour, Sire?" she exclaimed in alarm, and not impressed in the least by the King's august majesty.

"Old fool! do you as our gracious liege commands," cried Cornélius. "And shall the King lack flour?"

"My good flour!" grumbled she, as she descended the stairs. "Is this for what I buy fine flour?"

Then she returned and said to the King:

"Is it, Sire, only a royal fancy to examine my flour?"

Finally she reappeared, this time carrying one of those coarse flax-sacks, which from time immemorial have been used in Touraine to fetch and carry provisions to and from the market—nuts, fruit, or grain. The bag was half full of flour. The housewife opened it and showed it to the King, casting a viperous, venomous glance with which old maids, as one may say, seem to squirt venom on a man.

"It costs six sous the *septereé* or measure," said she.

"What, then, does that matter?" said the King. "Spread it upon the floor, but do it carefully so that it may be evenly strewn—as if it had been a light fall of snow."

But the old maid comprehended him not. This order dismayed her more than though the end of the world had come.

"My flour, Sire!—on the ground! But—why——"

Maître Cornélius was vaguely beginning to understand the intent of the King's doings. He grasped the sack and gently spread its contents on the floor. The old woman shuddered, but she extended her hand for the empty bag, and when it was given her by her brother disappeared step by step with a profound sigh.

Cornélius took a feather-duster and carefully smoothed over the flour till it lay like a sheet of snow; as he did this he stepped backward, the King before him, and who seemed much amused over the proceedings. When they reached the door Louis XI. said to Cornélius:

"Are there two keys to the lock?"

"No, Sire."

The King carefully examined the structure of the door, which was heavy and strengthened with plates of iron and strong bars of the same, all of which latter converged to a secret lock, the key of which Cornélius only possessed.

After scrutinizing everything thoroughly the King sent for Tristan; him he ordered to set a watch at night with the greatest circumspection and secrecy in the mulberry trees on the embankment and on the roofs of the adjoining houses; first, though, to assemble at once the rest of his command and escort him back to le Plessis, so that it might appear that the King did not stay to sup with Cornélius. Then he told the miser to close his windows with extreme care, so that not a single ray of light might escape through them, and to give orders that he be served with a light repast to continue the deception. Then the King departed in much pomp for le Plessis by way of the embankment, and privately returned with only two of his suite to the house of the *torçonnier*. These precautions were so well taken and carried out that the good folk of Tours and the courtiers really believed that the King had returned to le Plessis, and that he was to sup on the morrow with Maître Cornélius. The miser's sister still further confirmed this by buying some green-sauce from the best maker, who had a store near the *quarroir aux herbes*, afterward known as the carroir de Beaune, in honor of a splendid white marble fountain which was sent from Italy as an ornamentation for the capital of his Province by Jacques de Beaune.

About eight o'clock that evening, as the King was supping with his physician, Cornélius, and the captain of the Scottish Guard, conversing jollily and forgetting for the nonce that he was Louis XI., ill and in danger of death, profound silence was without, and all passers, even the cleverest thief, might have taken it that the house was uninhabited by any but its usual inmates.

"I hope," said the King laughing, "that my chum the silversmith may this night be robbed, so shall my curiosity be satisfied. See to it, my lords, that no one leaves his chamber to-morrow morning without my order under pain of condign punishment."

Thereupon all went to bed.

The next morning Louis XI. was the first to leave his chamber, and he at once proceeded to the door of the treasury. He was more than astonished to see, as he went along, the imprint of a large foot along the stairway and corridors of the house. He carefully avoided these so precious footmarks, but traced them to the door of the miser's closet; this he found locked and without any sign of violence or fracture. He examined the direction of the steps, but they became gradually fainter and ultimately left not the faintest trace; it was therefore impossible to discover whither the robber had escaped.

"Ha! crony," cried the King to Cornélius, "you have been robbed most excellently this time, for sure!"

At these words the old Fleming, terrified out of his senses, hurried out. Louis XI. made him look at the footprints on the pavements, and while again examining himself for the second time, the King by chance observed the old man's slippers and there recognized the shape of the sole of which so many copies were spread before him on the stairs. He said not a word and restrained his laughter, for he remembered the number of innocent men who had been hanged for this.

Cornélius now hurried to his treasures. When he was in the room the King caused him to make a new mark alongside those already there, and he soon proved to him that the thief of his treasure was none other than himself.

"The pearl necklace is missing! There is sorcery in this," cried Cornélius. "I never left my room."

"We'll soon learn as to that, now," said the King. The evident sincerity of the silversmith quite mystifying him.

He at once summoned the men of the watch and asked:

"Marry, now, what saw you during the night?"

"Ah, Sire!" said the lieutenant, "a most amazing sight! Your majesty's silversmith crept down by the side of the wall like a cat; so lightly withal that he seemed but a spectre."

"I?" exclaimed Cornélius; this one word he uttered, then remained silent, and stood stock-still and rigid like a man who has lost all use of his limbs.

"Begone now, all of you," said Louis, addressing the bowmen, "and tell Messieur Conyngham, Coyctier, Bridoré, and also Tristan to leave their rooms and come here at once to mine. You have incurred the penalty of death," said he to Cornélius, who very happily did not hear him. "You have ten such on your soul!"

Thereupon the King grimly, but noiselessly, laughed, then paused. But as he remarked the strange pallor that overspread the old man's face, he said:

"Be not uneasy; you are more valuable to bleed than to kill. You may escape the fangs of *my* justice in consideration of a good round sum paid into my treasury by you; but, mark you, if you build not at least one chapel to the Virgin, you are more than like to find that things are made hot for you throughout all eternity."

"Twelve hundred and thirty and eighty-seven thousand crowns make thirteen hundred and seventeen thousand crowns," replied Cornélius, absorbed in his calculations. "Thirteen hundred and seventeen thousand crowns hidden—where?"

"He must have buried them in some hiding-place," muttered the King, who began to think the sum as royally magnificent. "That was the lodestone that ever attracted him back to Tours. He smelt his gold."

At this moment entered Coyctier. Noticing the attitude of Maître Cornélius, he scrutinized him keenly, the while Louis XI. narrated the adventure.

"My liege," replied the physician, "there is naught of the supernatural in this. Your silversmith is a sleep-walker. This is the third case I have come across of this so singular malady. If you would amuse yourself by watching him at such times, you might see the old hulks stepping without danger on the verge of the parapet to the roof. In two other cases I have already studied, I could observe a curious connection between the actions of the nocturnal existence and the interests and occupations of daily life in which they were engaged."

"Ah! Maître Coyctier, you are indeed most wise."

"Am I not then your physician?" he insolently retorted.

On hearing this reply, Louis XI. made a slight gesture habitual with him when a good idea struck him—he hastily shoved up his cap.

"At such times," continued Coyctier, "persons transact their business when asleep. As this friend of ours is fond of hoarding, he has simply carried out his darling hobby. He would most probably have an attack when, during the day, he has felt much alarm for the safety of his treasure."

"*Pasques-Dieu !* and such a treasure!" exclaimed the King.

"Where is it?" asked Cornélius, who, by a singularity of our nature, heard all the remarks of the King and his physician, while yet practically in a state of torpor, caused by thought and the shock of his misfortune.

"Ah!" cried Coyctier, with a diabolically coarse laugh, "somnambulists never have recollection of their acts when they awake."

"Leave us," said the King.

When Louis XI. was alone with Cornélius, he glanced at him and ejaculated a cold chuckle.

"Be it known, Worshipful Master Hoogworst," said he, bowing ironically low, "all treasure-trove in France is the property of the King."

"Yes, my liege, all is yours; you are the absolute master of our lives and fortunes; but thus far you have been merciful, and have only taken what you needed."

"Listen to me, old crony mine; if I assist you in recovering this lost treasure, you can surely, in all confidence and without fear, agree to divide it with me."

"No, Sire, I will not divide it; I will give it all to you at my death. But what scheme have you for finding it?"

"I myself will watch you when you take your nocturnal walks. You doubtless would fear to intrust any but me."

"Ah! Sire," exclaimed Cornélius, flinging himself at the King's feet, "you are the only man in the kingdom whom I would trust in such service; and I shall try to prove my gratitude for your goodness to your so humble servant, by doing my utmost to promote the marriage of the heiress of Burgundy with Monseigneur the Dauphin. She indeed would bring you a noble treasure, not of crown-pieces, to be sure, but of lands which would round off your dominions to their greater glory."

"Pshaw, Dutchman, you think to hoodwink me!" said the King, his brow growing threatening, "or you have hitherto played me false."

"Nay, Sire, can you then doubt my devotion—you the only man I love?"

"Words, words!" retorted the King, turning to face the miser, and looking him in the eye. "You ought not to have waited for this moment to be of use to me. You are selling me your influence—*Pasques-Dieu!* to me—Louis the Eleventh. Are you, then, the master? Am I the servant? I wish to know."

"Ah! Sire," said the old man, "I was but waiting to surprise you most agreeably with the news of arrangements I had made for you in Ghent; I was looking for confirmation of it from Oosterlinck through that apprentice. What has become of him?"

"Enough!" said the King. "This is but a blunder the more. I do not like that persons should interfere, uncalled for, in my affairs. Enough! leave me; I must think it all out."

Maître Cornélius found the agility of youth to fly to the lower rooms where he made sure of finding his sister.

"Ah! Jeanne, dear soul, we have a hoard hidden somewhere in this house; I have put away thirteen hundred thousand crowns in jewels somewhere. I—I—I am the thief."

Jeanne Hoogworst rose from her stool and stood erect as if the seat had been red-hot iron.

The shock was so violent for an old maid, accustomed as she was to reduce herself by voluntary privations and fasts, that she trembled in every limb; horrible pains seized her back. By degrees her paleness increased, and her face—the wrinkles of which made any change difficult to discover—became quite distorted while her brother told her the malady to which he was a victim, and the perplexing situation in which he was placed.

"King Louis the Eleventh and I," said he in conclusion, "have just been lying to each other like two miracle-mongers. You see, child, if he watches me, he will learn the secret place of my hidden treasure. Only the King may watch my nightly wanderings. I am not so sure that his conscience, near as he is to death, could withstand the temptation of thirteen hundred and seventeen thousand crowns. We must be beforehand with him; *we* must find this nest and send the treasure to Ghent, and you alone——"

Cornélius stopped suddenly short; he seemed to be weighing the heart of his sovereign, who at twenty-two years of age had dreamed of parricide. When he had made up his mind about Louis XI., he rose abruptly like a man in haste to escape a pressing danger. At this moment his sister, too weak or too strong for such a crisis, fell stark; she was dead.

Maître Cornélius raised her and shook her with violence, saying:

"This is no time for dying. You will have time enough for that later on. Oh! it's all over. Old hag, she never could do the right thing at the right time."

He closed her eyes and laid her on the floor. But then the good and noble feelings which lay cumbered over in his heart came back to him, and, almost forgetting his hidden treasure, he pathetically cried:

"Ah! my poor companion, have I really lost you? You who understood me so well! Oh! you were my real treasure. There, there, lies my real treasure! With you goes my peace of mind, my affections—all are gone. If only you had known what good it would have done me for you to have lived two days longer, you would surely have remained alive, if only to please me, my poor sister. Ah! Jeanne! thirteen hundred thousand crowns! Won't that wake you? No, she is indeed dead!"

Thereupon he sat down and said no more; but two great tears welled in his eyes and rolled down his hollow cheeks; then, with many an ejaculation, he locked up the room and returned to the King. Louis was startled by the expression of grief on the damp features of his old crony.

"What now?" he asked.

"Alas! Sire, misfortunes never come singly. My sister is dead. She's gone below before me," said he, pointing to the floor with a terrible gesture.

"Enough!" cried Louis XI., who disliked any mention of death.

"I make you my heir. I have now nothing for which I care. Here are my keys. Hang me, if such be your good pleasure. Take all; ransack the house; it is full of gold. I give it all up to you——"

"Come, come, old friend," said the King, half moved by the sight of this strange grief, "we shall yet find your treasure some of these fine nights; the sight of such riches will give you a further heart to live. I will come again in the course of the week."

"When it pleaseth you, my liege."

At this answer the King, who had made a few steps toward the door, turned sharply around, and the two men looked at each other with an expression that pen or pencil would vainly try to reproduce.

"Adieu, my crony!" said Louis XI. at last, in a curt voice, pushing up his cap.

"May God and the Virgin keep you in their good graces!" replied the usurer humbly, as he conducted the King to the door.

After so long a friendship the two men found a barrier raised between them, erected of suspicion and gold; though they had always been as one man on matters of suspicion and gold. But then they knew each other so well, they had so completely the habit, as one might say, of intimacy, that the King could divine from the tone of expression in his voice as he said: "When it pleaseth you, my liege," the repugnance he would henceforth feel when he visited the silversmith, just as the latter recognized a declaration of war in the manner of the King's saying: "Adieu, my crony!"

Thus Louis XI. and his treasurer parted in much doubt as to what their future conduct would be to each other. The monarch, for a truth, knew the secret of the Fleming; but he, on his part, could, by means of his connections, bring about one of the greatest acquisitions that any King of France had ever made; namely, the domains of the house of Burgundy, which were, at that time, the coveted of every European sovereign.

Cornélius' gold and influence could most powerfully aid the negotiations now begun by Desquerdes, the general appointed by Louis XI. to the command of the army then encamped on the Belgian frontiers. The celebrated Marguerite's choice would be guided by the good people of Ghent and the inhabitants about her. Thus these two master-foxes were like two duelists whose arms are paralyzed by some stroke of fate.

Now, whether it was that from that day the King's health began to fail and got steadily worse, or that Cornélius did assist in bringing into France Marguerite of Burgundy—who arrived at Amboise in July, 1438, to be married to the Dauphin to whom she was betrothed in the chapel of the castle—certain it is that the King took no steps toward finding the treasure; further, he levied no tribute on his silversmith, and no trial was held; so the pair remained in a cautious condition of armed neutrality.

Happily for Cornélius, a rumor spread around Tours that his sister was proven to have been the robber; and that she had secretly been put to death by Tristan. Otherwise, and if the true history had become generally known, the whole town would have arisen as one man and hastened to destroy the Malemaison before the King could have taken means to defend it.

But, though these historical guessings may have had some foundation as regards the inaction of Louis XI., it was not so as to Cornélius Hoogworst. He was not supine. The first few days which succeeded the fatal one the silversmith spent in a ceaseless hurry. Like a carnivorous beast confined in a cage, he went and came, he smelt for gold in every cranny of his domicile; he sounded the walls; he studied the crevices; he besought the trees of the garden, the foundations of the house, the turret roofs, earth and heaven, to give back his treasure. Often he stood motionless for hour upon hour, casting his eyes around on every side, plunging them into space. He essayed the miracles of second-sight and sorcery; he tried to see his riches through space and solids.

One overwhelming thought constantly absorbed him; he was consumed by a single desire that gnawed his vitals; he was more cruelly racked by the everlasting agony of the duel he fought with himself since his passion for gold had turned upon and rent him. It was a species of incomplete suicide, embracing all the pangs of living and dying.

Never was a vice so trapped by itself: a miser who by inadvertence locks himself in his subterranean stronghold that contains his treasure has, like Sardanapalus, the happiness of dying in its midst. But Cornélius, the robber and the robbed in one, knowing neither the secret of the one nor the other, possessed, and yet possessed not, his treasure—a novel, whimsical, but ever-continuing form of torture.

Sometimes, when he forgot himself, he would leave the little gratings of his door open, and then the passers in the street could see the little, weazened old man planted on his two legs in the middle of his untilled garden, absolutely motionless, and looking on any one who stopped to gaze at him with a fixed, glaring stare, the luridness of which froze them with terror. If by any chance he walked about the streets of Tours, he seemed like a stranger there; he knew not where he was, nor did he know whether the sun or moon shone on him. Oftentimes he would ask his way of those he met, believing himself to be still at Ghent; everywhere he seemed on the hunt for his lost treasure.

The most perennial and the most corporeal of all human ideas—that by which man reproduces himself by creating outside and apart from himself the fictitious being known as Property—that mental demon had its claws of steel perpetually clutching at his miser-soul.

In the midst of this torture, Fear arose, with its accompanying train of sentiments. Two men possessed his secret—the one that he himself knew not. Louis XI. or Coyctier could post their spies to watch his movements when he slept, they might thus discover the unknown gulf into which he had cast his riches, that wealth that he had watered with the life-blood of so many innocent ones: and Remorse stood beside Fear.

To prevent during his lifetime the abduction of his lost riches, during the early days after his disaster, he took every conceivable precaution to avoid sleeping; beside, his commercial relations put him in the way of procuring the most powerful anti-narcotics. His wakeful nights were most terrible, his struggles to keep awake awful—alone with night, silence, Remorse, Fear, with all the thoughts that man, instinctively it may be, has most embodied, in obedience to some moral truth, as yet devoid of certain proof.

At last, this man so powerful, his heart so calloused by politics and commerce, this genius (unknown to history), was doomed to succumb to the horrors of the torture he himself had created. Crazed by some reminiscence more agonizing than any he had as yet resisted, he cut his throat with a razor.

His death was almost exactly coincident with that of Louis

XI.; thus there was nothing to restrain the violence of the mob. The populace, unrestrained, pillaged Malemaison, the Evil House. A tradition exists among the older inhabitants of Touraine that a revenue-farmer, named Bohier, had discovered the old usurer's treasure and used it in building the castle of Chenonceaux, that marvelous mansion which, in spite of the lavish wealth of several kings, and the taste of Diane de Poitiers and her rival Catherine de' Medici, remains unfinished to this day.

Happily for Marie de Sassenage, the Comte de Saint-Vallier died, as we all know, during his embassy to Venice. The family did not become extinct. After the departure of the count the countess gave birth to a son, whose career was famous in the history of France under the reign of King François I. He was saved by his daughter, the celebrated Diane de Poitiers, the illegitimate great-granddaughter of Louis XI., and who became the morganatic wife, the adored mistress of Henry II.: for love and bastardy were hereditary in that noble family.

CHÂTEAU DE SACHÉ, *November and December*, 1831.

GAMBARA.

TRANSLATED BY JNO. RUDD, B. A.

To Monsieur le Marquis de Belloy.

NEW YEAR'S DAY 1831 was throwing around its packets of sugared-almonds; four o'clock was striking; great crowds thronged the Palais-Royal, and the restaurants were filling up. At this time a coupé stopped at the entrance and a young man of noble bearing alighted; a foreigner undoubtedly, or he would not have had as attendant an aristocratic chasseur wearing a plumed hat, neither would the panels have displayed the coat-of-arms, which the heroes of July still sought for the purpose of attack.

Our stranger entered the Palais-Royal and followed the crowd around the wooden galleries, evidently not caring to notice the slow progression he was compelled to make by the sauntering mass of humanity; he seemed born to the noble gait, called in derision the "ambassadors' strut," and yet his dignity had a touch of the theatrical. Although his face was grave and handsome, his hat, under which showed a mass of black, curling hair, tipped the least bit too much over his right ear, belying his gravity with a touch of rakishness. His inattentive, half-closed eyes let fall an occasional contemptuous glance upon the crowd.

"There's a handsome young fellow," said a grisette to another one in her company, as they drew aside to let him pass.

"And right well he knows it, too," responded aloud the companion, who was very plain.

After having made a turn through the arcades, the young man alternately looked at his watch and at the sky; he seemed to be impatient, and at last went into a tobacconist's store, lit a cigar, and stood for a moment before the mirror to glance over his apparel, which was more ornate than the French law of good taste could tolerate. He pulled down his collar and black velvet vest, over which hung many festoons of those heavy gold chains made in Genoa; then, with one jerk of his left shoulder, he satisfactorily arranged his velvet-lined cloak in graceful folds, and resumed his promenade, paying not the slightest attention to the glances of the inquisitive bourgeois.

When the store windows began to be illuminated and the dusk seemed dark enough, he walked to the open square of the Palais-Royal with an appearance of avoiding recognition; he kept close to the wall as far as the fountain, under cover of the hackney-coaches, to thus reach the entrance of the Rue Froidmanteau, a dirty, dark, and disreputable street—a moral sewer which the police tolerate near the purified precincts of the Palais-Royal, the same as an Italian major-domo allows a negligent servant to leave the sweepings from a suite of rooms in a corner of the staircase.

The young man hesitated. He had something of the air of a middle-class wife in her Sunday best clothes when she fears to cross a gutter swollen by the rain; yet the hour was not ill-chosen in which to indulge some questionable whim. Earlier in the day he might have been detected; later, he might be cut out. To have been tempted by a glance more encouraging than alluring; to have followed a young and pretty woman for an hour, perhaps for a day; to set her on a pedestal in his own mind and giving a thousand flattering excuses for her light conduct; to find one's self believing in a sudden, irresistible affinity; to imagine under the flame of a passing excitement the beginning of a love-adventure at an epoch when romances are written because there no longer exists the slightest trace of romance; to have dreamed of balconies, guitars, stratagems, and bolts and Almaviva's mantle; to have written, in fancy, a poem in honor of this divinity; and, after all this, to stop at the door of a house of ill-fame; to find in the decorum of his Rosina a reticence enforced by the police, is surely a history, a delusion; is it not, I ask, an experience of many a man, much as he would desire to deny it?

Our most natural feelings we confess the least willingly; chiefest is self-conceit. When the lesson goes no further than the door, a Parisian profits by it or forgets it; so no great harm is done. With a foreigner, though, this is not so; he begins to think his Parisian education may cost him altogether too dear.

The saunterer was a noble of Milan, banished his country, where some pranks of liberalism had led the Austrian government to suspect him. The Comte Andrea Marcosini had been welcomed in Paris with that French cordiality always shown to one of a witty, amiable nature and of a high-sounding name, especially so when accompanied by an income of two hundred thousand francs a year and a prepossessing appearance. To such a man exile meant but a pleasure tour; his property was only sequestrated, and his friends took means to let him know that after the course of a year or two he could return to his own country without risk.

After rhyming *crudelli affanni* with *i miei tiranni* in a dozen or so sonnets, after also assisting as many of the poorer Italian refugees, Comte Andrea, who for his misfortune was born a poet, thought himself released from patriotic concerns. So since his arrival he had given himself up without discretion to the pleasures of every kind that Paris so kindly offers gratis to everybody who may be rich enough to buy them. His talents and attractive person won him success with many women, whom he collectively loved, as was natural to his age, but among all of which he had, as yet, not selected a particular one. Beside, in him the taste for such pleasures was subordinate to the love of music and poetry, gifts which he had assiduously cultivated since childhood; he thought success in these realms more difficult of attainment and more glorious than the triumphs of gallantry, since nature had spared him the difficulties which most other men take a pride in vanquishing.

Of a complex nature, like many another man, he let himself be charmed by the comforts of luxury, without which he could hardly have lived; he held just as tenaciously to the social distinctions rejected by his political creed. Thus his theories as an artist, a thinker, and a poet were often in direct contradiction to his tastes, his feelings, and his habits as an opulent man of rank; but he consoled himself for this seeming inconsistency by recognizing the same traits in many Parisians— men who are Liberals from self-interest and aristocrats by nature.

Hence it was not without some misgivings that he found himself on foot, on December 31st, in a thaw, following at the heels of a woman whose dress betrayed abject poverty—an inveterate, long-accustomed poverty—and who was not one whit handsomer than others to be seen on any evening at the Bouffons, the opera, or in society, and she certainly was not as handsome as Madame de Manerville, with whom he had an assignation that self-same day, and who, most probably, was at that moment awaiting him.

But there was a something in the glance, half-wild, half-tender, rapid yet intense, which that woman's black eyes had furtively shot at him; a world of buried sorrows and stifled delights was there; she blushed so fiercely when, emerging from a store where she had lingered a little while, her eyes met those of Marcosini, who was outside awaiting her return, but her look met that of the count's with equal candor. There were, in short, so many incentives to curiosity that the count, seized by one of those crazy temptations for which no language has a name, not even in that of the orgy, followed in pursuit of the woman exactly as an old Parisian runs a grisette to earth.

As he went along, sometimes before, sometimes in her rear, he examined the details of her person and dress, he tried to dislodge the absurd and frenzied desire that had taken possession of his brain; but soon his scrutiny felt a keener pleasure than he had experienced the day before as he stood gazing at the perfect shape of a woman he loved, as she took in her bath. Sometimes the unknown fair, bending her head, would throw on him a glance like that of a kid tethered with its head near the ground; then, still finding him in pursuit, she hurried on as if to escape him. Nevertheless, when a block caused by carriages or persons crowded together brought Andrea beside her, he saw that she turned away from his gaze without any sign of annoyance. These signals of repressed emotions spurred on the unruly dreams which were running away with him, and he gave them a free rein as far as the Rue Froidmanteau, down which, after many windings, she suddenly disappeared, trusting that her pursuer would thus find the scent killed for him; he was astonished at this move and had lost trace of her.

It was dark. Two highly rouged women, who were drinking a liqueur of black-currant in a grocery, saw the young woman and called to her. She paused a moment on the threshold, replied to their greeting by a few gentle words and passed on. Andrea, who was close behind her, saw her vanish in one of the darkest courts in the street, of which he knew not the name. The repulsive appearance of the house which the heroine of his romance had entered turned his stomach. He stepped back a few paces to examine the surroundings, when, finding a villainous-looking fellow at his elbow, he asked for information. The man rested one hand on a knotty stick, and ironically answered in two words:

" Droll dog !"

But catching a full view of the Italian, who stood in the light of a street lamp, his face suddenly assumed a wheedling expression.

" Ah! your excuses, monsieur," said he, at once changing his tune; "there's a restaurant in that house, a kind of *table d'hôte* is there served, where the cooking is horribly bad and they put cheese in the soup. Monsieur, perhaps, is in search of that place—for it is easy to see that monsieur is an Italian—and Italians are fond of velvet and cheese. If monsieur would like to know of a better eating-house, I can show him one; my aunt lives near by, and she is very fond of foreigners."

Andrea drew his cloak as high as his nose and rushed out of the street, driven by the disgust he felt for this filthy creature, whose clothing and gestures were in keeping with the squalid house into which the unknown woman had disappeared. He returned with delight to the comforts and elegancies of his suite of rooms, and passed the evening with the Marquise d'Espard, to cleanse himself, if possible, of the pollution of the fancy that had taken such hold upon him.

Nevertheless, afterward when he was in bed, in the silence of the night, his evening vision arose before him, brighter, clearer, more vividly than the reality. Before him walked his divinity; at times as she crossed the street gutters she slightly raised her dress and displayed a shapely leg ; and her beautifully mouldered hips swayed at every step. Once more Andrea wished to speak to her and dared not. He, Marcosini, a noble of Milan! Then he saw her once more enter the dark court and the wretched house, and blamed himself for not following her farther.

"For," said he to himself, "if it was that she avoided me and tried to put me off the scent, surely it is a sign of her loving me. With women of this kind coyness is proof of love. Possibly though if I had gone further with the adventure it might have ended in disgust. I'll just sleep in peace."

The count was in the habit of analyzing his keenest sensations, as all men born with a good headpiece involuntarily do when their brain equals their heart : he was greatly surprised to still find himself thinking of the strange damsel, not in the ideal glamour of a vision, but in all the reality of the naked facts. And yet, if his fancy had stripped her of the misery of wretchedness, the woman herself would have been spoilt for him; for he wanted her, he desired her; he loved her—muddy stockings, broken shoes, her battered straw bonnet, all! He longed for her in that very house which he had seen her enter.

"Am I then enamored of vice?" he asked himself with horror. "Nay, I have not come to that, I am but three-and-twenty; there is nothing of the senile stage about me."

The very vehemence of the caprice of which he was the plaything seemed to somewhat reassure him. This curious struggle, these reflections, this love on a run may be an enigma to some persons who imagine they know the ways of Paris; but let such bear in mind that Count Andrea Marcosini was not a Frenchman.

Brought up as he was by two pious abbés, by the instruction of a pious father, who had seldom permitted him out of their sight, Andrea had not fallen in love with a cousin at eleven, nor had he seduced his mother's waiting-maid at twelve; he had not studied at those colleges where the most consummate teaching is not prescribed by the State; he had lived in Paris but a short time, and he was yet on the watch against those sudden and deep impressions against which the education and customs of a French education are such a powerful ægis.

In Southern lands great passions are often born at a glance. A Gascon gentleman who had tempered his sensibility by deep reflection, and owned a horde of little recipes against the sudden apoplexies of the head and heart, had one day advised Marcosini to indulge at least once a month in a wild sensual orgy, so he might avert those storms of the soul which, without such precautions, were apt to burst forth at inconvenient times. Andrea well remembered this advice, and, as he sank to sleep, muttered to himself:

"Well, I'll begin to-morrow, January the 1st."

This will explain why it was that the Comte Andrea Marcosini so furtively skirted the line of hackney-coaches to get at the entrance of the Rue Froidmanteau. The man of fashion hampered the lover; he hesitated for some time, but, after a final appeal to his courage, the lover advanced with a firm step to the house, which he easily recognized. There he again stopped. Was the woman what he took her to be? Might it not be that he was about taking a false step?

Just then he recollected the Italian table-d'hôte, and eagerly jumped at the middle course thus offered, and which seemed like to serve the ends of his desires and his repugnance.

He entered the place, intending to dine there; he made his way down a greasy passage, at the end of which he found, after groping about for some time, the damp and slimy steps of a stairway, and which, to an Italian nobleman, must have seemed little more than a ladder.

Attracted to the second floor by the light of a lamp placed on the floor, and by a strong scent of cooking, he pushed a door which stood ajar, and saw a large room dingy with smoke and grease, where a woman was engaged laying a table for about twenty customers. None of the guests had as yet arrived.

Glancing around the ill-lighted room, where the paper hung in strips from the wall, the nobleman seated himself near a stove which rumbled and smoked in a corner.

The major-domo of the place, attracted by the noise the count made in entering, now hustled into the room. Picture to yourself a thin, lank cook, very tall, blessed with a nose of extravagant dimensions, casting about him from time to time a feverish glance that he intended to seem cautious. At sight of Andrea, whose dress and appearance bespoke affluence, Signor Giardini bowed respectfully.

The count expressed an intention of habitually dining there with his compatriots; he paid for a number of tickets in advance, and gave a friendly tone to the conversation to enable him to achieve his purpose the quicker.

He had scarcely alluded to the woman he was seeking than

Signor Giardini made a grotesque gesture, looked knowingly at his customer with a wink, and let a smile curl his lip.

"*Basta!*" he exclaimed. "*Capisco!* You, signor, are brought hither by two appetites. The Signora Gambara will not have wasted her time if she has managed to interest a gentleman so generous as you seem to be. I can tell you in one word all that we know here of the woman, who is truly to be pitied.

"The husband was born, I think, at Cremona, but he came here from Germany, quite recently. He has been endeavoring to get the *Tedeschi* to try some new music and a new kind of instrument. It is pitiable, eh?" exclaimed Giardini, shrugging his shoulders. "Signor Gambara, who believes himself a great composer, does not seem to me to be particularly smart in other directions. A fine fellow enough, occasionally good-natured, full of commonsense and wit, especially when he has drunk a glass or two of good wine— a not frequent occurrence, for he is frightfully poor. He toils night and day in composing imaginary operas instead of working for a living as he should do. His poor wife is reduced to working for all sorts of people, prostitutes and the like—sewing she does. Well, it can't be helped, she loves her husband like a father and cares for him like a baby.

"Lots of young men have come here to dine in hopes of being able to pay court to madame, but no one has as yet succeeded," he said, with a significant emphasis on the last word. "La Signora Marianna is virtuous, sir; much too virtuous for her own good, worse luck. Nowadays men give nothing for nothing. The poor creature will die in poverty

"You would naturally suppose that her husband would reward such fine devotion, wouldn't you? Bah, he doesn't even give her one smile. The cooking is done at the bakery, for, see you, this devil of a husband never earns a sou, but he spends his whole time in making instruments, which he cuts and lengthens, and shortens and fits, and sets up and takes to pieces again till they give out squeaks that would scare a cat; then only is he happy. And yet you will find him the kindest and gentlest of men; he's not a bit lazy, no indeed, he's alway busy. To speak truth, he's mad and doesn't know it. I have seen monsieur filing and forging those instruments of his and chewing away on his black bread with an appetite that I have often envied—I, monsieur, who keep the best table in Paris.

"Your excellenza shall learn before an hour passes over your head the man I am. I have introduced a number of refinements into Italian cookery that will amaze you. Excellenza, I am Neapolitan, which is saying, a born cook. But of what good is instinct without science? Science! I have spent thirty years in acquiring it. See, then, to what it has brought me! My history is that of every man of talent. My efforts, my experiments, have ruined three restaurants in succession—one at Naples, the others at Parma and Rome. Again reduced in this city to making a trade of my art, I practice in my ruling passion more than before. Some of my finest ragouts I give to these poor refugees. I ruin myself. Folly! you would say? I know this, but, then, can I help myself? Genius is stronger than I; is it possible I can restrain myself from creating a dish that smilingly allures me? And they always know it, the scallawags! I can make oath to you that they know at once whether it was my wife or I who handled the ladles.

"And what now is the consequence? Out of the sixty or more guests whom I used to see at my table-d'hôte every day when I first opened this wretched place, barely twenty remain, and most of these want credit.

"The Piedmontese, the Savoyards, have quit me, but the persons of taste, the Italians proper, remain. And for these what sacrifices would I not make! I often give them a dinner at five-and-twenty sous a head that has cost me double that to prepare."

Signor Giardini's little speech was so redolent of Neapolitan cunning that the count was tickled immensely; he could have fancied himself back at Gerolamo's.

"If such be the case, my good host," said he familiarly to the chef, "and since accident, chance, and your good-nature have let me into the secrets of your daily sacrifices, permit me the honor of paying double."

Thus speaking, Andrea flung a forty-franc piece on the table, out of which Signor Giardini solemnly returned him two francs and fifty centimes in change, with a mysterious ceremony which enchanted the young man.

"In a few minutes," continued the signor, "you shall behold your *donnina*. I'll seat you next the husband; if you wish to get in his good graces, talk music; I have invited both of them for this evening, poor souls. For New Year's Day celebration I have prepared a dish for my guests in which I may say that I have surpassed myself."

The words of Signor Giardini were drowned in the noisy greetings of the said company, who streamed in singly or in pairs, irregularly, after the manner of tables-d'hôte. Giardini stood ostentatiously by the count and pointed out to him the regular company. He was liberal with his quips and quirks, and tried by his humorous remarks to bring a smile to the lips of this man whom, as his Neapolitan instinct assured him, was a wealthy patron who might be turned to account.

"That man," said he, "is a poor composer who would much like to leave the ballad line for the realm of opera; but he can't. He abuses managers, music publishers, everybody but himself, who is his own greatest enemy. Don't you catch on to his rubescent complexion, what jolly self-conceit, how little firmness he displays? He's only cut out for a ballad-monger, and nothing else. The other man in his company, who looks like a match-vendor, is a great musical celebrity, Gigelmi—the greatest of Italian conductors. But he is now going deaf, and is ending his days most miserably, deprived as he is of all that is attractive to him. Ah! and here comes our Ottoboni the great, the most guileless old fellow on earth; and yet he is suspected of being the most vindictive of all those who are plotting for the regeneration of Italy. I should dearly like to know why ever they banished such a mild old gentleman——"

Here Giardini looked closely at the count, who, aware that he was being pumped on the political question, kept an impassibility that was truly Italian.

"A man who cooks for all the world is denied political opinions, excellenza," went on this culinary genius. "But any one seeing that worthy man, who looks more the lamb than the lion, would say as I do about him, even to the Austrian ambassador himself. Beside all, at this day liberty is no longer proscribed; it is *en route* again! At least that's what these good people here present fancy," he whispered in the count's ear, "and I, why should I daunt their hopes? Though I myself do not hate an absolute government.

"All great talent is for absolutism. Well, though Ottoboni is choke full of genius, he expends time and trouble in teaching Italy; he writes little books to teach the minds of children and the laboring classes, and he very cleverly gets them smuggled into Italy; he adopts every means to awaken a moral sense in our unlucky native land, where, after all, enjoyment is more desired than liberty—it may be they are right."

The count still retained his impassiveness, and the cook was unable to learn any of his political opinions.

"Ottoboni," he went on, "is a saint; very benevolent and helpful; all the refugees love him, for you must know, excellenza, that even a Liberal may have his virtues. Ah! here we have a journalist!" he exclaimed, interrupting himself, and pointing out a man who wore the attire generally attributed, perhaps more conventionally than truthfully, to the garret poet; his coat was threadbare, his shoes cracked, his hat shiny, his overcoat in senile decay. "Excellenza, that poor man is full of talent and incorruptibly honest! He was born in a wrong age; he tells the truth to the whole world; people detest him. He is the theatrical critic of two little journals, though he is smart enough to write for the great dailies. Poor fellow!

"The others are beneath your notice; your excellency will easily learn about them without my help," he hastily added, perceiving that the count was no longer paying attention to him, as the wife of the composer entered the room.

Seeing Andrea there, Signora Marianna visibly started and a blush tinged her cheeks.

"Here he is," said Giardini in an undertone, pressing the count's arm and motioning to a man of tall stature. "See how pale and grave he is, poor man! His hobby is evidently not cantering to his mind to-day."

Andrea's love-dream of Marianna was suddenly overpowered by the captivating grace which Gambara's presence exercised over every true lover of art. The composer was forty; but although his high forehead, from which the hair had flown, was furrowed with a few wrinkles, not deep, but in parallel lines, and in spite of the hollow temples where the blue veins showed through the clear, transparent skin, and of the sunken orbits of his dark eyes surmounted by heavy lids and light-colored lashes, the lower part of his face made him still appear young, so calm were the lips, so tranquil the outline. It could be recognized at a glance that this man had subserved passion by the curb of intellect; that he would only grow old from mental struggle.

Andrea stole a rapid glance at Marianna, who was watching him. The sight of her glorious Italian head, the exquisite proportion and rich coloring, revealed an organization where all the human forces were symmetrically balanced; he sounded the gulf which separated this pair accidentally joined together. More than pleased with this evidence of dissimilarity between husband and wife, he no longer combated the feelings which drew him to Marianna. But for the man whose only blessing she was, he already felt a touch of respectful pity, seeing, as he could not help doing, the dignified and serene acceptance of ill-fortune that was expressed in Gambara's melancholy and mild eyes.

Expecting to find, from Giardini's description, one of those grotesque beings so often set before us by German novelists and libretto poets, instead he found, to his great astonishment, a simple, reserved man, whose manner and demeanor were aught but eccentric, and possessed a dignity all their own. The dress of the musician, though it showed no trace whatever of luxury, was more seemly than his extreme poverty would lead one to expect, while his linen bore testimony to the tender care which watched over even the minor details of his being.

Andrea raised his moistened eyes to Marianna, who did not blush, though a half-smile curled her lips, perhaps called forth by the pride she felt in the young man's mute homage. Too seriously fascinated not to watch for the slightest indication that his feelings were returned, the count began to fancy himself beloved by her because he saw that she comprehended him. From this moment he set himself to the conquest of the husband rather than of the wife, directing all his batteries against poor Gambara, who unsuspectingly went on eating the *bocconi* of Signor Giardini without knowing their taste.

The count opened the conversation with some general remark; but from the first he was conscious that the man's intellect, supposedly blind on one point at least, was extraordinarily clear-sighted on all others, and he saw that it would be far more important to understand his ideas than to attempt any flattery of his whims.

The remainder of the guests, a hungry crew, whose wits were only sharpened by the sight of a dinner, were it good or bad, betrayed a positive animosity to Gambara, and only waited the end of the first course to give vent to their satire.

One refugee, whose frequent leers showed an ambitious scheme in connection with Marianna, and who seemed to fancy that he could entrench himself in her good graces by making her husband ridiculous, opened fire by trying to explain to Marcosini the lay of the land of the table-d'hôte.

"It is quite a long time since we have heard anything about the opera of 'Mahomet,'" he exclaimed, smiling at Marianna. "Can it be that Paolo Gambara is wholly given up to domestic affairs, the charms of the *pot-au-feu*,* and so neglects his superhuman genius, thus allowing his talent to grow cold and his imagination to stale?"

Gambara knew all the company; he felt that he lived in a sphere high above them; he therefore no longer took the trouble to repel their attacks, he made no answer.

"It is not given to everybody," said the journalist, "to have an intellect that can comprehend the musical efforts of Monsieur Gambara; it is for this reason, doubtless, that our divine *maestro* hesitates to produce his works for the worthy Parisians."

"And yet," put in the ballad-monger, who up to now had only opened his mouth to cram into it all the food that was within reach, "I know some men of talent who think much of the judgment of these same Parisians. I myself have something of a reputation as a musician," he added diffidently; "I owe it solely to my little songs in vaudevilles, and the great success of my quadrille music in drawing-rooms; but I propose to very soon present to the world a mass composed for the anniversary of the death of Beethoven, and I anticipate a better understanding in Paris than elsewhere. You, monsieur, may perhaps do me the honor of hearing it?" he said, addressing Andrea.

"Thank you," replied the count. "I am afraid that I am not endowed with an understanding necessary for the appreciation of French music. But if you were dead, monsieur, and Bee-

* The stock-pot; really meaning the chimney-corner.

thoven had written your mass, I should have pleasure in attending the performance."

This retort effectually stopped the skirmishing of the enemy, who wanted to start Gambara off on his hobby-horse so that his gambols might furnish amusement to the new guest. Already it was repugnant to Andrea's feelings to see a madness so gentle and pathetic, if madness it were, at the mercy of this vulgar wit. It was not then with any baseness that he carried on a desultory conversation, in the course of which Giardini's nose not infrequently interposed between two replies. When Gambara gave expression to a paradoxical idea, the cook would poke his head forward, to glance pityingly on the composer, and to wink knowingly at the count as he whispered in his ear:

"*E matto!*"

Presently, though the second course demanded the attention of the chef, and as he attached extreme importance to this, he was interrupted in his sapient remarks. During his absence, which was only a short one, Gambara leaned toward Andrea and said in his ear:

"Our worthy host threatens us to-day with a dish of his own concoction, which I would advise your avoiding, though his wife has had her eye upon him. The honest fellow has a mania for innovations in cookery. He has ruined himself by experimenting; the last one compelled him to flee from Rome without a passport, a thing he never talks about. After buying the good-will of a famous restaurant, he was engaged to cater for a banquet given by a lately created cardinal, whose household was in an incomplete state. Giardini thought the time had come for him to distinguish himself; he succeeded. That very evening he was accused of trying to poison the whole conclave and was forced to leave Rome, and Italy, without packing his trunk. That misfortune was the last straw, and now——" and Gambara laid his forefinger on his forehead and shook his head.

"In other respects," he added, "he is a right good fellow. My wife can inform you that we are under numerous obligations to him."

And now came in Giardini, carefully carrying a dish, which, with much elaboration, he laid upon the centre of the table; then he modestly resumed his seat by Andrea, who was first helped. When the count took just one taste of the mess, he felt that an immeasurable abyss separated him from the next mouthful. He was much embarrassed, and, being anxious to avoid annoying the cook, he kept his eye upon him and studied. Though a French restaurateur may trouble himself but little about what his guests may think of his cooking, for which they must needs pay anyhow, it is otherwise with an Italian *trattore*, who is scarcely satisfied with perfunctory praise.

To gain time, Andrea paid extravagant compliments to Giardini; he leaned over to whisper in his ear, and as he did this slipped into his hand a gold-piece, begging him to go out and himself purchase some champagne, giving him the freedom to announce to the company that it was his own treat.

When, after a while, the cook reappeared, every plate was cleared, and the room reëchoed with praises for the mastercook. Under the influence of the champagne the Italian tongues were soon unlimbered, and the conversation, till now more or less subdued in the stranger's presence, leaped the barriers of suspicious reserve, and wandered wildly hither and thither over the broad fields of political and artistic theories. Andrea, who was guiltless of all intoxicants but love and poetry, soon controlled the attention of the company, and cleverly led the discussion to matters musical.

"Monsieur will, perhaps, kindly inform me," he said to the composer of dance-music, "how it is that the Napoleon of petty tunes can bemean himself to a struggle with such people as Palestrina,[*] Pergolese, and Mozart—poor creatures,

---

[*] Much of this composer's music is still popular in the United States.

who must go, bag and baggage, on the advent of this stupendous mass for the dead?"

"You see, monsieur," replied the composer, "a musician finds it difficult to reply when his answer needs the coöperation of a hundred skilled performers. Mozart, Haydn, and Beethoven, without an orchestra, would have been no great shakes."

"No great shakes!" cried the count. "Why, man, the whole world knows that the immortal composer of 'Don Giovanni' and the 'Requiem' was named Mozart; but I am so unhappy as to be in ignorance by what name the inventor of fashionable country dances is known——"

"Music is a being independent of its execution," said the ex-conductor of orchestras, who, despite his deafness, had caught a few words of the conversation. "Take the C-minor symphony by Beethoven, the musical mind is borne onward into Fancy's realm on the golden wings of the theme in G-natural, repeated by the cornets in E. He sees a whole nature illuminated in turn by dazzling jets of light darkened by clouds of melancholy, inspirited by heavenly strains."

"Beethoven is outclassed by the new school," said the ballad-monger scornfully.

"Beethoven is not yet understood," said the count. "How, then, can he be excelled?"

Here Gambara drank a large glass of champagne, accompanying his libation with a covert glance of approval.

"Beethoven," the count went on, "has extended the limits of instrumentation, and, as yet, none have followed in his path."

Gambara assented with a slight nod.

"His works are specially remarkable for simplicity of construction and for the manner in which the theme is worked out," continued the count. "In the works of most composers the instrumentation is vague and at random, an incoherent blending for a specious effect; they do not carry forward the progression of the harmony in the movement by any regularity and system. Whereas, Beethoven assigns to each part its tone-quality from the inchoation. The same as various regiments assist by disciplined movements in the winning of a battle, so do the various orchestral scores of a symphony by Beethoven over the general command for the interest of the whole, and are subordinate to an admirably conceived plan.

"In this respect he may be likened to another genius. We often find in Walter Scott's noble historical romances that the personage who appears to have less to do with the action of the story than any other character is, at the proper moment, brought forward, and leads up to the climax by threads woven into the plot."

"*E vero!*" said Gambara, whose commonsense seemed to return inversely to his sobriety.

Being anxious to test the musician still further, Andrea for the nonce abandoned his own predilections and proceeded to attack Rossini's European reputation. He disputed the position which the Italian school had captured by storm, night after night for thirty years on a hundred stages. He soon found he had enough on his hands. At his first words a strong murmur of disapproval arose; but neither interruptions nor exclamations, nor frowns, nor contemptuous looks were now able to check this determined advocate of Beethoven.

"Compare," said he, "the productions of the sublime composer with what is by common consent called the Italian school; what a paucity of ideas, what a limp in the style! Listen to those monotonous measures, those trite cadences, the endless bravura passages flung out haphazard irrespective of the dramatic situation, the ever-recurring *crescendo* brought into vogue by Rossini, and which is now become an essential in musical composition, and, last of all, those trills, vocal fireworks, all combined in a chattering, pattering, vaporous music, the sole merit of which consists in the fluency of the singer and his agility in vocalization.

"The Italian school has lost sight of art's highest mission. Instead of elevating the world, it has condescended to the crowd; its fame is won by seeking the suffrages of the multitude, and by appealing to the perverted taste of the majority. Its fame is a street-corner celebrity.

"To say all, the compositions of Rossini, in which this music is embodied, as well as of those writers who derive more or less of their style from him, seem to me to be worthy only of collecting a street crowd around a barrel-organ or keeping step to the capers of a punch-and-judy show. I prefer French music even to that; I can't say more. Long live German music!" he cried, "—— when it is tuneful," he muttered ironically to himself.

This sally was the summing up of a long argument in which Andrea soared metaphysically with all the ease of a somnambulist on a roof. Gambara, keenly interested in such subtleties, had not missed a word of the argument. At the instant that Andrea dropped it he took it up, and the attention of the company was at once arrested; a few who were about leaving the room returned to listen.

"You attack the Italian school most vehemently," said Gambara, who was warmed to his work by the champagne he had supped, "but that to me is a matter of indifference. Thank God. I stand outside all these frivolities of melodious frippery. Yet for a man of the world you show but little gratitude to the land from which Germany and France derived their first lessons. While the compositions of Carissimi, Cavalli, Scarlatti, Rossi, were being played through all Italy, the violinists of the French opera enjoyed the singular privilege of being allowed to play their instruments with gloved hands. Lulli, who so much extended the realm of harmony, and who first gave the rule of discords, on arriving in France found only two men, a cook and a mason, who had voice and intelligence enough to execute his music; of the first he made a tenor, and the latter he made a bass. At that time Germans, always excepting Sebastian Bach, were ignorant of music. But, monsieur," added Gambara, in the humble tone of a man who realizes that his remarks will be received with scorn, if not ill-will, "you must, although young, have studied the higher questions of musical art for a long time, or you could not so clearly explain them."

These words caused a smile in many of the hearers, for they had not understood the fine distinction of Andrea's views. Giardini, convinced that the count was only talking at random, nudged him warily, laughing in his sleeve at the hoax in which he thought himself an accomplice.

"There is much that strikes me as being very true in what you have said," Gambara went on; "but take care. Your argument, while it brands Italian sensualism, seems to incline somewhat to German idealism, which is a not less fatal error. If men of imagination and good taste, like yourself, desert one field only to stray into the other, if they cannot remain neutral between two extremes, we shall always be subject to the satire of the sophists who deny progress and liken human genius to—to this table-cloth, which, being too short to wholly cover Signor Giardini's table, decks one end at the expense of the other."

Giardini bounded in his chair as though he had been stung by a gad-fly, but quick reflection restored his dignity as a host; he raised his eyes to heaven and again poked the count, who was beginning to think the cook more crazy than Gambara.

The serious and even religious manner in which the latter spoke of art interested Marcosini extremely. Seated between these two manias, one so noble, the other so vulgar, and making game of both, to the great amusement of the crowd, the count felt as if he was continually being tossed about from the sublime to the ridiculous—the two extravaganzas of the comedy of human life. Suddenly breaking the chain of the fantastic events which had led him to this smoky den, he fancied himself the victim of some strange hallucination, and began to believe that Gambara and Giardini were two abstractions.

Presently, after a last piece of buffoonery on the part of the deaf orchestra leader, directed at Gambara, the company retired amid roars of laughter; Giardini went off to make coffee he intended offering his guests remaining and his distinguished patron; and his wife meanwhile cleared the table. The count was seated near the stove and between Marianna and Gambara, and in the precise position that the latter had declared to be so desirable—midway between sensualism on the one hand and idealism on the other. Gambara, who for the first time met a man who did not laugh at him to his face, soon left off generalizing and began to speak of himself, his life, his toil, and his hopes of a final musical redemption of which he believed himself to be the Messiah.

"Hearken to me," said he, "ye that have thus far not laughed me to scorn; I will tell you my life—not that I may extol a constancy which does not emanate from my own self, but for the glory of One who has placed this force in my soul. You seem to be good and reverent; if you cannot believe in me, you at least can extend me your sympathy; pity comes of man, faith is God."

Andrea, who blushed crimson, turned and withdrew his foot which had been seeking Marianna's, and fixed his gaze upon her while he listened to her husband.

"I was born at Cremona," continued Gambara, "the son of an instrument-maker; a fairly good performer of music, but a far better composer. I had thus at an early age mastered the laws of composition in its dual aspect, the spiritual and material; and, with the natural curiosity of my age, I paid attention to many things which I afterward applied in my more mature manhood.

"The French invasion drove us, my father and myself, from our home. We were ruined by the war. From the age of ten

I began that wandering life to which all men are condemned who revolve in their brain reforms in art, science, or politics. Fate, or the natural instincts of their minds, which never gee with those of ordinary comprehension, leads them onward, providentially, to points where they receive instruction. Led by my passion for music I wandered through Italy from theatre to theatre, living on little, as men can live there. Sometime I played the violoncello in orchestras; often I formed one of the chorus; or worked in the wings with the carpenters. Thus I studied music in its every aspect, learned the tones of the human voice and instruments, in what manner they differed from each other; I listened carefully to the scores and noted the harmonizing, always applying the rules taught by my father. Often, again, I traveled through the country mending instruments. It was a hard life in a land where the sun ever shines, where art permeates the air and money is not—at least for the artist, since Rome is no longer, save in name only, the sovereign of the Christian world.

"Sometimes I was gladly welcomed, at times driven forth because of my poverty; yet I never lost heart; I heard an inner voice foretelling fame. Music to me seemed but in its infancy. That opinion is still retained.

"All that we still have of the musical efforts anterior to the seventeenth century demonstrates to me that ancient composers knew melody only; they were ignorant of harmony and its vast resources. Music is both science and art. It is rooted in physics and mathematics, hence a science; its inspiration makes it an art, unconsciously employing the propositions of science. It derives from the physical by the very essence of the matter on which it subsists. Sound is air in motion; air is made up of elements which undoubtedly find within us analagous constituents which respond to them, which sympathize with and augment them by the power of the intellect. Thus air must contain as many varieties of elastic molecules, capable of vibrating in as many diverse periods as there are tones in all sonorous bodies; and these particles, put in motion by the musician and received by the ear, respond to our ideas in accord with our several organizations. It is my opinion that the nature of sound is identical with that of light. Sound is light under a different form; both act by vibrations which are sentient to man, and which he transforms in his nerve-centres into ideas.

"Music is analogous to painting, making use of materials that possess the property of freeing this or that property of the birth substance in suggesting a picture. So in music the instruments perform this part, as does color in the painting. Now, as all sound produced by a reverberating body is invariably accompanied by its major third and fifth, whereby it acts on grains of sand spread upon a plain of stretched parchment and arranges them in geometrical figures—always the same in form according to the pitch—regular when the harmony is a true chord, but without definity under the influence of discords, I say that music is an art conceived in Nature's very womb."

Gambara's calm eyes were fixed upon Marcosini, who listened with rapt attention.

"It is that music is subject to both physical and mathematical laws," he went on. "The physical laws are but little understood, the mathematical laws are somewhat more fully comprehended; and, since their relationship has been more studied, it has enabled those creations of harmony to be effected which we owe to the genius of Mozart, Haydn, Beethoven. and Rossini, men of glorious genius. whose music is unquestionably nearer perfection than that of their predecessors. for it must be admitted that the latter's genius is incontestable. The old masters could create melody, but they had none of the resources of art and science at command—that noble alliance which blends into a grand whole the beauties of melody and the power of harmony.

"Now, if a knowledge of the mathematical laws of music

gave these four musicians to us, to what height may we not attain if we can succeed in discovering the physical laws by virtue of which (please note this) we may store up in a greater or less quantity, according to the proportions required, a certain ethereal substance diffused in the air, which gives us music as it gives us light, the phenomena of vegetation and animal life! Do you grasp my meaning?

"These new laws would arm the composer with new powers; it would supply him with instruments superior to those now used, and, more than possibly, with a potency of harmony than that which dictates the realm of music at this time. If every modulation obeys a power, we must need learn that power that we may be enabled to couple these forces in accordance with their appropriate laws. Just now composers are working on substances unknown to them.

"Why should an instrument of metal and one of wood, say a bassoon and a cornet, have so little resemblance of tone, though they act on the same matter, in the same manner, on the constituent gases of the atmosphere? Their dissimilarities must come either from some decomposition of these gases or by the assimilation of affinities, whence they return modified by the influence of some force unknown to us. Could we only discover what those faculties are, then science and art would be immense gainers. Whatever extends science enhances art.

"Well!" he exclaimed, after a short pause, "as to these discoveries! I have traced, I have made them! Yes," said Gambara, with more and more vehemence, "up to now man has noted the effect less than the cause. If he could but penetrate cause, music would be the greatest of the arts. Is it not the one that drives deepest in the soul? In painting you see no more than the picture shows; in poetry you hear only what the poet speaks; music goes far beyond this—it forms thought, it rouses torpid memory. Take a thousand souls present at a concert; a strain speeds forth from Pasta's throat, executing so masterly the thoughts that shone in Rossini's soul as he wrote the passage; that single phrase of the master, transmitted to attentive souls, develops in them as many diverse poems. To one it shows a woman long dreamed of and desired; to another some shore anon he traversed, where rising before him are the drooping willows, its clear waters, and the hopes that danced with him beneath the leafy coverts. This woman is recalled to the throng of feelings that tortured her in an hour of jealous rage; another one sees the unsatisfied longings of her heart, which is painted by her mind in the rich hues of a dream, the ideal lover to whom she would fain abandon herself with the rapture of the woman in the Roman mosaic, who is seen embracing a chimera; yet another dreams of desires about to be gratified, she plunges in anticipation into a torrent of delight whose raging waves of feeling surge about and break upon her burning bosom. Music alone has power to make us return unto ourselves; all other arts give but limited pleasures. But I am digressing.

"Such, then, were my first ideas, vague it may be, for an inventor in his inception only catches a faint glimpse of the dawn. I kept these glorious ideas at the bottom of my knapsack; they gave me spirit to eat the dry crusts as I gayly soaked them in the waters of a spring. I worked, I composed airs, and after I had played them on some instrument, the first one to hand, I resumed my travels through Italy. At last, when I was two-and-twenty, I settled in Venice, where for the first time I enjoyed rest and gained a fair competence. There I made the acquaintance of a Venetian nobleman, who was taken with my ideas; he encouraged me in my investigations and procured me employment at the Fenice theatre. In Venice living is cheap and lodgings cost but little. I had a room in the Palazzo Capello whence the celebrated Bianca issued one night to become the Grand Duchess of Tuscany and Queen of Cyprus.

"And there I would dream that at some future time my hidden fame would issue thence to be like her, crowned.

"My evenings were spent at the theatre, my days in work. But disaster came. The representation of an opera, 'The Martyrs,' in which I had experimented with my music, was a failure. No one could understand my score. Place Beethoven before the Italians and they cannot gauge him. No one had the patience to await an effect to be produced by the different *motifs* given out by each instrument, all intended to at last unite in one grand harmony.

"I had founded my hopes on the success of the 'Martiri,' for we ever discount success, we disciples of the azure goddess—Hope. When a man thinks himself destined to produce great thoughts, it becomes difficult to believe that they are not achieved; the cask has chinks through which the light will shine.

"In the same palace resided my wife's family; and the hope of winning Marianna, who frequently smiled on me from her window, had greatly stimulated my efforts.

"I now fell into a state of dark melancholy, as I sounded the depths of the abyss into which I had fallen; for before me I saw naught but a life of poverty—a ceaseless struggle in which love must perish.

"Marianna acted as genius does; she bounded over every obstacle, both feet at once. I will not speak of the slender happiness which gilded the early days of my misfortunes. Dismayed by my failure, I felt that Italy was but dull of comprehension and too much under the influence of the routine chorus to be prepared to receive the innovations I meditated; so I turned my thoughts to Germany.

"As I traveled to that country, which I did by way of Hungary, I paid heed to the manifold voices of nature; I tried to reproduce those sublime harmonies by the assistance of instruments which I wholly constructed or changed for the purpose. These experiments necessitated enormous outlay, and soon exhausted our slender savings. And still this was the happiest time of our lives; I was appreciated in Germany. Never was my life so glorious as then. I know of nothing to compare with the tumultuous joys that filled me in Marianna's presence, whose beauty was then in all its celestial radiancy and power. I was happy.

"More than once during these hours of weakness I expressed my passion in the language of terrestrial harmony. I even composed some of those melodies which resemble geometrical figures, which are so much prized in the world in which we live. But so soon as I gained success, insurmountable obstacles were placed in my path by rivals, envious or unappreciative.

"I had heard of France as a country which welcomed innovations; thither I resolved to go; my wife provided the means and we came to Paris.

"Before this no one had ever actually laughed in my face; but in this dreadful city I had to undergo this new form of torture, to which was added the keen anguish of miserable poverty. Compelled to sojourn in this fever-stricken quarter, for many months we have lived on Marianna's work; she does sewing for the wretched prostitutes who make this horrid street their stamping ground. Marianna tells me that she is treated with deference and generosity, which I, for my part, ascribe to the ascendency of a so pure virtue that even vice itself must needs respect it."

"Hope on," said Andrea. "Perhaps you have reached the end of your trials. My efforts shall be united to yours. and it may be that your labors will yet be seen in their true light; permit me, in the meanwhile, as a compatriot and an artist like yourself, to offer you in advance some part, however small, of your inevitable future gains."

"All that has to do with my material life is my wife's affair alone," replied Gambara. "She it is who must decide whether without humiliation we can accept the assistance of an honorable man, as you seem to be. For myself, who have been led to make you this long-drawn confidence, I must beg your permission to retire. A melody beckons me; it starts dancingly before me; bare, quivering, like a beautiful girl entreating her lover for the clothes he has hidden. Adieu, I go to dress my mistress. My wife I leave with you."

He hastened away like a man who blames himself for losing valuable time, and Marianna, somewhat embarrassed, prepared to follow him.

Andrea dared not detain her.

Giardini however came to the rescue.

"But, signorina," said he, "did not you hear your husband tell you to settle some business with the signor count?"

Marianna resumed her seat, but without looking at Andrea, who hesitated about addressing her.

"And will not Signor Gambara's confidence," he at length said, in a voice of emotion, "also win for me that of his wife's? Will *la bella* Marianna refuse to give me the history of her life?"

"My life?" answered Marianna; "my life, it is that of the ivy. If you would ask the story of my heart, you must suppose me equally devoid of pride and modesty after listening to what you have just heard."

"Of whom then shall I ask it?" cried the count, whose passion was blinding his wit.

"Of yourself!" replied Marianna. "You have either understood me, or you never will. Ask yourself."

"I will, but you must listen to me. I take your hand, it is to lay in mine so long as I tell your story truthfully."

"I listen," said Marianna.

"The life of a woman begins with her first passion," said Andrea. "And my dear Marianna began to live only on the day when she first saw Paolo Gambara. Her nature needed a deep passion to afford it joy; more than all she needed some pathetic feebleness to sustain and protect. The lovely female nature with which she is endowed is perhaps less amenable to passion than maternity.

"You sigh, Marianna; have I then laid a finger on an open wound? You took upon yourself a noble part, young as you were, in protecting a noble, distraught intellect. You said to yourself: 'Paolo shall be my genius, I will be his common-sense; between us we shall almost be that well-nigh divine being that men term angel; that sublime creature which enjoys and comprehends, while reason never stifles love.'

"In the first transports of youth, you heard the thousand voices of nature which your poet longed to reproduce. Enthusiasm seized your soul when Paolo spread before you those treasures of poetry as he vainly searched for their equivalent, striving to embody them in the sublime but limited language of his art. You admired him as an ecstatic rapture carried him high above you, for you loved to think that all this errant energy would finally fall and alight upon you as love. You did not realize the tyrannous and jealous empire which thought maintains over the minds of those who are subject to it. Gambara before he knew you was the slave of that proud, vindictive mistress with whom you have been combating against for him to this day. Once, for an instant, happiness was opened before you.

"Paolo, fallen from the lofty sphere where his mind was ever soaring, was amazed to find a reality so sweet; so sweet that you may well have believed that his mania would forever slumber in your arms. But ere long music clutched her prey. The dazzling vision which carried you suddenly into the thrilling delights of mutual passion made the solitary path on which you had started look only the more arid and desolate.

"In the story just narrated by your husband, as from the striking contrast between your person and his, I can readily divine the secret anguish of your life, the painful mysteries of that ill-assorted union in which you have taken the lot of suffering upon yourself alone. Marianna, though your conduct is and has been unfailingly heroic, and though fortitude never deserts you in the performance of your cruel duties, perhaps in the silence of your solitary nights the heart which only now is beating so violently in your breast may from time to time have rebelled.

"Your husband's worthiness is your worst torture. Had he been less noble, less pure, you might have deserted him; but your virtues are supported by his. It may be that you have at times speculated which of the two heroisms will first give way.

"You pursue the real grandeur of the task while Paolo is chasing his chimera. If you had only the love of duty to sustain and guide you, perhaps triumph might seem the easier; to kill your heart and carry your life into the region of abstractions might possibly suffice you; religion would absorb the rest; you would have lived for an idea, like those saintly women who extinguish at the foot of the cross all the instincts of their nature. But the pervading charm of Paolo's person, the elevation of his soul, his rare and affecting proofs of tenderness, constantly drag you down from that ideal world where virtue tried to keep you; they have excited forces within you which are being incessantly exhausted in contending against the phantom of love. But now the time has come in which you must no longer deceive yourself. You never suspected this. The faintest glimmer of hope kept you in the pursuit of this sweet dream.

"Year after year of disillusion has undermined your patience; an angel would long ago have lost it. To-day the phantom so long pursued is naught but a shadow without substance. Madness so closely allied to genius can never know a cure in this world. You have at last become aware of this fact, you have glanced backward on your vanished youth, lost, if not sacrificed; you bitterly perceive the blunder of nature that gave you a father only when you sought a husband. You ask yourself whether you have not gone beyond the duties of a wife in keeping yourself faithful to a man who knows no mistress but science. Marianna, let your hand remain in mine; all that I have told you is true. You have looked around you—but now you were in Paris, not in Italy, where only men know how to love——"

"Oh! let me finish the tale," cried Marianna; "it were better fitting that I say these things myself. I will be frank; I feel that I address my truest friend. Yes, I was in Paris when all you have so lucidly explained took place within me, for nowhere had I met the love I had dreamed of from childhood up.

"My poor dress, my so poor abode, concealed me from the notice of men like yourself. The few young men I met here, whose position did not allow of their insulting me, are odious to me; these scoff at my husband as a rambling old dotard; some only court him the more easily to betray him; all aim at getting me separated from him; none of them all can understand the adoration I have vowed to that soul which is so far away from us only because it is so much nearer heaven; nor the love I feel for that friend, brother, whose handmaid I would ever be. You alone have understood the tie that binds me to him. Tell me that your interest in my Paolo is sincere, without an object——"

"I accept your praises," interrupted Andrea, "but do not go further; do not compel me to contradict you. I love you, Marianna, as we know how to love in that glorious country where you and I were born. I love you with all my soul, with all my strength; but before I tender you this love, I intend to make myself worthy of your affection.

"I will make a last effort to give back to you the man you have loved since childhood, and whom, most probably, you will never cease to love. While awaiting success or defeat, accept, with no trace of shame, the modest comforts which I can give you both. To-morrow we will look out a suitable abode for him.

"Is your esteem sufficiently great to allow me to be a sharer in your guardianship?"

Marianna, astounded by such generosity, held out her hand to the count; he took it, and departed, endeavoring to evade the civilities of Giardini and his wife.

Next day Andrea was taken up to the room in which Gambara and his wife lived. Though Marianna fully recognized the noble nature of her lover (for there are natures which can quickly read), she was too good a housewife not to show embarrassment on receiving so great a gentleman in so humble a chamber. But it was exquisitely clean. She had spent the morning in dusting her motley furniture, the handiwork of Signor Giardini, who had devoted his moments of leisure in constructing it from the woodwork of instruments which had been discarded by Gambara.

Never in his life had Andrea seen anything so amazing. To keep a sober countenance he was compelled to turn away his eyes from a bed, so grotesquely manufactured by the ingenious cook out of the case of an old harpsichord, to look at Marianna's narrow couch, of which the single mattress was covered with a white lawn counterpane, a circumstance which surcharged his mind with sad, but some sweet thoughts.

He wished to talk of his plans and morning's work; but the enthusiastic Gambara, who believed that he had at last found a willing auditor, seized upon the count and made him listen to an opera which he had written for the Parisians.

"In the first place, monsieur," said Gambara, "allow me to explain the subject in two words. Here in Paris people who receive a musical impression do not work it out in their own minds, as religion teaches us to develop sacred texts, by meditation and prayer. It is therefore very difficult to make them understand that there exists in nature an eternal theme, disturbed only by fluctuations independent of the Divine will, as passions are uncontrolled by the will of men.

"It became necessary that I should seek some vast framework in which to combine cause and effect, for my music aims at presenting a picture of the life of nations taken at its loftiest points of view. My opera, for I myself wrote the *libretto* (as no poet could have fittingly developed the subject), gives the life of Mahomet, a personage who unites the magic of ancient Sabæanism and the Oriental poetry of the Jewish Scriptures, resulting in one of the grandest of human epics—the dominion of the Arab.

"Mahomet, without a doubt, borrowed the idea of despotic government from the Jews, and the progressive movement which created the brilliant empire of the caliphs from the pastoral or Sabæan religions. The prophet's destiny was stamped upon him at his birth—his father was a Pagan, his mother a Jewess. Ah! my dear count, to be a great musician one must also be very learned. Without education there can be no local color; in fact, no musical ideas. The musician who only sings to sing is but an artisan, not an artist.

"This magnificent opera is a continuation of the great work I had already commenced. My first opera was called 'The Martyrs;' I intend to write a third one on 'Jerusalem Delivered.' You can of course discern the beauty of this triology and the manifold motives it affords. The Martyrs, Mahomet, Jerusalem! The God of the Occident, the God of the Orient, and the struggle of their religionists about a tomb. But let us not speak of my fame for ever gone. Listen to the argument of my opera."

He paused.

"The first act," he went on, "shows Mahomet as a porter living in the house of Khadijah, a rich widow with whom his uncle has placed him. He is in love and ambitious. Driven from Mecca he flies to Medina, and dates his era from the time of his flight, the Hegira.

"The second act presents him as a prophet founding a religion militant. The third shows him disgusted with all things; having exhausted life, he seeks to conceal his death that he may be deemed a god, last effort of human pride.

"Now you shall judge of my method of expressing in sound a great fact which poetry can only imperfectly render in words."

Gambara seated himself at the piano with a calm and collected air, and his wife brought the voluminous sheets of the score, which, however, he did not open.

"The whole opera," said he, "is founded on a base as on a fruitful soil. Mahomet must therefore have a majestic bass voice, and necessarily his first wife must have a contralto one. Khadijah was quite old—twenty! Attention! Here is the overture. It begins *andante*, C-minor, triple time. Do you hear the sadness of the ambitious man whom love cannot satisfy? Through his plaints, by a modulation to E-flat, *allegro*, common time, are heard the cries of the epileptic lover, his ravings, mingled with certain warlike sounds; for the all-powerful scimitar of the caliphs begins to gleam before his eyes. The charms of the single wife give him that idea of the plurality of love which so forcibly impresses us in 'Don Giovanni.' As you listen to this theme do you not already catch a glimpse of the paradise of Mahomet?

"Now we have, A-flat major, six-eight time, a *cantabile*, fit to create emotions of delight in those rebellious to all musical feeling; Khadijah comprehends Mahomet! Then Khadijah announces to the multitude the prophet's conferences with the angel Gabriel—*maestoso sostenuto*, in F-minor.

"The magistrates and priests, power and religion, feeling themselves attacked by the reformer, as Christ and Socrates attacked the effete, expiring religions and powers, turn upon Mahomet and drive him forth from Mecca—*stretto* in C-major. But now, pay heed! comes my glorious dominant—G, common time. Arabia hears her prophet, the horsemen gather—G-major, E-flat, B-flat, G-minor, still common time. The mass of men gathers like an avalanche. The false prophet practices on one tribe the deceptions he is so soon to impose upon a world—G-major.

"He promises univeral dominion to the Arabs; they believe him because he is inspired. The *crescendo* begins—in the dominant still. Listen to the fanfare of the trumpets—C-major; brass instruments woven into the harmony, strongly marked, and asserting themselves as an expression of the first triumphs of victory. Medina is conquered for the prophet, the whole army marches on Mecca—burst of martial music—still in C-major. The whole power of the orchestra is worked up to a conflagration; every instrument gives voice; do you hear the torrents of harmony?

"Suddenly the *tutti* is interrupted by a graceful air—minor third. You hear the last strains of devoted love! The woman who upheld the great man dies, concealing her despair; dies, dies at the triumph of the man in whom love had become too mighty to be content with one woman; she adores him enough to sacrifice herself to the grandeur that destroys her. Soul of flame!

"But now behold! The desert invades the world—C-major again. The orchestra takes up the score in the terrific fifth of the fundamental bass which dies away—Mahomet is satiated; he has tasted all, he has exhausted all! But he craves to die a god. Arabia adores him in prayer; we fall back upon my first sad strain to which the curtain rose—C-minor.

"Do you not discern in this music," said Gambara, ceasing to play and turning toward the count, "in this vivid, picturesque music, abrupt, jostling, melancholy, fantastic, but always grand, the expression of an epileptic frantic after enjoyment, unable to read or write, making his very defects a stepping-stone to his grandeur, transferring blunder and disaster into triumphs? Do you not obtain from this overture—an epitome of the opera—an idea of his seductive power over a greedy and lustful race?"

The face of the maestro, at first calm and stern, on which

Andrea had been trying to divine the meaning of the ideas he was uttering with an inspired voice, though the chaotic flood of notes estopped his hearer from comprehending, grew even more animated until it took on an impassioned, fiery glow which infected Marianna and the cook. Marianna, deeply affected by the passages in which she read her own position, could not hide the agitation from Andrea.

Gambara wiped his forehead and threw his glance with such force to the ceiling that he seemed to pierce it and rise upward to the skies.

"You have seen the vestibule," said he; "now we enter the temple. The opera begins:

"ACT I. Mahomet, alone on the stage, sings an air—F-natural, common time, interrupted by a chorus of camel-drivers, who surround a well at the rear of the stage—contrary time, twelve-eight. What majestic grief! It touches the heart of the most frivolous woman, piercing the soul if she has no heart. Is not this the very expression of repressed genius?"

To Andrea's very great amazement (for Marianna was accustomed to it) Gambara contracted his larynx so violently that choking sounds issued thence, something like the attempted growl of a watch-dog which has lost its voice. A light froth arose on the composer's lips and caused Andrea to shudder.

"His wife appears—A-minor. Magnificent duet! In this number I make it known that Mahomet has the will, his wife the brains. Khadijah announces that she is about undertaking a work which will bereave her of the love of her young husband. Mahomet aspires to conquer the world: his wife divines his purpose; she seconds his endeavor by persuading the people of Mecca that her husband's epileptic fits are due to his commerce with the angels. Chorus of Mahomet's first disciples, who press forward to promise him their help—C-sharp minor, *sotto voce*. Mahomet *exeunt* to speak with the angel Gabriel—*recitative* in F-major. His wife encourages the chorus—*aria*, accompanied by chorus; gusts of chanting voices sustain Khadijah's grand, majestic song—A-major.

"Abdallah, the father of Ayesha, the only maiden that Mahomet has found to be a virgin, whose name he thereupon changes to Abu-Bekr, the father of the virgin, comes forward with Ayesha and sings against the chorus, taking up Khadijah's in contrapuntal treatment. Omar, father of Hafsah, another virgin who is to be Mahomet's concubine, follows Abu-Bekr's example; he and his daughter join in and form a quintette. The virgin Ayesha is first soprano; Hafsah, mezzo soprano; Abu-Bekr is a bass; Omar a baritone.

"Mahomet returns inspired.

"He sings his first bravura *aria*, the beginning of the *finale* —E-major; he promises the empire of the world to those who believe in him. The prophet sees the two maidens, by a soft transition—from B-major to G-major; he turns to amorous tones. Ali, Mahomet's cousin, and Kâhled, his greatest general, both tenors, now appear and announce the persecution; the magistrates, the soldiers, and rulers have banished the prophet—*recitative*.

"Mahomet now makes an invocation to the angel Gabriel in C. He declares that the angel is with him, and points out a pigeon flying above his head. The chorus of believers make reply in tones of devotion—modulating to B-major. The soldiers, magistrates, and officials arrive—*tempo di marcia*, B-major. Struggle between the two forces—*strette* in E-major. Mahomet, in a succession of diminished sevenths in a descending theme, yields to the storm and takes to flight. The savage, sombre color of the *finale* is raised somewhat by the phrases of the three women, who utter predictions of Mahomet's triumph; and these *motifs* will be found further accentuated in the third act, where Mahomet is found enjoying the delights of splendor."

Tears arose in Gambara's eyes; he controlled his emotion and resumed:

"Act II. Behold religion is now established. Arabs guard the prophet's tent, who confers with God—chorus in A-minor. Mahomet appears—prayer in F. What a majestic and noble strain underlies this chant in the bass voices, in which, I believe, I have enlarged the limits of melody! It seemed necessary to express the marvels of that immense uprising which created an architecture, a poetry, a music; with its own manners, customs, and morals.

"As you listen you walk beneath the arches of the Generalife and thread the vaulted portals of the Alhambra. The *fiorituri* of the melody paint the exquisite Moorish arabesques, the gallant and warlike religion which was presently to meet in battle the noble and valorous chivalry of Christianity. A few brass instruments now sound the first notes of triumph—by a broken *cadenza.* The Arabs, on their knees, worship the prophet—E-flat major. Khâled, Amrou, and Ali enter—*tempo di marcia.* The armies of the Faithful have taken many towns and conquered the three Arabias. Such a sonorous *recitative.* Mahomet rewards his generals by giving them maidens.

"And here comes in," said Gambara, ruefully, "one of those wretched ballets which cut the thread of our finest musical tragedies. But Mahomet—B-minor—redeems it by his transcendent prophecy, which that poor Monsieur de Voltaire describes in these words:

"'Arabia's day at last has come.'

"The chorus of Arabs breaks triumphant—six-eight time, *accelerando.* Now the tribes in multitude come on; horns and brass join in the orchestra. General rejoicings ensue, by degrees all the voices take part, and Mahomet declares polygamy.

"In the midst of all this triumph the woman who has done so much for Mahomet pours forth a magnificent *aria*—B-major. 'And I,' sings she, 'am I no longer loved?' 'We must part,' he responds. 'Thou art a woman, I am a prophet;

slaves I may have, equals never.' Hearken to this duet—G-sharp minor. What anguish! The woman realizes the grandeur to which she has been the means of elevating Mahomet; she loves him enough to sacrifice herself to his glory, she adores him as a god, she judges not, she murmurs not. Poor woman! his first dupe, his first victim! What a subject for the *finale*—B-major.

"Behold the sombre grief standing out against the acclamations of the chorus, mingling with the tones of Mahomet as he flings his wife aside as a used-out instrument, and yet causes us to understand that he can never forget her. What fireworks of triumph, what red fire of joyous, rippling songs gush from the voices of Ayesha and Hafsa (*premiere* and *mezzo* soprano), further sustained by Ali and his wife, by Omar and Abu-Bekr. Weep, rejoice! Triumph and tears! Of such is life."

Marianna could not restrain her sobs; Andrea was so deeply moved that his eyes grew moist. The Neapolitan cook, shaken by the magnetic current of ideas generated by the spasmodic accents of Gambara's voice, was overcome by emotion like the rest.

The composer turned around to the group; he smiled.

"You understand me at last!" cried he.

No conqueror haled in triumph to the Capitol, amid the purple radiance of his glory and the acclamations of a nation, ever wore such an expression when the crown was placed upon his head as Gambara did at this time. His face had the halo of a martyred saint. None undeceived him. A dreadful smile flickered on Marianna's lips. The count was appalled by the artless, blind insanity.

"Act III.," said the rapt musician, again seating himself at the piano:

"Solo, *andantino*, Mahomet unhappy though in his seraglio surrounded by women. Quartette of houris—A-major. What pomp of harmony, what trills as those of a happy nightingale!

It modulates into F-sharp minor. The theme is given on the dominant (E) and is then repeated in A-major. Here all delights are grouped visibly to the senses and produce a grand contrast to the sombre *finale* of the first act.

"After the dances Mahomet arises and sings a grand *bravura*—F-minor. He regrets the singleness and devotion of his first wife, but acknowledges himself as wedded to polygamy. Never did musician have so grand a subject. The orchestra and women's chorus express the joys of the houri; meanwhile Mahomet reverts to the sad strain of the beginning.

"Where is Beethoven?" cried Gambara; "where, then, is that soul who only could understand the majestic overturning of my opera upon itself. See how completely all depends upon the bass; thus did Beethoven construct his symphony in C.

"But his heroic movement is purely instrumental, while mine is sustained by a sextette of glorious human voices, and a chorus of believers who are on guard at the gate of the sacred dwelling. I have here collected all the treasures of melody and harmony, vocal and orchestral. Listen to the utterance of all human life, rich or poor: BATTLE, TRIUMPH, SATIETY.

"Ali enters; everywhere the Koran is triumphant—duet, D-minor. Mahomet places himself in the hands of his two fathers-in-law; he is weary of all; he will abdicate and die in secret after he has consolidated his religion. Magnificent sextette—B-flat major! He bids all farewell—solo in F-natural. His two fathers-in-law, appointed his vicars or caliphs, summon the people. A grand triumphal march. Prayer of the Arabs kneeling before the sacred dwelling, the Kasba, whence a pigeon takes its flight—same key. This prayer, sung by sixty voices and led by women—B-flat—crowns my stupendous work, which so well expresses the life of men and nations. Here you have heard every emotion, human or divine."

Andrea was overcome with sheer amazement. He was much affected by this good man's mania, he colored, and stole a glance at Marianna; while she became pallid and turned her eyes downward, silently weeping. Had he not been shocked by the irony which the man showed as he presented the feelings of Mahomet's wife and yet not perceiving the same emotions in Marianna, the madness of the husband was eclipsed by the craziness of the composer. There was not the least resemblance to musical or poetical ideas in the loud blathering which oppressed his ears. All the principles of harmony, the first rules of composition, were quite ignored in this formless creation. Instead of a theme scientifically worked out such as had been described by Gambara, his fingers had brought out a succession of fifths, sevenths, octaves, major thirds, progressions of fourths, minus the sixths in the bass—a jumble of discordant sound, randomly made, as though intended to destroy the ear of the least sensitive of listeners. It is impossible to attempt a description of this grotesque execution; new words must needs be coined to portray this impossible music.

During its execution he had closed his eyes in ecstasy; had smiled upon his piano; had frowned at it; put out his tongue after the manner of an inspired performer. He had been, in fact, intoxicated by the poetry of the thoughts that peopled his brain—he had vainly endeavored the utterance of them. The strange discords had evidently been to him celestial harmonies. Beyond any doubt the vision of his inspired blue eyes in rapt enjoyment of another world; the rosy glow of his cheeks; above all, the heavenly serenity stamped upon his lofty features, would have led any deaf man to believe that he was present at the improvisation of some maestro. The illusion would have been the more perfect because the mechanical execution of this crazy music required immense skill in fingering. Gambara must have worked at it for years.

His hands were not alone employed; his feet were constant

in the pedaling; perspiration streamed down his face as he labored to fully emphasize a *crescendo* by all the feeble means which a decrepit piano afforded. He stamped, snorted, puffed, and shouted; his fingers darted hither and thither like the forked fangs of a snake; finally, as the piano uttered its last growl, he flung himself backward and let his head rest on the back of the chair.

"*Per Bacco!* I am stunned, dizzy," cried Andrea, escaping from the chamber. "A child dancing on the keyboard would make better music."

"Certainly," said Giardini. "All that chance could do couldn't manage to avoid hitting two notes in concord than that devil of a fellow has done during the hour now gone."

"How comes it that the regular features of Marianna's beauty remain?" muttered the count to himself. "Such an incessant hearing of so hideous melody must change anything. She will grow ugly."

"*Signor conte*, she must be saved from that," cried Giardini.

"Yes," said Andrea, "I have been thinking of that. But to be sure that my plans are not built upon the sands, I must test my thoughts by yet another experiment. To-morrow I will return and examine the instruments he has invented; after dinner we will have a little supper (*medianoche*). I provide the wine and a few fancy dishes."

The cook bowed low.

The next day was spent by the count in arranging the suite of rooms in which he intended domiciling the poor household.

He returned in the evening to the Rue Froidmanteau and found the wine and so forth set out by Marianna and Giardini, displaying some little taste. Gambara with much pride showed him some little drums, on which lay grains of gunpowder, by which means he made observations on the pitch and temperament of the sounds emitted by his instruments.

"Do you see," said he, "by what simple means I am able to demonstrate a great proposition? Acoustics by this means reveal actions analogous to sound on every object which that sound affects. All harmonies start from a common centre and always retain an intimate relation to each other; rather, harmony, like light, is decomposed by our art as a ray is by a prism."

Here Gambara proceeded to show Andrea the instruments constructed according to his principles, and he explained the changes he had made in their shape and material. Finally he announced, with gravity, that, to properly conclude this preliminary evening, which had thus far only gratified the curiosity of the eye, he would allow all then present to hear an instrument which was capable of taking the place of an entire orchestra; he called this the *panharmonicon*.

"If it is the arrangement in that case which causes a grumbling of all the neighbors," said Giardini, "when you are working on it, you won't do much playing thereon, for the police will interfere. Bear that in mind."

"If that unhappy idiot remains in the room," whispered Gambara in Andrea's ear, "it will be impossible that I should play."

The count made a pretext to get rid of the cook by promising him a present if he would stay downstairs and prevent the police and neighbors from interfering. Giardini, who had not stinted his own allowance of wine while pouring out for the others, willingly complied.

The composer, while not intoxicated, was in that elevated condition when every function of the brain is overexcited; when the opaque walls become transparent, the garret roofless, and the soul takes flight into the world of spirits.

Marianna, not without difficulty, uncovered an instrument about the size of a grand piano; but with an upper manual and a great double case, not altogether unlike the boxing of an organ. This curious machine was also provided with stops for various instruments, and the bent elbows of a number of tubes or pipes.

"Will you play for me the prayer which you say is so fine, the *finale* of your opera?" asked the count.

To Andrea's great astonishment and Marianna's surprise, Gambara commenced with a few chords in perfect harmony that proclaimed him a master; their astonishment was succeeded by admiration and in turn by complete rapture; they entirely lost sight of the place and performer. The effects of a full orchestra would have been less fine than the reedy tone of the wind instruments, which swelled like an organ and formed a marvelous blend with the string harmonies. But the unfinished state of this machine prevented the full development of the composer's ideas, which seemed the greater for the sense of incompleteness. It may be remarked that certain perfections in works of art seem rather to detract from than improve the unfinished sketch; for one may then add the deficiency by his own thoughts.

The purest and sweetest music that Andrea had ever heard rose from under the impact of Gambara's fingers like incense from an altar. The composer's voice became again youthful; so far from marring the fine melody, it expounded, supported, and directed it; as the quavering voice of a reader like Andrieux gives scope to the meaning of some great scene by Corneille or Racine by lending it a personal and sympathetic emotion.

This angelic music revealed the treasures that lay hidden in the grand opera which could never be understood so long as this man persisted in the endeavor to explain it in his normal state of dementia.

Marianna and Andrea, equally divided between delight of the music and surprise at the strange instrument with its hundred-voiced stops, in which a stranger might think a choir of young girls was hidden, so closely did some of the tones resemble the human voice, dared not exchange ideas either by word or look. Marianna's countenance was radiant with a glow of hope, which revivified the beauty of her youth.

This new birth of beauty, in connection with the luminosity of her husband's genius, cast a shadowy tinge of sadness over the pleasure that this mysterious hour had given the count.

"You are our good spirit!" Marianna whispered to him. "I am tempted to think that you inspire him, for I, who am never away from his side, have never yet heard anything like this."

"Khadijah's farewell," said Gambara; who now sang the *cavatina* which he had the previous evening described as being sublime, and which now brought tears to the eyes of the lovers, so perfectly did it express the noblest sentiments of devoted love.

"Who can have inspired you with such music?" cried the count.

"The spirit," answered Gambara. "When he appears, flame is all around me. I see the melodies face to face; fresh, beautiful, in floral coloring. They sparkle, they echo—I listen. But an infinity of time is necessary to reproduce them."

"Play on," said Marianna.

Gambara, who seemed not to feel fatigue, played without effort or untowardness. He executed the overture with such facility and skill, he showed such new and undiscovered musical effects, that the count was dazzled by what he heard; he began to believe in some magic like that controlled by Liszt and Paganini—a genius of execution which can change all musical conditions and create of it a poetry transcendent of all conditions of music.

"Well, excellenza, and can you cure him?" asked Giardini, when at length Andrea went down.

"I shall soon be able to say," replied the count. "The man's intellect has two windows: one is turned toward the earth and is closed; the other looks in upon heaven. The first is music, the second poetry. Until now he would stand stubbornly before the closed window; we must get him to the other. It was you, Giardini, that first put me on the track of this truth, by letting me know that his mind was clearer after a few glasses of wine."

"Yes," cried the cook, "and I can guess your scheme, excellenza."

"If it is not too late to make poetry ring in his ears to the sound of a glorious harmony, we must put him into a condition to hear and judge of it. Now it seems to me that only intoxication can bring this about. Will you assist me in this? You won't be any the worse for it, eh?"

"What is your excellency getting at?"

Andrea made no answer, but went away laughing at the perspicacity of the crazy mind of the Neapolitan.

On the following day Marcosini came to fetch away Marianna and show her the lodging he had secured. She had used the morning in fixing up a simple but decent dress, into which she had put the whole of her little savings. The change would have been the disillusion of a mere dangler; but the fancy of the count had now become a settled passion.

Marianna, stripped of her picturesque poverty, was transformed outwardly into a mere bourgeoise, and gave Andrea visions of a wedded life; he gave her his hand in assisting her into the hackney-coach, and acquainted her with his ideas. She smiled and approved; she was happy at finding her admirer more lofty, more generous, more disinterested than she had dared to hope. He soon reached the new dwelling, where Andrea had endeavored to keep himself ever in her thoughts by adding a few of those little elegancies which beguile the most virtuous of women.

"I will never mention my love to you until we despair of Paolo's sanity," he said to her, as they returned to the Rue Froidmanteau. "You shall be witness to the sincerity of my efforts. If these prove successful, I may be unable to keep up my part as only your friend. If this happens I shall flee you,

Marianna. I have firmness enough, I think, to work for your happiness, though I may not have enough to look upon it."

"Do not say such things," said Marianna, with difficulty keeping back her tears. "Has not generosity its dangers, also? But are you going so soon?"

"Yes," said Andrea, "seek your happiness without my drawback."

If Giardini is to be believed, the excellent change of air and living was favorable to both husband and wife. Every evening after his wine, Gambara appeared less absent-minded, talked more, and was more sedate; he even proposed to read the papers. Andrea quaked in his shoes at each manifestation of his success; but, though his distress made him aware of the strength of his passion, this did not cause him to relax his virtuous resolution. He now came every evening to learn the progress of this singular cure. On one occasion the state of the patient gave him satisfaction, but his pleasure was dazed by Marianna's beauty, for her life being rendered less onerous had restored her brilliant loveliness.

He joined each evening in the conversations, grave or gay, in which he argued coolly and dispassionately against Gambara's singular theories. He used the remarkable lucidity of the latter's mind, on every point that did not touch upon his malady, to make him clearly perceive and acknowledge principles in other branches of art and which he afterward demonstrated were equally applicable to music.

All went well so long as the composer's brain was under the influence of the fumes of wine; but just as soon as he became perfectly sober his reason was dethroned—he was again the maniac. And yet, in the main, Paolo was more easily aroused by impressions from the outer world: his mind even began to employ itself on a greater diversity of subjects.

Andrea, who took all an artist's interest in his semi-medical treatment, thought at length that it was about time to try a master-stroke. He resolved to give a dinner at his own house, to which he intended inviting Giardini for the purpose, as he told himself, of not separating the sublime and the ridiculous. He selected the day that "Robert le Diable," an opera he had already heard in rehearsal, was for the first time given in public.

After the second course Gambara was already half-seas over, he was laughing at himself with a good grace, while Giardini was admitting that his own culinary innovations were of the devil.

Andrea had neglected no means to bring about this twofold miracle. Flagons of Orvieto and Montefiascone, expensive wines which are easily spoiled if carelessly carried; liqueurs of Lachrymæ Christi, and Giro, and other heady liqueurs of *la cara patria* or the beloved country, soon caused the double intoxication, in these excitable minds, of grape and reminiscence. At dessert the musician and the cook mutually abjured every heresy; one hummed a *cavatina* from Rossini, the other piled confectionery on his plate and washed them down with maraschino from Zara, to the honor of the *cuisine Française*.

The count took advantage of Gambara's happy frame of mind to carry him off to the opera, whither he allowed himself to be led like a lamb.

With the first notes of the introduction Gambara's inebriety vanished, and gave place for the feverish excitement which at times brought his judgment and imagination into harmony; the habitual discord of which was the undoubted source of his insanity. The dominant idea of that great musical drama appeared to him in all its radiant simplicity, like a flash of lightning breaking through the clouds of darkness in which he lived. To his unsealed eyes the music seemed to sweep the immense horizons of world in which he found himself for the first time, though he recognized it as what he had seen in his dreams.

He fancied himself transported to those slopes of his own

dear native country where *la bella Italia* commences, and which Napoleon so appropriately termed the "glacis of the Alps." His memory took him back to the day when his young, vigorous brain was not yet troubled by the fervid imagination; he listened in reverent awe, unwilling to miss a word. The count respected the travail of his soul. Till after twelve o'clock he sat so motionless that the opera-house audience might have taken him for a drunken man—which he was. On his way home the count began to attack Meyerbeer's masterpiece, trying to arouse Gambara, who was now plunged in the half-torpid state of drunkenness.

"What is there in that incoherent score that it makes a somnambulist of you?" said Andrea, when they arrived at his house. "The story of 'Robert le Diable' is not altogether without interest, I'll admit. Holtei has very happily worked out with much skill a well-written drama, full of strong and moving situations, but the French librettists have managed to make it the most absurd bundle of nonsense. No libretto of even Vesari or Schikaneder has ever equaled in absurdity the words of 'Robert le Diable;' it becomes a dramatic nightmare, which oppresses the hearer without arousing any deep emotion.

"Meyerbeer's devil plays too prominent a part. Bertram and Alice represent the contest between right and wrong, the good and evil spirit. That antagonism offers a splendid opportunity to the composer. The sweetest melodies, placed side by side with harsh and crude airs, is the natural consequence of the libretto; but, unfortunately, in the score of the German composer the devils sing better than the saints.

"The heavenly inspirations give the lie to their origin; when the composer leaves the infernal lay for a moment, he returns as speedily as may be, worn out with the effort of trying to be rid of them. Melody, the golden thread that should never be broken in so vast a scheme, is often strained to the vanishing point in Meyerbeer's work. Sentiment is absolutely lacking; the heart has no part in it; we find few of those delightful inventions, those artless themes which touch our sympathies and leave a tender impression on the soul.

"Harmony reigns supreme, instead of being the groundwork from whence should issue the melodious groups of the musical picture. Those discordant notes, far from moving the hearer, only excite in him a sentiment similar to the one he would experience in seeing a tight-rope walker hanging, as it were, midway between life and death. The soothing arias never come at the right moment to quieten this nervous agitation. One might well believe that the composer had no other object in view than to produce a bizarre effect, not troubling himself about musical truth or unity; or about the capability of the human voice, which is overwhelmed in this flood of instrumental hurly-burly."

"Hush, my friend!" said Gambara, "I am still under the influence of that glorious chorus of hell, made still more terrible by those long trumpets—a new instrumentation. The broken *cadenzas* which add such vigor to Robert's scene, the *cavatina* in the fourth act, the *finale* to the first, still hold me in the clutch of some superhuman power. No, even Gluck's compositions never produced so powerful an effect; I am amazed at such skill."

"*Signor Maestro*," said Andrea smiling, "permit me to contradict you. Before Gluck wrote he pondered long; he calculated the chances and adopted plans which might afterward be modified under his inspirations in their details, but he never allowed himself to stray from the marked-out path. Therein lies his power of emphasis; that elocution of music which has life and truth in every beat.

"I agree with you that the science of Meyerbeer's opera is very great; but science becomes a defect when isolated from inspiration; I think I can see in that opera the painful work of a cultivated craftsman, who in his music has interlarded gems from many forgotten sources, or from damned operas;

these he has extended, remodeled, or concentrated. But he has fallen into the usual error of the plagiarist, an abuse of good things. This clever gleaner in the harvest-fields of music is prodigal in discords, which, when too frequently introduced, end by annoying the ear; it becomes habituated to startling effects, such as a composer should he chary in giving, so that he may obtain the full benefit when the situation demands it.

"This inharmonic phrasing is repeated to satiety, and the abuse of the plagal cadence* detracts from the religious solemnity of the work.

"Of course I am well aware that every composer has his particular methods to which he will return again and again in spite of himself; but he should watch and guard himself against that blunder. A picture that had none but blues and reds in it would be unfaithful to nature, beside fatiguing to the eye. Thus the constantly recurring rhythm of the score of 'Robert le Diable' gives monotony to the whole. As to the effect of the long trumpets, of which you speak, it has long been known in Germany, and what Meyerbeer gives us for novelty was constantly utilized by Mozart, who makes his chorus of devils in 'Don Giovanni' sing in that manner."

By these contradictions and renewed libations Andrea strove to bring Gambara back to his proper musical senses: he endeavored to show him that his so-called mission to the world was not to regenerate an art beyond his powers, but to seek expression for his ideas under another form, by poetry, in fact.

"You, my dear count, do not understand the least thing about that stupendous musical drama," said Gambara airily.

He stood in front of Andrea's piano, struck the keys, listened to the tone, then seated himself, meditating for a few moments as if to collect his ideas.

---

* The chord of the sub-dominant followed by that of the dominant. — TRANS.

"In the first place you must know," said he, "that a trained ear like mine perceived at once that labor of setting of which you speak. Yes, this music has been lovingly selected from the store of a rich and fertile imagination into which science has squeezed ideas which are to bring out the very essence of music.

"I will illustrate this."

He rose to move the wax-candles into the adjoining room, and, before returning to his seat, he drank a large glass of Giro, a wine of Sardinia, as full of fire as any old Tokay has ever been.

"It is this," said Gambara, "this music was not written for skeptics nor for those who know not love. If you have never in your life experienced the vehement assaults of an evil spirit, who ever moves the object at which you are about to take aim, who brings to a painful end your liveliest hopes— in one word, if you have never felt the devil's tail whisking about the world—the opera of 'Robert le Diable' must be to you what the Apocalypse is to those who think that all ends when they do. But if, persecuted and wretched, you understand that spirit of evil, that so great ape which hourly is engaged in destroying the work of God; if you imagine him as not having loved, but of ravishing an almost divine woman, and gaining from that deed the joys of paternity; as so loving his son that he would rather have him miserable to all eternity that he might be with him, than to think of his being in eternal happiness with God; if, again, you can imagine the soul of the mother hovering around her son to draw him away from the atrocious temptations offered by his father, you, even then, will have but a faint idea of that stupendous poem, in which little is wanting for it to become the rival of Mozart's 'Don Giovanni.'

"'Don Giovanni' is, I admit, the superior by the perfection of its form. 'Robert le Diable' represents ideas: 'Don Giovanni' arouses sensations. 'Don Giovanni' is still the only musical work in which harmony and melody are exactly balanced. In this lies its superiority to 'Robert le Diable,' for 'Robert' is the richer work.

"But to what good are these comparisons, since both works are beautiful in their own way? To me, subject as I have been to the oft-repeated assaults of the demon, 'Robert' speaks more powerfully than to you; I find it at once vast and concentrated.

"Thanks to you, I have been transported to the land of dreams, where our senses expand, where the universe unfolds in gigantic scale in comparison with man."

He was silent for a moment.

"I am still quivering," continued the unlucky artist, "at the sound of those four measures of the cymbals, which shook my very being when they open that short, abrupt introduction where the trombone solo, the flutes, oboes, and the clarionet cast a fantastic color over the soul. The *andante* in C-minor is a foretaste of the invocation of spirits in the abbey; it gives grandeur to the scene by its announcement of a purely spiritual struggle. I shuddered!"

Gambara struck the keys with a firm hand and developed Meyerbeer's theme in a masterly *fantasia*, a kind of explosion after the manner of Liszt. The instrument was no longer a piano, it was an orchestra they heard—the Genius of music rose before them.

"That is Mozart," he cried. "Hear how that German handles his chords; see through what intricate modulations he raises the image of terror to come to the dominant of C. I can hear all hell there!

"The curtain rises.

"What do I see? The only spectacle to which we can give the epithet infernal: an orgy of Knights in Sicily. The chorus in F contains every human passion let loose in that bacchanalian *allegro*. Every thread by which the devil holds us is pulled. That is the kind of joy that comes over men when they dance on the verge of a precipice; they whirl themselves into vertigo. What 'go' in that chorus!

"From that chorus, the reality of life, an artless bourgeois of every-day existence stands out—G-minor—in the song by Raimbaut, full as it is of simplicity. That worthy man, who is the representative of the fresh verdure of plenteous Normandy, refreshes my soul as he recalls it to Robert's mind in the midst of his drunkenness. The sweetness of that beloved land shines like a thread of gold in the dark texture of the scene.

"'Now comes the marvelous ballad in C-major, accompanied by the chorus in C-minor, so expressive of the theme. Then the outburst '*Je suis Robert*'—I am Robert. The rage of the prince offended by his vassal is no longer a natural fury; but presently it calms down, for memories of childhood arise, with those of Alice, in that gracefully pretty *allegro*—A-major.

"Do you not hear the cries of the persecuted innocent as it enters this infernal drama? 'No, no!'" sang Gambara, and making the piano echo him. "His native land and its sweet memories bloom anew in Robert's heart; his mother's shade now arises, bringing in its train soothing religious thoughts. Religion it is that inspires that beautiful song in E-major, with its miraculous progressions in harmony and melody, in the words:

> 'Car dans les cieux, comme sur la terre
> Sa mère va prier pour lui.'*

The struggle begins between the mysterious powers and the only human being who has the fire of hell in his veins to resist them. To make this quite clear, as Bertram comes on, the great musician gives the orchestra a *ritornello* reminiscent of Raimbaut's ballad. What art! What cohesion of every part! What strength of construction!

> * For in the skies as on the earth
> For him his mother prayeth.

"The devil is beneath all; he hides, he squirms. With the terror of Alice, who recognizes the devil of the image of St. Michael in her own Norman village, the conflict of the powers antagonistic begins. The musical theme develops—in what varied phrases! The antithesis so necessary in every opera is emphatically shown in a grand *recitative*, such as Gluck might have composed, between Bertram and Robert:

> 'Tu ne sauras jamais á quel excès je t'aime.'*

In that diabolical C-minor, Bertram, in his terrible bass, which countermines and destroys every effort of the vehement, passionate man, is, to me, terribly appalling.

"Must the crime become possessed of the criminal? Will the executioner clutch his prey? Must misfortune swallow up the genius of the artist? Will the disease kill the patient? Can the guardian angel save the Christian?

"Now the *finale*, the gambling scene, in which he torments his son by rousing him to terrible emotions. Robert, despoiled, angry, destroying everything around him, eager for killing, breathing blood, fire, and sword, is his own son; the father sees the likeness. What horrid glee we note in Bertram's words, '*Je ris de tes coup!*' or, 'I laugh at thy blows!' How the Venetian *barcarole* tinges this *finale!* Through what bold transitions that infamous parent is brought on the stage again to drag Robert to once more throw the dice!

"This first act is overpowering to those who follow out such themes in the profundity of their thought and gives them the breadth of meaning the composer intends to convey.

"Love alone could be in contrast with that grand symphony of song, in which you cannot detect any monotony nor twice the employment of the same means. It is one, it is many; it is characteristic of all that is grand and natural. I breathe freer; I reach the higher sphere of a chivalrous court; I hear

---
* Never wilt thou understand to what excess I love thee.

Isabella in charming phrase, fresh, but always melancholy; and the female chorus in two divisions, echoing each other, with a suggestion, it seems, of the Moorish influence on Spain.

"Here the terrifying music is softened to a gentler tone, like a storm dying away, till it comes to this dainty flowery duet, so sweetly modulated and entirely unlike the preceding music. After the turmoil of a camp of martial heroes and free-lances comes a fair picture of love. Poet! I thank thee! My heart could not have borne more.

"If I could not here and there have plucked the daisies of a French light opera, if I had listened to the sweet gayety of a woman able alike to love and charm, I could not have endured that terrible, deep note with which Bertram reappears, as he says to his son: '*Si je le permets!*' (If I permit it); when Robert has promised, in his hearing, the princess he adores, that he will conquer with the arms she gives him.

"To the hope of the gambler reforming through love, the love of the exquisite Sicilian—do you not note that falcon eye?—to the hope of the man hell answers in that awful cry: '*A toi, Robert de Normandie!*'

"Does not the sombre horror of those long-held, splendid notes excite your admiration in that: '*Dans la forêt prochaine?*' All the fascinations of 'Jerusalem Delivered' is to be found here, just as Chivalry appears in that chorus with the Spanish movement; and in the *tempo di marcia*. What originality in that *allegro;* in the modulation of the four cymbals in C-D, C-G! What grace in the call to the lists! The movement of the whole heroic life of the period is there; the soul unites with it; I read in it a romance, a poem of chivalry.

"The exposition now ends; the resources of the art of music appear to have been exhausted; and yet it was a homogeneous whole. You have had human life set before you in its one, its only real aspect. 'Shall I be happy or unhappy?' is the query of the philosopher. 'Shall I be saved or damned?' is that of the Christian."

Here Gambara struck the last chords of the chorus, which he brought forth in a lingering, melancholy way; he then rose and poured out and drank another large glass of Giro. This semi-African vintage again lit up the fires of his countenance, which had been somewhat paled by the passionate and wonderful sketch of Meyerbeer's opera that he had made.

"That nothing may be lacking to this composition," he resumed, "the great artist has given us the only *buffo* duet permissible for a devil to sing; that in which the unhappy troubadour is tempted. He puts a horror and a jest side by side, a jest that literally swallows up the only realism he had allowed himself in the weird opera—the pure, calm love of Alice and Raimbaut; their life is to be troubled by anticipatory evils. Only great souls can feel the nobility that animates these *buffo* airs.

"They have neither the gaudiness of our Italian music nor the vulgarity of our Parisian street favorites; they possess rather the divinity of Olympus. The bitter laugh of a divine being mocks the surprise of the Don-Juanized troubadour. Only for this dignity the return to the general tone of the opera would be too suddenly achieved, full as it is of terrible fury of diminished sevenths, and resolving into that infernal waltz, which at last brings us face to face with the howling demons.

"How vigorously Bertram's couplet detaches itself—B-minor—from the devil's chorus, in which is depicted the knowledge of paternity mingled in awful despair with demoniac voices! What an exquisite transition is the arrival of Alice, *ritornello* in B-flat. I still hear those voices of the angels in their heavenly freshness; it is the warble of the nightingale after the tempest.

"Thus is the leading idea of the whole worked out in detail; for what could better be done than the contrast with the tumult of demons in their den and the wonderful *aria* by Alice?

"The golden thread of the melody glides through the entire length of the grand harmony like a hope of heaven; it is embroidered on it with marvelous skill. She sings:

'Quand j'ai quitté la Normandie.'*

"Genius can never lose hold on the science that guides it. Here Alice's song in B-flat is taken up to F-sharp, the dominant of the chorus of devils. Do you hear the *tremolo* of the orchestra? Robert is being bidden to the rout of devils.

"Here Bertram reënters, and this is the culminating point of musical interest, a *recitative*, only comparable to the finest compositions of the greatest masters; comes the struggle in E-flat between the two combatants, Heaven and Hell—one in '*Oui, tu me connais!*' (Yes, thou knowest me!)—on a diminished seventh; the other in that sublime F, '*Le ciel est avec moi!*'—Heaven is with me! Hell and the crucifix are face to face.

"Then we have Bertram's threats to Alice, the most awful pathos ever written; the Genius of Evil complacently making himself known, and, as usual, tempting through self-interest. The arrival of Robert gives us the magnificent trio, unaccompained, in A-flat; this opens the struggle between the two rival forces for the possession of the man. Note how clearly this is effected," exclaimed Gambara, who epitomized the scene with such passion of execution as startled Andrea.

"All this avalanche of music, from the crash of the cymbals in common time, has rolled onward to this contest of the three voices. The spell of Evil triumphs! Alice flees. You hear the duet between Bertram and Robert—in D. The devil fixes his talons in Robert's heart; he rends it for his own; he decants on every feeling—honor, hope, eternal pleasure, all are in turn displayed before him; he carries him, as he did Jesus, to the pinnacle of the temple, he shows him all the treasures of the earth, that jewel-case of Sin. Finally he

* When I forsook my Normandy.

piques his courage, he stings him, and the noble instincts of the man is expressed in that cry :

> ' Des chevaliers de ma patrie
> L'honneur toujours fut le soutien.'
>
> (To the knights of my native land,
> Their mainstay was honor ever.)

To crown the whole opera comes in the same theme which so fatally prognosticated the work at its opening, that grand invocation to the dead :

> ' Nonnes qui reposez sous cette froide pierre,
> M'entendez-vous ? '
>
> (Nuns who sleep beneath that cold, cold stone,
> Hear ye me?)

Carried most gloriously through the career of the music, it ends equally gloriously in the *allegro vivace* of the bacchanal —D-minor. Here is the triumph of Hell! Roll on harmony! Swathe us in thy manifold cloak! Roll on, bewitching!

"The powers of the infernal have seized their prey. They hold him while they dance around him. The noble genius born to vanquish, born to reign, is lost! Devils rejoice, genius is stifled by povetry, passion wrecks the knight."

Here Gambara improvised a *fantasia* himself, cleverly varying the *bacchanale*, and accompanying the piano in a soft tone of voice, as if to give utterance to the sufferings he had known.

"Do you hear the celestial plaints of neglected love?" said he. "Isabella calls Robert from the midst of that grand chorus of knights wending their way to the tournament, where the *motifs* of the second act reappear to emphasize the fact that the events of the third act happen in supernatural spheres. Here is real life again. The chorus fades away as the enchantments of hell approach, which are brought by Robert with his talisman. Now develops the deviltries of the third act. First the viola duet, where the rhythm plainly depicts the brutal desires of a man who is omnipotent, while the princess, in plaintive moans, endeavors to recall her lover to reason.

"Here the musician has placed himself in a position that is very difficult to be brought out; but he surmounts it by the sweetest gem in the whole work. What exquisite melody in the *cavatina* '*Grâce pour toi!*' (Mercy for thee!) That one number would suffice to make any opera famous; for every woman feels that she is contending against a knight. Never yet was music so passionate, so dramatic.

"The whole world now rises against the reprobate. Some may object that the *finale* resembles too much that of 'Don Giovanni;' but there is this immense difference: a noble faith inspires Isabella, a perfect love that will rescue Robert, who scornfully rejects the talisman of hell confided to him, while, on the other hand, Don Giovanni persists in his unbelief. Beside all, this accusation has been made against every composer who has written a *finale* since the time of Mozart. The *finale* to 'Don Giovanni' is one of those classic forms that has been invented once for all time.

"At last we hear Religion, which arises omnipotent, in a voice that rules the universe, that calls all sorrow to come and be consoled, all repentances, that they may have peace.

"The whole house is stirred by the chorus:

> '*Malheureux ou coupables,*
> *Hâtez-vous d'accourir!*'
>
> (Now wretched, guilty men,
> Haste to approach!)

Hitherto, in the fearful tumult of unchained passions, the Holy Voice had not been heard; but at this critical moment it booms out like thunder; the Catholic church divine rises glorious in light. And I am astonished to here find at the close of such a lavish use of harmonic treasures a new vein of gold in that grand masterpiece of chorus: '*Gloire à la Providence!*' written in Handel's style.

"Robert, distracted, rushes on the stage with his heart-rending cry: '*Si je pouvais prier!*' (Could I but pray!) But, constrained by the edict of hell, Bertram pursues his son and makes a final effort. Alice calls up the vision of the Mother. Now you hear the glorious trio to which the whole opera has gradually advanced, the triumph of soul over matter, the victory of the spirit of Good over the spirit of Evil. The strains of faith prevail over the chorus of hell; joy reappears in majesty. Here the music weakens. I but see a cathedral instead of hearing a concert of angels in bliss; a divine prayer of souls delivered, consecrating the union of Robert and Alice. We ought not to be left under the spells of hell, we should be able to leave the scene with a heart of hope.

"Myself a Catholic and a musician, I needed for my soul another prayer like the one from 'Moses in Egypt.' Also would I fain have seen Germany contending with Italy—what Meyerbeer could do to rival Rossini.

"However, the writer may say, in justification of this defect, that, after five hours of such solid, substantial music, a Parisian prefers a bon-bon to a musical masterpiece. You heard the applause that followed the performance; it will run five hundred nights. If the French really understand that music——"

"It is because they have ideas," said the count.

"No, it is because it powerfully sets forth in definite shape an image of that struggle in which so many souls are worsted; and because all individual existences are connected with it by memory, as it were. Therefore is it that I, unhappy one, grieve that at the end I do not hear the sound of those celestial voices I have so often heard in dreams."

Here Gambara fell into a musical ecstasy; he improvised the

most lovely, melodious, and harmonious *cavatina* that Andrea should ever hear; a song divinely sung, on a theme as graceful and full of charm as that of *O filii et filiæ;* but with such added beauties such as none but musical genius of the highest order could have rendered.

The count was lost in rapt admiration; the clouds were breaking; the celestial blue shone out; now angelic forms appeared and raised the veil that hid the sanctuary; the light of heaven descended.

Silence reigned again.

The count, surprised at the music suddenly ceasing, looked up at Gambara, who, with fixed, staring eyes and rigid form, stammered the word: "GOD!"

The count quietly awaited the moment when the composer returned from celestial glory, whither the prismatic wings of inspiration had borne him, resolving to illuminate his mind with the very truths that he himself should bring down.

"Well," said he, pouring out another bumper of wine and clinking glasses with him, "this German has written, as you say, a sublime opera without troubling himself about theory; whereas musicians who write grammars of music are, more than often, like literary critics—atrocious composers."

"Then you do not like my music?"

"I don't say that. But, if instead of perpetually dissecting the method of idea expression—which carries you beyond the mark—you would simply awaken our sensations, I feel sure that you would be better comprehended, unless, that is, you have not entirely mistaken your vocation. You are a great poet."

"What!" cried Gambara. "What, are five-and-twenty years of study simply wasted? Am I then to learn the imperfect utterance of man—I who hold the key to the language of heaven? Ah! should you be right—then I crave to die!"

"No, no, not you. You are great, you are strong. You shall begin a new life, and I, your friend, will sustain you.

We will show to the world the rare and noble alliance of a rich man and an artist who comprehend each other."

"Do you speak truth?" asked Gambara, rigid in a sudden torpor.

"As I have already said, you are more poet than musician."

"A poet, poet! That is better than nothing. But truly tell me, whom do you most esteem, Mozart or Homer?"

"I admire them equally."

"On your honor?"

"On my honor."

"H'm! One word more. What think you of Meyerbeer and Byron?"

"You have judged them by naming them together."

The count's carriage was at the door. The composer and his titled physician were driven to Gambara's residence. They ran upstairs and were soon in Marianna's presence.

As they entered Gambara threw himself into his wife's arms, who withdrew a step and averted her head. The husband also drew back, and, beaming on the count, said, in a husky voice:

"You might at least have left me my madness, monsieur."

Then his head drooped and he fell.

"What have you done?" cried Marianna, casting a look at her husband, in which disgust and pity were equally blended. "He is dead drunk!"

The count with the help of his valet raised Gambara and laid him upon the bed; then Andrea left the house, his heart glad in horrid rapture.

The next day he purposely let the hour of his daily visit pass by; he was beginning to fear that he had been duped by himself, and had paid too dearly for the comfort and virtue of that humble couple whose peace he had for ever destroyed.

At length Giardini came bringing a note from Marianna.

"Come," she wrote, "the harm done is not so great as you desired, cruel man."

"Excellenza," said the cook, while Andrea was dressing,

"you entertained right royally last night. But you must allow that, apart from the wines, which were excellent, your *maître d'hôtel* did not produce a single dish worthy an epicure's table. You won't deny, I suppose, that the dish placed before you, on the day you honored my table with your presence, was superlatively better than those that sullied your service of plate last evening? Consequently, when I awoke this morning, I remembered the promise you had made me to become your chef. I henceforth consider myself as one of your household."

"I have had the same thought in my mind for the past few days," replied Andrea. "I have mentioned your name to the Austrian ambassador, and you will be allowed to recross the Alps as soon as you please. In Croatia I have a castle which I seldom visit. There you may combine the offices of porter, butler, cook, and steward, with two hundred crowns a year. This emolument will also be that of your wife, who can do the rest of the work. You can there try all your experiments *in anima vili*—that is to say, on the stomachs of my vassals. Here is a cheque for the costs of your journey."

Giardini kissed the count's hand, in the Neapolitan fashion.

"Excellenza," said he, "I accept the cheque, but not the position. It would be dishonoring in me to give up my art and lose the good opinion of the most perfect epicures, who are undoubtedly those of Paris."

When Andrea arrived at Gambara's apartments the composer arose and came forward to meet him.

"My generous friend," said he frankly, "either it is that you took advantage of the weakness of my head to play a joke on me last night, or else your brain is no whit stronger, when testing the heady fumes of our native Latium, than mine is. I choose the latter hypothesis: I prefer to doubt your stomach than your heart. Be this as it may, I from this renounce the use of wine—for ever. Last evening the abuse of good liqueur led me into culpable folly. When I call to mind that I nearly degraded ——" He glanced in terror at Marianna.

"As to that wretched opera you took me to hear, I have thought it over; it is naught but music made by very ordinary methods; a heap of piled-up notes—*verba et voces*. It is but the dregs of the nectar which I quaff in deep draughts as I reproduce the heavenly music that I hear. I know the origin of those patched-up phrases. That Gloire à la Providence is too like Handel; the chorus of knights on their way to the lists is closely related to the Scotch air in 'La Dame Blanche.' In short, if the opera is pleasing, it is simply because the music is borrowed from everybody and is therefore generally known.

"I must now leave you, my dear friend. Since morning I have had an idea seething in my brain which bids me rise to God on the wings of song; but I wished to see you and say this much to you. Adieu! I go to ask forgiveness of my Muse. We shall meet this evening at dinner; but no more wine—at least not for me. Oh! I am firmly resolved——"

"I give him up," said Andrea, blushing violently.

"You enlighten my conscience," said Marianna, "I dared not question it. My friend, my friend, the fault is not ours; he *won't* let us cure him."

Six years later, in January, 1837, such musical artists as were unlucky enough to injure their wind or string instruments were in the habit of taking them to the Rue Froidmanteau, to a squalid, disreputable house where the said instruments were repaired by an old Italian named Gambara, who resided on the sixth floor.

For the past five years this man had lived alone, his wife having deserted him. An instrument, called by him a *panharmonicon*, from which he expected fame, had been sold at auction by the sheriff, on the Place du Châtelet, in addition to a great pile of musical manuscript thickly scrawled. The day after the sale, this said paper appeared in the markets wrapped around pats of butter, fish, and fruits.

In this manner the three grand operas—of which the poor man would often boast, though a once-celebrated Neapolitan cook, now a vendor of broken victuals, declared they were but a mass of rubbish—were scattered throughout Paris in the baskets of hucksters. But what matter?—the landlord had gotten his rent, the sheriff's men their fees.

The Neapolitan victual-monger, who had as regular customers the prostitutes of the Rue Froidmanteau for his warmed-up scraps, which were the crumbs from the fine banquets given by society on the previous night, was always ready to tell that Signora Gambara had gone off to Italy with a nobleman of Milan, and no one knew what had become of her. Weary of poverty and wretchedness, she was more than likely ruining the count by a career of extravagant luxury, for they adored each other with so fierce a passion that he had never in all his Neapolitan experience beheld the like.

Toward the end of this same month, January, one evening as Giardini was chatting with a girl, who had chanced in to buy her supper, about the beautiful Marianna, so pure, so glorious, so nobly self-devoted, and who had, notwithstanding, gone the *way of all the rest*, the street-girl and the wife of Giardini noticed in the street a tall, thin woman, with a sunburnt, dusty face; a nervous walking skeleton, who was peering at all the numbers and trying to recognize a house.

"*Ecco la Marianna!*" cried Giardini.

Marianna recognized the one-time cook in the poor object, but gave no heed to the misfortunes which had reduced him to his present wretched trade as a dealer in second-hand food. She went in and sat down; she had walked from Fontainebleau; she had walked fourteen leagues that day, after begging her bread from Turin to Paris.

The sight of her horrified that miserable trio. Of all her marvelous loveliness naught now remained but a pair of fading, anguished eyes. The one thing faithful to her was misfortune.

The old mender of instruments heartily welcomed her; he greeted her with inexpressible joy.

"Here you are, my poor Marianna!" he said affectionately. "During your absence they sold my instrument and my operas."

It would have been a difficult job to kill the fatted calf for the prodigal returned; but Giardini produced the fag-end of a salmon, the street-walker paid for the wine, Gambara found the bread, Signora Giardini lent a table-cloth, and these diverse unfortunates supped together in the musician's garret.

When questioned about her adventures, Marianna refused to reply, but she raised her fine eyes to heaven and whispered to Giardini:

"He married a ballet-girl."

"And how do you mean to live?" asked the girl. "The journey from Milan has killed you and——"

"Made me an old woman," said Marianna. "No, it is not fatigue, not poverty, it is grief that has done this."

"Bah! why then did you never send your man here any money?"

Marianna only answered by a look, but it stabbed the woman to the heart.

"She ain't proud at all! oh, no!" she exclaimed. "But much good it has done her," she whispered in Giardini's ear.

That year it seemed that every musician took extraordinary care of his instrument, and the business of repairing them dropped to *nil*, or to less than sufficient to provide for the daily bread of that poor household. The wife earned little by her needle, and they were compelled to turn their talents to account in the meanest occupation.

In the dusk they would go together to the Champs-Élysées and sing duets, and Gambara, poor soul, accompanied on a wretched guitar. On the way thither Marianna, who always concealed her head under a sort of veil of lawn, would take her husband to a grocery in the Faubourg Saint-Honoré and give him two or three nips of brandy to make him tipsy; otherwise he could not play but intolerably. Then they would stand up together before the gay world seated on chairs along the esplanade, and the greatest genius of the day, the unrecognized Orpheus of modern music, played fragments of his operas to the crowd. These were so remarkable that they were able to extract a few sous from Parisian supineness.

One day a *dilettante* of the Bouffons happened to be sitting there, and, not recognizing from what opera they were taken, questioned the woman in the Grecian head-dress, when she held out the stamped, round metallic plate on which she collected her charity.

"I say, my dear, from what music is that?"

"From the opera of 'Mahomet,'" Marianna replied.

As Rossini had composed an opera, "Mahomet II.," the gentleman remarked to the lady:

"What a pity that they will not give us at the Italiens those works of Rossini that are known the least. Certain it is that this is glorious music."

Gambara smiled.

A few days ago it was necessary for this poor couple to pay the paltry sum of thirty-six francs as arrears of rent due on their miserable garret. The grocer refused to give credit for the brandy with which Marianna plied her husband to enable him to play. Gambara was thus so atrociously bad that it became insufferable; the ears of the rich were irresponsive— the tin bottle-stand remained empty.

It was nine o'clock in the evening when a beautiful Italian, the Principessa Massimilla di Varese,* took pity on the poor creatures. She gave Marianna forty francs and questioned both, after discovering from the wife's thanks that she was a

* See "Massimilla Doni."

Venetian. Prince Emilio, who accompanied his wife, would learn the history of their distress, and Marianna detailed all, making no complaints against God or man.

"Madame," said Gambara, who was not drunk, "we are the victims of our own superiority. My music is good; but so soon as music rises from sensation to idea, only persons of genius should be the hearers, for only they are capable of responding to it! It has been my misfortune to hear the chorus of angels; I believed that men could understand those strains. It is thus with women when their love assumes a divine aspect: men can no longer comprehend them."

These words were well worth the forty francs bestowed by Massimilla; she drew out another gold-piece from her purse, saying, as she gave it to Marianna, that she would write Andrea Marcosini.

"Do not write him, madame!" exclaimed Marianna. "And God grant you may be beautiful for ever!"

"Let us provide for them," said the princess to her husband; "this man has remained faithful to the IDEAL which *we* have killed."

When Gambara saw the gold he wept; then there came to him a vague reminiscence of some old scientific experiment, and the wretched composer, as he wiped away his tears, uttered these words, which the attendant circumstances make piteous:

"Water is produced by burning."

www.ingramcontent.com/pod-product-compliance
Lightning Source LLC
Chambersburg PA
CBHW032003300426
44117CB00008B/886